The Future of Quality News Journalism

"This impressive work of scholarship and analysis spotlights the essential role that quality journalism and news organizations plays in civil society and focuses urgently needed attention on the challenges of sustaining such enterprises."—Eric Freedman, Michigan State University

In the face of the continuously changing challenges of the digital age, it is difficult for quality news journalism to survive on any significant scale if a means for adequately funding it is not available. This new study, a follow-up to 2007's *The Future of Journalism in the Advanced Democracies*, includes a comparative analysis of possible alternative business models that may save the future of the quality news business across the developed, intermediate, and developing worlds. Its detailed evaluation encompasses also the different ways in which wider key issues are affecting the prospects for quality news as a core ingredient of effectively working democracies. It focuses on the United States, the United Kingdom, South Africa, India, Kenya, and selected parts of the Arab World, providing a detailed cross-cultural survey of different approaches to addressing these various issues. To keep the study firmly rooted in the "real world" the contributors include distinguished practitioners as well as experienced academics.

Peter J. Anderson is Reader in News Media and Research Coordinator for the School of Journalism and Digital Communication at the University of Central Lancashire, UK.

George Ogola is a Senior Lecturer in Journalism at the University of Central Lancashire, UK.

Michael Williams is a Senior Lecturer in Journalism at the University of Central Lancashire, UK, and continues to practise as a national newspaper journalist.

Routledge Research in Journalism

1 Journalists, Sources, and
  Credibility
  New Perspectives
  *Edited by Bob Franklin and
  Matt Carlson*

2 Journalism Education, Training
  and Employment
  *Edited by Bob Franklin and
  Donica Mensing*

3 Network Journalism
  Journalistic Practice in Interactive
  Spheres
  Ansgard Heinrich

4 International News in the
  Digital Age
  East-West Perceptions of a New
  World Order
  *Edited by Judith Clarke and
  Michael Bromley*

5 Digital Media and Reporting
  Conflict
  Blogging and the BBC's Coverage
  of War and Terrorism
  Daniel Bennett

6 A Global Standard for Reporting
  Conflict
  Jake Lynch

7 The Future of Quality News
  Journalism
  A Cross-Continental Analysis
  *Edited by Peter J. Anderson,
  George Ogola, and
  Michael Williams*

The Future of Quality News Journalism

A Cross-Continental Analysis

Edited by Peter J. Anderson,
George Ogola, and
Michael Williams

Routledge
Taylor & Francis Group

NEW YORK AND LONDON

First published 2014
by Routledge
711 Third Avenue, New York, NY 10017

Simultaneously published in the UK
by Routledge
2 Park Square, Milton Park, Abingdon, Oxon OX14 4RN

*Routledge is an imprint of the Taylor & Francis Group,
an informa business*

© 2014 Taylor & Francis

Library of Congress Cataloging-in-Publication Data

The future of quality news journalism : a cross-continental analysis / edited by
  Peter J. Anderson, George Ogola, and Michael Williams.
    pages cm
  Includes bibliographical references and index.
  1. Journalism–History–21st century.   2. Journalism–Management.
  3. News audiences—History—21st century.   4. Online journalism.
  5. Citizen journalism.   I. Anderson, Peter J., 1954- editor of compilation.
  II. Ogola, George, editor of compilation.   III. Williams, Michael, 1948-
  editor of compilation.
    PN4815.2.F88 2013
    070.4090'05–dc23
    2013011732

ISBN: 978-0-415-53286-0 (hbk)
ISBN: 978-0-203-38270-7 (ebk)

Typeset in Sabon
by Apex CoVantage, LLC

Printed and bound in the United States of America by Publishers Graphics,
LLC on sustainably sourced paper.

In Memoriam, Robert Stephens Beers

Robert S. Beers enjoyed the sort of journalistic career that many imagine but few experience. Robert began as a newspaper reporter and never lost his love for the printed word, but he will be remembered for his work as an award-winning television correspondent, documentary producer and, latterly, a respected and much-loved teacher.

During a career that spanned decades, the job—Robert always regarded journalism as a "job"—took him from reporting conflict in Central and South America to shining a light on the darkness of the former Soviet Union. He covered four American presidential elections and interviewed a raft of world leaders, from Fidel Castro and Yasser Arafat to Indira Gandhi and the former Shah of Iran. His documentaries and special reports from virtually all over the globe gave viewers fascinating insights on the world's hot spots as well as demonstrating his rare clarity and understanding of the events.

Like many journalists, Bob had a mistrust of authority and 'spin', a dislike of bureaucracy and paperwork. He adored travel, films and writers such as Steinbeck, Hemingway and Le Carré. Like any reporter, Robert loved gossip, but he was also a wonderful raconteur, regaling colleagues and students with affectionate stories about the Hollywood greats: Burt Lancaster, Sophia Loren and Orson Welles. Everything and everyone fascinated him whether he was in New York, Delhi or Edinburgh. This gentle and self-effacing man also adored his family.

Robert joined the University of Central Lancashire in 2004 and helped develop the first postgraduate International Journalism course in the United Kingdom. Students from around the world appreciated his wisdom and kindliness, and through them Robert's commitment to rigorous journalism lives on.

He finished his contribution to this book shortly before his death in February 2013, and we dedicate it to him. We hope it is a fitting tribute to a cherished colleague and inspiring teacher.

Contents

Acknowledgments xi

Introduction 1
PETER J. ANDERSON

SECTION I
What Is Quality News Journalism? 5

1 Defining and Measuring Quality News Journalism 7
PETER J. ANDERSON

2 From the Insight Team to Wikileaks: The Continuing Power
of Investigative Journalism as a Benchmark of Quality
News Journalism 35
PAUL LASHMAR

SECTION II
Funding Quality News Journalism in the Face of Significant
Economic and Technological Change 53

3 Finding Viable Business Models for Developed World Print
and Online Newspaper Sectors 55
CHRIS BLACKHURST

4 Finding Viable Business Models for Developed World
Broadcast News 67
PAUL EGGLESTONE

5 Finding Viable Business Models for Intermediate
   and Developing World Broadcast, Print and Online
   Newspaper Sectors   88
   MOTILOLA AKINFEMISOYE AND SALLY DEFFOR

SECTION III
A Critical Overview of Current Quality Levels in the
Journalism of Sample Developed World States, and
What Needs to Be Done to Maintain or Improve Them   101

6 Quality Journalism in the UK, in Print and Online   103
   MICHAEL WILLIAMS

7 One Newsroom, Many Possibilities: How the Merging of
   Digital and Print Journalism in American Newsrooms is
   Shaping the Future of U.S. News Media   127
   ALEX ORTOLANI

8 American Broadcast News and the Future   143
   ROBERT BEERS

9 How the Audience Saved UK Broadcast Journalism   162
   DEBORAH ROBINSON AND ANDREW HOBBS

10 U.S. Citizen Journalism and Alternative Online News Sites 184
   CLYDE BENTLEY

11 UK Social Media, Citizen Journalism and Alternative News 202
   CLARE COOK AND ANDREW DICKINSON

SECTION IV
Current Quality Levels in the Journalism of South Africa
and Kenya, and What Needs to Be Done to Maintain or
Improve Them   225

12 The Future of Quality News Journalism and Media
   Accountability in South Africa and Kenya   227
   GEORGE OGOLA AND YLVA RODNY-GUMEDE

13 Citizen Journalism in South Africa and Kenya: The Quandary
of Quality and the Prospects for Growth   248
HARRY DUGMORE AND DINA LIGAGA

SECTION V
Case Studies from India and the Arab World   265

14 Where More Is Not Better: Challenges Facing Quality
News Journalism in 'Shining' India   267
PRASUN SONWALKAR

15 (Re-)framing the 'Quality' Debate: The Arab Media
and Its Future Journalism   282
GEORGE OGOLA

Conclusion   297
PETER J. ANDERSON

Bonus Chapter—More Core Material Available by Web Link   306
Why Mainstream News Still Matters, and Why New Business
Models Must Be Found
PETER J. ANDERSON, AVAILABLE AT: HTTP://CLOK.UCLAN.AC.UK/7824

Contributors   307
Index   313

Acknowledgments

Thanks are due to Andrew Hobbs for stepping in at short notice to help with some key editorial work when one of life's many unpredictabilities, in the form of ill health, temporarily took one of the team out of the book. The lead editor would also like to thank his co-editor for the predecessor volume, Geoff Ward, and Andrew for their detailed reading and commentary on chapter one, which helped decide the final shape that it took and also Fred Mudhai of Coventry University for his detailed and helpful comments with regard to chapter five. Thanks are due also to the contributors for their dedication and commitment to the project. Finally, the editorial team is grateful to the University of Central Lancashire for providing the flexibility that enabled a complex project to be completed within a reasonable deadline.

Introduction

Peter J. Anderson

The key purposes of this project are to evaluate critically the current state of quality hard news journalism within the core case study societies, together with the chances of preserving, enhancing and spreading some of the best practices within it that currently are visible to the various contributing authors. Given the fundamental importance of economics in underpinning quality news operations of any size and range, one of the key questions that will be addressed asks to what extent sustainable business models can be found for this type of journalism in the various forms in which it exists.

Obviously, it is impossible to cover all of the world's continents in a book of this size, while simultaneously retaining depth as well as breadth of analysis, and to cover anything other than key states from within those continents that are actually analysed. A selection has to be made, therefore, from among the large number of potential case studies that is clearly supportable by a clear logic.

The inclusion of the USA is not only due to the fact that it is the most long-standing democracy in the Americas, and now one of the oldest in the modern world, but also because of its status as the most powerful single political, military and economic actor on the global stage, despite the rise of new challengers aspiring to its status. It is argued that it is vital that such a powerful entity has within it adequate means to keep its electorate informed about what is done in their name abroad as well as domestically, and that quality hard news journalism has a vital role to play in this regard.

Amongst the reasons for the UK's inclusion as Europe's representative—something that might seem ironic, given British attitudes towards the European Union—is the fact that it is home to the most powerful, respected and influential of the news providers within the democratic world, the BBC, together with two global quality newspaper brands in the form of the print/online Guardian and Financial Times. No other European country is in a position to match these claims for inclusion.

South Africa chooses itself almost from within Africa, given its position as a democracy with one foot in the developed world and one very firmly still in the developing part of the global economy and its status as an emerging, if troubled, regional superpower. It is also a new democracy in comparison to the much older examples of the UK and the USA, and this in itself makes for a useful point of contrast.

Kenya, on the other hand, provides a fascinating example of a democracy that is still very much in the developing world, and this provides a useful comparison with, and contrast to, its more economically advanced South African colleague. It is attempting to manage a complex tapestry of political, ethnic, cultural, historical and economic forces and influences that together create a very distinctive context for its news media and the role that they play within Kenyan society. As such, it forms a study that introduces readers outside Africa to some of the subtle nuances and details of the relationship between democracy and journalism that so distinguish this continent from the others within the book, and it is for this reason that Africa is represented by two states within the study.

India's position as an emerging economic and media superpower with the potential to rival non-democratic China justifies its position as the selected Asian case study, together with the fact that some of the key trends in media development within it appear to be running counter to those in other crucial parts of the world. As such, it will provide a useful contrast to some of the other case studies.

Finally, the 'Arab Spring' and its consequences, both promising and otherwise, have highlighted the changes, innovations and continuities in the role and potential of the news media within one of the most crucial regions on the planet. The timeliness of these, together with the significance of the growing demands for democracy within key countries within the region, justifies its inclusion as an additional case study.

The most attention, in terms of chapter numbers, will be given to the United States and the United Kingdom, given their continuing status as the leading democratic global news media players. Two chapters are devoted to Africa as a result of the need to accommodate a detailed study of two countries in one chapter for the reasons stated previously *and* the complexity of some of the new media developments that are occurring in parts of the continent, something that the editors felt required a chapter in itself for adequate analysis. The vastness of India and its media networks make it impractical to try and fit detailed coverage of all of its diverse media structures and themes into a book of this size, so the focus instead is on identifying the key trends within Indian quality news journalism and investigating the extent to which they appear to be mirroring or running counter to the journalism of the other case study countries. While India is given only one chapter, that chapter not only provides useful insights into the key developments and the potential of the country's news media, but also throws valuable light on their implications for wider trends in the news media internationally.

The space limitations of the book leave only one chapter for the Arab World, also. However, as with India, that chapter is a substantial one and will focus on the key trends within the region and the problems and opportunities that they offer for quality news journalism and its political and economic sustainability.

It should be emphasised that the exclusion of the democracies of Australia, New Zealand and Japan, for example, does not mean that they are regarded as insignificant in a global news media context, particularly given Japan's continuing leading role within the global economy. They are not included simply because of the limitations of space and the necessity to make difficult choices within that context.

In terms of its structure, the book begins with a detailed examination of how quality hard news journalism can be defined, conceptualised in its various forms and measured. This provides a theoretical underpinning that all of the other chapters draw upon as necessary. This is followed by an exploration of the current and likely future state of what is often regarded as the pinnacle of hard news journalism: investigative journalism. For those readers who would like some additional discussion of the continuing importance of the quality news media, which is impossible to include in a book of this size, an extra chapter by the lead editor has been provided via a web link (http://clok.uclan.ac.uk/7824).

The next section of the book looks at one of the key enabling factors that determines the extent to which quality hard news journalism can survive and grow: the business models that fund it. Three chapters explore the core economic questions currently facing the different sectors of the news industry within the developed, intermediate and developing worlds. In line with the overall philosophy behind the book, the authors within this section include a leading practitioner from within the news business, and, as in the next section, the chapter formatting is deliberately flexible to include this mix. This mixture of academics and practitioners enables the book to keep its proverbial feet firmly within the 'real world'. The detailed country-by-country studies then follow in the manner outlined previously, with each relevant section analysing the current quality levels in the hard news journalism of the various case study states and what needs to be done to maintain or improve them in the future. Overall conclusions are drawn at the end of the book, which also includes an appropriate contribution to the debate concerning the future of quality news journalism within democratic societies.

In addition, it should be mentioned that, wherever relevant, the role and value of external news providers (that are additional to the BBC and are alleged to provide a quality news product) within case study countries and continents will be critically assessed. These include such well-known names as Internews, CNN, Radio Free Asia, Reuters, Associated Press, Agence France-Presse, Bloomberg and Al Jazeera.

Section I
What Is Quality News Journalism?

1 Defining and Measuring Quality News Journalism

Peter J. Anderson

INTRODUCTION

This book focuses on the question of how quality hard news journalism[1] can survive in the face of formidable economic and technological challenges that confront it in many parts of the world. However, the term 'quality news' is often used extremely loosely to include forms of journalism, or the outputs of specific newspapers, programmes, and so forth that many critics of the news industry would find it difficult to rate as providing high quality material. The intention here, therefore, is to consider in some detail just what 'quality' hard news journalism involves from the specific viewpoint of this book. The chapter will set out to determine the primary characteristics of quality hard news journalism as they are relevant here and the key processes that affect the likelihood of their being realised. It will discuss appropriate and practical means of establishing the extent to which quality news exists in the output of news organisations. Overall, it will provide a clear understanding of *the overall framework of quality* from *which the various usages of the term within this book will be derived,* as well as a precise view of what the project would see as justifying the description of 'quality hard news'.

This book does not fall into the trap of assuming there was a past ill-defined 'golden age' of journalism against which the current news media should be judged. Nor, in line with McNair's cautions (see, for example, McNair 2000), will it fall prey to the assumption that quality news is subject to an inevitable process of 'dumbing down' as a result of all of the commercial and technological pressures now facing it. Instead, it starts from the premise that quality journalism can be conceptualised in a variety of different ways and that some of the available definitions are more relevant than others within specific national and cultural contexts. In light of this, the chapter seeks to provide a framework that will set down some of the various ways in which quality journalism can be conceptualised and measured in the developed, intermediate and developing countries that are most relevant to the case study chapters in this book.

In the developed world and for most of the developing/intermediate world case studies, for instance, and for reasons that will be explained, the media's normative function of information provider will be the primary benchmark for our analysis. The understanding of the term 'information provider' will be one that bears in mind the nuances and insights relating to this role that have been developed by Stromback (2005) and others, most particularly those relating to participatory democracy. These are relevant equally to both the developed and the developing/intermediate world. However, there is a need to emphasise that in focussing primarily on this role we are not simplistically assuming that it is the only role of journalism that can be regarded as important. Many writers, for example, James Carey (1989) and David Paul Nord (2001), see this as only a small part of what journalism is about. However, in any study that sets out to analyse particular aspects of journalism in some depth, it is not feasible to look at every key way in which it is conceptualised if that depth is not to be lost. Therefore, it is important to make clear what we are not looking at within this study. The book will, for example, be looking at the idea of journalism as a forum in some of its chapters, but primarily from forums' partial role as information providers. It will not be looking at journalism as a means of identity formation, nor will it be addressing news audiences' emotional engagement with journalism. These are all important additional perspectives on the possible roles of journalism, but to include them as well would leave insufficient space to consider adequately what we have selected as the main focus for the present study.

The book will, however, be focussing in some detail on a specific nuance of the idea of information provider that relates most to journalism in parts of the intermediate and developing world. As will be demonstrated in the relevant chapters, specific historical events (that will be explained within them) have shaped the journalism practised in some of the sample countries in a way that affects significantly quality measurement. It requires quality also to be evaluated in terms of the extent to which news providers supply the kind of information and forums that facilitate the *continuing development* of democratic structures in the intermediate and developing economies of South Africa, India, the Arab World and Kenya.

It is possible also for the function/role of the fourth estate to be a characteristic of a quality news provider. But this idea has been so often abused by 'press barons', such as Beaverbrook and Murdoch, that a great deal of care has to be exercised before concluding that a news provider is genuinely adopting a position that stands up for the interests of 'the people' in the face of powerful elite interest groups who would exploit them. The main concern in this book will be with the information provider role, although carefully qualified attention will be given to the fourth estate role where appropriate.

For reasons that will be explained in some detail, the quality measure applied to Kenya will include also an economic developmental component.

The question of how journalism can reconcile its information provider/ fourth estate roles within a developmental paradigm while operating in a new market–based economy will be asked. Because of its unique status with regard to Kenya from among our case study countries, this aspect of news quality will be discussed specifically within that chapter and not here.

Fundamental to the underlying rationale for the choice of this informational benchmark as the primary focus is the argument that the specific understandings of it set down within the chapter can be seen to be core requirements for the functioning of democracy to the fullest extent that it would appear is possible in a considerably less than perfect world. Quality will, therefore, be broadly measured according to the extent to which journalism performs the information provider role. For instance, to what extent do the news media in the United States, the United Kingdom, Kenya, South Africa or Kenya sufficiently focus on and interrogate news directly related to political and civic citizenship?

Our first point of departure is the question of how quality should be defined.

DEFINING QUALITY

Quality is a highly contested topic in the context of news journalism, as is illustrated effectively in Shapiro's literature review of definitions of quality (2010), which demonstrates, among other things, the variety of different views on how quality should be measured. It is alleged frequently to be lacking as a result of the presence of bias within news reports (see the carefully qualified argument in Anderson and Weymouth 1999, for instance). Such bias can be argued to be the result of what is excluded from reports as well as what is included (Anderson and Weymouth 1999; Fairclough 2001, 58). However, this view on quality is contested by others who argue that *declaredly* biased journalism is ethically sound and realistic quality news reporting. This is contended to be particularly the case given the problems with achieving balance and objectivity in any human record of events. But it can only be quality journalism within the terms of this understanding if it is based on rigorous sourcing and evidence building with a dedication to fact checking (see, for example, Starkey 2007, 59–60).

Different qualities and levels of news information are argued to be necessary for different types of democracy. For example, Stromback (2005) has systematised the available literature to produce a four-fold typology of democracy. We have discussed this in some detail in the predecessor volume (Anderson and Ward 2007) and shall therefore re-present it only in summary form here. In Stromback's typology, at one end of the spectrum, 'procedural democracy' simply requires that journalism should monitor the carrying out of election procedures and report any instances of malpractice or incompetence in this regard.

Then there is what he defines as competitive democracy. For this to exist, journalism should meet the democratic need for rigorous, in-depth information providers/watchdogs with regard to the platforms and records of political parties and the key political players (Stromback 2005).

Near the other end of the spectrum he outlines the concept of 'participatory democracy'. This carries extra expectations. A journalist's job should be not simply to assess the fairness of election procedures and report competently on rival political parties' competing records and platforms, but also to supply voters with a sufficiently high level and quality of information for them to become participants in their domestic political systems between elections, as well as during them. If elected politicians and the bodies they are responsible for break their promises or under-perform, or if justice and order within the society they govern breaks down, then quality news journalism has very specific responsibilities. It must provide voters with both the key details of what is going wrong and the information that is necessary for them to hold those elected and their officials to account. Within participatory democracy, journalists should frame politics as a process that is open to the active participation of everyone.

Stromback (2005) outlines also a fourth category, deliberative democracy, but this is so enormous in terms of its demands upon government and society that it is difficult to think of an example where it might at some stage exist as part of 'real world' politics and governance. As one of the authors has pointed out elsewhere (Anderson and Ward 2007), 'it assumes a degree of rationality, impartiality and deliberative discussions among all sections of the public and their representatives that is unlikely to be realised in an imperfect world' (47). Despite its overall impracticalities, however, some of its individual requirements of journalism are practical insofar as they dovetail with key declared aspirations of BBC-style news provision, namely the fostering 'of public discussions characterized by rationality, impartiality, intellectual honesty and equality' (Stromback 2005, 337, 341).

The most ambitious form of democracy from within these category types that can be argued to be realisable to one extent or another on the basis of existing evidence is participatory democracy. Variations of this version of democracy exist to one extent or another in a number of countries across the world, including prominent states such as the USA, the UK, Germany and France. Equally, there are clear examples of journalism that is regularly tuned in to this form of democracy, including most obviously the best of the BBC's news output on the multiple platforms that it is presented. *Therefore, the specifications for the expected roles of journalism in a participatory democracy mentioned previously will be the ones that will form the core of the definition of quality news journalism appropriate for developed states' democracies that will be used within this study.* Stromback's summary of these is an excellent guide to the basics of what is required. For some developing and intermediate societies, these specifications would be extended to include also the provision of the kind of information and forums that facilitate the continuing development of democratic structures, as will be seen in the relevant chapters.

NECESSARY CONDITIONS FOR QUALITY NEWS JOURNALISM

This section of the discussion will do three things. First, it will look at some of the key processes that affect negatively or positively the chances of quality news journalism being produced, accessed and understood, with the latter two things being as crucial as the first. In doing this it will attempt to refine and, where necessary, redesign some of the established relevant theoretical insights on the topic. Second, it will look at the question of how the content of quality news should be measured and introduce a new framework for doing this that is specifically relevant to this study. Third, bearing in mind that there is little use in producing high quality news if it is in a form that very few people want to access, it will examine the issue of how quality can be measured *meaningfully* in a way that looks at the extent to which high quality content actually succeeds in reaching its target audience.

a)   New Light on Journalism Processes: Story Boxes and Mind Boxes

We would argue that a useful way of looking at the key requirements for quality news journalism is through our idea of 'story boxing'. **Story boxes** are an enhancement of the notion of frames. The literature on framing has been richly developed in recent years (see, for example, D'Angelo and Kuypers, 2010), and Nisbet (2010) has offered a useful caution against the continuous reinvention of ways of conceiving frames, arguing that agreement should be reached on ways of doing this in order that comparative data can start to be built using a uniform approach. However, the argument here is that where a specific research purpose requires a refinement and expansion of existing ideas, then it would obstruct the development of greater understanding if this was 'forbidden'. The notions of story boxes and mind boxes explained here provide such a refinement and expansion for the specific quality focussed concerns of this chapter and are justified on those grounds. It is not claimed that they would fit necessarily the needs of other research questions and concerns, and the literature provides a rich set of analytical tools from which analysts *can choose according to their needs*.

What the concepts of story boxes and mind boxes do is avoid the distraction of the (for many other purposes, highly effective) wider framework(s) of framing theory and focus in directly on the *constraining factors* that are most useful in helping us think very specifically about news quality, which is the core concern of this chapter.

Story boxes are the 'boxes' *into which information is selectively put* for the audience to view as news stories. 'Boxes' are a more helpful metaphor than 'frames' *for the specific purposes of the quality focussed research concerns of this chapter* because they remind analysts that the box within which the story has been packed *has to be opened* by the audience before it becomes relevant. The box's packaging has to be of the right quality if it is to attract interest. If the audience does not go to the web page, print page, television/radio news programme or whatever that contains the story and 'open the box' within which it is contained, it has no impact (a point that is elaborated more fully in a later stage of this chapter). So when the audience chooses to view news, they effectively open story boxes that are in turn viewed through 'mind boxes,' or pre-existing ways of categorising reality within their own heads.

The idea behind mind boxes is that when a news consumer opens a story box, the consumer looks out from his or her mind box into another box: the story box. He or she processes journalism based on a view of the world that is, to varying degrees, circumscribed or, obviously, 'boxed in'.

The Walls of the Boxes and What They are Made of

It is the *process* of story-boxing that most concerns us in this first part of the discussion. It includes *all the factors that affect decisions on what to include and what to exclude within news stories, for example, changing technology, resources and ideology, including the way in which the limitations and opportunities of particular technological platforms, such as smart phones, affect the information selection and presentation process.*

Crucial also are the budgetary parameters within which stories are constructed. If there is not sufficient financial resource to invest in the high quality journalism that is necessary for news coverage of the best standard, then that will limit the information that goes into the story boxes in the most fundamental way.

Equally basic are the ideological parameters within which the societies hosting news producers operate. Those that are most to the right of the free market capitalism spectrum, such as the United States, view news as a social good that is best provided as a commercial good, with little or no commitment to public service news provision. That, in turn, can be a serious limitation on the range and depth of information going into the story boxes that are offered for the U.S. public to open and access, as is illustrated in some depth in Robert Beers's chapter on the U.S. broadcast media.

Sitting more in the middle of the spectrum, the UK obviously has the guaranteed public service provision of the BBC across radio, television and online. That, in turn, ensures that there is at least a safety net in place should, for example, the quality press collapse over the next three or four years as a result of the difficulties of finding long-term, viable business models in the internet age. In the British case, it means that, providing the far right marketeers within the UK Conservative party do not get their way and begin to damage the BBC any more than recent cuts already have done, the UK's audience should continue to have access to story boxes containing a broad range of in-depth hard news material from a 'brand' with a reputation that, prior to the Savile and McAlpine scandals,[2] was widely trusted. Nevertheless, a BBC faced with less domestic competition would not be ideal from the perspective of liberal democracies theoretically being the hosts for a plurality of views and interpretations regarding the political world. Nor would it be desirable in terms of it being kept on its toes, although it would, of course, be aware that if it became a lazy provider, parts of its audience would begin to gravitate away towards the various other forms of news communication that are still in the process of emerging and developing on the internet.

Common to both story boxes and mind boxes are the limitations occasioned by the 'omnivision deficit'. There is a danger, when viewing things from a theoretical perspective, of assuming that there is a correct way of telling a news story that will enable all of the key causal factors to be identified and explained in a manner that is comprehensive enough to reveal 'the truth' at the heart of every issue. The question as to what extent it is possible for journalists to report 'the truth' has long been at the heart of quality news journalism. Postmodernists have argued that knowledge and truth are mere social constructs and that their composition will vary according to the different socially constructed perspectives of groups and individuals as to what 'the truth' is (Axford 1995). Equally, leading historians have contended that historical 'truth' is no more than the consensus of eminent historians at any one time as to what the historical facts of a situation are and can change from one generation of historians to another. These viewpoints suggest that there is no 'one truth' for journalists to discover. However, other schools of thought have argued that the postmodernist view is flawed because if all of the ideas that are described as knowledge and truth are mere debateable social constructs, then this must be equally true of postmodernism. Therefore, it cannot be used as an argument to establish *beyond doubt* that the discovery of 'the truth' is impossible (Axford 1995).

The reality of the matter is that the search for 'the truth' behind human actions, whether they be decisions affecting war or peace, or the raising of higher education tuition fees, is made immensely difficult both by the complexities of the human brain and, ironically, by its limited ability to handle complexity. The former can make it extremely problematic to try and untangle the reasons for human actions when the interplay of logic and emotions within the mind of the perpetrator of an action, when combined with the fallibilities of human memory, can make it difficult for even them to understand precisely why they acted in the way they did, never mind a journalist or anybody else. When an action of immense consequences, such as the decision to embark on a war, involves a number of minds with a range of such complex interactions going on within them, the scale of the problem is multiplied several-fold. When whole societies are involved, the level of complexity is such that the answers to many questions concerning their collective actions can at best be well-evidenced possible explanations rather than 'the truth'. An example is the continuing quest to discover precisely how the people of one of the most civilised countries on earth could have allowed the rise to power and the brutal domestic, as well as foreign, excesses of the German Nazi Party during the 1930s.

With regard to the limited ability of the human mind to deal with complexity, psychologists have long pointed out that the information-processing ability of each individual is affected by their 'cognitive complexity' (Burleson and Caplan 1998). Famously, for example, there is the contrast between presidents Roosevelt and Reagan; the former had the capacity to read and absorb significant quantities of complex documentation himself before making decisions, whereas the latter relied on one or two pages of summary documentation provided by his advisers to help him navigate his way through the day's business. Even the most brilliant mind, such as that of Einstein, lacks the ability to unlock all of the mysteries of the universe and is thereby limited by its own cognitive complexity. In short, the simple fact that nobody has the 'omnivision' of an all-seeing god means that there are automatically going to be limits on what goes into story boxes and equally on how the minds of the audience can judge and interpret what they find there. No matter how good the quality of the storytelling and the journalism behind it, those limits can at best be mitigated, but not eradicated.

The story boxing process includes also the factors traditionally identified as part of the framing process, such as the way in which family, educational and wider societal socialisation processes and ideological beliefs affect the way that news selectors choose what goes into particular story boxes and what is left out.

Also important in understanding the process of story boxing is the literature on primary definers and their role in determining how news is shaped by attempting to present the details of a story in a manner that they hope will persuade journalists to portray relevant issues and events in a way that favours their interests (Hall et al. 1978). The most obvious example of this is the worryingly commonly observed phenomenon of busy journalists on 'downsized' regional and local newspapers taking with little question the carefully spun documents of PR companies operating on behalf of powerful vested interests and printing their contents as news. When this happens the relevant primary definers have succeeded in channelling the news item into a story box of their own devising that restricts the portrayal of reality to their particular vision of what it should be like. If the journalist concerned had instead challenged the facts as presented to them and compared them with alternative views from other sources, then the story would have gone into another, bigger box, this time one that gave the audience a much broader picture of reality. The more representative of the range of perspectives that are available regarding the story it is then, from a participatory democracy point of view, the higher quality will be the journalism offering provided for the audience. These are the most obvious and basic forms of story boxes.

At the high end of quality news journalism the most sophisticated practitioners are aware also of the importance of such things as ideological story boxes. Frequently, for example, the news is presented only within the broad confines of the dominant economic ideology of the day, without looking at how the facts might appear within alternative ideological perspectives, or via *alternative nuances of perspective within* the current dominant ideology. That results in story boxes that scholars such as Fairclough (2001) would argue reflect and reinforce the status quo and, by so doing, the interests of currently dominant elites. Journalism that truly sets out to facilitate a fully working participatory democracy would make its audience aware that there are different answers to problems and different diagnoses of the causes of those problems within different economic ideological viewpoints. It would make them aware also that it might be worth at least considering whether some of the alternative views offer solutions that could be adapted to the needs of problems that are being inadequately solved within a current dominant economic ideology. Whether the audience would be able to see beyond an existing ideological prism would of course determine the extent to which such journalism had an impact, but the principle that they should at least be given the opportunity to be aware of such a step change in terms of alternative views is an important ingredient of participatory democracy.

A good example of journalism that uses story boxes that present issues via *alternative nuances of perspective within* the current dominant ideology is coverage of the post-2008 crash and economic crisis affecting the developed states. Coverage, for example, of the plight of the U.S. or UK economies that uses story boxes limited to a consideration of the issues within the Anglo-Saxon version of free market economics, that is, that which has limited the ability of the U.S. and British economies to reduce their exposure to the financial services sector via boosting domestically manufactured exports, runs up against a brick wall. This takes the form of an economic outlook that says production should always be moved to wherever wage and other production costs are cheapest, no matter what the impact on domestic jobs and the negative impact (via consequent unemployment) on domestic spending power. However, when the post-1945 (originally West-) German economic model is offered as a contrast within a broader story box, it becomes immediately apparent that there are other ways of doing free market economics than those practised by the British and the Americans that might well produce far better results for their economies. The best of

BBC economic reporting uses such story boxes, for example. That at the more mediocre end of the spectrum does not, and that coverage arguably is not fully facilitating participatory democracy.

The extent to which such a sophisticated approach to story boxing is possible is going to be dependent on a number of things, the most obvious obstacle being, of course, ideological limitations imposed by a particular news organisation or other provider of journalistic services. However, even in cases where a news provider is concerned to be as free of ideological obstacles to such examples of quality news provision as it can be, the extent to which this is possible is going to be dependent upon it having journalists with the necessary in-depth knowledge and skills across the range of key hard news topic areas—and editors wise enough to make full use of those skills. Where this aspect of its 'human resources' is seriously lacking, for financial or other reasons, then the quality ambitions of the service provider are going to remain mere aspirations to the extent that the required expertise is absent.

Mind boxes comprise all of the factors that 'box' ideas and information (relating not only to news, but everything else besides) into particular configurations within the minds of both news selectors and their audience. They include the frames that result from the 'boxing' process but go far beyond them. *The notion of mind boxes sees the mind 'at the heart of the box' in a dynamic, often unpredictable interpretive role, trying to get to grips with a reality that is mediated frequently by inaccurate or incomplete information.* The rich literature on framing includes excellent analyses of the full interactive and pluralistic relationships that are involved in, for example, a situation in which the journalist as a watcher of the world around has their view framed by the news and social interactions that directly influence them and then, in turn, frames news for an audience, news that is influenced by the way that the world has been framed to them (as the news producers), the news values that have been framed by their news organisation, and so forth. This can provide an in-depth and multilayered understanding of the framing process. However, for the specific news quality related purposes here, something with an extra layer of directly relevant 'quality targeted' insight to that available within the existing literature is required. That takes the form of the idea of mind boxes, which conveys more effectively than pre-existing analytical tools the way that individuals' views of the world are limited and constrained—'boxed in' in the most literal sense—by a wide and still growing variety of influences. They are to a considerable extent the other side of the coin to story boxes and story boxing processes, insofar as the latter are the means by which stories are shaped for *presentation to* the interpretive minds of the audience and can become *part* of the mind boxing process. However, as pointed out earlier, mind boxes also play a role in determining how news selectors choose the information that they include in or exclude from story boxes. Our concern here is with the importance of mind boxes for the way the audience views the news.

Quality news producers try to find ways of accessing an audience whose attention can be difficult to grab, even for the limited purposes of grazing. Mind boxes are useful insofar as they provide a fuller picture of the news producer's task and the levels at which it can be approached. These levels are constantly evolving *in tandem with such things as the continuously developing technologies that play an increasing role in helping shape them.*

However, a deterministic view of technological development and its impact would be simplistic. The effect of new technology on news interpretation, accessing or avoidance is determined significantly by *user practices/cultures*, which can vary over time and between societies. Mind box walls include the 'add-ons' to traditional framing factors that help shape the mind's options regarding such factors, particularly, for example, with respect to the technological tools and toys that the current generation of 18–30 year olds rely on for everyday communication, social networking and information accessing in the developed world and within the wealthier sections of society in the less developed world. These both expand and limit their view of the world. They limit it, for example, via what may be loosely termed 'Dark Angel' or 'Lucifer factors'. These are the added distractions (as compared to periods when technologies and 'leisure alternatives' were less developed and less numerous) that these add-ons provide, pulling users yet further away from the serious information highways on which the news that is an important part of the heart blood of participatory democracies travels, with a range of alternative ways of spending their time. The use of such colourful terms is not frivolous and is derived from the sobering 'in extremis' memory of the ways in which Hitler's rise was facilitated by parts of the German population of the time who allowed themselves to be distracted from the dangerous realities that were developing around them and simplistically saw the answer to their economic and other problems in a tyrant (Kershaw 2008). These Lucifer factors are not only much larger in number than those available to previous generations, but *always with them,* insofar as smart phones are for many almost a piece of 'interactive clothing', constantly worn on their person. Equally, while the online/ mobile format in some ways expands the possibility of news access via the extreme portability of the platform devices, in others it could be argued to limit the way that this happens, not least because of the limited extent to which quality news can be headlined within even the most generous of smart phone screens (although *The Guardian* [2012] in particular has been working on ways round this).

But, to stretch the biblical allusions a little further, technology also presents its users with 'Seraphim factors', or potential benefits of the use of new technologies that can expand citizens' understanding of the key issues at the heart of the democracies in which theoretically it is hoped they will want to fully participate. Most obvious of these is the potential of the internet, unparalleled in history, for providing users with instant access to huge volumes of primary and secondary information on everything ranging from government policies on climate change or defence to local planning regulations relating to garden sheds. In theory this provides them with most of what they need to become effective participants in the political process if they choose to access it.

However, the available research suggests that this is a potential that is a minority pursuit. One of the problems is that *the dizzyingly large range of possible things to do and look at* that all internet users are confronted with presents them with far more things than there is time to examine and consider in detail, or properly absorb, thereby encouraging the grazing approach to news access that, for example, Pew research shows as characterising the news accessing habits of those aged between 18 and 29 in the USA (Pew Research Center for the People and the Press 2012) and Michael Williams's chapter shows to be the dominant usage of online news sites within the UK. The detailed accessing of hard news takes time that could be spent on more pleasurable activities such as Facebook conversations, Twitter updates, and so forth. News producers' awareness of the pulling power of social media is demonstrated by all of the ways in which sites like BBC online try and reference it and interact with it in an attempt to attract the attention of its international mass membership of users.

A sub-category of Lucifer factors, in the form of 'herd-pull' factors, are often at work here, and Facebook is indeed a classic example of what they involve. They are the magnetically attractive fads, forums and fashionable goods, services or practices that frequently come to dominate (in particular) youth cultures, whose impact is magnified exponentially by the internet as a viral communication tool spreading new trends and desires. They can be spontaneous, created by users themselves and/or manipulated by skilful manufacturers such as Apple, with its successful transformation of iPhones and iPads into 'must haves' for millions of users across the world. Like all Lucifer factors, they can be powerful distractors from things like news, reducing or eliminating its accessing via their competing and often massive demands on user time and attention. Because they can be fleeting and subject to change between one generation and another, or due to the replacement of one fashionable technology by another, they can make it particularly difficult for commercial news producers to make stable projections for their business and to evolve reliable means of accessing different key parts of their target audience (see Boaden, quoted in chapter nine, page 164).

In addition, such factors as *the context of the times* are potentially important in shaping mind boxes. For example, it is a logical expectation that news accessing will rise during startling and horrific events such as 9/11. What potentially can be increased in such times is the *receptiveness* to news, if only relating to the specific events concerned. Equally, when the culture of contentment (Galbraith 1993) predominates within sectors of society, it is argued frequently that the receptiveness to serious news declines and 'the contented' switch their attention to more frivolous matters.

Also present within mind boxes are generational experience factors—those who have lived through wars and other traumatic experiences directly impinging on them as participants or victims have a greater primary evidence base within their heads regarding the importance of the political world, the economy, and so forth than those who have lived through relatively calmer times without such traumas directly impacting on them. Educational factors are pertinent as well. If the day-to-day direct relevance of politics and economics and the basis of how to understand these subjects is not taught at school level and beyond—and taught in an interesting way—then that also can be dis-incentivising as far as the accessing of hard news is concerned.

Finally, an interesting although as yet unproven proposition advanced by David Nicholas and others is that our brains are being 're-wired' in the way that they select and process information as a result of their interaction with new technologies (*The Telegraph* 2010). If this speculation turns out to be correct, then obviously that too will have an impact on the mind boxes of news media users, reducing the ability of the mind to concentrate for sustained periods of time on substantial bodies of data.

b)   The Quality of the Content

One of the key questions at the heart of this book asks, how can we measure the quality of hard news journalism in a readily usable and reasonably effective way?

A variety of perspectives on news quality and how to evaluate it are on offer within the literature. There is space here only to permit the selection of some of those that are most relevant to this study. Bogart, for example, published a particularly interesting analysis and review of industry, reader and academic views of news quality in 2004 that emphasised, above all else, the difficulty of measuring it in the absence of any truly objective way of doing this. One frequently favoured way of measuring news quality historically has been to research editors' views of what it consists of, and he compares the results from two studies of these, set 25 years apart, one conducted by himself in 1977 and one conducted by Meyer and Koang-Hyub in 2002. Both used the same set of criteria. The 1977 study surveyed 746 members of the American Society of Newspaper Editors and, as its core measure, asked them to rate seven measures of editorial quality. Of the top four, accuracy, came first, followed by impartiality in reporting, investigative enterprise and specialised staff skills. The 2002 study was a smaller study of 285 editors. While the size difference should introduce a degree of caution regarding the findings, it was interesting that Meyer and Koang-Hyub found little change in the views of the 2002 editors to those from 1977 (Bogart 2004, 45–46). Bogart points out that the key quality attributes used in his 1977 study have been used by a variety of other researchers as well with 'rather consistent results' (Bogart 2004, 47).

Another, more recent, excellent review of news quality issues, which contains also a proposal for a news quality evaluative framework that builds on the classical study of rhetoric, was published by Ivor Shapiro in 2010. His framework is organised within five "faculties": discovery, examination, interpretation, style and presentation. A specific evaluative topic is associated with each of these faculties, as are potential standards ("quality journalism is independent, accurate, open to appraisal, edited and uncensored") and criteria of excellence—"the best journalism is ambitious, undaunted, contextual, engaging and original" (Shapiro 2010, 143 and 152–158). The framework is both provocative, in terms of challenging the reader to contemplate a well thought out adaptation of the ancient to the purpose of evaluating the modern, and useful, with regard to the number of items that both journalists and academic theorists of journalism would agree are important to one extent or another in the critical evaluation of journalism quality that it contains. However, it could be argued to lean too much into the academically theoretical for practitioners to be persuaded either to use it in the broad initial form that it is sketched out, or even to extract from it some of its key components for precisely targeted evaluative purposes.

We might look also at the 'matrix' developed by two of the authors within this book (Anderson and Egglestone 2012) for the monitoring, maintenance and enhancement of the quality of BBC text-based and audio-visual online journalism. The aim behind this is twofold. First, to produce a more comprehensive framework for the monitoring and evaluation of the quality of specific, key aspects of the corporation's online hard news output than currently exists. It is intended to be usable not only by expert outsiders looking in at the BBC's standards, but, with a little basic training, by the organisation's editorial staff, should the corporation choose to consider its merits and agree its adoption. The second aim is to provide a means of helping maintain and increase the quality of the same key aspects of BBC news output at the stages of reporting and editorial decision-making within ongoing stories. Implicit and explicit within this is a detailed understanding of core fundamentals of quality news journalism that are necessary to meet the requirements of participatory democracy.

However, the matrix was designed for use within a news organisation with resources that exceed those of most others around the globe. While many will not have the resources to implement it to the extent envisaged for the BBC, it can still be used successfully for monitoring both the text-based and audio-visual news quality standards of any online hard news provider by those wishing to monitor quality 'from the outside looking in', whether they do this via their own resources, if they are sufficiently well funded, or with the assistance of the type of crowd sourcing that is explained within the details of the matrix's various requirements (Anderson and Egglestone 2012).

However, even were this framework to be espoused as suitable at least for the monitoring of quality *online* news journalism in the specific and limited circumstances outlined previously, the question remains as to how news producers with considerably less resources than the BBC—and indeed external news monitors without the time or resources to apply the matrix in its full form—can effectively monitor the quality level of hard news that is being produced. Equally, from the point of view of this study, while both Shapiro's framework and the preceding work of authors such as Bogart contain elements that can be used, to one extent or another, for the purposes here, the precise nature of those purposes do not fit easily with *all* of those elements. What will be done, therefore, is to choose from the work of Bogart, Shapiro, Anderson and Egglestone and other relevant frameworks those components that can be argued to best fit the immediate needs of this book and to devise new ones where they are necessary, or adapt and modify existing ones where this would seem to be appropriate. Of these various studies, it is argued that the Anderson and Egglestone matrix is the most practical of the quality frameworks that we have looked at, for the reasons that are set out in the article containing it (2012), and that the best strategy would be to use as much of this as possible, together with relevant components from the framework of Shapiro and others, to create something that would most fit the needs of this book. These, of course, go beyond the online focus of the matrix study, and this will affect the choices made.

Accordingly, it is argued that a framework based on what we term 'the five Cs and one A' (comprehensibility, context, causality, comparativeness, comprehensiveness and accuracy) provides an acceptable, simpler, stripped-down version of the matrix-style comprehensive framework. This new framework is explained later in this chapter. It is partially derived from the matrix but also constitutes a standalone framework designed for the purposes of this study and serves to show how news producers can viably and effectively monitor their content in a manner that does two important things. First, it gives them a workable and adequate means of solidifying their claim to be quality brands. Second, it provides news consumers and other interested parties with an *effective* way of establishing and monitoring the quality of the news 'products' at the heart of the democratic process. This should enable them to establish not only which 'products' are most likely to be of use in helping them access reliable information and commentary on key hard news events, but the extent to which participatory democracy, as defined by Stromback, is being facilitated or hampered by the allegedly quality news media of a society. The relevant components are equally applicable in an online or offline context. The exposition that follows will in its detail demonstrate the logic that underpins these contentions.

It is important to emphasise that it is automatically assumed that, in the case of developed states, part of the broader quality assessment equation will involve checks to ensure that, over any given year's coverage, major news producers will have covered the majority, if not all, of the key issues that potentially could have a significant impact on the lives, concerns and interests of their target audience. Ideally such checks should ensure that this is done in a manner that enhances the audience's ability to participate in the debates and policy-making processes relating to them (see following section). It will most certainly need to do this to meet the requirements of the assessment criteria set down within the 'five Cs and one A' framework. The range of coverage that is evaluated *in detail*, using this, will depend on the resources available to those doing the evaluation. The monitoring of those stories that are chosen for assessment will include ongoing news reports, periodic backgrounders, and so forth, but will exclude those items specifically referred to as comment. In the case of the sample developing and intermediate societies, checks will need to be made also to ensure that, during the same period, major news producers will have provided the kind of information and forums that facilitate the continuing development of democratic structures within those societies.

AN EFFECTIVE NEWS QUALITY CONTENT MONITORING FRAMEWORK FOR ORGANISATIONS/INDIVIDUALS WITH MODEST RESOURCES

The first question to ask about any quality monitoring process obviously is why have its components been chosen from the considerable range of candidates for inclusion that are available within the literature and the quality related documents produced by the industry, or the quality regulatory/advisory bodies relating to various parts of it.

The answer in this case is that it is important to emphasise that the following process is not claimed to be the only way of assessing quality for the purposes stated in this chapter, or with the level of resources implied here. What is argued, however, is that its components are those most necessary if the audience is to be given sufficient high quality information for it to be empowered in a meaningful sense, that is, to the extent that is necessary to fully enable a participatory democracy. Each criterion underpins vital parts of the structure of participatory democracy.

Some industry quality preferences, such as having a reputation for being first with the breaking news, therefore, are eschewed in favour of indicators that measure the quality of the information and analysis.

The other argument that is advanced in favour of the framework set out here is its ease of use.

It was stated previously that the framework is based on five Cs and one A. The A is what Helen Boaden, the former BBC Head of News, and other key figures in the news industry have argued to be the first and most sacred principle of quality hard news: accuracy (Anderson and Ward 2007; Bogart 2004, 45). Some news producers who value being first with the news above everything else are prepared to sacrifice immediate accuracy on the grounds that the internet allows all errors to be rapidly corrected.[3] Too many inaccuracies can cost a news producer the trust of its audience and the reputation upon which it depends. Accuracy requires proper sourcing and verification, and, arguably, the range of sources used should not be decided purely on a numerical basis, but wherever possible should reflect the range of voices on an issue, or at the very least those that are representative of what might reasonably[4] be argued to be the key arguments and concerns.

The first of the five Cs is comprehensibility. The writing and/or audio/visual story construction must be of a high enough quality in terms of logical structure and the clarity of exposition for the news report to be readily comprehensible to readers/listeners/viewers of the average to high level of intelligence or education (bearing in mind that many people can be of a high level of intelligence but disadvantaged in things like the tradition of news accessing as a result of social/educational deprivation) that would be the range of the expected audience for quality news journalism.

The second is context. There must be sufficient context, either within the report itself, or across the range of related running reports/backgrounders, to enable the audience to see the issues that are raised in the story within the key contexts—whether these be economic, political, historical, cultural, or whatever—that are necessary for their understanding.

The third is causality. The story must convey to the reader, in a well explained manner, the key and most likely causal factors at work within the events and/or issues reported, insofar as they can reasonably be known at the time of the report being filed.

The fourth is comparativeness. As was elaborated in the notion of 'story boxes' earlier, key issues are poorly covered if they are reported within only one 'ideological prism' when others of a practical, logical and well-constructed nature are available that could offer the reader alternative ways of viewing the matters at the heart of the report for comparative purposes. Again, the example of judging the U.S. and UK economies within the German vision of free market economics and not only the Anglo-Saxon model, is appropriate.

The fifth is comprehensiveness. A useful evaluation of the range of questions monitored across a story's life and development can be made by relevant specialist correspondents and professionally or academically qualified members of the audience. They can assess the extent to which what might reasonably be argued to be the *key* questions relating to a news topic have been covered across the range of its coverage. It would be worth exploring whether retired correspondents, together with interested academics and others, would be interested in helping set up and participate in web panels dedicated to the monitoring of representative samples of stories from quality news producers, covering such issues as comprehensiveness. Our initial soundings suggest that there would be interest in this idea.

CHECKING FOR THE FIVE CS AND ONE A—COLOUR-CODED CONTENT ANALYSIS

The colour-coded content analysis system explained below is an approach borrowed from the matrix mentioned earlier and simplified for the more modest human and financial resource scale envisaged here. Content analysis in its 'full blown' academic form would have a zero minus chance of being used by busy working news organisations on a week-to-week basis. However, the 'user-friendly' version being advocated here is relatively manageable and would allow news editors, journalists and interested parties monitoring their quality performance from outside to see at a glance how a representative sample of claims for quality journalism are matching up to the reality. It is in essence a system of colour highlighting, plus simple scoring, which allows those using it to see quickly and easily the approximate amount of each of the five criteria outlined previously that are present in any ongoing story that is being monitored.

Some examples (in colour) of how it would work can be seen at http:// clok.uclan.ac.uk/7825. As will be seen from the examples, the colour-coding system would work hand in hand with a simple numerical coding system. In the case of these sample case studies, the *amount* of context within each story would be shaded in turquoise to give a crude but nevertheless usefully indicative and highly visual picture of the extent of its presence, using the simple word/sentence shading facility available on MS Word programmes. The *extent* to which *adequate context* was provided for the average audience member (as judged via existing audience research for the news provider concerned) would be indicated by a scoring of 1 to 6, with 1 denoting an unacceptably low provision of context and 6 an excellent provision. The scoring would be marked in turquoise bold large superscript at the end of each individual piece. Where adequate context had been provided by an earlier report in a continuing story, the score would be raised to reflect that, but put in brackets to alert the reader to the fact that this is a judgment that relates to quality across the range of the coverage and not just within the individual report. A scoring for comprehensibility using the same sliding scale of 1 to 6, with 1 representing an unacceptably poor performance and 6 an excellent one, would also be made in bold large superscript at the end of each report, this time in blue.

Similarly, sentences including explanations of relevant causal factors would be highlighted in green. The adequacy of the quality of the causal explanations, in terms of coverage of an adequate number of possible causes in a well-explained manner, would be indicated again by the use of the 1–6 scale in large superscript bold, this time obviously in green, at the end of the story.

The same approach would be used for the remaining Cs. With regard to comparativeness, the 1–6 scale would be used to indicate the extent to which the alternative key ideological prisms through which a story might be viewed have been included across the range of a topic's coverage. In this case the colour coding would be in yellow, with the content containing alternative prisms being highlighted in this colour, as well as the overall rating at the end. Finally, in relation to comprehensiveness, the same scale would be used to assess the extent to which *key* questions and issues relating to a topic in the news have been raised across the range of a story's coverage, and the colour used in this case would be purple. Again each key question would be highlighted in this colour at the point where it appears in the story.

As with context, where adequate degrees of any of the aforementioned criteria have been provided across the range of on-running coverage of a story, then, in instances where their presence in an individual story is limited, the overall quality reading could be inserted at the end of the piece, but again in brackets to make it absolutely clear that the judgment is based on the coverage as a whole, not the single item.

As far as accuracy is concerned, any inaccuracies should be both underlined and highlighted in red. The quality assessment of the sourcing should, wherever the nature of the issue makes it appropriate in quality terms, include a rating for the extent of the representative range of the sourcing, which should be provided in the usual way (a scoring on the basis of 1–6) at the end of the report and highlighted in orange.

To revisit briefly the issue raised previously as to who would best be placed to make the judgments in each of the previous cases, if the resources of relevant news producers were available in-house to do a number of random samples across the range of their coverage on a monthly basis, for example, then this would at least give an indicative picture of the quality of coverage being provided that would be useful both for the self-monitoring of quality standards and for using in response to criticisms of the news producers' quality levels from outside. However, unless the range of staff willing and able to do this job effectively is reasonably large, as is the case generally at the BBC, there would be problems with the credibility of the results. In smaller organisations, and most have been 'downsizing' in the face of the economic challenges of recent years, there would be a strong likelihood of the producers of the reports having a significant role in judging themselves and not spotting things that they had left out or done poorly for the same reasons that they did not see them or cover them adequately in the first place. For this reason, ideally the judging would be done by the kind of independent web panels suggested previously, comprising retired leading correspondents, academics, and so forth working in conjunction with the industry, either on a voluntary independent basis, or on a funded basis that avoids any dependent or interest-based link with individual news producers. Another possible model would be an organisation such as Full Fact, which is a fact-checking organisation funded by charities such as the Rowntree Trust, overseen by a cross party body of people experienced in making relevant professional judgments and with a small but effective staff to do the 'donkey work' (Full Fact 2013a). To give the exercises some attractiveness in terms of traditional media industry ways of doing things, the latter two models could be tied in to an awards scheme, the 'news Oscars' perhaps, that is specifically linked to the judgments that they produce. The question of who should fund such a scheme is a matter of debate, but the prestige accruing to those who might fund it as a result of their name being publicly attached to the awards may well be tempting for some.

There is no way of producing absolutely 'objective' judgments regarding the one A and the five Cs, for all the reasons that have been exhaustively re-hearsed within the literature relating to the inevitable presence of subjectiv-ity within qualitative judgments (see Bogart 2004, for example). However, what can be done is to ensure that those judgments are as rigorously and as transparently arrived at as possible. Those providing the quality ratings would need to make available the rationale behind their judgments so that those with the expertise and interest necessary for the provision of cross-checking would be able to interrogate and independently evaluate the data and its quality.

c)   The Other Half of the Equation: Measuring Quality Meaningfully—Received Quality News Journalism

On the one hand, the standards that should be aspired to in order to meet the content requirements of a specific form of quality news journalism can be agreed for the purposes of a book such as this. On the other, as pointed out earlier, there is little point in simply setting out to meet the standards in a box ticking fashion. In practice they are meaningless unless the quality jour-nalism that has been produced actually reaches its target audience. It could be argued, therefore, that a distinction needs to be made between *produced* and *received* quality news journalism and, in turn, between a failed and a successful communication of quality news. If very few of the target audience actually access the quality news being sent their way, then no matter how well it is produced in terms of literary or audio/visual style or journalistic quality, it is failing to fulfil the purposes required of it within a participatory democracy and is relatively meaningless in terms of its contribution to the enlightenment and empowerment of citizens.

This proposition suggests that *a fully refined system* of defining and mea-suring quality news journalism in the context of a participatory democracy, whether this is applied in the case of developed, developing or intermediate societies, should include the extent to which it is actually accessed.

For the purposes of this book, quality news journalism is received in a 'meaningful' sense where there is evidence that it reaches, on average, a significant part of its target audience. Some news programmes, such as Sky news, are often referred to as reaching a 'significant audience' in the form of journalists and opinion makers, but, given the concern with facilitating and extending participatory democracy here, significance is seen purely in terms of size.

If resources permit, a reasonably nuanced picture can be built up, with quality news coverage being broken down on a topic-by-topic basis and the extent to which each topic is received being analysed individually. In statistical terms it would seem appropriate to be generous in measuring such reception in a world where much of the audience is heavily time pressured by work or other commitments. A hit rate of 51% of the target audience would therefore seem reasonable to use as the outer boundary of the meaningfully received category of quality news journalism. At this level of 'target finding', while ideally the hit rate would have been higher, at least an 'absolute majority' of the target audience has been reached. A lower hit rate of 25%–50% would seem to merit the title of semi-received quality news journalism. The degree of audience reception is not irrelevant, but in failing to reach the majority of the target audience, its impact is much less significant. A hit rate of below 25% would seem worthy of being described only as 'declaratory' quality news journalism. It is a form of journalism that should tick all of the boxes in terms of meeting the requirements for news content quality within participatory democracies set out earlier within this chapter, but that fails to merit the description of being meaningful or semi-received simply because of its very low rate of target audience penetration.

The size of the overall target audience within individual countries, together with that of the domestic target audiences for individual news producers and their various news 'products', also is of relevance here. The precise nature of the former as part of the measurement would vary obviously in accordance with such things as the size of the country involved, its culture, the quality of its educational system and levels of access to it, and the ways in which news is consumed within it (the UK, has, for example, a much smaller population and territory than the USA, but more national quality newspapers). There is no fault-proof way of deciding on how the size of the overall target audience for quality hard news in any specific country should be measured. For quality hard news, within the UK, for example, the news producer with the greatest reach in terms of the target audience is the BBC, according to audience research (Full Fact 2013b). Should the *maximum recorded reach* of its quality news across the potential UK audience, together with that of other quality news organisations whose audience can be counted in millions (ITV news, Sky News, Channel Four News), be regarded as the overall approximate maximum size of the target quality hard news audience in that country on a practical, evidence-supported basis (given that the audience for quality alternative news blogs/sites generally is relatively small and only marginal in the counting)? Much of the audience for the only other significant (in terms of audience size) quality news organisations, the quality national newspapers, overlaps with the audience for various BBC and/or ITV, Sky, Channel Four quality news offerings, and there is some evidence that this situation is at least partially replicated online (Ofcom 2012). It would not seem sensible to double count by adding them on to the figures for the news providers listed previously.

However, it would need to be remembered that the maximum recorded reach of news producers such as the BBC occurred during times when the competition from 'Lucifer factors' was much less, and this would need to be factored into the calculations so that a target that is still actually potentially reachable can be set. Changes in population size over the years also would need to be taken into account.

What it would not make sense to argue is that the overall target audience should be equivalent to the entire adult population of a society, given that the available evidence suggests that there is always a sizeable minority within societies who are quite happy to live without quality news, or educationally or intellectually disadvantaged and therefore unable to appreciate its value, or make adequate sense of it. For example, in the United Kingdom, around 16% of the population (5.2 million people) are described as functionally illiterate (National Literacy Trust 2013).

If the case of the UK is used for illustrative purposes, therefore, three of the main ways in which received quality hard news could be measured are as follows: first, with regard to the proportion of the overall target quality news audience for the country that hard news output as a whole reaches; second, with regard to the slice of this overall target audience that individual quality news products (in the form of newspapers/sites, news channels, programmes, etc.) wish to try and reach and the extent to which they succeed in doing this; and third, in relation to long-established individual news producers, it is possible to argue, for example, that their maximum recorded historic reach could be used (with the aforementioned cautions being taken into account) as the yardstick against which their current performance could be measured within their very specific sector of the overall quality news market.

As with every measure of news performance, these approaches have their limitations, but they have useful illustrative value here and demonstrate that received quality news is a measurable concept as well as a crucial means of determining whether quality news journalism that ticks all of the boxes in terms of content quality is actually 'meaningful' in the sense of provoking significant numbers of the audience to access it.

All of this means, of course, that there are additional requirements involved in the successful communication of quality hard news other than the core process of the production of the relevant pieces of journalism themselves. They can be summarised as follows:

- The first is the responsibility of the news producers themselves. It is the need to find ways of accessing a core audience that in many cases will not only be multitiered in terms of generations, news platform preferences and usage habits, but significantly fluid in terms of the means needed to reach it due to the way that continuous technological development and social change, among other things, affects audience behaviour.

- The second is the responsibility of politicians and other elected representatives within participatory democracies. Where, as is often the case, there is a significant level of citizen non-participation within elections and other key parts of political life due to the actions and inactions of key politicians having bred cynicism, disillusionment, feelings of powerlessness or of being marginalised, and so forth, this can make it extremely hard to interest significant sectors of the population in the accessing of quality hard news concerning the relevant political/economic/social issues. Politicians cannot complain about low levels of interest in the affairs of legislatures and others if they have failed to take adequate steps to increase the credibility of themselves and the institutions within which they operate. Part of the responsibility for increasing the level of received quality news journalism is theirs.

- The third is the responsibility of all of those interested in and involved in the education of the young within participatory democracies. Where it is the case that educational systems are producing children who are, for the most part, economically and politically illiterate, no matter what their intelligence level, and who are unaware of the dangers of low levels of active citizen monitoring of the policies and other actions of governments and other elected authorities via key information routes, such as the news media and the wider range of quality information sources available on the internet, then the reasons for this have to be properly researched and means found to address them. If this is not done, then there is a danger that there will be a further decrease in the level of received quality news journalism within the relevant societies.

- Finally, there is a fourth critical area that needs attention if the breadth and depth of the reception of quality hard news is to be increased. That is something that so far has been running more or less out of control and that has been left almost entirely to the governance of market forces and the resources devoted to product innovation. It is the rate of technological development in the field of mass retailed media hardware and software. This affects news and means and levels of news and current affairs access in a range of often radical and increasingly varied ways. An obvious example is the way that the rise of the iPhone and the smart phone in general has led to the reshaping of appropriately targeted news from the BBC and other providers into a mobile readable format. One of the most significant technology-facilitated shifts occurred in the UK, for example, when satellite television was introduced by Sky during the 1980s; thereafter, it became possible to watch a growing number of television channels that had no news bulletins whatsoever. For those who ignored news-carrying television channels, radio, newspapers and subsequently, of course, the news-carrying parts of the internet, it was now perfectly possible to live their lives without any direct familiarity with local, national or international news.

With regard to the first of these requirements, which is an issue at the forefront of every mainstream news producers' agenda, the key to getting the audience's attention is, as always, the finding of an effective hook and then a suitably powerful means of storytelling to keep them on board. As seen earlier in the section covering 'Lucifer factors', the huge range of competitors for the audience's attention, most particularly in the developed states, but increasingly also in key developed and intermediate societies, is making this an increasingly difficult task for news producers to achieve. However, this does not mean that it is impossible. One strategy for attracting the interest even of those potential members of the audience for quality hard news who currently are uninterested in it, for example, can be to attempt to communicate issues at the heart of the news and current affairs initially via other routes than 'the news' itself. Those can be used to try and interest the 'non-accessors' enough in the specific issues concerned to make them want to access traditional hard news to find out more information. There is a well-established debate, for example, about the extent to which news and current affairs issues should be built into popular soaps in order to introduce those parts of the audience who otherwise would not pick up on them to their importance and relevance in their daily lives (see, for example, Toynbee 2012). UK soap writer Phil Redmond has long been an advocate of this approach (Millington 2013), and the BBC's longest running soap opera, *The Archers,* was originally launched in collaboration with the Ministry of Agriculture to educate farmers in more efficient food production (BBC 2013). The importance of thinking of ways to transform a high level of commitment to news focussed factual accuracy, analysis and explanation into new entertaining formats is further elaborated by, for example, Clay Shirky in an interview in *The Guardian* (Shirky 2012).

With regard to the second level of requirements, that pertaining to politicians, there is a profound need for those in political life to establish a strong bond of trust between themselves and the electorate via demonstrably kept promises and pledges, competence in the daily business of government and opposition and the complete avoidance of corruption. If they deliver on all of these fronts, then they can use the power of such platforms as Twitter to correct more rapidly than ever before false statements about themselves in the mainstream news media. Former UK Deputy Prime minister John Prescott, for example, has demonstrated how social media can be used to force major newspapers to correct inaccurate reports (Prescott 2012). If politicians come across merely as articulate spokespeople for governments, short on workable ideas or genuine commitment, then they should not be surprised if their words fall on deaf ears and the news reports containing themselves and their claims for the virtues of their policies are largely unreceived.

As far as the third set of requirements is concerned, arguably one potentially effective way of engaging the long-term interest of school pupils in the news is via what might be termed the 'consequences approach' to teaching about the news media and its role in helping people monitor what governments do in their name. This approach gets around the party political difficulties that can arise in countries like the UK regarding teaching anything relating to politics. It does this by using examples of the types of decisions that governments of any political persuasion need to make to show how the chain of responsibility for their consequences includes those entitled to vote (as soon as they reach voting age), as well as the government itself. Arguably, where matters of life and death are concerned, and where the teaching is of an appropriately high level in quality terms, the potential of this is, at the very least, interesting.

Finally, with regard to the fourth set of requirements, if ideological arguments for and against the idea of the primacy of market forces in deciding the pattern of news provision are put aside for one moment, and the horrifically violent record towards their own peoples of the governments of key parts of Europe and the Americas where liberal democracy collapsed, or failed to develop at all, during the first and second halves of the twentieth century, is recalled—the Stalinist Soviet Union, Fascist Spain and Germany, together with the murderous period of the generals in Argentina, for example—then a specific conclusion presents itself. Anything that threatens to undermine significantly the commitment of ordinary citizens to forms of governance that have protected their rights needs to be rethought and modified to reduce as radically as possible the chances of any such potentially catastrophic social side effects. Communications software and hardware manufacturers need to be brought into a constant debate and discussion about possible negative social and political impacts of their ever-evolving technologies and ways of mitigating these. Most particularly, it could be argued from this point of view that, where such negative effects potentially include a serious deleterious impact on the chances of quality hard news being accessed, then there should be a new requirement of manufacturers. That should be that, in future, 'the blue sky thinking' of their product development teams must include ways of building into their hardware and/or software credible ways of counteracting the dangers of such effects. It is arguably irresponsible to contend that as manufacturers their only responsibilities are product safety and consumer satisfaction. Where there is clear evidence that technological developments negatively and seriously impact on the frequency and depth of news consumption, it could even be argued that such a requirement should have legal backing. The practicalities or otherwise of such a suggestion will be investigated in the concluding chapter.

CONCLUDING COMMENTS

This chapter has set out the primary characteristics of quality news journalism as they are relevant here and the key issues and processes that affect the likelihood of their being realised. The latter are too many and detailed to be examined in detail within the context of every chapter. A key purpose in outlining and explaining them has been to provide an overview that can be drawn on, where relevant, to illuminate both specific chapters and the conclusions that are drawn at the end of the book. Among other things, they help to demonstrate the nature and scale of the obstacles that lie in the way of attempts to realise the types of quality news journalism espoused within this volume. They include a number of insights, conceptual enhancements, or innovations that help develop the existing literature with regard to such concepts as framing.

The chapter has discussed also appropriate and practical means of establishing the extent to which quality news exists in the output of news organisations that can be applied by those news producers and monitors who are not blessed with the substantial resources of the BBC. Obviously, these are not for application within this specific volume but provide a clear understanding of the overall framework of quality from which the various usages of the term within this book will be derived, as well as a rigorously formulated view of what the project would see as justifying the description of 'quality hard news'. This will inform all relevant sections of the discussion that follows. They demonstrate also that, for the purposes of this book, it can be shown that such quality is measurable in a rigorous, albeit necessarily subjective way. The fact that this is demonstrated to be the case will help ensure that the discussions of quality in the chapters that follow are built around an interpretation of the concept that is rooted, as far as possible, within practicality.

NOTES

1. Quality hard news journalism can be defined in a variety of different ways. For the purposes of this book hard news will refer to news about issues, processes, events and people that have an actual or potential significant political, economic or social impact on people's daily lives and wellbeing within local, regional, transnational and/or global contexts. As such it can include coverage of such things as crime and punishment, decisions affecting taxation and public spending, healthcare, welfare, conflict within or between states, education policy, etc. What we mean by *quality* hard news will be discussed and explained as the chapter progresses.
2. The Savile disaster of 2011–12 revolved around Peter Rippon, the then editor of the BBC flagship 'Newsnight' programme, dropping an investigation into a former BBC presenter who was discovered to have been guilty of serious sexual crimes. Both his decision and its timing caused major problems for the BBC subsequently. The McAlpine affair of November 2012 was another serious blow to the programme's reputation after its coverage

led to a Conservative Party peer being wrongly identified as guilty of child sex abuse. A timeline relating to the two sets of issues can be found at: http://www.guardian.co.uk/media/2012/dec/19/jimmy-savile-crisis-bbc-timeline

3. Anonymous industry source.
4. What is 'reasonable' is always a subjective matter open to debate. In this case what might 'reasonably' be argued to be the key arguments and concerns are those which are so in the majority view of a body of professionals (including journalists), academics and others *with expertise in the relevant field relating to an issue.* How such a body might be constituted for the purposes of this framework is explained below within the outline of its fifth keystone, comprehensiveness.

REFERENCES

Anderson, Peter, and Paul Egglestone. 2012. "The Development of Effective Quality Measures Relevant to the Future Practice of BBC News Journalism Online." *Journalism* 13: 923–941.

Anderson, Peter, and Geoff Ward. 2007. *The Future of Journalism in the Advanced Democracies.* Aldershot: Ashgate.

Anderson, Peter, and Anthony Weymouth. 1999. *Insulting the Public? The British Press and the European Union.* Harlow: Longman.

Axford, Barrie. 1995. *The Global System: Economics, Politics and Culture.* Cambridge: Polity Press.

BBC. 2013. "Frequently Asked Questions about the Archers." Accessed 20 February 2013. http://www.bbc.co.uk/programmes/b006qpgr/faq

Bogart, Leo. 2004. "Reflections on Content Quality in Newspapers." *Newspaper Research Journal* 25(1): 40–53.

Burleson, Brant R., and Scott E. Caplan. 1998. "Cognitive Complexity." In *Communication and Personality: Trait Perspectives,* edited by James C. McCroskey, John A. Daly, Matthew M. Martin, and Michael J. Beatty, 233–286. Creskill, NJ: Hampton Press.

Carey, James. 1989. *Communication as Culture: Essays on Media and Society.* New York: Routledge.

D'Angelo, Paul and Jim A. Kuypers. 2010. *Doing News Framing Analysis: Empirical and Theoretical Perspectives.* New York: Routledge.

Fairclough, Norman. 2001. *Media Discourse.* London: Arnold.

Full Fact 2013a. Homepage. Accessed 20 February 2013. http://fullfact.org/

Full Fact 2013b. "Is the BBC the Dominant Force in News Media?" Accessed 3 January 2013. http://fullfact.org/factchecks/bbc_sky_news_corp_audience_share-2831

Galbraith, John K. 1993. *The Culture of Contentment.* London: Penguin.

The Guardian. 2012. "Guardian Relaunches Mobile Site." Accessed 20 February 2013. http://www.guardian.co.uk/media/2012/nov/26/guardian-new-mobile-site

Hall, Stuart, Chas Critcher, Tony Jefferson, John N. Clarke, and Brian Roberts. 1978. *Policing the Crisis: Mugging, The State and Law and Order.* Basingstoke: Palgrave Macmillan.

Kershaw, Ian. 2008. "How Democracy Produced a Monster." *The New York Times.* Accessed 20 February 2013. http://www.nytimes.com/2008/02/03/opinion/03iht-edkershaw.1.9700744.html?_r=0

McNair, Brian, 2000. *Journalism and Democracy: An Evaluation of the Political Public Sphere.* Abingdon: Routledge.

Meyer, Philip and Koang-Hyub Kim. 2003. "Quantifying Newspaper Quality: I Know It When I See It." Unpublished paper, University of North Carolina, 19 November.

Millington, Bob. 2013. "Redmond, Phil." *The Museum of Broadcast Communications*. Accessed 20 February 2013. http://www.museum.tv/archives/etv/R/htmlR/redmonsphil/redmondphil.htm

National Literacy Trust. 2013. "How Many Illiterate Adults Are There in England." Accessed 20 February 2013. http://www.literacytrust.org.uk/adult_literacy/illiterate_adults_in_england).

Nisbet, Matthew C. 2010. "Knowledge into Action: Framing the Debates over Climate Change and Poverty." In *Doing News Framing Analysis: Empirical and Theoretical Perspectives*, edited by Paul D'Angelo and Jim A. Kuypers, 43–83. New York: Routledge.

Nord, David Paul. 2001. *Communities of Journalism: A History of American Newspapers and Their Readers*. Urbana: University of Illinois Press.

Ofcom. 2012. "Users Access Multiple Sources of News Online." Accessed 20 February 2013. http://stakeholders.ofcom.org.uk/market-data-research/market-data/communications-market-reports/cmr12/internet-web/uk-4.59

Owens, John. 2012. "Reputation Survey: The BBC—a mixed reception for Auntie Beeb." Accessed 22 February 2013. http://www.brandrepublic.com/analysis/1137518/

Pew Research Center for the People and the Press. 2012. "In Changing News Landscape, Even Television is Vulnerable. Trends in News Consumption, 1991–2012." Accessed 20 February 2013. http://www.people-press.org/2012/09/27/section-3-news-attitudes-and-habits-2/

Prescott, John. 2012. "Let Twitter Monitor the Press." *Reader's Digest*. Accessed 20 February 2013. http://www.readersdigest.co.uk/magazine/readers-digest-main/the-maverick-let-twitter-monitor-the-press

Shapiro, Ivor. 2010. "Evaluating Journalism." *Journalism Practice* 4(2): 143–162.

Shirky, Clay. 2012. "Clay Shirky on Student Journalists." *The Guardian*. Accessed 20 February 2013. http://www.youtube.com/watch?v=qT1v46LCK9w

Starkey, Guy. 2007. *Balance and Bias in Journalism: Representation, Regulation & Democracy*. Basingstoke: Palgrave.

Stromback, Jesper. 2005. "In Search of a Standard: Four Models of Democracy and Their Normative Implications for Journalism." *Journalism Studies* 6(3): 331–345.

The Telegraph. 2010. "Students' brains 'rewired' by the internet." Accessed 20 February 2013. http://www.telegraph.co.uk/technology/news/7205852/Students-brains-rewired-by-the-internet.html

Toynbee, Polly. 2012. "If Only Soap Operas Didn't Wash Their Hands of Politics." Accessed 20 February 2013. http://www.guardian.co.uk/commentisfree/2012/nov/12/soap-operas-wash-hands-politics

2 From the Insight Team to Wikileaks

The Continuing Power of Investigative Journalism as a Benchmark of Quality News Journalism

Paul Lashmar

INTRODUCTION

The purpose of this chapter is to examine the current state of a very specific form of news provision, quality hard news investigative journalism, and to evaluate the extent to which it still has a future. This type of journalism is regarded by many as the pinnacle of the profession and is seen as providing the monitoring of power and its exercise that is crucial to the effective working of the participatory democracy outlined in chapter one. Equally, in its most highly professional form, it conforms to the key quality criteria set down within that chapter. For the purpose of this exercise, the author will take one of the world's oldest democracies, the United Kingdom, as his case study, not least because he worked for 30 years as a member of some of its leading investigative reporting teams and is therefore able to offer an insider perspective as well as an academic analysis.

The discussion starts with Donal MacIntyre, a television investigative journalist best known for infiltrating a vicious gang of football hooligans, who observed that the imminent extinction of his trade has been prophesised many times:

> The death of investigative journalism was predicted with the creation of commercial television in 1954. All through the 1990s I heard it while at BBC documentaries and *World in Action*. For the last decade as budgets got tighter and the information world changed at lightning pace the same arguments that gained currency in 1954 have now have become an accepted truth. (Mair and Keeble 2011, 2)

It has been common practice to describe hard news investigative journalism as in its death throes, starved of resources and far too serious and expensive to survive in a media world of celebrity superficiality. Certainly, if investigative journalism was an intensive care patient, its struggle for life would be akin to a particularly dramatic episode of *Holby City*.

By 2008 there was a general agreement that the quality of the traditional media was in decline, and that was supported by a growing body of empirical research (Lewis, Williams, and Franklin 2008; Davies 2008). One of the most disturbing findings was the high percentage of stories in the national mainstream news media that, while by-lined with a reporter's name, were in practice taken directly from PR material or news agencies. Around the same time, the Reuters Institute published a detailed analysis of the likely impact of the digital revolution on the economics of news publishing in the UK. Among the conclusions reached in the report was that in the UK and elsewhere, news publishers are increasingly building digitally mechanised factories, equipped to feed content to a range of media platforms, all day and all week. "Under pressure to exploit content across multiple platforms, many publishers are morphing into a form that favours the processing rather than the generation of content" (Currah 2009).

Also in 2008, former *Sunday Times* investigative journalist Nick Fielding commented that "very little serious investigative journalism is going on" in the UK. Citing job losses at *The Guardian* and industry speculation over the future of the Independent newspaper, Fielding said of the British Press, "It's an industry which is massively in crisis at the moment" (Lashmar 2011). He was right, and worse was to come. The tabloids were obsessed with 'kiss and tell' and celebrity stories (many, we now know, were the product of phone hacking), and these obsessions infected the middle market and even the broadsheets, too. There was profound concern that the traditional media either no longer had, or wished to employ the resources to maintain, a sustainable level of investigative journalism. The dismal jingoist reporting that accompanied the Iraq War (see Lashmar 2008a) and complete lack of early warning of the 'credit crisis' (see Lashmar 2008b) had revealed the desperate need for better in-depth reporting. Investigative journalism was in a coma with few signs of life.

Among news and current affairs professionals it was widely believed that investigative journalism had suffered disproportionately. Former *Sunday Times* Insight team editor Stephen Grey claimed that cutbacks have severely reduced the number of investigative journalists able to work in the UK. "I think it's been absolutely savage in Great Britain. It's quite a long trend that's been going. You have seen major investigation shows in Britain collapse. There is very little investigation going on—telly as well as newspapers" (Stourton 2009).

In a 2009 paper, *The Crisis in Investigative Journalism*, I estimated that the number of serious journalists in the traditional media who could be called investigative, had fallen from around 150 during the 1980s to fewer than 90. I remarked, "even the most optimistic apostle for the resilience of investigative journalism would recognise that the genre is fighting for a sustainable future. The crisis for investigative journalism falls within the wider seismic changes occurring in the media, where newspapers face decline and TV is accused of no greater ambition than to be a ratings machine" (Lashmar 2009).

If we take 2011 as the next stop on this rollercoaster hospital drama, we find former BBC producer John Mair very positive in his prognosis for the patient:

Its death has been much predicted and is long in coming but Investigative Journalism in Britain is still in rude health.

In the last year alone we have seen Rupert Murdoch catapulted to crisis by 'Hackgate', (FIFA's) Sepp Blatter forced into a corner and Jack Warner out of FIFA, a policeman prosecuted for the unlawful killing of a bystander at the G20 demonstrations in 2009, a quarter of a million previously secret diplomatic cables released by WikiLeaks, Winterbourne View, a 'care' home exposed and closed by *Panorama* and more wrongdoers brought to justice all thanks to the diggers of the journalistic world.

The *Daily Telegraph*, not renowned for its anti-Establishment positions, did splendid work on the MP Expenses Scandal in 2009 where it simply bought the purloined data from an insider and exploited it on the page slowly, surely and deliberately. Six Members of the Mother of Parliaments are serving or have served prison sentences as a result of those revelations. (Mair 2011)

But within months the patient was to suffer another series of life-threatening setbacks. Take Wikileaks: at first this appeared to be a fascinating, even compelling, new response to the misuse of power, particularly by the U.S. government, using the global reach of new technology to protect whistle-blowers. It was a huge collective, international effort that revealed what American foreign policy really meant. Within a year of the disclosure of hundreds of thousands of U.S. classified diplomatic cables, Wikileaks had dissolved into a farce centering on its founder, Julian Assange, and his increasingly desperate efforts to avoid extradition from the UK to Sweden to answer some difficult questions over alleged sex offences. Then take the philanthropically funded Bureau of Investigative Journalism; in early 2010 it appeared to be as a beacon in the darkness, a new response in the UK to funding high quality journalism, a reason for optimism. Then, suddenly, an ill-considered tweet by the Bureau's editor about the possible naming of a senior member of the British Conservative party as a paedophile and a terrible error of judgement within the BBC over a *Newsnight* programme on child abuse left the Bureau in a critical condition. It was involved in the second public relations disaster as well as the first, and its reputation was deeply and possibly irreversibly sullied as a result.

What all this shows is that investigative journalism is in such a fragile state in the UK that a very small number of negative episodes such as the previously outlined can dramatically change the perception of whether the patient will live, particularly when so much is reliant on so few in terms of the number of people actively involved still in hard news investigative journalism. Therefore, prophesying the survival of investigative journalism is a risky undertaking. Nonetheless, with careful framing, a series of nuanced expectations can be suggested.

There are certainly reasons to be miserable. The area within UK journalism where investigative journalism has prospered in recent years has been towards the bottom end of the market, and the recent Leveson Enquiry has exposed the extent to which the techniques used to secure personal information within this previously over-resourced and under-controlled branch of UK journalism had become not only increasingly ruthless, but illegal. The situation hit proverbial rock bottom when it was discovered that a journalist had hacked the phone of a murdered schoolgirl, accidentally causing considerable distress to the family. Worse, the phone hacking scandal that started with the *News of the World* was soon found to extend to most other newspapers. This led not only to the reputation of the UK news media as a whole being dragged into deep and very public disrepute via the Leveson Enquiry and the media's own coverage of its embarrassing revelations, but to such truly damaging events as the charging of former News International Chief Executive Rebekah Brooks with perverting the course of justice. Overall, this huge and sordid scandal brought investigative journalism *as a whole* into disrepute. Such was the concern, the Lords Select Committee on Communications undertook an inquiry in 2011 into the future of investigative journalism. Some 40 people, including the author, gave oral evidence. The report, published in February 2012, summarized the status quo: "The role and practices of investigative journalism have received unprecedented scrutiny over recent months. Its long history of exposing issues that are not in the public domain and speaking truth to power has come under the microscope as the phone-hacking scandal, perhaps the greatest political media scandal of a generation, has gradually unfolded, raising a plethora of questions surrounding the public interest, privacy and media ethics" (House of Lords 2012, 5).

There are however, some reasons to be optimistic. This chapter will examine some very positive moves. First, in the campaigning sector, where pressure groups, consumer groups, charities and NGOs increasingly are undertaking their own investigative journalism to great effect.

Secondly, despite the 2012 crisis of the Bureau of Investigative Journalism, there is still hope for investigative journalism units funded by donations or subscriptions. In the United States, a number have been successful (though not all), like ProPublica. Exaro, another UK-based philanthropically funded outfit is performing well at the time of writing.

Thirdly, a whole generation of web savvy journalists is emerging who use new investigative techniques to interrogate public interest issues. Datascraping, crowd-sourcing, the network effect and using social media have really taken off as powerful tools for investigative journalism.

Fourthly, there is the rise of international yet informal networks of investigative journalists.

A SHORT HISTORY

If investigative journalism is in decline, that presupposes there have been better times. It has a long history. The origins of investigative journalism can be traced back to the government inspectors in China in 700 AD sent to report on economic and social conditions in the empire. In the UK the roots go back at least to the 17th century pamphleteers and thereafter include the activities of such notable individuals as William Cobbett and Charles Dickens (de Burgh 2008, 27).

Modern investigative journalism is often epitomized by the Watergate scandal in the United States during the early 1970s, which showed what an important role journalism can play in society. Over in the UK in the same period, the *Sunday Times*, under Editor Harold Evans, was seen as the epicentre of investigative journalism, with famous detailed investigations. These included the Thalidomide scandal, where the paper fought legal suppression to publish the facts about the drug responsible for serious birth defects in children whose mothers had used it to reduce sickness in pregnancy.

The 1970s saw UK television create a high quality, fiery brand of investigative journalism whereby individuals like John Pilger, and high profile investigative programmes like *Panorama, World in Action* and *This Week* took on the Vietnam war, torture and fascism, industrial disease and injury, child labour, miscarriages of justice and corruption stories. As will be discussed later, the tabloids were also producing a distinct vibrant form of investigative journalism, some of which was in the public interest. The Lords Committee commented that some witnesses described the 1960s to 1980s as the 'golden age' of investigative journalism. According to Gavin MacFadyen, Director of the Centre for Investigative Journalism, "It should be said that, for the last 20 years, investigative reporting, as I am sure everybody here knows, has been in major decline in Britain from what it was—major television programmes like *World in Action, This Week* and *Panorama*—to where we are now; we have nothing, really, that is comparable, or at least comparable with the depth and frequency that those programmes were" (House of Lords 2012, 21).

Professor de Burgh also identifies a boom in TV investigative journalism in the mid-1990s. "A systematic trawl of a database for 1995 (Programme Reports, 1995) suggests that in that year along alone on UK terrestrial television there were 300 discrete programmes that could be classified as investigative, this total excluding magazine programmes with investigative elements" (de Burgh 2008, 6). Whether there was a 'golden age' of investigative journalism is a matter of debate. Investigative journalism has always been a struggle, but at some times more than others.

THE ROLE OF INVESTIGATIVE JOURNALISM

It is hard to over-estimate the importance of investigative journalism. It is the most pure manifestation of the *fourth estate* role of the news media. For all their faults, the news media is the only group that has consistently shown the independence and heterogeneity to monitor the excesses and corruption of the establishment and even errant parts of its own industry. The Victorian politician and commentator Lord Acton famously observed, "Power tends to corrupt. Absolute power tends to corrupt absolutely," and there you have the succinct manifesto and justification for investigative journalism. For the author, with 30 years of experience as an investigative journalist, it is simple—without hard news investigative journalism and the monitoring of the powerful and the very public exposure of wrong doing that it provides, there can be no democracy as corruption will inevitably spread through the body politic. Investigative journalism may account for a very small part of the outpouring of the news media, but it is the benchmark that all other journalism is judged by.

> Investigative Journalism has helped bring down governments, imprison politicians, trigger legislation, reveal miscarriages of justice and shame corporations. Even today, when much of the media colludes with power and when viciousness and sensationalism are staples of formerly high-minded media, investigative journalists can stand up for the powerless, the exploited, the truth. (de Burgh 2008)

Roy Greenslade has encapsulated the nature of the investigative journalist:

> The best journalistic output is often created by individuals who are driven by a conviction that they alone have a handle on 'the truth'. They are usually single-minded, sometimes bloody-minded, often preferring to work alone, even if they are nominally part of a newspaper team. Wise editors know that certain reporters have qualities that place them apart and, despite the difficulties that sometimes causes, they give them their head. Nowhere is this more evident than in the overlapping fields of investigative and campaigning journalism. These are the provinces of lone-wolf reporters and, of course, the individual editors who publish their work. In an internet age, reporters can self-publish, but the results of their labours—if it is to cause ructions and bring about real change—presently require traditional media publication. (Greenslade 2010)

THE ELEPHANT IN THE ROOM

The appalling and illegal practices of the *News of the World* have resulted in a certain airbrushing of the history of investigative journalism. There is tendency to ignore the fact that tabloids do produce high quality real investigative journalism, as sparse as it might have been in the latter years. When giving talks or lectures, it is easy for practitioners and lecturers to avoid the subject and make investigative journalism purely the remit of the 'serious' media, such as *The Guardian, The Daily Telegraph, The Times,* Channel 4 and the BBC. But tabloid investigative journalism has on occasion had a serious hard news impact. When the Lords Committee picked out eight significant and relatively recent pieces of investigative journalism, two were from the tabloids, and both from the Murdoch stable.

- The *News of the World's* 'sting', exposing corruption by Pakistani cricketers, published on 29 August 2010; and
- *The Sun's* investigation, published on 14 September 2006, which exposed that an HIV-positive security guard had knowingly infected six women.

The Pakistani cricket sting was organized by one of the best known and the most controversial of UK undercover reporters, Mazher Mahmood, who spent 20 years working for *News of the World.* He has been dubbed as 'Britain's most notorious undercover reporter'. The *News of the World* claimed that Mahmood had brought more than 250 criminals to justice. (Though this figure has been challenged, as has his own accuracy in making such claims.) Mahmood is also known as the 'fake sheikh' because he often disguised himself as a sheikh in order to gain his target's trust. He posed as an Indian businessman to expose a cricket bookie by the name of Mazhar Majeed in August 2010, who named Pakistani cricketers Mohammad Amir, Mohammad Asif, Salman Butt and Kamran Akmal as having engaged in spot-fixing during Pakistan's 2010 tour of England. The team was accused of deliberately bowling three no-balls. Mahmood's targets have also included various society figures, including Sophie, Countess of Wessex in 2001 and, more recently, Sarah, Duchess of York in 2010.

Mazher Mahmood may be controversial, but he reflects a tradition of reporting that goes back a long way to such distinguished names in UK tabloid investigations as Laurie Manifold. Manifold joined *The People* in 1958 as news editor, later becoming investigations editor. Roy Greenslade is one of the few academics to document investigative journalism in the 'Red-Tops'. He says of Manifold, "It is no exaggeration to describe him as the father of modern popular paper investigative journalism. He trained a legion of journalists in a range of investigatory techniques, which they went on to practise in other newspapers, such as the *News of the World* (Trevor Kempson, Mike Gabbert and Mazher Mahmood), and on television, notably *The Cook Report* (Clive Entwistle)" (Greenslade 2008).

In order to investigate difficult stories, Manifold innovated with the use of subterfuge, covert tape recording and the setting up of fake companies. "He left nothing to chance," says Greenslade. "He devised special techniques to persuade reluctant sources to spill the beans. He drew up sets of rules for reporters on how they should behave." Greenslade spoke to and corresponded with eight former members of Manifold's staff, all of whom revere him as the wiliest and wisest of mentors. One spoke of him having "a mind like steel trap" (Greenslade 2008).

Manifold oversaw hundreds of investigations, and probably the pinnacle of his career was the exposure of high-level Scotland Yard corruption. "With the revelation in 1972 that the head of the Flying Squad, Commander Kenneth Drury, had been on holiday with a pornographer who had paid for the trip, the investigation ballooned as informants came forward to reveal widespread corruption within the force. It proved to be a drawn-out affair but it eventually resulted in the suspension and early retirements of 90 officers, and the convictions of 13 policemen, who were sentenced to a total of 96 years," says Greenslade. He notes that in 1978, Manifold and his team were recognised for their work with a special What The Papers Say award (Greenslade 2008). This tradition is what has been lost with the drive to celebrity reportage by the tabloids and the industry disaster that is the phone hacking scandal.

THE BBC TRAGEDY

Since the Lords Committee reported, there has been the BBC debacle. The editor of BBC's *Newsnight* spiked what appears to have been a piece of very serious journalism on child abuse committed by celebrity broadcaster and former disc jockey Jimmy Savile. Instead, the BBC ran a series of tributes to the recently deceased celebrity over Christmas 2011. The error of judgment in killing the investigation became blatant when rival ITV broadcast the story in September 2012 in a new investigation strand.

In a separate fiasco, a month after the Savile fiasco broke, *Newsnight* broadcast a programme interviewing Steve Messham, who alleged child abuse committed by a senior Conservative politician at a North Wales home at which Messham had been a child resident in the 1970s. While *Newsnight* did not name the politician, the way in which the programme was conducted resulted in the name of Lord McAlpine, an innocent man and senior Conservative grandee, spreading across the social media. The BBC was forced to issue a public apology, and Director-General George Entwistle resigned, as did the director of the Bureau of Investigative Journalism, Iain Overton, who had had input into, though no editorial control over, the item. As the BBC report says, some "basic journalistic checks were not completed" (Burrell 2012). Lord McAlpine received £185,000 in damages from the BBC.

It now transpires that while high quality investigative journalism has continued within the BBC and especially at *Panorama*, the actual number of experienced reporters and producers has dropped. The NUJ's Michelle Stanistreet said in November 2012 of the swingeing Government imposed cuts, "Even flagship programmes have not been ringfenced—at *Newsnight*, for example, the budget in real terms has halved over the past five years and the number of reporters and senior journalists has been cut relentlessly. These are simple facts. With fewer journalists, many employed on a casual basis, it means there is no time for that extra telephone call, no time to double-check the facts, no time to reflect properly before a programme goes out" (Turvill 2012; see also Lashmar 2012).

SURVIVAL AND EVOLUTION

If investigative journalism does have the capacity to survive, it is because of its continuing ability to evolve. The author can see that some of the early major investigations he undertook as a working journalist would be of little interest to the public now. For example, he can remember when the public were genuinely shocked by the idea of a police officer being corrupt. It took a long while for them to accept that, while it was not routine, it was too commonplace in some forces. Now, in the experience of the author, the public has a more jaundiced view of the police than do reporters. Therefore, you will rarely see an investigation into police corruption. They are the most difficult of investigations. If journalists make a mistake in framing allegations of corruption or misconduct, the cost of defaming a police officer is exceptionally high. Investigative journalism is not static or a given; it evolves to survive. So, as some editors ask when a reporter suggests an investigation into police corruption, "why go to a lot of trouble to tell the public what they already know?" The former editor of Channel 4's *Dispatches*, Dorothy Byrne, has said that she believes it is more and more difficult to surprise audiences with investigative journalism because they increasingly believe corruption to be widespread (Byrne 1999).

Various editorial tactics have been tried to make investigations more exciting and relevant for the present-day viewer to whom little, arguably, is a surprise after the revelations of recent years. The use of secret filming has been very influential, though it has tended to spawn story lines chosen for their undercover filming potential rather than actual public interest. Another is the rise of the celebrity investigative journalist. Roger Cook was the first, but Donal MacIntyre probably reflects most the obvious attempt to create an on-screen journalist 'superhero'. This is evolution to survive and be relevant. Methods used by investigative journalists have also evolved. Here I have identified a range of new ways in which high quality investigations are being conducted.

NGO JOURNALISM

In November 2012 Greenpeace secretly recorded the Conservative MP running the party's by-election bid in Corby apparently supporting the campaign of a rival candidate. This became a front-page story in *The Guardian*.

Chris Heaton-Harris, campaign manager for the Conservatives in Corby, was recorded saying he encouraged an anti-wind farm candidate to join the election race against the party employing him, adding, "Please don't tell anybody ever" (Lewis and Evans 2012).

This is a small example of the new breed of non-governmental-organisations' (NGOs) investigators at work. Importantly, there are an increasing number of NGOs, pressure groups, social justice groups, consumer groups and charities that conduct investigations and analysis on matters of local, regional and international concern. Organisations in this sector have become increasingly effective in bringing political and economic pressure to bear on errant governments and companies. Such campaigning, once the province of enthusiastic amateurs, is rapidly becoming highly professionalised and a core activity. They are waking up to the full potential of investigations as a campaigning tool. Some NGOs have been supplying investigative material to the traditional media for a long time. But NGO managers say there has been a sea shift, and they now often have to provide the whole package.

Paul Bradshaw, award-winning blogger and visiting professor at City University, argues investigative journalism does not have to be pursued—or funded—in one particular way. "The newsroom investigative journalist was an endangered species well before the internet arrived, while over the last decade NGOs and activist organisations have taken on an increasing role in funding investigations" (Mair and Keeble 2011, 246). The Lords Committee was interested in the migration of investigative journalists to NGOs who were sponsoring investigations into areas within their own sphere of interest. The author told the committee: "NGOs . . . have the money and the patience to do these things well . . . there are seven or eight [investigative journalists] that I can think of immediately who are now working for NGOs and doing really good work . . . they are using their expertise and bring professionalism and they now work with the media and are much more proactive" (House of Lords 2012, 54).

Other NGOs make extensive use of investigative techniques. The Environment Investigation Agency (EIA), an independent campaign group, has a great track record of undercover filming across the world. International NGO Global Witness uses investigative techniques to expose links between natural resource exploitation, conflict, poverty, corruption, and human rights abuses worldwide and has an inquiry team that includes former investigative journalists. Clive Stafford-Smith, the founder of prisoners' rights group Reprieve, told the author, "Reprieve places a huge emphasis on investigation—important cases are won by facts to a far greater extent than they are by law. My own view is that many NGOs, pressure groups and charities could be more effective by developing their investigative skills. Likewise, the symbiotic relationship between NGOs and journalists could do with a re-emphasis, particularly now that print media spends so much less on its own investigations, and depends to a greater extent on NGOs such as Reprieve" (Lashmar 2011).

NOT-FOR-PROFIT INVESTIGATION BUREAUX

The author was part of a group of investigative journalists who met in a London pub in 2009 to discuss the perceived perilous state of investigative journalism. The group examined the American experience, where long-standing, non-profit organisations like the Center for Public Integrity and the Centre for Investigative Journalism have used the combined foundation and donation funding model. One attractive model from the United States was ProPublica, which employs a substantial number of experienced journalists funded by a wealthy philanthropist—but the question was how to raise the money in the UK? Two public-spirited people, the former *Sunday Times* writer Elaine Potter and her husband, David, the developer of the Psion computer, intervened and put £2m of seed money from their charitable foundation into the project. The Bureau of Investigative Journalism was born.

In 2011, John Lloyd, at the Reuters Institute for the Study of Journalism, spoke of the "extremely encouraging signs of not-for-profit money coming in to investigative journalism in particular. In this country, it is not in a huge way, but in a significant way, in the Bureau of Investigative Journalism, which is attached to City University, and in the States there is much more" (House of Lords 2012, 53).

The then editor of the Bureau, Iain Overton, told the Lords Committee,

> We get commissions . . . to do broadcast journalism. We have worked with all of the major national papers. We have been operating since April 2010. We have had 26 front page stories in that time. We have won an Amnesty Award and a Thomson Reuters Award. We have just been nominated for a Foreign Press Association Award. We have been mentioned around 12,500 times in different articles internationally. (House of Lords 2012, 53)

However, the fate of such initiatives is dependent on how well they are led and managed. Unfortunately, at the time this chapter was written, the Bureau was in crisis. Iain Overton had tweeted an ill-considered message before the *Newsnight* child abuse programme went out (see previous discussion). As pointed out earlier, he resigned as a consequence. The Bureau has used much of its funding from the Potter Foundation and unfortunately has not been able to claim charitable status. Certainly, charitable status would encourage more not-for-profit journalism. Peter Preston (2012) says the bureau will only survive if it finds the funds to keep going. Whether it will or not is now dependent partially on the extent to which it is able to recover its reputation after the severe damage it inflicted on itself during 2012.

DIGITAL INVESTIGATIVE JOURNALISM

Social media has also become a useful tool in the investigative journalists' toolbox. Probably the reporter best known for using it in this way is *Guardian* reporter Paul Lewis. He has written extensively about the use of social media in piecing together the events that lead to the death of the news vendor Ian Tomlinson during the anti-G20 protests and also the death of Jimmy Mubenga, a deportee from the UK who died after being forcibly restrained on an aircraft. Lewis makes the point that in the pre-internet age, journalists mostly sought sources; now with social media, sources can seek out journalists (Lewis 2012).

Clare Sambrook, a freelance journalist, spoke of the benefits of using social media to publicise investigative reports. She said,

> There are lots of very good online publications and then also online we can promote the work through Twitter, for example. So, if you get a really astonishing piece—like we had a . . . piece on the Breivik massacre—and it just went . . . around the world. We got loads and loads of people reading that. It was a piece that would not have appeared in a national newspaper, a piece by a Norwegian giving context to what had happened very, very quickly. It would have been extraordinarily difficult for him, as somebody unknown to a national newspaper, to get that kind of space. So, there are all sorts of benefits to online publication and online research, massive benefits. (House of Lords 2012, 58)

The power of the internet has breathed new life into investigative journalism. Bradshaw thinks that we may finally be moving past the troubled youth of the internet as a medium for investigative journalism. He points out that for more than a decade observers looked at this ungainly form stumbling its way around journalism and said, "It will never be able to do this properly" (Bradshaw 2011). Now the internet is growing up, he says,

> finding its feet with the likes of Clare Sambrook, Talking Points Memo, PolitiFact and VoiceOfSanDiego all winning awards, while journalists such as Paul Lewis (the death of Ian Tomlinson), Stephen Grey (extraordinary rendition) and James Ball (WikiLeaks) explore new ways to dig up stories online that hold power to account. As these pioneers unearth, tell and distribute their stories in new ways we are beginning to discover just what shape investigative journalism might take in this new medium. (Bradshaw 2011)

Few of these journalists work for the traditional media. A new world of web-based journalism, with niche interests that parallel traditional investigative journalism, is emerging.

A massive amount of information, much of it statistics, is now made available online by public bodies as part of the UK Government's Open Data agenda. This is an opportunity for investigative journalists. Jeremy Hunt MP, former Secretary of State for Culture, Olympics, Media and Sport, said, "If we unleash citizen journalists on vast swathes of government data we are opening up big, big opportunities both to hold Government to account and also to learn things about our society that we never knew before. It is a very, very big opportunity" (House of Lords 2012, 59).

Professor Jon Crowcroft, Marconi Professor of Communications Systems in the Computer Laboratory at the University of Cambridge, also told the Lords Committee,

> Vast amounts of data are not necessarily a barrier to making some forms of investigative journalism easier, because the vast amount of computing power that is very cheaply available, almost freely available, offsets that . . . the biggest barrier seems to me, as in many walks of life, that to do anything reasonably new you might need to do some new piece of computing that might need some extra skills and resources in the journalism world that they might not have. (House of Lords 2012, 60)

Bradshaw argues that the internet has made it possible to separate the "investigative" from the "journalism": students, bloggers, activists, and anyone else with a burning question can begin to investigate it. "They can raise questions openly with thousands of others online; submit Freedom of Information requests at the click of a button or analyse datasets and documents with free tools, regardless of whether or not they are employed as a journalist. The vast majority do not want to be a journalist. What they want are answers" (Mair and Keeble 2011, 257).

GLOBAL NETWORKS

On 28 November 2010, WikiLeaks and five major newspapers from Spain (*El País*), France (*Le Monde*), Germany (*Der Spiegel*), the United Kingdom (*The Guardian*), and the United States (*The New York Times*) started to simultaneously publish the first of 251,287 leaked confidential—but not top-secret—diplomatic cables from 274 U.S. embassies around the world, dated from 28 December 1966 to 28 February 2010. This was one of those rare events that creates such a momentum that it changes the whole paradigm. It gave an enormous boost to investigative journalism before descending into the conflicted cult of personality described previously. It showed investigative journalism working internationally.

Even before Wikileaks, there were a growing number of international networks of investigative journalists spluttering into life. Some estimate that there are as many as 50 of these now in play. The author particularly watches Global-L, which has a charming air of diversity and occasional amateurism. Some of the participants are quite amazing in their innovation and collegiality—Henk van Ess of the University of Rotterdam, for example, who created the 'cablesearch' engine for full-text retrieval of the Wikileaks cables. It is a great journalistic response to the globalisation of capital and crime. There is also Paul Cristian Radu of the excellent Organized Crime and Corruption Reporting Project in the Balkans. They have devised the 'Investigative Dashboard' (2011) to help journalists track information and individuals across the world. For example, a short video tutorial explains how to find out if citizens of your own country are involved with companies based in the offshore haven of Panama. It uses Daniel O'Huiginn's scraped database of Panama companies. This is a follow-up to a previous video tutorial that shows how to navigate the more complicated Panama official registry of companies.

What also becomes clear is that these groups are part of the expansion of investigative journalism across the world and the willingness of journalists in one country to help journalists in another. The number of journalists who have been killed in countries like Pakistan and Mexico while pursuing their profession in recent times puts the problems of UK journalists in perspective. Hannah Storm, Director of the International News Safety Institute, said in November 2012 that 119 journalists had been killed worldwide that year: "We are heading for one of the darkest years on record in terms of the safety of journalists, with that number of casualties this year among our colleagues" (Storm 2012).

CONCLUSION

Asked whether investigative journalism is dead, former BBC reporter Barnie Choudhury said, "My response to that is an emphatic *no*. Basically, we will have investigative journalists so long as reporters maintain their insatiable curiosity" (Mair and Keeble 2011). The mainstream media are still delivering these stories. David Levy, of the Reuters Institute for the Study of Journalism, told the House of Lords committee that although technology offers many new opportunities for journalists and news organisations, "the main model for investigative stories will continue to be larger organisations that are seeking to enhance their brand by putting themselves, as they would see it, at the cutting edge of journalism" (House of Lords 2012, 62).

However, the Lords Committee was less optimistic and concluded, "With increasing economic pressures facing both the newspapers and broadcasting industries and a cultural shift in the way in which people receive news and information, large dedicated teams of investigative journalists within traditional news organisations no longer seem affordable. However, this does not mean that important issues cannot be uncovered by journalists, either working alone or as part of smaller, flexible teams" (House of Lords, 2011, 14).

Above all, investigative journalism is suffering from a lack of proper investment and organisational support. The Lords Committee suggested that the Charities Commission should look favourably on charitable status for not-for-profit investigative agencies. They also suggested, "To offer some respite from the funding crisis, we recommend an investigative journalism fund. Any fines which are levied for transgression of journalistic codes of conduct—including fines that might be introduced under a new system of press self-regulation and a proportion of fines issued for breaches of the Ofcom code—should be allocated to this fund which might be used for investigative journalism or for training investigative journalists" House of Lords 2011, 5). Lord Inglewood, the Lords Committee Chairman said, "We are encouraged, nonetheless, by the number of new funding and organisational initiatives that have started to materialise as a means of promoting investigative journalism, and believe it is vital that measures are taken to support and foster further initiatives which are independent of public subsidies or state support" (House of Lords 2011, 6).

Updating my 2009 estimate, I believe the number of reporters making their living from investigations in the mainstream media has increased and is probably more than 100. However, it is doubtful that this is enough to enable the participatory democracy outlined in chapter one. While the commercial news media might be argued to have an economic excuse for the cutbacks in resources going into hard news investigative journalism over recent years, given the current pressures on the industry, the same cannot be said for the BBC and the government's treatment of it. The corporation has long been seen as providing a safety net for democracy, helping fill the gaps in terms of impartiality and the range of issues reported that are left within the coverage of the commercial news media that surrounds it. But for that role to remain both credible and adequate, neither government nor the BBC itself should at any time have considered as being acceptable the argument that when there are budget cuts, news and investigative journalism must take their share of them along with everything else. The argument is fallacious by virtue of the simple fact that it legitimises the partial undermining of one of the key means of monitoring the honesty and proportionality of the exercise of power within the UK—both nationally *and regionally*—and therefore reduces the ability of the quality news media to enable a participatory democracy. This is most particularly the case in the face of the aforementioned decline of investigative reporting over the years within the commercial media—and even while new sources of such reporting have grown up in the UK and elsewhere, these cannot on their own do the job that a better resourced mainstream media can, a fact that was perhaps emphasised both by the near disaster that befell the

Bureau of Investigative Journalism in 2012 and the continuing uncertainty of its long-term funding. In addition, as pointed out earlier, the very fact that the BBC was having to use the Bureau in its abuse investigations, together with the feeling that the disasters that befell Newsnight in 2012 were an accident waiting to happen as a result of severe cutbacks in its investigative journalism budgets over recent years, would seem to emphasise the utter folly of treating the news budget as something that should be cut in the same way as anything else. Arguably, it is the BBC's performance in the field of news and current affairs that defines the public's trust in the corporation.

Equally, the Lords committee's position on the funding of quality hard news investigative journalism in general stops short of what is needed to make its position secure as part of the recognised monitoring framework that is essential to the proper functioning of a participatory democracy. There is no reason why there should not be adequate public funding set in place to help support this kind of reporting across a number of different platforms and suppliers, and not just with regard to the BBC. It is hardly beyond the wit of government, the media and other interested parties to come up with adequate safeguards and an interference-free formula for funding that would protect such essential financial underpinnings from those who would try and misuse political or administrative powers to make the granting of finance dependent on the favouring of one view over another, or the avoidance of "inconvenient" lines of enquiry. This remains an area that needs to be explored more fully.

These comments and criticisms aside, there are signs of life in the old dog yet. Outside the mainstream much is going on. NGOs in the UK have about half a dozen former mainstream media investigators on their staff, but have somewhere between 12 and 20 homegrown investigators to all intents and purposes undertaking investigations. Then there are the media investigators who do not operate in the traditional way and produce investigations in innovative and unexpected ways on a range of platforms.

At the time of writing, it is not possible to judge what impact the Leveson Report will have on regulation and how that will affect investigative journalism. As the standards of proof are high for quality, public interest investigative reporting, it will have less impact than on the more salacious end of the news media.

This chapter finishes as it started with Donal MacIntyre, who says investigative journalism should be celebrated: "The *Guardian*'s campaign against the undue influence and the corrupt practices of some *News of the World* journalists has resulted in arguably the most dramatic shift in power in this country over the last three decades. Against that backdrop how can it be said that investigative journalism is at death's door? Judging by the fruits of its labour, the future of investigative journalism appears to be very bright indeed" (Mair and Keeble 2011).

For that future to be as bright as MacIntyre hopes, however, the kinds of funding issues outlined previously need to be given more genuine and serious attention than has so far been the case. There is also a need to draw a clear line in the public perception between the disreputable, downmarket end of news investigations exposed during the Leveson Enquiry and the high quality work that has been the trademark of the Sunday Times Insight Team, World in Action, Panorama and the other benchmark names of UK journalism of the past 50 years. And while there is still a core need for traditional, mainstream hard news investigative reporting of this type, the future of quality investigative journalism will include also a variety of other providers on a range of platforms. Together their role is essential given the role of high quality investigations in preserving, promoting and periodically shaking up democracy.

REFERENCES

Bradshaw, Paul. 2011. "Has Investigative Journalism Found Its Feet Online?" Part 1. *Online Journalism Blog*, 23 August. Accessed 7 February 2013. http://onlinejournalismblog.com/2011/08/23/has-investigative-journalism-found-its-feet-online-part-1

Byrne, Dorothy. 1999. Guest lecture, MA Investigative Journalism course, Nottingham Trent University, 29 April.

Burrell, Ian, 2012. "Basic Journalism checks were not carried out." *The Independent*, 12 Novermber, accessed 13 May 2013 at: http://www.independent.co.uk/news/media/tv-radio/basic-journalistic-checks-were-not-carried-out-bbc-begins-disciplinary-proceedings-over-unacceptable-failings-by-staff-8306067.html

Currah, Andrew. 2009. *What's Happening to Our News: An Investigation into the Likely Impact of the Digital Revolution on the Economics of News Publishing in the UK*. Oxford: Reuters Institute for the Study of Journalism.

Investigative Dashboard. 2011. "How to Fish for People in Panama." Accessed 7 February 2013. http://www.datatracker.org/2011/03/how-to-fish-for-people-in-panama

Davies, Nick. 2008. *Flat Earth News: An Award-winning Reporter Exposes Falsehood, Distortion and Propaganda in the Global Media*. London: Chatto and Windus.

De Burgh, Hugo, ed. 2008. *Investigative Journalism: Context and Practice*. Oxford: Routledge.

Greenslade, Roy. 2008. "People Power." *British Journalism Review* 19: 15–21.

Greenslade, Roy. 2010. "Investigative Journalism is Still Thriving in the Internet Era." *London Evening Standard*, 27 October.

House of Lords. 2012. "The Future of Investigative Journalism." Select Committee on Communications, 3rd Report of Session 2010–12, Paper 256.

Lashmar, Paul. 2008a. "From Shadow Boxing to Ghost Plane: English Journalism and the 'War on Terror'. In *Investigative Journalism: Context and Practice*, ed. Hugo de Burgh, 191–214. Oxford: Routledge.

Lashmar, Paul. 2008b. "Sub-Prime—the Death of Financial Reporting or a Failure of Investigative Journalism?" Paper presented at the Future of Journalism conference, University of Bedfordshire Luton, 17–18 October.

Lashmar, Paul. 2009. "Investigative Journalism: A Case for Intensive Care?" Paper presented at the Journalism in Crisis conference, University of Westminster, London, 19–20 May.

Lashmar, Paul. 2011. "The Future of Investigative Journalism: Reasons to be Cheerful." *Open Democracy*, 11 June. http://www.opendemocracy.net/ourkingdom/paul-lashmar/future-of-investigative-journalism-reasons-to-be-cheerful

Lashmar, Paul. 2012. "Tragedies of the Fourth Estate." *Open Democracy*, 20 November. http://www.opendemocracy.net/ourbeeb/paul-lashmar/tragedies-of-fourth-estate.

Lewis, Justin, Andrew Williams, and Bob Franklin. 2008. "Four Rumours and an Explanation." *Journalism Practice* 2: 27–28.

Lewis, Paul. 2012. Talk to Media Education Summit, Bournemouth University, Bournemouth, 12 September.

Lewis, Paul, and Rob Evans. 2012. "Tory MP Running Corby Campaign 'Backed Rival in Anti-Windfarm Plot.'" *The Guardian*, 13 November. http://www.guardian.co.uk/politics/2012/nov/13/tory-mp-corby-anti-windfarm-film

Mair, John. 2011. "Is Investigative Journalism Dead or Alive?" *Huffington Post*, 26 August. http://www.huffingtonpost.co.uk/john-mair/is-investigative-journali_b_937968.html

Mair, John, and Richard Keeble, eds. 2011. *Investigative Journalism; Dead or Alive?* Bury St Edmunds: Abramis.

Preston, Peter. 2012. "Journalism Once Had Woodward and Bernstein. Now it's Guns for Hire." *Observer*, 18 November. http://www.guardian.co.uk/media/2012/nov/18/bureau-of-investigative-journalism-newsnight-bbc.

Storm, Hannah. 2012. "We are Heading for One of the Darkest Years on Record in Terms of the Safety of Journalists." International News Safety Institute, 23 November. http://www.newssafety.org/news.php?news=20586&cat=press-room-news-release

Stourton, Ed. 2009. "Investigative Journalism." *The Media Show*, BBC Radio 4, 14 April.

Turvill, William. 2012. "NUJ: Newsnight Budget has Halved Over the Last Five Years." *Press Gazette*, 12 November. http://www.pressgazette.co.uk/nuj-newsnight-budget-has-halved-over-last-five-years

Funding Quality News Journalism in the Face of Significant Economic and Technological Change

3 Finding Viable Business Models for Developed World Print and Online Newspaper Sectors

Chris Blackhurst

INTRODUCTION

This chapter confronts the conundrum of how to make quality print and online news journalism pay in the developed world. There have been various experiments to see how this might be achieved, including the creation of paywalls (paying for the use of web sites), the investigation of the possibilities of subscription models and charging for "apps" on tablet computers, such as the iPad. But, as also is pointed out in other chapters within the book, so far no successful model has been found for monetising the internet, other than with regard to those few newspapers with high value, niche markets, such as the *Financial Times* (FT), nor for restoring the newspaper revenues of pre-internet days. As a result, budgets for producing quality news have been slashed.

Many of the problems that afflict putative new business models for the developed world's newspaper industry have been addressed in some detail already within trade and academic literature, and there seems little point in simply re-treading these here (see, for example, Kaye and Quinn 2010; Nel 2010). What the chapter will do instead is provide an insider's view of one approach that has been taken recently within the UK newspaper industry, with the involvement of transnational investment capital. It is pertinent because it shows in some detail that all is not doom and gloom, that new ideas can be found that work if the courage is present to try them and that they may provide at least part of the solution to helping keep in place the traditional print news platform at the high quality hard news end of the newspaper industry. While the example is taken from the United Kingdom, as will be shown, significant parts of it are transferable to other parts of the world.

It is not claimed that the new ideas outlined here furnish all of the answers to the question of how to preserve and even expand the role of those elements of the news industry that have for the longest period of time provided, to varying degrees—according to title, owners, editors and financial circumstances—the quality information and analysis that is necessary to enable the kind of participatory democracy outlined in chapter one. Indeed, as will be shown with regard to the *London Evening Standard*, some of those ideas are workable only in very specific metropolitan circumstances. It will be suggested also that an old mainstay of the newspaper industry, the proprietor who is prepared to invest in highly uncertain outcomes, is still a desirable presence and an even more desirable one if the individual concerned is prepared genuinely to provide the titles involved with editorial freedom. But the tune that will be played here is not the all-pervasive requiem for an industry doomed to extinction by the rise of an internet that cannot be adequately monetised. New means of survival are out there and need new qualities of mind to find them.

What will be presented here is a strategy for the survival of quality news that is characterised by a three-layered approach. The first focuses on a so far proven and successful means of resurrecting and reinvigorating a dying big city print title and making it into something that people want to read again and advertisers are anxious to get into. The second centres on the reinvention of the quality paid-for print national newspaper in a format and at a price that has been highly successful with the 'difficult-to-reach' younger audience and those who had started to abandon print newspapers as they became increasingly expensive. The third layer of the strategy is the least developed and as yet the least successful and as far as the generation of new ideas is concerned, represents still a work in progress. That focuses on the halting or at least slowing of the declining sales of a major, traditional format national print newspaper and the development of its previously undernourished companion web site. Like nearly all traditional quality national print titles and their online siblings, the case study newspaper is still hunting for a formula that will stabilise its sales and advertising position and then begin to redirect them towards some at least modest growth, and the chapter here does not pretend that the situation is anything otherwise. But, on the positive side, what it will do is note the extent to which, in the meantime, the two successful layers of the survival strategy might help create a support structure that keeps the traditional paid-for title afloat until answers to the conundrum of how its own long-term survival can be achieved are found. Finally, with regard to its web-based sibling, there will be some discussion also of the possibilities for a more successful online strategy.

FROM THE IFLR TO THE INDEPENDENT

In a 28-year journalistic career, since entering the trade in 1984, the author has worked on every type of print format. His first job was as deputy editor on a highly-specialist law magazine (his degree was in law, and he had worked in a City law firm), International Financial Law Review, part of Euromoney Publications. Back then, IFLR, as it was known, came out 10 months a year, cost £185 by subscription only and had a full-time staff of just two. It had around 2,000 subscribers (split between lawyers in firms and those working in-house for large companies) and made a profit of £200,000 a year. Each issue was approximately 40 pages, of which two-thirds would comprise articles written by financial lawyers on a deal they'd been involved in or a legal conundrum they'd come across, for free. The other third was generated by the staff, usually consisting of a diary listing appointments and hirings in financial law, office openings and so on, and a feature or two, which would be a survey of law firms in a particular country. There was some, very limited, advertising.

IFLR was typical of its breed, a specialist journal very close to its readers, relying on their goodwill as well as their money. In many respects, it fulfilled the role of a 'quality' publication. Its contents dealt with complex matters and were full of legal terminology. There was little room for humour, none at all for tittle-tattle. Nor was there any scope for questioning, revelatory, investigative pieces that might be critical of a particular lawyer or their employer. That is not to be critical, either. Such articles were not expected by the readers. The magazine did a good job in keeping them informed and abreast of developments in their field. That was what they wanted, and that was what they received.

Next came a non-specialist monthly. Its title was Business, and it was owned jointly by Conde Nast and the *Financial Times*. While the masthead suggested specialisation, it was written and produced to appeal to the generalist. Big and glossy in scope, and lavishly illustrated, it was like Vanity Fair is today (the Conde Nast influence). Business concentrated on people, the rich and powerful of the commercial world. But it was also serious: running investigations, publishing detailed features on someone's fall from pre-eminence, exposing fraud and wrong-doing. It was a new title, launched in 1986, with big ambitions (and overheads). But as a non-specialist publication, it could not command the cover price to make a profit. Its aim was to appear current and up to the minute, but that was impossible with long lead times. By the time they came out, pieces in the magazine had frequently been overtaken by events. There were issues, too, with advertisers. A magazine that was looking to partner giant corporate names could not then turn round and tear apart boardroom culture the next. After a short, fraught life, Business closed in the early 1990s.

Following that came a Sunday flagship: *The Sunday Times*. In many ways, a weekly is the perfect vehicle for quality journalism—allowing as it does, the time to develop and explore subjects, and, without the need to follow a daily agenda, the space in which to present them. Certainly, the Sunday format—and the author subsequently worked at the *Sunday Express, Observer, Daily Express, Independent* and *Independent on Sunday*—is best suited to the research and breaking of hard news stories, and in-depth retrospectives or looking ahead pieces. There are important caveats, however. Such journalism requires resources. Investigations by their very nature carry risk—the story may not be true or may lack sufficient evidence to satisfy a libel lawyer. In a market that is rising in terms of sales and advertising revenues, dedicating staff to work that might not in the end make the newspaper is an easier task than in a period in which the market is falling, when resources are tighter. Sunday newspapers have had to contend in recent years with all the competing pressures besetting the industry—digital, social media, 24-hour TV news—plus one that is unique to them. Proprietors have identified Saturday as a day for packaging their products, adding advertising-driven and circulation attracting arts and lifestyle sections and supplements. This has had a negative impact on the Sundays, meaning their sales have been hit even harder than those of the dailies. Consequently, their budgets have tightened, resulting in cuts to reporting teams.

There is one further factor: arguably, the UK Sundays have not helped themselves by relentlessly pursuing exclusive stories. In some cases, this has seen pieces hyped and overblown, to the extent they break down on scrutiny and are not followed up and have minimal impact. Not only is this a waste of valuable journalistic time and effort, but it can have a negative bearing on a title's reputation. Within the daily format, which the author experienced with *The Independent* as Westminster Correspondent and as deputy editor, and now as editor, it can be difficult to find room for groundbreaking journalism. Sometimes the sheer demands of the daily schedule, from politics, the courts, City and sports can be so over-bearing as to stifle any original endeavour. While reporters are exhorted to find exclusives, they are also expected to cover their beat, to not miss anything on the diary. It's a matter of balance, but the tendency always will be to err on the side of reporting the daily news. Perhaps this is a mistake, but no daily newspaper has set out to ignore the agenda entirely in favour of articles from left-field.

That's not to say an editor does not want exclusives. At *The Independent*, where the author is editor, each day he is looking for a mix of stories that are ours alone and ones that are from elsewhere but must be covered. The greatest lever in this regard is cost. As sales have fallen across the piece, so too have editorial budgets. Not just in terms of manpower. Space has also declined—newspapers are not as large as they once were. Advertising to editorial ratios have shifted so that papers today carry more advertising in relation to editorial.

In many respects the paid-for evening title is no different to the paid-for morning. The one, crucial difference is lack of time. Stories tend to break in real time, during the hours when most offices are open, Parliament is sitting, the Stock Exchange is operating (in the case of business reports, this is often ahead of the stock market opening, on the official news service, at 7 am). Inevitably, press conferences are called during these hours. This means that for an evening paper that goes to bed at mid-day, only those announcements that occur during the morning will make that day's edition. Those that are made in the afternoon and evening will be dealt with in a more reactive, discursive, analytical fashion in the following day's paper. However, the nature of the cycle is that these can be quickly dropped in favour of a breaking story the following morning—which must then be turned around for the noon cut-off.

Evening papers, though, by and large, are in sharp decline. Today's commuters almost certainly know the main news stories of the day by the time they take the bus, Tube or taxi home. They leave offices where they've been staring at screens with access to digital news sites and sometimes Twitter and Facebook all day; invariably, the premises will contain flat-screen TVs showing 24-hour news bulletins. The last thing they want to do when flopping in the seat for the journey home is to be greeted with serious news stories—what they'd like is to be able to switch-off from work.

RAISING THE (NEARLY) DEAD—THE LONDON EVENING STANDARD

These of course are generalities, but they contributed to an environment in which evening newspaper circulations fell. It was against this backdrop that the Russian Lebedev family bought the *London Evening Standard* in 2009. The newspaper was heading for oblivion—sales had fallen so drastically that there was no future for it; closure was very much on the cards. But the Lebedevs were encouraged by CEO Andy Mullins to be bold and brave, to take the paper free. It was widely assumed in the market that the *Standard* would cut its editorial costs as a result. In fact, the editorial budget was only slightly reduced. The main cuts were in distribution. In the past, the *Standard* sold through 4,000 outlets across Greater London and parts of the South-East. Every afternoon, a fleet of vans would head off, dropping off copies at newsagents en route to outlying areas of the capital. On some journeys, so few copies were sold that the exercise did not even pay for the petrol. Instead, under the free model, the 4,000 sales points became 400. Some free papers—for instance, *Metro*—follow the "out to in" approach. They distribute the paper in the outer suburbs for people travelling in. The *Standard*'s "in to out" distribution is less expensive, covering a much smaller area, and it can be managed more efficiently. The 400 tend to be in an extremely tight, Central London geographical zone—covering the main professional, working areas of the City and West End and Canary Wharf. The distribution time was also slashed: the paid-for *Standard* would go on sale at 2 pm and could still be sold at 8 pm in the evening. The free version would be handed out from 4 pm, when office workers tend to start going home. The targets were the busiest London Underground and main-line stations.

At Holborn Tube, one of London's commuting hubs, before the paper went free, it was selling about 300 copies on a good day. Today, every weekday, 16,000 copies are handed out at Holborn station. It's the same story at Oxford Circus—where more than 30,000 copies go every working day.

In order for the *Standard* to succeed as a free product, it was vital that it attracted display advertising. That would only be achieved if it could be shown that copies were not only picked up by commuters but also read. Central to that aim was the maintenance not just of editorial costs but standards. It was billed as the 'world's first free quality paper'. How do you judge the success of a free newspaper? Two rules of thumb are, how long does it take to hand out every copy so none are left (the quicker the better), and how many are discarded? What was remarkable about the *Standard* going free is that the pick-up was very fast—the paper was hit with complaints from regular readers who simply could not find a copy when they left work—and there was virtually no litter. Previous free newspapers in London had been fined by the transport authority for creating litter and extra work for the cleaners. This was not the case with the *Standard*.

Did anything change, editorially, as a result of the *Standard* going free? Mostly, no, is the answer. But there were two barely perceptible shifts. The paper became more inclusive. Perhaps this was as much to do with a change in editor that occurred when the Lebedevs acquired the paper, to the campaigning Geordie Greig and then to Sarah Sands. However, there was a sense that this was now a more community-based title. Also, crucially, for the first time, its audience was clearly and narrowly defined: they were people going home or out for the evening from their places of work; they were commuters. As a commuting newspaper, transport issues were more to the fore. It was also more London-centric—everyone picking up the paper was in central London, not outlying areas.

Another, subtle shift was in terms of internal power. Under the paid-for model, editorial was king. Now, with only one source of revenue, advertising, the commercial department had a greater voice. It was not a huge difference, but it was real: perhaps previously, an advert may have been turned down because it hampered editorial. In the new, free, era, that was less likely to occur. It would be wrong to over-stress this—the editorial team still determine what goes in their newspaper. But there's no doubt that the advertising sales people carry more muscle than they did before.

The Lebedevs' gamble was a colossal one. At a stroke, by going free, they forfeited all the paper's future sales income. They were left entirely dependent on the cycles of the advertising market. There was no fall-back, alternative revenue stream. But the management team, led by Andrew Mullins, the CEO, had created a brilliantly efficient model that left no detail unchecked. Proof of that came in October 2012, when for the first time in decades, the *Standard* turned a profit. It's a model that could be rolled out anywhere in the world, where there is tight, high-density distribution to a large, mainly ABC 1 audience in a narrow timeframe—anywhere, in short, where there are lots of office workers going home using mass transport systems. New York, Paris, Shanghai and Mumbai are just four major cities that fit into this category.

Extending the free *Evening Standard* across the UK would be challenging. It could not be a nationwide free evening paper—the problems of distribution are too great, logistically, and too onerous, financially. But versions could be rolled out in the UK's largest commuting conurbations: Birmingham, Manchester, Leeds and Glasgow.

In terms of the quality of its journalism, a "free" *Standard* poses no difficulties, except the one of upsetting the advertiser—something that all titles that carry advertising face. In the case of the *Standard*, the potential for damage is greater because it only has advertising income, it does not have circulation revenue. Realistically, however, the chances of an investigation or story annoying an advertiser to the point where they will pull their advertising are slight. In the author's experience, it does happen, but rarely—it's something that journalists like to ponder upon and debate, but the actual occurrence is nowhere near as common as they might imagine.

There are conflicting arguments as to whether "free" journalism is the future. Certainly, in the UK, the Metro has proved successful in the middle-market in the mornings: City AM has established a reputation as a specialist title servicing commuters to London's Square Mile, and the *Standard* has proved there is a viable commercial raison d'être for a free quality product. The reasoning goes, in some quarters of the media, that there will be more titles going free, that as readers are so used to receiving their online news and information for free, they expect the same of print. It is certainly the case, as well, that by going free in print, it is impossible therefore to charge for the web site. Declining print sales would suggest this view is correct and that it's only a matter of time before other paid-for newspapers follow the *Standard* example and go free.

But advocates of this argument miss the point about the *Standard*: it's worked precisely because it is not a national newspaper but one blessed with a very large ABC 1 target audience in a small geographical space at the same moment. Anybody following suit nationwide, in any country, would be faced with punitive distribution costs. The only possible solution would be part-paid, part-free—those not in the central population districts would pay, while those in the biggest cities would get their paper for free.

THE TRADITIONAL PRINT FLAGSHIP—THE INDEPENDENT

Being Editor of *The Independent*, as the author was between July 2011 and June 2013, when he was made Group Content Director, should, if doom-laden forecasts are correct, be a job without a future. Founded in 1986, on a vision of offering principled, entirely objective journalism, sitting firmly at the very top of the market in terms of quality, *The Independent* has not made a penny profit on any day in its history. Its high-point, circulation-wise, was in March 1992, when it overtook *The Times* at 440,000. This was after the general election, and it says much about "The Indy's" pitch that this was only the second domestic national ballot it had covered, yet it had already carved out a USP as a paper that people turned to in a period of great debate. Unfortunately, that success was followed almost instantly by a declaration of war from *The Times'* owner Rupert Murdoch: he cut the price of his flagship. The response of *The Independent's* management was not reply in kind, but to go in the opposite direction: while *The Times* dropped its cover price, *The Independent's* went up. The idea behind this counterintuitive move was to stress the price gap, to highlight that one was a quality product demanding a quality price. Plus, the mood at *The Independent* was one of defiance—the title was young, an upstart that was not going to be pushed around by the mighty Murdoch.

However, the belief that, as one senior *Independent* executive, said "our readers will not be moved by price" proved to be wrong. The paper lost around 30% of its sale as readers defected to the much cheaper *Times*. Unable to compete with the more muscular Murdoch, The Indy's owners turned to another group for help, and to realise their equity, combined with the Mirror Group. While the latter provided much-needed financial and logistical ballast, it was the wrong partner for *The Independent*. Pooling distribution, for instance, on paper represented a considerable saving for *The Independent*. However, it meant that the determinedly upmarket broadsheet was sharing the same network that serviced the working-class tabloid *Mirror*. Reports ensued of newsagents in industrial areas, the *Mirror's* heartland, holding piles of *The Independent*, while outlets in university towns, the Indy's core audiences, complained of not having enough copies.

From the unhappy ownership of the Mirror Group, the Indy went to the Irish company, Independent News & Media. Under the control of entrepreneur Tony O'Reilly, INM had built up a stable of newspapers across the world. For 12 years, from 1998 to 2010, INM owned *The Independent*. It was a timeframe that exactly coincided with the birth and surge of the internet, and the decline in demand for print media. While the Irish owners covered *The Independent's* annual losses—the whole marriage cost INM more than £200m—they did not invest heavily. Crucially, they displayed little belief in the likely hegemony of digital—while other groups pushed ahead with "internet first" strategies and diverted financial and staffing resources towards online, The Indy was slow to react. In 2010, they sold *The Independent* and its sister *Independent on Sunday* to the Lebedevs for £1.

REINVENTING THE PRINT NEWSPAPER—THE RISE OF THE I

But while sales fell, the standing of *The Independent* nationally and internationally has remained high. It's a newspaper whose image and status far outweigh its circulation. It's one of the few UK titles not to be tainted by the hacking scandal, for example. The strategy of the Lebedevs was to build on that position. They developed online, making the web site much more immediate and vital and adding Independent Voices, a campaigning, comment and discussion forum. And they launched the *i* newspaper. Costing 20p versus the Indy's £1.20, the new product is an abridged version of its parent. *i* is comprised of shortened stories from *The Independent*'s journalists. Together with heavier usage of graphics, it provides a faster read without losing the quality element. It also does not have any editorial or "leader" column—*i* readers want their news quickly; they do not want to be assailed with opinion. A typical *i* will have 56 pages, less than *The Independent*, which can be anything from 64 to 96 pages. It has a small, dedicated team, but all Indy staff are expected to work for *i* as well.

The success of the new paper has been remarkable. In two years it's achieved a daily, Monday to Friday sale of around 290,000 (Audit Bureau of Circulations 2013) (reduced on Saturdays because its buyers are commuters, people on the move during the day, and Saturday is a day of leisure). This has meant that paid-for *Independent* journalism now outsells The Guardian's and is close to reaching *The Times'*—objectives that were previously unthinkable. Advertising can be sold into both the *Independent* and *i*. Both papers carry the same copy (with one or two exceptions of commentary—the *i* does have a few of its own columnists), but one version is longer than the other.

In 'marketing speak', what the new title supplied was brand stretch. However, research shows that *i* is a brand in its own right—70% of its readers, for instance, do not know there is any connection with *The Independent*. Its market is younger than the Indy's—students are a prime target—although many of its readers are older people who do not want to pay so much for a newspaper. They are loyal and engaged—the *i* enjoys a high degree of interactivity with its audience.

What this has achieved for the company is a strong portfolio. Where once there were the struggling *Independent/Independent on Sunday* with declining sales, there are the flagship titles where the financial losses and falling circulation have slowed, online growth and a buoyant *i*. The commercial department is fully integrated between the *Standard* and *Independent*, and the process of combining editorial has begun, with the business and sport journalists now working for the *Standard* and *Independent* titles. These desks were selected because it was felt that the news flow in business and sport was ideally suited to integration. Business news tends to occur in the morning and sport in the afternoon and evening. Also, management was mindful of the need to maintain the special flavour of their titles—business and sport were not thought to be as vital in that regard as, say, comment. However, that is likely to be a factor in terms of how far they can go in integrating all the departments.

The Lebedevs have displayed courage and commitment—ownership of the *Standard* and *Independent* titles has so far cost them in the order of £100m. That is their own money. But the papers they acquired are now in a much stronger position: the *Standard* is making a surplus, compared to losing £18m a year when they bought it; the *Independent* has a growing online presence and a burgeoning, cheaper sibling.

The pressing issues all newspaper groups face are how to halt the decline in print, in circulation and revenues, and to monetise the internet. The latter is more urgent than the former because it represents the guarantee of existence and sustainability.

MONETISING THE INTERNET

At present, *The Independent* is free to internet. It's possible that may change and a pay-wall is introduced, although this has to be weighed carefully. There is still no sign of any news provider (with the exception of the specialist *Financial Times*) having broken through with a charging digital model that achieves scale volume in subscribers and income. The upside of charging is a revenue stream, loyalty of the purchaser, which can be enhanced by the provision of additional "subscription only" material, and the creation of a community of subscribers who can then be targeted with advertisers' offers and promotions. The downside is a lack of accessibility and reduced number of hits. *The Independent*'s preferred route, currently, is to build online presence, from what was a low base.

What there is not is a plan to stop printing. There may be other factors why a title could close—it's hard to see how accumulating losses can be met by some owners—but merely ceasing to print because paper is a declining medium and online is growing, does not have credibility. Even with their sales falls, most national newspapers still enjoy high volumes. They would no longer 'be', they would not enjoy anything like the same attention presently paid to them by TV and radio, they would slip into becoming A N Other news provider on the internet.

Crucially, too, they would lose a source of revenue at a time when internet cash-flow remains unproved. The optimum model, at present, is to treat print as another platform, alongside digital. This multiplatform approach has to be the most efficient, with journalists supplying copy online and in print.

CONCLUSION

These case studies deliver a number of insights that are relevant to one extent or another for the future of print and online newspaper business models in the developed world. The relevance of the *Evening Standard* experience has been carefully qualified in terms of the range of market conditions to which it can be profitably applied, but the success of the turnaround does suggest that this is a solution to one very specific part of the sector's problems, if approached in the right, highly targeted manner, backed up by detailed pre-research and appropriate staffing levels.

The *i* also has shown that the combination of real 'blue sky thinking', dovetailed with detailed market research and a preparedness to take well-balanced risks, can lead to successful reinventions of the print newspaper for new and previously lost parts of the market. In some months, such as November 2012, sales of more than 300,000 have been reached (Audit Bureau of Circulations 2013), and that level of market penetration starts to create a situation where advertising prices can be levered upwards to help generate increasing amounts of the income that inevitably are forfeited by the very low cover price. Whether there is space for more than one *i* in national newspaper markets such as that of the UK is an interesting question, however, and it is notable that so far none of *The Independent*'s competition has responded with their own equivalents.

Finally, with regard to the flagship national title, while there is no sign of *The Independent* beginning to reclaim lost territory in terms of its print sales, its decline has been greatly slowed. This has been achieved by a variety of means, three of the principal ones arguably being a redesign that helps make it stand out visually at sales points and communicate more effectively graphically between the covers and a concentration on its core strengths in terms of *truly independent* quality news journalism. *The Independent*'s online sibling also has been redesigned and brought more in line with its competition in terms of such things as visual appeal, but like most other newspaper online presences has yet to crack the problem of how to make the site pay. *However, the fact that this hasn't been achieved so far does not mean that it never will be.* The internet itself is a continuously evolving platform, and that very evolution continues to open new routes into audience engagement. The trick for newspapers is to find a way of attaching themselves to, adopting or becoming a creator of those new routes as they evolve and discovering ways within them of being able to charge for content. Something as simple as the creation of a virtual news world in which the reader can become part of the story, for example, is one route through which a paying audience might be attracted online. The 'virtual' possibilities of newspaper storytelling as yet have hardly begun to be explored.

What remains to be found is a balance of products and business models that enables the operation as a whole—the *Evening Standard, Independent* and *i*—to break even and thereby sustain the flagship into the future. This chapter has shown that the *Independent* and its siblings are part of the way there, and the route that they have taken offers some lessons and examples that can be adopted by others. What it has shown also, however, is the continuing importance of a proprietor who is prepared to 'take a hit' financially while the news operation tries to reorganise itself in such a way that high quality hard news journalism can be sustained over the medium-longer term. In that regard, the Lebedev's have provided a vital underpinning of the titles' finances without which they would have ceased to exist. But they have added another vital ingredient that the previous owners failed to provide, and that has been a preparedness to take the level of risk that was necessary for the launch of the *i* and the re-launch of the *Evening Standard*. That is perhaps one of the most potent lessons of *The Independent*'s experience—the need for a well-resourced ownership that looks beyond the immediate 'bottom line' when it plans for the future of its news business.

REFERENCES

Audit Bureau of Circulations. 2013. Accessed 3 February 2013. http://www.abc .org.uk/

Kaye, Jeff, and Stephen Quinn. 2010. *Funding Journalism in the Digital Age*. New York: Peter Lang Publishing.

Nel, Francois. 2010. "Where Else Is the Money? A Study of Innovation in Online Business Models at Newspapers in Britain's 66 Cities." *Journalism Studies* 4(3): 360–372.

4 Finding Viable Business Models for Developed World Broadcast News

Paul Egglestone

I am pleased to announce to the board of directors, a plan for the co-ordination of the main profit centre with the specific intention of making each division more responsive to management. Point 1. The division producing the lowest rate of return has been the news division, with its $98m budget and its annual deficit of $32m. I know that historically news divisions are expected to lose money, but to our minds this is a wanton fiscal affront to be resisted.

(Frank Hackett played by Robert Duvall
in Sydney Lumet's *Network*, 1976)

INTRODUCTION

The purpose of this chapter is to provide an overview of the situation facing quality hard news in the television sector of the broadcasting industry across the developed world. The scale of the task means that it is not possible to include radio, which is briefly discussed in chapters eight and nine.

The approach here will be to move in from a macro-level summary analysis of the pressures facing the quality hard news industry as a whole within the relevant societies, to more micro-level summary diagnoses of the problems and opportunities within the television hard news sector, specifically. These will focus on such key issues as problems of ownership and the continuing and surprising strengths of television as a platform, together with the growing challenges resulting from the accelerating rate of technological development, changes in audience behaviour within younger age groups, and the inadequate responses from news producers to some of these. It will conclude by outlining and evaluating a number of new and emerging business models/ways of accessing the audience and by considering the future prospects for quality television broadcast news across the developed economies. This will provide a backdrop, drawn both from summary and original research, against which the later country-specific chapters develop their themes in depth.

THE ECONOMIC AND TECHNOLOGICAL CHALLENGES FACING THE NEWS INDUSTRY

According to Mark Thompson, former Director General of the BBC and now Chief Executive at the *New York Times,* the impact of multichannel television on news programming is still one of the biggest challenges to TV news operations.

> What we're seeing so far in Britain and the US in TV news is not so much the impact of the Internet, it's actually multichannel television. Audience fragmentation has definitely hit news pretty hard. It turns out that given the choice of non-news programmes of a wide variety, instead of news, viewers will often go for non-news programmes. (personal interview, 5 February 2013)

This is already a worrying pattern of behaviour for TV news operations. If the existing multichannel television environment has created an appetite for choice, new and emerging technologies connecting viewers to the Internet must accelerate the trend away from news to alternative forms of entertainment.

In October 2012, speaking at Mipcom, the TV industry's annual international programme fair, YouTube's Robert Kyncl (2012) told an audience of TV executives that "producers who do not create content for the (YouTube) platform will be left behind". "Charlie Bit My Finger" is the most watched minute of video made in the last five years, receiving almost 500 million views on YouTube (http://www.youtube.com/watch?v=_OBlgSz8sSM). It was shot on domestic video equipment, was not edited and was distributed by its creators without any advertising or assistance from professional marketing companies. Charlie and his dad, Howard Davies-Carr, have earned around £120,000 ($190,000) from the 57-second video clip. YouTube claims its "skippable" adverts are now generating as much advertising revenue as U.S. cable networks. The so-called digital revolution has arrived on TV's doorstep.

The disruptive impact of digital technologies and changes in the ways audiences receive and view news has recently prompted a focus on the economic challenges facing quality news journalism. Nightingale and Dwyer (2007), Jenkins (2006) and Macnamara (2010a) acknowledge that the evolution of digital media has created a different communication paradigm. McNair (2006) anticipates the opportunity of this new paradigm to challenge dominant ideologies and power elites. It is this "cultural chaos" that is disturbing traditional media companies and undermining the way they do business. And it is creating the type of behavioural response from media organisations articulated by Curran (2010) and paraphrased here as (1) total denial, (2) extreme pessimism, (3) selfish opportunism, and (4) naive optimism.

If these are the symptoms of the global news industry confronting an unfamiliar world, Macnamara (2010b) is emphatic that any cure needs identifying and administering quickly if the patient is to survive. In their quest for a cure, Kaye and Quinn (2010) explore a series of dominant and emergent media business models, looking for an elixir to better suit the constitution of a digital media landscape. Downie and Schudson (2009) offer a range of publicly funded initiatives designed to stop the bleeding—a bitter pill for taxpayers to swallow in the current economic climate. In France, President Sarkozy implemented a policy of subsidies for newspapers. McChesney (2010) concludes that changing public policy and finding public funding that recognises and sustains reporting as a public good is the only medicine up to the job. The prognosis even appears bleak enough for Levy and Picard (2011) to wonder whether contemporary news organisations would be better restructuring their businesses, changing their legal status and setting themselves up as charities.

The thought of television news executives forced to stand outside department stores waving collecting tins may appease some members of the public disillusioned with current media practices. These include the treatment of Princess Diana, the UK newspaper phone hacking scandal embroiling the Murdochs' media empire, the prison sentences hanging over Silvio Berlusconi and the failure of the BBC *Newsnight* programme to air accusations of child abuse against the late BBC presenter Jimmy Savile.

However, if the kind of participatory democracy outlined in chapter one is to be the ideal, then it is crucial that high quality broadcast news survives and—in light of the observations immediately above—improves and is strengthened. The global overview that this chapter is designed to provide means that the questions of how to improve quality (as defined in chapter one) will be left to the individual chapters that cover broadcast news in the various case study countries. What will be investigated here are the current and emerging clues as to the likely economic sustainability of quality broadcast news in the face of increasing technological and other challenges over the short term to medium term.

BROADCAST NEWS AND WHAT THE RESEARCH LITERATURE DOESN'T TELL US

Much of the literature in the field of emerging business models for quality news journalism embraces the practice of journalism as "media" without focussing on the individual platforms of print, television, radio or online (Boler 2008; Macnamara 2010a; Pavlik 2008). Whilst this broader perspective reflects the diversity of news outputs across a range of technologies, it conceals the capabilities and relative effectiveness of individual platforms to reach different audiences. It also ignores the corporate structures of news companies that tend to have a single platform at the core of their business whilst endeavouring to leverage their brand and distribute content across multiple platforms at the periphery of their operations. When there is a focus on a single platform (Franklin 2012; McChesney 2010), studies tend to favour print journalism. The more generic approach of the majority of work broadly mirrors reports like the Open Society Foundation's "Mapping Digital Media" (2012), which analyses the impact of digital technology on the core provision of quality journalism in 60 countries. The emphasis is on "quality journalism" rather than a particular delivery platform. Similarly, Foster (2012) examines the impact of digital technology on the plurality of news, and whilst the data draws largely on online news sources, its findings are not platform-specific. The Reuters Institute report on Digital News (Newman 2012) makes a significant contribution to the data for online news consumption, whilst discounting digital news on, for example, smart internet-connected TVs. Geneits (2010) does study broadcast news, but covers eight countries in just two continents. Further, the rapid evolution of digital technology that has created internet-connected "smart" TVs, "Over The Top" (OTT) TV and the applications that have enabled broadcast programmes to be received on tablets and mobile devices makes it difficult to define in any meaningful way what we mean by "television" anymore.

Our analysis starts at the top of the media tree and looks at the actual and potential impact of specific forms of ownership on the current state of broadcasting.

THE GROWTH OF CORPORATE OWNERSHIP OF TELEVISION NEWS OPERATIONS AND ITS ECONOMIC IMPLICATIONS: AN AMERICAN WARNING

> We are no longer an industrialised society; we aren't even a post-industrial or technological society. We are now a corporate society, a corporate world, a corporate universe. This world is a vast cosmology of small corporations orbiting around larger corporations who, in turn, revolve around giant corporations, and this whole endless, eternal, ultimate cosmology is expressly designed for the production and consumption of useless things.
>
> (Howard Beale, played by Peter Finch in *Network*)

For some time television networks and their news divisions have largely ceased to be independent businesses. Since the 1950s media companies have sought to develop strategic partnerships with competitors and grow their operations through a series of mergers and hostile takeovers. In the United States the increasingly global television industry has witnessed the horizontal integration of related media corporations through takeovers and mergers on an alarming scale. Ever larger corporations do "revolve around giant corporations". Meanwhile the TV news divisions within these organisations are dwarfed by their commercially lucrative siblings, too often contracting in size to stem their financial losses, or seeing their budgets spread ever more thinly to fund new digital offerings. Barely a year passes without a significant change in the structure, and occasionally ownership, of media companies. Such changes are driven by shareholder calls for the rationalisation of production and distribution costs, and the leveraging of collective brands for profit. It is something they do with considerable commercial success.

Comcast and GE, joint owners of NBC, posted revenues of $55.8bn from their stable of media companies in 2011 (Comcast Annual Review 2012) with operating profits of a little more than $3bn. In July 2012, under the NBC News umbrella, NBC News Digital (formerly owned by Microsoft) joined the news network's television properties, including *Today, NBC Nightly News, Meet the Press, Dateline* and *Rock Center* and its cable arm, MSNBC TV. MSNBC TV will launch a new digital service in 2013. The digital presence will be an extension of the MSNBC TV on-air brand. MSNBC Digital Network will be incorporated into NBC News's current operation in New York to create multiplatform teams and promote the sharing of resources and cross-platform reporting between the network's broadcast and digital properties. Whilst strategically this corporate shift looks set to align the company with audience consumption patterns, the challenges of changing the culture within previously independent mono-media newsgathering operations are not insignificant. Aligned to these changes will inevitably be the job losses that follow as individual roles are redefined and duplication is eradicated.

NBC News also plans to build what will become the NBC News Innovation Center. This centre will focus on digital innovation and technology. NBC News will continue to build its digital businesses, focusing on a model of user engagement through social networks and creating more "premium" content with an emphasis on video. Speaking after the takeover, President of NBC News Steve Capus said, "NBC News enters a new phase of its history better positioned to compete and grow in a digital environment, as well as deliver consumers and clients a multi-platform news experience unlike anything else in the industry" (UPI 2012). Exactly what this might look like remains to be seen. News Corporation's revenues exceeded $33bn in 2011, making a net profit of $1.06bn in the last quarter of 2011, up from $624m in 2010 (News Corporation 2011). Similarly, CNN International's owner Time Warner generated revenues of $29bn over the same period, whilst international revenues for its Turner and HBO networks alone were $3bn, with operating profits of $650m (Time Warner 2011).

In light of all this, Jenkins's (2006) optimism for a more inclusive and pluralistic media landscape post web 2.0 looks misplaced. The stifling dominance of "legacy" media conglomerates across the television news business in the developed world continues in much the same vein as it did before it was rudely interrupted by disruptive digital technologies like the internet and mobile. In the American case, the shareholder-driven mission of the conglomerates to deliver an audience to advertisers with low-cost content has reduced space for even mainstream political news (Bennett 2003; Patterson 1993, 2000; see chapter eight). McChesney (2010) amplifies the argument that, left to the market, news will fail. For him, legislation and public funding are its only salvation once the philanthropists and venture capitalists have moved on. In the UK, also, independent regional television companies and their news operations have nearly all gradually been swallowed up by ITV plc. This has led to some reduction in regional variation, but no obvious decline in journalistic quality (see chapter nine). However, it is the UK that reminds us also that there is a real, vital alternative to the commercial ownership model in the form of the BBC. Therefore, it is to public funding models that we next turn in our overview of the current state of television news media ownership.

PUBLIC FUNDING MODELS FOR BROADCAST NEWS

Publicly funded broadcasting in Western Europe and one or two other countries whose broadcasting system is very similar, like Japan or to a degree Korea, Australia, New Zealand and Canada, according to Thompson,

> [remains] a pretty good business model. You've still got some public support for broadcasting with varying degrees of constitutional protection for the independence of the broadcaster. It's very strong in the UK, pretty strong in most of the other English speaking countries and weaker in some European countries. Although it's disputed in many countries—because particular newspaper proprietors don't like it—public support for some level of public funding in broadcasting is still quite high. (personal interview, 5 February 2013)

Thompson believes audiences' expectations of a public broadcaster have a direct impact on quality as they are pressurised to deliver "really good coverage of serious news at home and abroad".

The public funding approach to supporting quality news journalism is not unproblematic. Advocates of publicly funded media point to the importance of a media unaided and therefore uninfluenced by commercial imperatives. McChesney and Nichols (2010) are proponents of state aid for the news (print) industry akin to the subsidies paid to protect and secure jobs in the manufacturing sector. At an estimated cost of $35bn in the United States alone, there is unlikely to be much public appetite or political will within the American government to pursue this course of action in an age of austerity (McChesney 2010). Nevertheless, in August 2012, Singapore's government announced a 35% increase in funding for Public Service Broadcast (PSB) content, amounting to S$630m or around £400m over five years (Singapore Ministry of Communication and Information 2012).

Similarly, Qatar's healthily state-funded Al Jazeera continues to expand. Al Jazeera now has 65 bureaux (35 more than CNN) and 400 journalists worldwide. The station broadcasts to 220 million households in 100 countries. Mark Orchard, editor of Al Jazeera English, said, "Our trajectory is expansive and forward-looking, whereas some other networks unfortunately have seen decades of contraction in foreign news" (Ricchiardi 2011). Thompson sees this contraction as a troubling development:

> I think people correctly worry that news organisations, which are disinvesting (for example) in foreign bureaux, may be compromising, in some respect, the quality of their output. It's very easy to cover the world effectively without having a significant number of foreign correspondents. But if you're reliant entirely on agency video and you only bus people in for the very biggest stories, they're unlikely to give you as good coverage as someone covering a country, like Pakistan, who is based there and can get to know it. (personal interview, 5 February 2013)

Despite these concerns, public service broadcasting (PSB) organisations like the BBC in the UK are adjusting to delivering their services for less. The current licence fee of £145.50 per household was frozen for six years in 2010. Taking even relatively low rates of inflation into account, this figure adds up to a 16% real terms cut in BBC funds. Tough economic conditions in 2011 saw BBC World News revenue and profits fall (BBC Annual Report 2011/12), whilst the impact of "a significant cost saving plan" across the company further reduced operating budgets across departments.

This is a neat illustration of the downside of public funding models. When economies come under pressure—in the UK as a result of the lingering impact of the 2008 financial crash—so do those reliant on public funding, in this case the BBC. Clearly, therefore, no model is without its problems, although the breadth and depth of the BBC's news offering continues to exceed considerably that provided by the major American commercial broadcasters (see chapter eight). Indeed, as has been shown in the previous section, the United States, with its absence of a public service broadcaster on the scale of the BBC, is a powerful example of the problems that can arise on the commercial side of the fence. Having looked briefly at an overview of the owners, we can now move to the other side of the fence and assess the state of the television news platform itself.

TV IS DEAD—LONG LIVE TV: THE CONTINUING STRENGTH OF TELEVISION AS A HARD NEWS PLATFORM—AND EMERGING WEAKNESSES

The majority of additional research material here draws on interviews, company and consultancy reports and datasets from ratings agencies like the Broadcast Audience Research Board (BARB) or Nielsen in the United States.

Even if these sources were completely reliable (ratings agencies excepted), much of the information in them refers to television output in generic terms. Authors use categories like 'Entertainment', 'Documentaries' or 'News and Current Affairs'. Whilst these labels identify particular styles of programming within TV organisations, the taxonomies are difficult to interrogate, open to question and unlikely to be universally accepted.

Despite the emergence of internet-enabled devices like tablets, smartphones and PCs, and the myriad new ways to receive news and information, television remains—by a considerable margin—the primary source of news and information in developed and developing democracies. In the McTaggart address to television executives at the 2011 Edinburgh TV festival, Executive Chairman of Google, Dr. Eric Schmidt (2011), conceded that "In 2010, UK adults spent as much time watching TV in 4 days as they did using the web in a month. TV is still clearly winning the competition for attention!" Deloitte's analysis for the Edinburgh TV festival reported a rise in TV viewing in the UK every year since 2006 (Deloitte 2011). The same report noted that total television viewing in the UK had gone up by 6% over the same period—an increase of 364 million hours.

Revenues from pay TV in the BRIC nations (Brazil, Russia, India and China) will rise by 20% to more than US$17bn, Deloitte (2012) says. In the United States, Pew Research Center's 2012 State of the News Media project reported the kind of growth in TV news audience that mirrored TV viewership generally. Drawing on Nielsen's Media Research data, the report concluded all television news viewership increased in 2011. Networks, rather than local news stations, were the main beneficiaries, with average evening news viewership across ABC, CBS or NBC increasing by 4.5%, or around one million viewers in 2011. An average of 22.5 million people watched news on ABC, CBS or NBC every night in 2011. Even the global economic collapse seems to have benefited television as people stay at home, turn on and tune in to avoid the expense of going out. Research performed by French company IDATE in 2011 claimed the global TV industry's revenue will grow by 12.1% between 2012 and 2016, around 2.9% annually (IDATE 2012). In 2012 it will total €340.1bn. A 20% growth in TV advertising revenue is predicted over the same period (Ofcom 2011). Kanter Media UK reported a 7.7% growth in TV advertising revenue in the fourth quarter of 2011 (up 2.4% for the year), making IDATE's estimates appear conservative.

Clearly, television news viewership has not yet seen the decline witnessed by newspapers in many countries. In the United States, where much of the available data comes from, Pew's researchers recorded little change in the number of people claiming they had watched the news or a news programme on TV the previous day (Pew Research Center 2011). Of those surveyed in 2012, 55% said they watched TV news, only marginally down on the previous survey. More worrying is the significant fall in the number of young people watching news on TV. Whilst this research does not specify whether the same demographic consumed any news at all, the popular assumption is that they either watched TV news on a different device or merely time-shifted viewing. Not according to Patterson (2007): "Our findings suggest that some news surveys have overestimated either the amount of news young adults consume or the capacity of non-traditional media to take up the slack from young people's flight from traditional news sources". Patterson's research concluded that young people today pay less attention to daily news than their predecessors. It also contests the notion that young people are merely changing their consumption patterns, moving from receiving or reading news on legacy news platforms and migrating to consuming digital news online, on mobile and on demand. The results of two national surveys into news consumption habits amongst young people in the United States also demonstrate the contradiction between the verbal claim by teenagers themselves that the internet is their primary source of news, and the evidence drawn from their behaviour, which shows they receive most of their news by watching television—though the total volume, breadth and depth of news they watch is pitifully small and woefully insufficient to create informed citizens in the sense set out in chapter one (Patterson 2007).

So while claims that the death of television is imminent are wide of the mark, certainly in the case of the United States, there is clear evidence that in the medium to longer term the future of television news is very much in question unless it can find new ways of attracting a younger audience. A young audience aged 25 to 54 is essential to TV because they are the demographic group advertisers want to attract. Thompson points out that the current style and editorial approach of news programmes aimed at an older age group of 55 and above is hampering their endeavours to appeal to young people and, therefore, limiting their ability to attract advertising revenue:

> The advertising that commercial channels sell is often sold against a desirable demographic and the American network news might be getting nine million viewers but only two and a half million will be in the attractive demographic the advertisers want to buy. The ageing population of TV news audiences is playing into the problems that the network broadcasters here (in the US) and other commercial broadcasters have got. (personal interview, 5 February 2013)

The ageing population of TV news audiences and the sometimes-misplaced belief that young people are getting their news in other ways are compounding the problems facing quality TV news operations. We will now look at this loss of the younger hard news viewer in more detail, before moving on to look at another key way in which technology has been impacting on television news: the long-established route of pay-for-view.

THE IMPACT OF TECHNOLOGY ON TELEVISION NEWS

i) The Interactive Dimension

> TV news in this country (USA) has lost almost all its viewers under the age of 40, and it is frankly the TV news organisations' fault. It's an industry that makes you listen to an hour's programme before you get to the bits you're interested in when other technology allows you to click or scroll directly to it.
>
> (Professor David Klatell, Columbia Journalism School)

For some commentators and practitioners, new technology appears to offer television news a different lifeline, although the gap that TV news must span is a large one. Until relatively recently, television broadcasts have been entirely linear. Viewers in the countries of their national broadcasters were united as they simultaneously watched the same news stories from beginning to end with no control over what they were watching, other than the ability to change channels or adjust the volume. This is still true of the vast majority of television programmes. Television broadcasts are linear, and the viewer's consumption of news watched on their television sets—cathode ray tubes, LCD and plasma screens alike—is a linear experience.

Cover (2004) argues that "the rise of interactivity as a form of audience participation is a strongly held and culturally based desire to participate in the creation and transformation of the text that has been denied by previous technologies of media production and distribution". As an essentially passive medium, television and television news specifically has been remarkably slow to understand the principle of co-creation and audience participation, and particularly, the impact of second screen technology, namely tablets and mobiles on audiences' viewing experience. Ernesto Schmitt, the co-founder of the social TV app Zeebox, claims a third of all internet browsing happens while watching TV, whilst two-thirds of people regularly connect with their friends via social networks while watching TV (Smith 2012). They are doing this on their tablets and smartphones. This has brought a digital twist to television. Families may not sit on the sofa and watch programmes together anymore, but Twitter users wishing to share their thoughts and opinions about what they are watching simultaneously certainly do. As a genre, TV news would seem to naturally lend itself to engaging the Twittersphere. Encouraging conversation between television news viewers using digital technology at least creates some semblance of participation, though the level and tone of discussion confined to 140 characters is invariably low. A Twitter veteran usually initiates the most productive conversations with a large group of followers. By nature, most of these individuals do not work for large TV networks. And by nature, TV networks have tried to use second and third screens as another platform for their programmes, spectacularly missing the point of social media, alienating potential viewers and demonstrating the cavernous cultural gap between TV executives and second screen audiences.

ii) The Pay-for-View Dimension

Whilst the number of people who pay for TV in the United States has remained fairly stable, it has grown in other countries. Pay TV (PTV) is a form of linear broadcast channel that is only available to paying customers. PTV channels are available to cable and satellite customers in addition to their basic channels at extra cost. The average American PTV bundle costs around $100 a month. Since the 1970s, PTV audiences have also been able to select a particular scheduled TV programme and watch it on their television set for an additional one-off fee. Since the 1990s, viewers receiving their programmes via satellite, cable or fibre-optic cable—often referred to as broadband—have been able to watch what they want, whenever they like, through their TV providers' video-on-demand (VoD) service. This programming is not tied to the schedule. Viewers access programme content hosted by the broadcaster through a graphical TV interface that looks similar to the electronic programme guide. Viewers can watch, rewind, fast forward or pause individual programmes independently of the schedule. VoD networks usually operate on one of three business models: PTV, VoD or pay-per-view (PPV, sometimes referred to as pay-as-you-go—meaning viewers pay for each programme before they watch—and popular for live sports events and films), or a mixture of these. Canada's cable and speciality networks saw growth of 6% in their revenue and operating profits in 2009 according to statistics published in April 2010 (QFinance 2012). The Canadian Radio-television and Telecommunications Commission (CRTC) said the country's cable, pay-for-view, and speciality broadcast services posted revenue of C$3.1bn in 2009, up from C$2.9bn in 2008, despite a drop of 2.6% in advertising revenue over the same period (QFinance 2012).

However, this apparent good news will not last forever. Television, and more aptly television news, whether it be on pay-for-view or other access routes, will not avoid the impact of disruptive digital technologies that previously toppled major labels in the music industry. The challenges include changing consumer demand, outmoded business models, converged competition and the aggressive evolution of "Over The Top" (OTT) and Internet Protocol TV or IPTV. OTT involves the delivery of audio-visual content over the internet without the need for a special infrastructure. IPTV consists of audio and/or video signals delivered to viewers using internet protocol technology that is also used to access the internet via computers (IPTV is typically a 'closed intranet', rather than the 'open or public internet'). These technologies change what, where, when and how we watch TV. *Crucially, they change how we pay for it.* Viewers can buy individual programmes, specific channels or bundles of channels. They can choose to pay for what they watch when they watch it, using online payment methods, or they can pay monthly or annually for channels bundled together by broadcasters.

News is often subsidised rather than profitable. Traditionally, the range of additional channels and services offered to audiences by the network pays for news operations. In the context of pay-for-view, many news programmes survive only as part of 'bundles' to cable and satellite viewers. In some territories, notably the United States and the European Union, legislation forces broadcasters to include news services as part of a range of channels they sell to people whose primary purchase may be a series of entertainment or sports channels. Under these agreements, heads of TV news can support their operation by claiming a share of revenue from the subscription fee. Thompson believes the status quo is likely to be maintained in the foreseeable future, but he also raises the spectre of what type or style of news programme will appeal to cable operators either forced or wishing to carry news on their channels:

> I think it's inevitable that news channels in the US will still be available on basic cable. Cable companies quite like having news in the mix. You definitely can see intense competition in news and it's probably fair to say that one of the dynamics of the competition is that noisier, brighter, more controversial news services like Fox News feel that they're much more competitively tuned to the new world of American cable than CNN, which began with a rather BBC-like editorial impartiality. The way competition is playing out is to favour the rather gaudier version of news—but it's not news in any sense that we would identify as traditional news. (personal interview, 5 February 2013)

PPV and VoD technology is, in theory, making it easier to strip away unwanted programming. These technologies already afford viewers the opportunity to buy one-off event-based programmes or download individual episodes of soap operas or period dramas. Thompson thinks it unlikely that people will pay per view or pay a subscription just for TV news on its own. "The idea of consumers paying for TV news is quite hard to believe. I suspect that unless there's some level of public funding, the remaining broadcasters of news are going to have to find ways of getting advertising and sponsorship to cover it". Whether they will be able to remains a troubling question.

In light of audience/funding uncertainties such as these, the next sections investigate some of the ways through which quality television news might be supported.

NEW SOURCES OF INCOME AND BUSINESS MODELS

1. Television and Data Harvesting—A Means of Generating Income via Increased Advertising, or an Unacceptable Invasion of Privacy?

Cable television originated in the United States in 1948. It was intended to improve the poor reception of broadcast television signals in remote and mountainous areas. As cable, broadband, satellite and digital terrestrial TV technologies have evolved, so has the relationship with audiences viewing content via any set-top box. What started as a means of improving the technical quality of television and extending its reach to deliver a larger audience to advertisers has morphed into a sophisticated method of gathering audience data about people's viewing habits. In some cases this data is sold to advertisers (TiVo 2012). Where the technical infrastructure supports it, this data could be used to deliver highly targeted "premium" advertising to individual households based on their media consumption patterns. The more sophisticated the set-top box, the more accurate the data. In homes with superfast broadband and wi-fi, the box is not only recording what is being viewed on TV, but it is also able to retain and transfer information about how people are using other devices, such as mobile phones and tablets connected to the internet wirelessly via a home network. All this begins to build a reasonably rich picture of people's consumption patterns across devices and over time and, through its obvious attraction to advertisers, potentially could be used to negotiate an increased spend by the advertisers.

TiVo is perhaps the company most associated with producing set-top boxes that harvest people's viewing data and sell it to advertisers. However, while acting in an enabling capacity to advertisers on the one hand, on the other they also did something that threatened the income that much of the television news industry earns from television adverts. TiVo introduced one of the first Digital Video Recorders (DVR) with a built-in function that enabled viewers to "skip" TV commercials. Turf wars and standoffs between technology companies, PTV operators and network executives have been commonplace since. Most recently, in May 2012, the Fox network took out a legal case against Dish Network, whose DVR also came with automated advert skipping software. Speaking in June 2012 at the Cannes International TV Advertising conference, Chairman of NBC Broadcasting Ted Harbert said that "we can no longer ignore time-shifting" within what Cheredar called "the business model to drive ad revenue. The problem with 'time-shifted' (a.k.a. DVR) devices is that the industry doesn't have enough control to make sure those commercials will play for an audience the way they do for live broadcasting" (Cheredar 2012).

Network executives continue to buy TiVo's data whilst campaigning against ad skipping software. Whilst TiVo was among the pioneers of the data harvesting model, it is now commonplace wherever a TV set-top box can be plugged into a digital telephone line. Apple has sold more than 2.5m of its Apple TV devices in the United States, as has Roku, whose set-top box retails at around $50. YouView, a multichannel collaboration between broadcasters in the UK, has just launched. It, too, is capable of recording viewing habits.

OTT companies are evolving their own policies on what data they harvest whilst we watch TV using one of their devices. Your.TV in the Netherlands issue this information on their website: "In addition to your personal data, we collect and store information relating to your viewing habits. For instance, we monitor which programmes you watch on a regular basis to provide you with viewing suggestions and offers tailored to your viewing habits."

There is public concern over the issue of data collection, exploitation, privacy and the security of personal data collected by set-top boxes. There is also deep concern within the academy as scholars, including Battelle (2005), Chester (2006), Clarke (2006) and Hirst and Harrison (2007), warn of the potential abuse of privacy as a new generation of digitally connected technologies move beyond their Web 2.0 capabilities to Web 3.0. The current self-regulatory framework is believed by many to be inadequate (Mills 2008), but the process of legislating for future technologies and consumer behaviours is fraught with difficulty. Regulation that prevents perceived improvements for one group, whilst seeking to protect the privacy of others, will clearly be contentious and probably unworkable. Anecdotal evidence from viewers accustomed to receiving targeted advertising on social media sites like Facebook, for example, suggests they have few issues over the collection of data on their viewing habits. They are happy if it is used to provide more relevant content, including advertising. The commercial value of audience data delivered directly to networks providing the programmes and advertising airtime, when coupled with the technology to target specific adverts at individual customers, would appear to tip some of the commercial balance in TV's favour and help provide a workable business model for the future. However, Deloitte (2012) predicts that targeted TV advertising will account for less than $200m from a global TV advertising market of $227bn. The high cost of producing multiple versions of expensive TV commercials for individual customers is likely to be a major disincentive.

The quest for more reliable audience data continues nevertheless, and, with a new generation of Smart TVs, it is about to get even more sophisticated. In the United States, TV ratings agency Nielsen is loved and loathed in equal measure by television producers and advertisers alike. The accuracy of its data has come under attack by some network programmers, who argue that its polling system of 50,000 homes is antiquated in the digital age. NBC's Chairman Ted Harbert criticised the TV industry's standard for content ratings through Nielsen, saying, "We're participating in many initiatives to try and crack the measurement code because we just can't wait—and wait some more—for Nielsen to do it" (Cheredar 2012). Harbert recognises data itself has value beyond tailoring programming and ad breaks for customers; technology companies developing new products and health organisations researching 'couch potatoes' would all like access to what people are watching, what device they are watching on and how long they spend each day doing it. Consequently, there is a willingness among some TV executives to experiment with delivery platforms that might offer even better data on how people consume television and that, in turn, potentially can be sold to help fund their television platform.

NBC has joined Toyota and Samsung Mobile as companies interested in an idea developed by Microsoft. Microsoft plans to launch a new advertising system called NUads that aims to get viewers to participate in advertisements. The adverts will be featured on Microsoft's Xbox 360 game console plugged though a standard TV set and featuring the Kinect motion-tracking device. The Xbox system will enable companies to receive real-time feedback on how many people are watching and physically interacting with the adverts. The technology developed by Microsoft has a far greater means of measuring how people react to a piece of content than any current TV system. It can detect a person's facial expressions, record/sense audio reactions and transmit pieces of video. After launching NUads at the Privacy Innovations Identity (PII) conference in May 2012, Microsoft was quick to defend itself for the justifiable backlash from consumer groups and human rights organisations: "Microsoft has strict policies in place that prohibit the collection, storage or use of Kinect data for the purpose of advertising" (Callaham 2012). Around the same time as the PII conference in Seattle, Intel (who also make the microchips for Microsoft's Xbox 360) announced a similar product: "Intel is counting on facial-recognition technology for targeted ads and a team of veteran entertainment dealmakers to win over reluctant media partners for its new virtual television service" (Adegoke and Randewich 2012).

If data harvesting is to support high-quality TV news, it must generate a considerable amount of revenue, and its privacy issues must be resolved. As Thompson says,

> Issues of privacy almost become more important in the context of news than almost anything else, but I think the idea of news operations using viewing data to sell or cross-sell things is certainly worth exploring. E-commerce maybe another possibility here, though news isn't the most obvious genre. But even if all these things are possible—the sale of data or e-commerce—it's still hard to believe that the lion's share of revenues won't come from advertising. I think it will. (personal interview, 5 February 2013)

ii)   The Mobile Dimension

On Wednesday, 1 August 2012, 729,000 people watched on mobile devices as British cyclist Bradley Wiggins took gold in the men's cycling road time-trial at the London Olympics (O'Riordan 2012). Live video, usually transmitted using broadcast technology, was streamed to mobiles using the UK's overstretched 3G telephone network. In what has been billed as the first digital Olympics, the BBC's iOS and Android smartphone application was downloaded 1.9 million times. Of all daily browsers to the BBC's Olympic coverage, 34% were using mobiles, whilst the BBC received 12 million requests from mobiles for video throughout the Games. This is challenging for news. Research from Pew (2012) shows that whilst 70% of desktop/laptop owners in the United States get news on their computers, half of smartphone owners (51%) use their phones for news. Just as the portability of radio ensured its popularity as a news platform, the even greater flexibility of mobile suggests its ascendency is inevitable. Its impact on hard news will be economic. Revenues from web adverts are approximately 10% of "offline" legacy media platforms. Mobile is now a fraction of web advertising, and its revenue value is estimated at 1%. If, as Pew's research demonstrates, 51% of Americans are using mobile as their primary source for news—a platform that generates a hundredth of its offline predecessors' revenues—funds generated by mobile alone are clearly inadequate to even cover the costs of a quality news operation. But the lure of portability, flexibility and the way mobiles and smart phones are changing consumption habits make them impossible to ignore. Matthew Postgate, Controller, BBC Research and Development, offered a glimpse of the current thinking at the BBC in a recent interview:

> The reality is the mobile phone industry is at least ten times bigger than the broadcasting industry . . . we as broadcasters need to understand that broadcasting is a state of mind, it's an activity, it's not certain technologies. We need to understand how we continue to be a broadcaster but on Internet technologies rather than broadcast technologies. It's very rare that one of these things immediately supplants another but we are absolutely already in a world where the two have to coexist and we need to understand that. (interview with Deborah Robinson, 2 October 2012)

Future technologies will further transform what we currently understand as 'television'. After the struggles to cope with audience demand for 3G services during the 2012 Olympics, and in response to the growing trend towards mobile delivery, 5G technology is already in development in the UK. In September 2012, Surrey University was awarded a £35m research contract to create the network of the future. 4G is available in some countries now, including the UK. The impact of mobile on news consumption is explored elsewhere in this book, but television broadcasters will be an increasingly important component of mobile. They have the means to produce something consumers have an insatiable appetite for: video. Technology and the evolution of new platforms will create a different set of market conditions for licensing and syndicating TV news content delivered on mobile and online. Different contractual arrangements between broadcasters and mobile network operators need to emerge to share bandwidth for media-rich services in a converged digital media ecosystem—and within all of this are promising new opportunities for helping fund the operations of broadcasters, including their hard news services. As has been remarked elsewhere (Anderson 2007), paradoxically technological development is both an opportunity and a threat to the business models of news operations, and this is an example of a golden opportunity in waiting.

iii)   Alternative Funding Models

Allied to the evolving digital broadcast technologies are a number of alternative models for funding quality video news journalism delivered online and on TV, which are embodied within new providers of news. The positioning and editorial stance of these experimental, emerging news organisations enables them to offer some plurality. They generally originate stories and events overlooked by traditional TV news networks. One example is The Real News Network (TRNN). Established in 2009, TRNN claims to be the world's first independent, non-profit, viewer-supported daily video-news and documentary service. It provides "independent and uncompromising video journalism". Crucially, TRNN does not take advertising, government or corporate funding. It is financed by the kind of major individual and foundation gifts that were alluded to by McChesney. Its future relies on finding a global audience with shared values and deep pockets from which they will finance TRNN's ongoing production.

Another example is Link Media's launching of LinkTV in 1999. The not-for-profit, grant- and viewer-funded channel is dedicated to providing Americans with global perspectives on news and culture. Link TV is available online globally and on satellite TV in the United States at http://www.linktv.org.

In addition, ideas borrowed from online models like Dave Cohn's Knight Foundation-funded Spot.US, where journalists appeal to the public directly for financial support to cover a particular story, are surfacing sporadically. These are unlikely to become major income streams in their own right, but they could be part of the funding mix for local TV in the future. There are also global examples of partnerships between university media departments and community news groups and between philanthropic foundations like Knight and local TV news organisations, though these arrangements are largely perceived as cutting costs rather than increasing participation, audience engagement or improving the quality of TV news.

CONCLUSION

The biggest challenges to quality television news journalism will not come from changing consumption patterns, new and disruptive technology, increased competition or citizen journalism alone. The editorial intent and ambition of the news agenda within a television operation, an indicator of quality in its own right, is under threat because of the economic pressures that are playing on commercial news providers. As Thompson points out, "It's very hard for them to justify the expense on the type of TV that may not be very popular with audiences" (personal interview, 5 February 2013). This may well be the clarion call from within the corporations who own news operations, as directors respond to shareholder demands for efficiency savings and higher returns. Left to the free market, questions about the financial viability of news will continually frame the debate.

The embattled news editor fighting with corporate bosses for the resources to deliver depth as well as breadth is making a comeback, if they ever left. Only this time they are not just arguing with the drama department, tackling sport or fighting entertainment. Their depleted resource will also be spent on technologists and computer programmers developing mobile and tablet applications to carry their news programming. The explosion of new digital TV channels, which has meant creating more programming to fill airtime, has been complemented by a new series of content-hungry tablets, mobiles and smart TVs. Keeping pace with the sheer volume of these technologies is one thing, but the lack of standardisation of software and agreed protocols they use is expensive for broadcasters. In the UK, there are 550 different versions of iPlayer to ensure BBC digital content is available on Smart TVs from a range of manufacturers. TV networks want to be represented on all platforms. News divisions within corporations are paying to ensure their channels or programmes are included. In light of all this, increasingly, news editors will be required to produce ever more detailed business cases for covering stories as the rhetoric continues to frame news as a cost-constrained product and the organisations that deliver news as businesses. To quote Frank Hackett in *Network* (1976), "I know that historically news divisions are expected to lose money, but to our minds this is a wanton fiscal affront to be resisted."

For now, it is likely that state-funded broadcasters like Al Jazeera will continue to expand as other broadcasters retreat, due to lack of finance or corporate will to continue in the relatively expensive pursuit of quality news. PTV operations like Sky News in the UK, funded by subscription and advertising, will surely begin to supplement income by harvesting audience data and selling it to interested parties. In turn, the technology that enables this could be used to deliver individually tailored news programming and advertising—a kind of bespoke 'micro hyperlocal' TV, which may be of interest to advertisers. Current legislation prevents this, although the lobbyists within the corporate sector are already building. But this is not a future that serves well the idea of participatory democracy across our various case study countries. An effective resolution to the key problems for quality hard news (in the sense defined in chapter one) needs to be found. The chapters on broadcast news that follow assess the extent to which any resolution is in sight.

REFERENCES

Adegoke, Yinka, and Noel Randewich. 2012. "Insight: Intel's Plans for Virtual TV Come Into Focus." 8 June. Accessed 12 October 2012. http://www.reuters.com/article/2012/06/08/us-intel-tv-idUSBRE85706Q20120608.
Anderson, Chris. 2007. *The Long Tail*. New York: Hyperion.
Battelle, John. 2005. *The Search: How Google and its Rivals Rewrote the Rules of Business and Transformed our Culture*. Boston, MA: Penguin.
BBC Annual Report. 2011/12. Accessed 12 October 2012. http://www.bbc.co.uk/annualreport/download/.
Bennett, W. Lance. 2003. *News: The Politics of Illusion*. New York: Longman.
Boler, Megan, ed. 2008. *Digital Media and Democracy: Tactics in Hard Times*. Cambridge, MA: MIT Press.
Callaham, John. 2012. "Microsoft Issues Statement on Kinect NUads." 17 May 2012. Accessed 25 January 2013. http://www.neowin.net/news/microsoft-issues-statement-on-kinect-nuads.
Cheredar, Tom. 2012. "Microsoft Kinect's NUads Is What the TV Industry Needs to Survive the Future." *Venturebeat*, 16 May. Accessed 20 November 2012. http://venturebeat.com/2012/05/16/nuads-kinect-microsoft/.
Chester, Jeffrey. 2006. "Google, YouTube and You." *The Nation*, 16 October. Accessed 12 October 2012. http://www.thenation.com/article/google-youtube-and-you.
Clarke, R. 2006. "Introduction to Dataveillance and Information Privacy, and Definition of Terms." Accessed 12 October 2012. http://www.anu.edu.au/people/Roger.Clarke/DV/Intro.html.
Comcast Annual Review. 2011. Accessed 14 November 2012. http://www.comcast.com/2011annualreview/?SCRedirect=true.
Cover, Rob. 2004. "New Media Theory: Electronic Games, Democracy and Reconfiguring the Author-Audience Relationship." *Social Semiotics* 14: 173–191.
Curran, James. 2010. "The Future of Journalism." *Journalism Studies* 11: 464–476.
Deloitte. 2011. "TV Perspectives in Words and Numbers." Accessed 27 October 2012. http://www.deloitte.com/view/en_GB/uk/industries/tmt/5d44f5fe4e0f1310VgnVCM2000001b56f00aRCR D.htm.
Deloitte. 2012. "Technology, Media & Telecommunications Predictions." Accessed 28 January 2013. https://www.deloitte.com/assets/Dcom-Global/Local%20Content/Articles/TMT/TMT%20Predictions%202012/16264A_TMT_Predict_sg6.pdf.
Downie, Leonard, Jr., and Michael Schudson. 2009. "The Reconstruction of American Journalism." *Columbia Journalism Review*, 19 October. Accessed 4 February 2013. http://www.cjr.org/reconstruction/the_reconstruction_of_american.php?page=all.
Foster, Robin. 2012. "News Plurality in a Digital World." Oxford: Reuters Institute for the Study of Journalism.
Franklin, Bob. 2012. "The Future of Journalism: Developments and Debates." *Journalism Studies* 13: 663–681.

Geneits, Anne. 2010. *The Global News Challenge: Assessing Changes in International Broadcast News Consumption in Africa and South Asia.* Oxford: Reuters Institute for the Study of Journalism.

Hirst, Martin, and John Harrison. 2007. *Communication and New Media: From Broadcast to Narrowcast.* Oxford: Oxford University Press.

IDATE Research. 2012. World Television Market: Markets & Data 2008–2016: Fact sheet. July. Accessed 25 January 2013. http://www.idate.org/en/Research-store/World-Television-Market_668.html.

Jenkins, Henry. 2006. *Convergence Culture: Where Old and New Media Collide.* New York: New York University Press.

Kaye, Jeff, and Stephen Quinn. 2010. *Funding Journalism in the Digital Age: Business Models, Strategies, Issues and Trends.* Oxford: Peter Lang.

Kyncl, Robert. 2012. Keynote presentation given at MIPCOM, Cannes, 8 October. Accessed 13 February 2013. http://blog.mipworld.com/2012/10/liveblog-google-youtubes-robert-kyncl-at-mipcom/.

Levy, David A. L., and Robert G. Picard, eds. 2011. *Is There a Better Structure for News Providers? The Potential in Charitable and Trust Ownership.* Oxford: Reuters Institute for the Study of Journalism.

Macnamara, Jim. 2010a. *The 21st Century Media Revolution: Emergent Communication Practices.* New York: Peter Lang.

Macnamara, Jim. 2010b. "Remodelling Media: The Urgent Search for New Media Business Models." *Media International Australia* 137: 20–35.

McChesney, Robert W. 2010. "Rejuvenating American Journalism: Some Tentative Policy Proposals." *Perspectives on Global Development and Technology* 10: 224–237.

McChesney, Robert W. 2011. "Farewell to Journalism." *Journalism Studies* 13: 682–694.

McChesney, Robert, and John Nichols. 2010. *The Death and Life of American Journalism: The Media Revolution that will Begin the World Again.* New York: Nation Books.

McNair, Brian. 2006. *Cultural Chaos: Journalism, News and Power in a Globalized World.* New York: Routledge.

Mills, Elinor. 2008. "Don't Like Targeted Ads? Opt Out, says Online Ad Group." *CNET News*, 24 February. Accessed 13 October 2012. http://news.cnet.com/8301–10784_3–9877604–7.html.

Newman, Nic, ed. 2012. *Reuters Institute Digital News Report.* Oxford: Reuters Institute for the Study of Journalism. https://reutersinstitute.politics.ox.ac.uk/publications/risj-digital-report.html.

News Corporation. 2011. Annual Report. Accessed October 2012. http://www.newscorp.com/Report2011/2011AR.pdf.

Nightingale, Virginia, and Tim Dwyer, eds. 2007. *New Media Worlds: Challenges for Convergence.* Melbourne: Oxford University Press.

Ofcom. 2011. *International Communications Market Report 2011.* Accessed 25 January 2013. http://stakeholders.ofcom.org.uk/market-data-research/market-data/communications-market-reports/cmr11/international/.

Ofcom. 2012. *International Communications Market Report 2012.* Accessed 25 January 2013. http://stakeholders.ofcom.org.uk/market-data-research/market-data/communications-market-reports/cmr12/international/.

Open Society Foundation. 2012. "Mapping Digital Media." Accessed 5 February 2013. http://www.opensocietyfoundations.org/about/programs/media-program.

O'Riordan, Cait. 2012. "Digital Olympics: Week One in Numbers." BBC Online, 3 August. http://www.bbc.co.uk/blogs/blogbbcinternet/posts/olympic_statistics_traffic_week?filter=none

Patterson, Thomas E. 1993. *Out of Order.* New York: Knopf.
Patterson, Thomas E. 2000. "Doing Well and Doing Good: How Soft News and Critical Journalism are Shrinking the News Audience and Weakening Democracy—and What News Outlets Can Do about It." Faculty Research Working Paper Series, RWP01–001. Joan Shorenstein Center on the Press, Politics and Public Policy, Harvard University. Accessed 5 February 2013. http://shorensteincenter.org/wp-content/uploads/2012/03/soft_news_and_critical_journalism_2000.pdf.
Patterson, Thomas E. 2007. *Young People and News.* Cambridge, MA: Joan Shorenstein Center on the Press, Politics and Public Policy, Harvard University. http://shorensteincenter.org/wp-content/uploads/2012/03/young_people_and_news_2007.pdf.
Pavlik, John. 2008. *Media in the Digital Age.* New York: Columbia University Press.
Pew Research Center. 2011. *The State of the News Media 2011.* Project for Excellence in Journalism. Accessed 20 October 2012. http://pewresearch.org/pubs/1924/state-of-the-news-media-2011.
Pew Research Center. 2012. *The Future of Mobile News 2012.* Project for Excellence in Journalism. Accessed 4 January 2013. http://www.journalism.org/analysis_report/future_mobile_news
Postgate, Matthew. 2012. Interview with Deborah Robinson, 2 October 2012.
QFinance. 2012. Sector Profiles: Media Industry: Major Industry Trends. Accessed 22 November 2012. http://www.qfinance.com/sector-profiles/media.
Ricchiardi, Sherry. 2011. "The Al Jazeera Effect." *American Journalism Review*, 21 April. Accessed 25 January 2013. http://ajr.org/Article.asp?id=5077.
Schmidt, Eric. 2011. MacTaggart Lecture, Edinburgh Television Festival, 26 August. http://www.guardian.co.uk/media/interactive/2011/aug/26/eric-schmidt-mactaggart-lecture-full-text.
Singapore Ministry of Communication and Information. 2012. Press Release: "Government Accepts Recommendations by PSB Review Panel." Accessed November 2012. http://www.mci.gov.sg/content/mci_corp/web/mci/pressroom/categories/press_releases/2012/government_acceptsrecommendationsbypsbreviewpanel.html.
Smith, Chris. 2012. "Ernesto Schmitt: Focusing on the Second Screen Experience." *Guardian*, 16 February.
Time Warner. 2011. Annual Report. http://ir.timewarnercable.com/files/doc_financials/Annual%20Reports/TWC_2011_Annual_Report.pdf.
The Real News Network. 2013. http://therealnews.com/t2/about-us/mission. Accessed 14 May 2013.
Thompson, Mark. 2013. Interview with Paul Egglestone, January 2013.
TiVo. 2012. Press release: "TiVo Launches 'Next Day' TV Viewing Data." 27 February 2012. Accessed 25 January 2013. http://pr.tivo.com/press-releases/tivo-launches-next-day-tv-viewing-data-nasdaq-tivo-0856490.
UPI. 2012. "NBC News Now Fully Owns MSNBC.com." July 16. Accessed 25 January 2013. http://www.upi.com/Entertainment_News/TV/2012/07/16/NBC-News-now-fully-owns-msnbccom/UPI-73771342446751/.
Your.TV. http://www.cloudbroadcasting.tv/.

5 Finding Viable Business Models for Intermediate and Developing World Broadcast, Print and Online Newspaper Sectors

Motilola Akinfemisoye and Sally Deffor

INTRODUCTION

Studies on the media in intermediate and developing economies suggest a thriving mainstream broadcast media and newspaper industry, which is in contrast to current trends in the developed world (Stone, Nel, and Wilberg 2010). Some have attributed this contradiction to the varied business models that have been adopted by news organizations in the global North and South (see, for example, Collins 2011; Moro and Aikat 2010). Others point to the differing adoption and adaptation of new media technologies and multimedia platforms by the broader news industry. However, there is a paucity of critical scholarship on the business models that seem to be helping traditional media in the global South survive, even flourish in some regions, in these uncertain times for the news industry. This chapter seeks to tease out some of the business models currently used by media organizations in selected countries from the global South and further assesses their viability. In particular, the cases of Kenya, Nigeria, and Ghana are examined. Examples are also drawn from the Big Emerging Markets (BEM) of Brazil, China, India and South Africa.

THE MEDIA AS BUSINESS

Media organisations function as public watchdogs but are also business ventures. As such, media organisations employ business models that are best suited for their contexts. According to Chesbrough and Rosenbloom (2002, 530), the business model concept was born with Chandler's seminal work *Strategy and Structure* (1962). Since Chandler's work, business models have been variously defined in terms of strategy and organizational structure (see Morris, Schindehutte, and Allen 2005; Shafer, Smith, and Linder 2005; Zott, Amit, and Massa 2011). Many scholars have hinted at what business models should do as well as how firms should appropriate them. For Afuah (2004, 2), a business model refers to a "framework for making money". Chesbrough and Rosenbloom (2002, 529) contend that beyond being an outline of an organisation's strategy for maximizing profit, a business model is "the heuristic logic that connects technical potential with the realization of economic value". This suggests that firms must seek out strategies that are useful in meeting the bottom-line as the business model adopted is said to impact on the overall performance of the firm (Baden-Fuller and Morgan 2010). In determining how firms create value, Picard (2002, 26) advises that the business models firms adopt "need to account for the vital resources of production and distribution technologies, content creation or acquisition".

This chapter adopts Chaharbaghi, Fendt, and Willis's (2003) conceptualisation of business models to unpack how media organisations in BEMs and developing economies operate. They identify three interrelated strands for thinking about business models: characteristics of a company's way of thinking, its operational system and capacity for value creation. Nielsen and Bukh (2008, 6) note that these three strands "form the basis of a meta-model for business models".

In the light of this, we examined the products and services that these media in both the intermediate and developing economies provide, against the backdrop of the strategies that inform their choices. The chapter also examines the viability of those choices.

PROBLEMATIZING THE BUSINESS OF NEWS

The frames, slants and other newsroom cultures that journalists pursue in the news production process are ultimately guided by ensuring that the final product, the news, is well suited for the target market. Cranberg, Bezanson, and Soloski (2001, 2) argue that "the business of news is business, not news". As such, media organizations continue to "seek ways of maintain[ing] viability in a rapidly changing business and social environment" (Owers, Carveth, and Alexander 2004, 3–4). Media scholars thus question what this means for the roles and functions of actors in the sector (Gans 2003; Franklin 2008). Who then is a journalist, and what is the function of journalism as an institution?

The role of news has become increasingly problematic as media institutions strive to provide the most widely sought news via the most financially lucrative means. Phillips and Witschge (2012, 6) note that the "responsibilities [of the media] are to themselves or their shareholders, rather than their role in a functioning democracy". However, caution needs to be taken in the way such generalizations are made. Although the roles of media organizations may be undermined by economic imperatives, they still have a stake in functioning democracies and must therefore ensure that they carry out their traditional roles as watchdogs of society, for this may in fact determine their very existence. These dual roles "create tensions within media companies and among media policy-makers" (Picard 2005, 337), and as such there have been calls that "both roles [be looked at] at the same time" (Phillips and Witschge 2012, 4). In the next sections, we look at how media organizations in the global South attempt to reconcile these roles.

SELLING THE NEWS(PAPER) IN INTERMEDIATE AND DEVELOPING CONTEXTS

Unlike media organizations in the Global North who are "facing a long-term decline in their core revenue streams and . . . struggling to cover the underlying costs of original journalism" (Currah 2009, 37), the print media markets in intermediate and developing economies are relatively stable. It appears that where the economies are growing, the media industry also seems to be thriving. Moro and Aikat in their study of the media markets of China and India identified a parallel relationship between such economies and the "expansion in media audiences, providers and advertising spending" (2010, 357). In Brazil, for example, the industry has grown about 1/3% in recent years, and circulation figures are put at 8.2 million. In South Africa, readership is said to be increasing with the growth in income levels. The country's newspaper market grew by 5.7% in 2011, earning some 11.4 billion rand ($1.3 billion). There is also remarkable growth in China and India where combined circulation figures reach nearly 220 million copies daily (Moro and Aikat 2010). According to the World Association of Newspapers and News Publishers (WAN-IFRA) in its World Press Trends for 2012, newspaper sales have been on the increase in the Global South with a "3.5 percent increase in newspaper circulation in Asia and 4.8 percent in the Middle East and North Africa". While the expansion of the media markets is infinitely tied to the growing economies, including the expansion of the middle class and media audiences in general, the adoption of a diversified range of business models also accounts for the previous figures. The next section identifies some of these models.

TRADITIONAL SYSTEM MODEL

There is still a great appeal for the news provided by the mainstream media via the traditional routes of newspapers, radio and television broadcast. With particular reference to newspapers, indications point to the audience in the BEM and developing economies having a value system where newspapers are still regarded as a 'record of truth'. In India, people still fancy the art of reading a physical newspaper (Moro and Aikat 2010, 360). This spurs the continuing stability in circulations and readerships in these economies even with the penetration of the internet. According to a news report in 2011(BBC News 2011a), newspaper circulation figures in India as of 2009 stood at 107 million copies daily. In Brazil newspapers witnessed a significant growth of 6.5% in 2006 from the previous year (Moreira and Helal 2009, 97). Thus, newspapers remain an important product of the media industry in these economies. Moro and Aikat (2010, 360) take this argument forward by noting that newspaper circulation in India and China is growing because people "cherish their newspaper reading habit and have the time to read and inclination to buy a newspaper every day". In Kenya, Ghana and Nigeria, newspapers are still widely regarded as records of truth. For instance, in Nigeria during the 2012 *Occupy Nigeria*[1] protests, newspapers sold more copies because readers wanted to verify the events they had seen and read about on social media.[2] This sociological factor is partly the reason for the stable readership and sustainability of newspaper production in these economies.

In terms of packaging and distribution, some conventional models remain. In South Africa for instance, evening editions, classified sections and the wide broadsheet style newspapers still exist even as these trends wane in the developed world. In Nigeria and Ghana, traditional newspaper distribution networks such as vendors selling newspapers at newsstands are still in place. These mechanisms ensure that news organizations have a reliable source of generating revenues from newspaper sales. This established practice, unlike that of relying on revenues from their news websites, remains relatively consistent, offering steady revenues to newspaper organizations. Even in the developed economies where internet penetration is relatively high, news on the websites of news organization remains unprofitable. In Phillips and Witschge's words, "commercial news on the web appears to have limited options for recouping production costs through sales" (2012, 4). Taking this argument forward, Moro and Aikat (2010, 361) aver that "newspaper revenues are still through the traditional means of newsstand sales, advertising and subscription".

However, there is the recognition that in the Western world where newspapers are declining, they also once had these socio-cultural attachments to reading the newspaper. Therefore, perhaps the best explanation one can advance for why the traditional is still attractive can in a sense be attributed to technological factors. It is the advancement in internet use that separates the media in the developed world from that of the intermediate and developing, where in South Africa for example, internet penetration is at a low 17% (Miniwatts Marketing Group 2012). This said, the rates at which societies develop are unequal, and it is the way that they appropriate the use of new technologies that determines its relevance in that particular context. For example, mobile phone use as a money-transfer device is fully developed in Kenya (e.g., M-PESA) but it is only now emerging in the global North.

Again the business processes and procedures that enable production, distribution and revenue generation from methods other than the traditional, (as exists in the developed world), have not been well developed in much of the global South. As such, the traditional business model remains very much in place and viable. As of September 3, 2012, World Association of Newspapers and News Publishers (WAN-IFRA) noted on its website that, "print continues to provide the vast majority of newspaper company revenues with circulation alone accounting for nearly half of all revenues" (WAN-IFRA 2012).

NEW TECHNOLOGY MODELS

Mainstream media organizations in intermediate and developing countries (much like their counterparts from the developed world) are putting measures in place for business models that take advantage of technological advancements. In Brazil, the newspaper *Folha de S Paulo* has implemented the pay-wall system where readers are charged a nominal fee to access the online version of its printed editions. This service is also offered on its smartphone and tablets versions. It is the pioneer Brazilian newspaper to do this, and some Brazilian newspapers have expressed the desire to toe this line in search of new business models that generate revenue using digital media as opposed to relying heavily on revenues from print (Mazotte 2012).

The development of this model remains slow, and future growth is uncertain. Moro and Aikat (2010, 361) argue that news organizations have not quite worked out how this model could work financially and sustainably. For instance the *Times of London* struggled with implementing pay-wall because they were unable to sustain online readership and, most importantly, convert these readers into subscribers (Chittum 2012). In effect, publishers are still struggling with how to maximize profit from online news. In India and China, pockets of niche paid-content products exist (Moro and Aikat 2010, 360), but due to their low uptake, one can surmise that it is neither attractive nor viable in the short term. Moro and Aikat attribute this to low internet penetration and the attachment to reading newspapers (2010, 360). In the case of Nigeria, attempts at commercializing online news by making readers pay for access have been largely unsuccessful because of the low internet penetration and the newspaper-sharing culture of readers in the country.[3]

There seems to be strong indications that media organizations are going to keep pursuing more innovative means of generating revenues via digital media (Mazotte 2012). There is also growing recognition that, eventually, online news and online advertising will become a more integral part of the media industry (Gardam 2009). It has also been noted that newspapers in many markets are exploring ways of increasing online usage, which is one important way of ensuring increase in revenues from the digital space (WAN-IFRA 2012).

According to Franklin (2008, 310) advertising in the online media space exists globally and is growing. In South Africa, it is growing at twice the rate of newspaper advertising (Boyle 2011). There is evidence to suggest then that with current advancements in technology and internet access, and with sustainability thesis in mind, this product in a technology-based business model could be advanced. Though tentative, revenues from the online domain are expected and were projected to be nine percent of total ad spending at the end of 2008 (Ahlers 2006, 41). This fact highlights a somewhat sustainable business model that should be pursued. Though cautiously, advertising in the online domain will increasingly chip away at the newspaper base (Ahlers 2006, 43). Therefore, technology-driven models pioneered by newspapers may continue to be viable and perhaps sustainable in the long term.

Another reason for advancing a model that relies on the use of new technology is perhaps due to the fact that it is cheaper and more attractive to advertisers in terms of advertising. In Kenya, advertising on the *Daily Nation and Standard* online news site comprises mostly product placements of real estates, airlines and money transfer services targeted at Kenyans in the growing diaspora who are the most likely to be accessing the online news. This seems to be a practice that, over the long term, can be sustained in other intermediate and developing contexts, given the increasing number of audiences in the diaspora who want to be kept abreast of happenings at home. As The Central Bank of Kenya (CBK) reports, as at December 2012, remittances to Kenya grew by 24% and accounts for the fourth-largest source of foreign exchange to its economy (Central Bank of Kenya 2013). This is indicative of a large market for newspaper web sites in Kenya and explains why these newspapers have such ads on their web sites. As such, the investments of Kenyans in diaspora back home means that they become targets for online newspapers of the homeland.

Another element to this technology-driven model is where the increase in mobile phone subscriptions in Africa has seen media organizations in Kenya, Ghana and Nigeria providing SMS news alerts to those who subscribe to it. Mobile phones are ubiquitous in Africa and have recently been described as "the new talking drums of everyday Africa" (de Bruijn, Nyamnjoh, and Brinkman 2009). Mobile phones are relatively popular and continue to grow with a 65% penetration rate as of November 2011 (BBC News 2011b).

However, media organisations in Kenya, Ghana and Nigeria have yet to fully maximize the opportunities of selling news through the mobile platform. In cases where attempts have been made to explore the mobile platform, the media organizations themselves do not generate enough revenue due to the percentage revenue-sharing arrangement with the telecommunications providers who take up to 65% of the revenue generated, leaving the news providers with barely enough to make profit (WAN-IFRA 2011). It will be useful for media organizations in these developing countries to develop mobile news platforms so as to cash in on the growing mobile phone adoption rates.

DIFFERENTIATED-PRODUCTS MODEL

The differentiated-products model is perhaps the most specific to the newspaper industry (both print and online). In this model, newspapers organizations have taken to the development and marketing of specialized products with distinct styles that appeal to certain audience types. An easily recognizable one to mention here is the tabloid. Newspaper organizations in countries in the intermediate world such as Brazil and South Africa have taken to employing the tabloid approach, which boomed (and subsequently fell) in the developed economies of the United States and the United Kingdom. In Brazil, they are cashing in on a growing lower middle class that has a taste for vibrant and catchy publications (Moreira and Helal 2009, 97). Some Brazilian major newspapers with mainstream publications have launched additional publications—much cheaper tabloid versions—with which they cash in on this demand without taking away the substance of their main broadsheet publications. The Brazilian *Super Notícia* newspaper, for example, offers a mix of crime, football and gossip that the growing semi-literate audiences demand, according to Moreira and Helal (2009, 97). This tabloidization drive is an attractive prospect for publishers, not only in response to audience demand, but perhaps also to compensate for the decline in the revenues generated from broadsheet sales. In Brazil, the high-end, low cost tabloids are targeted at the growing lower middle class and are a mix between the popular broadsheet newspapers and traditional tabloid-style editions. There is a policy of 'complements rather than competes', where different styles of newspapers (broadsheets and tabloid) are produced by the same media conglomerates that target different audiences (Magro 2010). For example, the *Zero Hora* targets and produces content suited to the taste of upscale readers under 30 years of age, while its sister publication *Diário Gaúcho* aims for the middle and lower-middle classes. The pricing also reflects this differentiation with the former being much more expensive. The *Super Notícia* sells at a fraction of the price of trendier papers, such as the *Estado, Folha de Sao Paulo*, and *O Globo*, and features a collection of promotions and discount offers (Phillips 2009).

South Africa has also seen the growth of tabloid newspapers, which has dramatically changed the country's mediascape (Wasserman 2010, 1). Media Club South Africa noted on its web site in 2012 that this phenomenon is the future of South African newspapers. The popular *Daily Sun*, which has a readership of some 7.7 million, leads this 'revolution' (Wasserman 2010), and its massive success is well recognized in the industry. Other South African publications such as the *Son, Isolezwe, Ilanga* and the *Daily Voice* have taken a cue from the *Daily Sun*'s example and are relatively successful.

In terms of sustainability, it is necessary that we recognize that the tabloid model we are discussing here was also modeled in the developed economies that are now facing a decline in readership and circulation. However, it is pertinent to note that the income class that these tabloid newspapers appeal to is growing in these intermediate economies. Tabloids are able to respond more quickly to the tastes and interests of their teeming consumers. The news sourcing practices, for instance, which tabloids employ in contrast to the time-consuming investigative journalism of the broadsheet, mean that the cost of production is relatively cheap. Also, the focus on brevity and the visual make them appealing to their target market.

The place of the local newspaper in terms of content, community and language is another aspect to this business model. In India, Brazil and South Africa there is increasing appeal for local newspapers that carry local news and draw on the successes of the community-media model (Moro and Aikat 2010; Moreira and Helal 2009; Media Club South Africa 2012). In the developing economies of Kenya, Ghana and Nigeria, however, this is not the case as the market for local newspapers is still underdeveloped. One parallel between the two economies with regards to the local is the diversification into local language newspapers to cater for certain segments of the market. Examples include the South African *Ilanga* and *Isolezwe*, the Swahili daily in Kenya *Taifa Leo*, and the *Alaroye* newspaper in Nigeria. However, the reason the *Ilanga* and the *Isolezwe* newspapers seem to be faring relatively better from among the lot boils down to the tabloid nature and the local news dimension (Media Club South Africa 2012). In India and China, this genre of newspapers seems to be gaining popularity. However, in terms of financial viability, we raise questions about the viability of producing hyper-local content in an increasingly globalized and diversified economy such as exists in India and China. Nonetheless, this seems to be a strategy that could be pursued as a recognized viable newspaper business model, while taking into consideration the peculiarities of the country context in which it is advanced.

MEDIA OWNERSHIP AND FUNDING MODEL

The ownership structures that exist in media organisations help in understanding how funding is sourced and in turn "produces different operational and performance contexts" (Picard and van Weezel 2008, 23). We examine ownership here based on privately owned and publicly funded media organisations. With the exclusion of state-owned or subsidised media organisations, the economic imperative of media organizations is to make profits in order to continue to exist. As such, this impacts on the operational strategies that media organisations adopt. Publicly owned media organizations still largely adhere to their public-service mandate and have access to some state funding.

In Africa, particularly Kenya, Ghana and Nigeria, private broadcasters, for instance, are open to innovation. The competitive environment that the deregulation of the broadcast media in the 1990s made possible means that private broadcasters are able to create new products in order to remain afloat. This translates into flexible strategy decisions on production and distribution that they put in place. They are more able to take risks and thus continually make short-term investments in news production and distribution without feeling the pressure to show immediate returns. On the other hand, media institutions listed on the stock exchange are tied to the strict requirements of their investors. For example, in Brazil and South Africa, privately owned media organizations have proven to be able to be more flexible in experimenting with new ventures. They are also more resilient to difficulties in the media environment.

However, there is a case to be made for large media corporations. The Nation Media Group of Kenya, for instance, is a media conglomerate listed on the Nairobi Stock Exchange and own a number of media platforms across the East African region. These include the *Daily Nation* newspaper, EasyFM radio, QTV, among others. This concentration means that they are able to command a large share of the media market, generate large revenue and dominate the Kenyan media market. This factor adds a survival and resilience dimension to their operations and existence due to their extensive operation.

In terms of ownership and funding mechanisms in the broadcasting arena, state–owned public service providers modeled after the BBC's public service broadcasting have varying experiences with viability and sustainability. With the influx of privately owned commercial broadcasting following the deregulation of the broadcast sector in the 1990s in many sub-saharan African countries, the monopolies enjoyed by publicly funded broadcasters was broken. As Eko (2007, 12) explains, "public broadcasters tr[ied] to reinvent themselves to the new environment of globalization and market competition". As such, the notion of Public Service Broadcasting as a model where the organization is predominantly publicly funded is not necessarily the case anymore. Although state-owned media organisations exist, they also compete for advertisements with the privately owned media organisations in order to remain afloat. This move to find alternative funding sources is imperative, also due to the declining revenues from licensing fees. The Kenyan Broadcasting Corporation (KBC), for instance, initially funded by licence fee payers witnessed a drastic drop in revenues because of the proliferation of private broadcasters as consumers became unwilling to continue paying for services that are offered freely by the private broadcasters. Thus, public broadcasters in most developing economies grapple with funding challenges and are usually pressured into supporting the ruling party.

However, private broadcasters seem to be faring better not only because of their funding sources, but also due to operating small, lean structures in comparison with the public ones. This factor makes their operations more financially rewarding. Private broadcasters also have a cross range of funding sources available to them that includes subtle political funding mechanisms and live entertainment events. Additionally, they offer a variety of diversified programming that the emerging middle class prefer; examples include Ghana's *Viasat1* and *e.tv*, which are both foreign private broadcasters. Their line of programmes includes international sports tournaments, soap operas, and music. Collectively, the factors discussed previously make the private newspaper and broadcasting ventures a more viable option in these economies.

CONCLUSION

In this chapter, we have drawn out the identifiable business models in existence in the media environment in the Big and Emerging Market (BEM) economies of India, Brazil and South Africa and the developing economies of Nigeria, Kenya and Ghana. We have used specific case studies to show that viable business models are still in place to sustain traditional media despite the growing concerns of its inevitable decline. The business models we discussed may overlap in the sense that one or more of the models may be in place at the same time within the same organization. The traditional model examines the conventional dynamics that are still in place for news production and distribution, and are proving to be viable and sustainable, where the medium of the physical newspaper is still a financially attractive venture. This seems to be in sharp contrast with the new-technology model where the focus is on developing options for revenue generation from online news. Evidence from the case studies reveals that this is a model that is still in its gestation period and will only develop with time. The differentiated-products model centers on how various distinct publications are produced by the same media organizations that target different sectors of the market. The model that considers specifically the institutions behind the product in terms of how the particular ownership and funding schemes engender viability is the media ownership and funding model. This model contrasts the publicly funded against the privately owned and argues that a strong case can be made for the latter in that their operations are more likely to be profitable.

We conclude that although these business models can be labeled as sustainable or even growing, finding a uniform working business model remains elusive. This is because the countries studied in this chapter are at different stages of development, and their economies experience unique challenges. As Chaharbaghi, Fendt, and Willis (2003, 374) argue, the reading of business models should be context-specific, and this is what we sought to achieve in our discussion.

NOTES

1. Occupy Nigeria was a protest by Nigerians against the government's removal of the fuel subsidy in January 2012.
2. Newspaper editor, Nigerian newspaper, interview conducted in 2012.
3. A privately-owned newspaper in Nigeria, *The Punch* decided to implement an access fee for its online edition but failed because readers simply moved on to read their news from other websites (Newspaper editor, Nigerian newspaper, interview conducted in 2012).

REFERENCES

Afuah, Allan. 2004. *Business Models: A Strategic Management Approach*. New York: Irwin/McGraw-Hill.
Ahlers, Douglas. 2006. "News Consumption and the New Electronic Media." *Press/Politics* 11: 29–52. doi: 10.1177/1081180X05284317.
Baden-Fuller, Charles, and Mary S. Morgan. 2010. "Business Models as Models." *Long Range Planning* 43: 156–171. doi:10.1016/j.lrp.2010.02.005.
BBC News. 2011a. "Newspapers: Why India's Newspaper Industry Is Booming." Accessed 11 January 2013. http://www.bbc.co.uk/news/business-14362723
BBC News. 2011b. "Africa's Mobile Phone Industry 'Booming'." Accessed 25 November 2012. http://www.bbc.co.uk/news/world-africa-15659983
Boyle, Brendan. 2011. "Death of Newspapers Premature." *Times Live*, 15 December. Accessed 12 December 2012. http://www.timeslive.co.za/opinion/columnists/2011/12/15/death-of-newspapers-premature
Central Bank of Kenya. 2013. "Diaspora Remittances." Accessed 20 January 2013. http://www.centralbank.go.ke/index.php/diaspora-remittances
Chaharbaghi, Kazem, Christian Fendt, and Robert Willis. 2003. "Meaning, Legitimacy and Impact of Business Models in Fast-Moving Environments." *Management Decision* 41: 372–382. doi:10.1108/00251740310468013.
Chandler, Alfred D., Jr. 1962. *Strategy and Structure: Chapters in the History of the Industrial Enterprise*. Cambridge: The MIT Press.
Chesbrough, Henry, and Rosenbloom, Richard. 2002. "The Role of the Business Model in Capturing Value from Innovation: Evidence from Xerox Corporation's Technology Spin-Off Companies." *Industrial and Corporate Change* 11: 529–555. doi:10.1093/icc/11.3.529.
Chittum, Ryan. 2012. "Paywalls: Maybe Not So Complicated After All." *Columbia Journalism Review*, 17 January. Accessed 30 November 2012. http://www.cjr.org/the_audit/shirky_and_paywalls.php?page=all
Collins, Richard. 2011. "Content Online and the End of Public Media? The UK, a Canary in the Coal Mine?" *Media, Culture & Society* 33: 1202–1219. doi: 10.1177/0163443711422459.
Cranberg, Gilbert, Randall P. Bezanson, and John Soloski. 2001. *Taking Stock: Journalism and the Publicly Traded Newspaper Company*. Ames: Iowa State University Press.
Currah, Andrew. 2009. *What's Happening to Our News: An Investigation into the Likely Impact of the Digital Revolution on the Economics of News Publishing in the UK*. Oxford: Reuters Institute for the Study of Journalism.
de Bruijn, Mirjam, Francis Nyamnjoh, and Inge Brinkman. 2009. *Mobile Phones: The New Talking Drums of Everyday Africa*. Bamenda, CMR: Langaa.

Eko, Lyombe. 2007. "Africa: Life in the Margins of Globalization." In *The Media Globe: Trends in International Mass Media*, edited by Lee Artz and Yahya R. Kamalipour, 7–32. Lanham, MD: Rowman & Littlefield Publishers Inc.

Franklin, Bob. 2008. The Future of Newspapers. *Journalism Practice* 2: 306–317. doi:10.1080/17512780802280984.

Gans, Herbert J. 2003. *Democracy and the News*. New York: Oxford University Press.

Gardam, Tim. 2009. "Foreword," in *What's Happening to Our News: An Investigation into the Likely Impact of the Digital Revolution on the Economics of News Publishing in the UK*, by Andrew Currah, 3–4. Oxford: Reuters Institute for the Study of Journalism.

Magro, Maira. 2010. "Why is Newspaper Circulation Growing in Brazil As It Falls in the U.S?" Knight Center for Journalism in Americas Blog, 28 May. Accessed 15 December 2012. http://knightcenter.utexas.edu/blog/why-newspaper-circulation-growing-brazil-it-falls-us

Mazotte, Natalia. 2012. "First Brazilian Newspaper Implements Paywall to Charge for Access to Digital Content." Knight Center for Journalism in Americas Blog, 21 June. Accessed 15 December 2012. http://knightcenter.utexas.edu/blog/00-10539-first-brazilian-newspaper-implents-paywall-charge-access-digital-content

Media Club South Africa. 2012. "The Media in South Africa." Accessed 11 December 2012. http://www.mediaclubsouthafrica.com/index.php?option=com_content&view=article&id=110%3AThe+media+in+South+Africa&catid=36%3Amedia_bg&Itemid=54

Miniwatts Marketing Group. 2012. "Internet Users, Population and Facebook statistics for Africa." Accessed 15 November 2012. http://www.internetworldstats.com/stats1.html

Moreira, Sonia, and Carla Helal. 2009. "Notes on Media, Journalism Education and News Organisations in Brazil." *Journalism* 10: 91–107. doi:10.1177/1464884908098322.

Moro, Nikhil, and Debashis Aikat. 2010. "Chindia's Newspaper Boom: Identifying Sustainable Business Models." *Global Media and Communication* 6: 357–367. doi: 10.1177/1742766510384976.

Morris, Michael, Minet Schindehutte, and Jeffrey Allen. 2005. "The Entrepreneur's Business Model: Toward a Unified Perspective." *Journal of Business Research* 58: 726–735. doi:10.1016/j.jbusres.2003.11.001.

Nielsen, Christian, and Per N. Bukh. 2008. "What Constitutes a Business Model: The Perception of Financial Analysts." *Working Paper Series, Department of Business Studies, Aalborg University*. Accessed 21 January 2013. http://www2.business.aau.dk/digitalAssets/52/52602_38.pdf

Owers, James, Rod Carveth, and Alison Alexander. 2004. "An Introduction to Media Economics, Theory and Practice." In *Media Economics: Theory and Practice*, 3rd Edition, edited by Alison Alexander, James Owers, Rod Carveth, C. Ann Hollifield, and Albert N. Greco, 3–48. London: Lawrence Erlbaum.

Phillips, Angela, and Tamara Witschge. 2012. "The Changing Business of News: Sustainability of News Journalism." In *Changing Journalism*, edited by Peter Lee-Wright, Angela Phillips, and Tamara Witschge, 3–20. London: Routledge.

Phillips, Dom. 2009. "Brazilian Tabloids Show There Is Still Life in Print." *Financial Times*, 30 August. Accessed 5 January 2013. http://www.ft.com/cms/s/0/74117334-957b-11de-90e0-00144feabdc0.html#axzz2JIC9m82H

Picard, Robert. 2002. *The Economics and Financing of Media Companies*. New York: Fordham University Press.

Picard, Robert. 2005. "Money, Media and the Public Interest." In *The Institutions of Democracy: The Press*, edited by Geneva Overholser and Kathleen Hall Jamieson, 337–350. Oxford: Oxford University Press.

Picard, Robert, and Aldo van Weezel. 2008. "Capital and Control: Consequences of Different Forms of Newspaper Ownership." *International Journal on Media Management* 10: 22–31. doi:10.1080/14241270701820473.

Shafer, Scott M., Jeff H. Smith, and Jane C. Linder. 2005. "The Power of Business Models." *Business Horizons* 48: 199–207. http://dx.doi.org/10.1016/j.bushor.2004.10.014

Stone, Martha, François Nel, and Erik Wilberg. 2010. *World News Future and Change Study 2010*. Paris, France: World Association of Newspapers and News Publishers (WAN-IFRA).

Wasserman, Herman. 2010. *Tabloid Journalism in South Africa*. Bloomington: Indiana University Press.

World Association of Newspapers and News Publishers (WAN-IFRA). 2011. "Mobile Media Services at Sub-Saharan African Newspapers: A Guide to Implementing Mobile News and Mobile Business." Accessed 30 November 2012. http://www.africanmediainitiative.org/upload/Mobile.pdf

World Association of Newspapers and News Publishers (WAN-IFRA). 2012. "World Press Trends: Newspaper Audience Rise, Digital Revenues Yet to Follow." Accessed 30 November 2012. http://www.wan-ifra.org/press-releases/2012/09/03/world-press-trends-newspaper-audience-rise-digital-revenues-yet-to-follow

Zott, Christoph, Raphael Amit, and Lorenzo Massa. 2011. "The Business Model: Recent Developments and Future Research." *Journal of Management* 37: 1019–1042. doi: 10.1177/0149206311406265.

A Critical Overview of Current Quality Levels in the Journalism of Sample Developed World States and What Needs to Be Done to Maintain or Improve Them

6 Quality Journalism in the UK, in Print and Online

Michael Williams

This chapter is written from the point of view of a senior practitioner within the quality UK national newspaper sector who divides his time working as a journalist and as a senior lecturer in the Journalism School at the University of Central Lancashire. It reflects that fact within its structure and analytical content, as is the case in other chapters written by insider contributors, and does so as part of the flexible approach of the book, which blends together the expertise of academics and journalists in order to gain a fully rounded perspective on the key issues at its heart.

There has been much chatter over the past decade about the imminent death of newspapers. Seismic shifts have taken place, with falling advertising revenues and losses of circulation as audiences have moved online, encouraged by the rapid development of portable digital media. Without a successful model to monetise content in this new world, quality journalism—expensive to produce—has been seen to be at risk. Yet, this chapter argues, the decline of quality print journalism may have been overstated. Serious newspapers have not only survived one of the worst recessions in living memory, but imaginative and flexible new approaches are enabling quality print media to adapt and survive for what could be a considerable while yet.

Quality journalism as defined in chapter one, exhibiting comprehensibility, context, causality, comparativeness, comprehensiveness and accuracy, dates back to the mid-nineteenth century, if not earlier. The growth of advertising enabled London newspapers to refuse subsidies from political parties (Koss 1981) at a time when publishers realised that readers preferred balanced coverage rather than one-sided polemics (Chalaby 1998). The invention of news reporting, in which journalists proactively sought out stories rather than merely acting as stenographers, also developed in the mid-1800s, initially in the United States (Wiener 2011). These Victorian traditions have shaped the twenty-first-century press, including a preference for sourcing stories from those in power (Curran 1978).

The moment the British quality press entered the modern age can be timed precisely to January 26, 1986—but that date also heralded a crisis soon to unfold in the print press that many commentators believe may ultimately be terminal. It was then that Rupert Murdoch, already the biggest media owner in the UK, secretly moved the printing of his four national newspapers, *The Times*, *The Sunday Times*, the *Sun* and *News of the World*, to a new editorial headquarters at Wapping. The copy for the newspapers was input by journalists, thus removing an expensive and labour-intensive production process that dated back to Caxton. A bitter battle was fought with the print unions, who picketed the new offices for more than a year before finally being forced to accept that their era was over.

Lowering costs and removing restrictive practices did, however, lead to a temporary flowering of quality journalism. Pagination of papers such as *The Sunday Times* went up to the point where a single edition would contain more words than a fairly weighty novel, and a number of new newspapers were born, freed from the traditional overheads that had beset Fleet Street for decades. *The Times* and the *Guardian* were able to produce additional supplements supported by columns of classified advertising, folded inside the main edition, unhindered by industrial disputes that often accompanied increases in pagination.

At the same time the arrival of a bonanza of new titles was predicted since start-up costs were instantly lowered. One that made its way into print was *Today*, a tabloid newspaper modelled on *USA Today*, America's only national newspaper, which took advantage of the new technology to print in colour and present information in new ways, such as the use of information graphics. But *Today*'s publisher, Eddy Shah, failed to sustain the vision of quality journalism that he proclaimed at the outset, and his paper ended up as indistinguishable from others in the middle market (MacArthur 1988). The first high-tech, non-union paper was destined to fail, finally closing in November 1995. Other new enterprises of the period flopped, too. The *Sunday Correspondent*, a new Sunday newspaper pitched at the quality market, folded a little more than a year after its launch on September 17, 1989, and the *News on Sunday*, committed to presenting news from a left-of-centre viewpoint, also succumbed, surviving only seven months after launching in April 1987.

The single start-up survivor has been *The Independent* (along with its sister paper the *Independent on Sunday*). The daily title was launched on October 7, 1986, and the *Independent on Sunday* in 1990. Since then both papers have established themselves as a world brand signifying high-quality journalism, although their commercial existence continues to be precarious—in February 2013 the Sunday paper ceased to have an independent existence after the owners merged it into a seven-day operation. So, far from being groundbreaking, history now shows that Wapping was more a last gasp than a revolution. All the while there had been another infinitely more potent development incubating in the background, as nascent broadband networks started to improve and become more widely available in the mid-1990s. At the same time, newspaper buying habits were fast transmogrifying—victim of increasingly busy lives, more mobile work patterns and greater choice of media outlets. Rupert Murdoch brought U.S. cable-style rolling news to Britain on February 5, 1989, under his Sky News banner, offering headlines in quick bites round the clock. Sunday newspapers were particularly affected by changed social trends as they had to compete no longer just with church attendance, but with the weekly supermarket shop now available for longer, the gym, Premier League football, longer licensing hours and a host of other diversions as Britain headed into the 24-hour society.

Today the quality daily national newspaper press in Britain can be reckoned to comprise the following:

i. The *Daily Telegraph*, with a circulation of 587,040 copies a day in January 2012, compared with more than a million in the late 1940s, is the only remaining broadsheet quality paper (excluding the specialist *Financial Times*). Privately owned by the property developers the Barclay twins, it is both the largest selling and the only quality paper to make money. Regarded as the Conservative Party House journal, its readers are the traditional middle classes of Britain—in some ways similar to the mid-market *Daily Mail*, leading to the nickname the *Daily Mailygraph*. However, its readers see themselves as socially above the *Mail*'s, and the paper reflects this with its emphasis on a *Country Life* and 'Urban Sloane' agenda. Paradoxically, given its traditional social outlook, the paper was a pioneer in moving into multiplatform journalism and was the first of the nationals to reinvent its newsroom to meet the demands of the new convergent digital world. Its web site, which is one of the world's most successful newspaper sites, with 2,353,047 unique daily users in June 2012, took a first step towards a paywall in November that year.

ii. The *Guardian* is the leading quality newspaper of liberal Britain. It has a unique commercial structure with no proprietor, shareholders or distribution of profits, instead answering to the Scott Trust, which defines its role as "to secure the financial and editorial independence of the *Guardian* in perpetuity as a quality national newspaper without party affiliation; remaining faithful to its liberal tradition; as a profit-seeking enterprise managed in an efficient and cost-effective manner" (Guardian Media Group 2010). In this it is supported by a number of outside investments, which provide a cross-subsidy. The absence of the need to distribute profits has allowed it to invest heavily in its web site, which is one of the most viewed in the world with 3,374,984 unique daily users in June 2012. However, print sales have continued to decline heavily—the circulation in January 2012 was 215,988 compared with 494,000 in January 1987. There have been substantial redundancies among both editorial and commercial staff, and in February 2010, the Guardian Media Group was forced to sell its sister paper the *Manchester Evening News* (itself a standard-bearer for quality in the regional press), cutting umbilical ties with the city where it was founded. The editor Alan Rusbridger has hinted the future of the print edition may be finite. The strategy now is to extend the "brand" (see later section on business models) and the newspaper's influence worldwide, notably in the United States. That influence is described by a former deputy editor Peter Cole:

> It is scorned by its opponents, loved by its supporters. Millions who have never read it believe they know what it represents—and they are often wrong. It hangs its conscience on its sleeve. Its critics accuse it of an unworldly disconnection with the concerns of 'ordinary people', but then Guardian readers do not see themselves as ordinary people. (Cole and Harcup 2010, 76)

iii. **The *Times*** Once known as 'The Thunderer', it is Britain's most famous newspaper. Historically it has been a paper of record, gazetting matters of importance to the establishment—law reports, church appointments, the affairs of court and so on. It was famous for its letters page, known as the top people's 'tribal noticeboard'. Since it was bought by Rupert Murdoch in 1981, it has developed a more popular outlook, although still retaining some of its original features such as the 'Court Circular' and law reports. The circulation in January 2012 was 397,549, down from 821,000 in 1997.

iv. **The *Independent*** is the smallest of the quality newspapers (with a circulation of just 105,160 in January 2012, roughly a quarter of its peak of around 400,000 after its launch in 1986), but the newspaper still has an influence vastly out of proportion to its size. Founded in 1986 by three journalists from the *Daily Telegraph* who sought to change the model of traditional proprietorship after Wapping, it has moved far from its original pitch both commercially and editorially. Although its initial success derived from an appeal to the 'yuppies' of the Thatcher era (with the famous slogan 'It is, Are You?'), it has moved leftwards and through many metamorphoses of ownership, including a long period owned by the Irish entrepreneur Tony O' Reilly's Independent Newspapers. Unable to sustain heavy losses, O'Reilly sold it to a former Russian spy Alexander Lebedev in March 2010 for £1. The new owners cut costs still further by renting space in the offices of the *Daily Mail* and sharing back office services. Recently further economies required some staff to work from home to save costs. The paper was late into seeing the potential of the internet and has the least-developed web site, with 14.5 million unique monthly users in March 2012 (Hall 2012).

v. **The *Financial Times*,** known as the 'Pink 'Un', is a different product altogether—less newspaper than the brand behind one of the world's leading news and business organisations. It is unique among British quality newspapers in that it is owned by a public company, Pearson PLC. Although its circulation in January 2012 was 316,493, some two thirds live overseas. The FT is unusual in having a thriving web site with 4.5 million registered users and over 285,000 digital subscribers.

Beyond the nationals, in 2012 there were 79 daily regional titles and 1,083 weeklies (Newspaper Society 2012; the distinction between morning and evening titles has disappeared as most evening titles have switched to overnight printing to save costs). There are approximately 1,600 associated web sites. More people read the regional press than the national press (71% and 57% of adults, respectively; Leveson 2012a, 148), and the regional press is more trusted and seen as more influential by media managers (Franklin 2009, 4). The local and regional press could be considered as the plankton of news ecology, originating news stories that are reproduced and developed further up the food chain, by local radio, regional TV and national newspapers (Ofcom 2009, 76). Most local and regional newspapers are owned by only four large groups—Johnston Press, Trinity Mirror, Newsquest and Local World. Many regional publishers maintained profit margins in excess of 30% before the economic downturn, from high volumes of advertising and from relentlessly cutting costs, including editorial staffing (Gulyas 2012, 29; Oakley 2012b).

CIRCULATION AND REVENUES FACE IRREVERSIBLE DECLINE

Although all the UK quality titles are intrinsically different in ownership, readership and business models, there are two factors common to all: they are all experiencing irreversible decline in circulations and print revenue, forcing them to cut costs. At the same time, digital revenue growth has failed to offset print decline. By the second decade of the twenty-first century, a new generation of sophisticated portable devices, such as tablet computers and phones connected to 3G and 4G networks, had accelerated the decline still further, underlining the weakness of newsprint as a delivery platform for news. At the same time, most regional evening newspapers no longer print on the day of publication, switching to centralised overnight printing to cut costs, while harming their ability to report breaking news (Oakley 2012b, 63).

In the new multiplatform world, two key sources of revenue for quality newspapers—copy sales revenue (retail sales and subscriptions) and display and classified advertising—are both exposed to ever greater pressures. Circulation, as indicated previously, is in long-term decline and has accelerated since 2005, and cover price rises have been held back for fear of further circulation losses. Display advertising has been hit by economic recession and by new sophistication in advertising on the internet using new search and targeting techniques. Classified advertising has plummeted as it has moved to dedicated and more searchable web sites. Salient factors affecting press copy volume sales between 2005 and 2010 include the fact that PC-based internet-broadband adoption leapt from 34% to 68% of UK households, a deep recession in 2009 from which the consumer has yet to recover, and a lack of engagement with print news media by young adults, of which more later (Enders Analysis 2011). The circulation decline between 2005 and 2010 has been a consistent feature of all press categories, but larger at the quality nationals. Quality circulations are down by 24% compared with 17% for popular papers, which means that the qualities have lost national market share. By 2015, 75% of all adults are expected to have purchased a smartphone (iPhone or Android), and tablets will continue to enable mobile news activities on the internet. At the same time, it is reckoned that competition between newspaper titles will become more aggressive. However, some commentators believe that the newspaper industry's problems pre-date the internet and are caused by excessive profit-taking, editorial cuts, lack of investment and conservative attitudes among journalists and managers, leading to missed opportunities when the internet took off (Chisholm 2012, 11–12; Schlosberg 2012). More forward-thinking publishers in Finland and Norway, for example, transferred their advertising to their web sites before rival online-only advertising companies could be established (see also Oakley 2012b, 62–63, for missed online advertising opportunities in the UK regional press).

The circulations, profits and numbers of regional and local newspapers have declined even more steeply—yet they are still healthy; a 32% fall in the last five years (Chisholm 2012, 9) merely continues what began in the 1950s. Multiple local editions have been scrapped for many titles, further reducing sales. Revenues have also fallen more steeply than for the nationals, from £3,133m in 2004 to £1,599m in 2010 (Leveson 2012a, 150). More than 240 titles have closed in the last seven years, leaving towns such as Wellingborough and Port Talbot without a newspaper of their own (Oakley 2012a). However, the headline closure figures are misleading—70 new titles have been launched in the last five years (Oakley 2012a), and most closures have been of free papers or titles whose owners had more successful papers in the same local market (Ofcom 2009, 80). And, as the Leveson report notes, "despite this bleak picture, regional news provision remains essentially profitable" (2012a, 150).

In terms of profitability, the situation is worse for the quality nationals. By the end of the first decade of the twenty-first century, the quality press was losing money in large quantities, too. *The Times* and *Sunday Times* lost £45.1m pre-tax in 2010, before apparently improving to an £11.6m deficit in the year to 30 June 2011—although the true trading performance is more likely worse (Sabbagh 2012). Some industry estimates suggest it is possible that 2011 pre-tax losses were around £60m. For a rough comparison, the *Guardian* and *Observer* lost £43.8m in the year to 30 March 2011. The *Independent* titles also have been losing money, reckoned to be at least £10m a year. Of the general broadsheets in Britain, it is only the market-leading *Daily Telegraph* and its smaller Sunday sister that have made a significant profit: £47.9m in 2011. The *Financial Times*, as a specialist publication, is

not directly comparable. For the year 2011, profits at the newspaper were
£76m, helped by digital subscriptions, which were more than half the total
paid circulation (Sabbagh 2012).

ONLINE PUBLISHING IMPOSES NEW DEMANDS

The demands of online publishing have forced an entire re-evaluation of the
conventional news cycle, in which all activity was geared towards having a
newspaper on sale at breakfast time each morning. In the new web world,
deadlines have become redundant as news content is poured into the various platforms as soon as it arrives. "Web publication is changing the basic
forms of news writing in terms of how it is read, how it looks and how it
works" (Hall 2008, 196). Stories have become shorter, requiring a different
style of writing to accommodate the need for adding further content as a
story develops. Even headlines have had to change to fit in with the requirements of 'search engine optimisation', rendering them more prosaic in many
instances. Greenslade (2008) argues that this has not necessarily led to a
reduction in quality, since stories of almost infinite length can be accom-
modated, as the physical constraints of newsprint have disappeared, and
the web permits not only a fuller version of a story to be published but also
accompanied by context and links to other related material—the so-called
'long tail' (Anderson 2007).

One of the biggest impacts of all these changes has been in the area of
staffing, with hundreds of journalists losing their jobs over the past three
decades. Davies found that 20 years after Wapping, staff levels of national
newspapers were slightly lower, but the amount of space journalists were
filling in their papers had trebled:

> To put it another way, during those 20 years, the average time allowed
> for national newspaper journalists to find and check their stories had
> been cut to a third of its former level . . . That is a disaster. It shoves a
> blade right into the heart of the practice of journalism. If truth is the
> object and checking is the function then the primary working asset of
> all journalists, always and everywhere, is time. Take away time and you
> take away truth. (Davies 2008, 63)

Similar evidence of the impact of reduced reporting staffs was found
in the regional press (Franklin 1986; Fenton, Mtykova, Schlosberg, and
Des Freedman 2010, 14; Oakley 2012b, 63), although there is conflicting evidence from readers—Fenton et al. found that the public shared the
concerns of journalists and academics over a decline in the quality of local
news, while an Ofcom survey found a public perception of improved local
newspaper journalism (Ofcom 2009, 74). The impact of job losses on

specialisms has been particularly hard. No UK popular newspaper now has a staffed foreign bureau (in contrast to, say, the *Daily Express* of the 1950s—famous for its foreign bureaux in every continent of the world). Staff photographers are an almost extinct breed. *The Independent*, once world famous for the quality of its photography, no longer employs a single photographer.

THE DUMBING DOWN DEBATE

The combined pressure of reduced staffing, increased workloads and the commercial pressures of a more competitive market have led to what many commentators have labelled 'dumbing down'—a general driving down of standards across the board.

The former *Times* editor Harold Evans told the Leveson inquiry in 2012 that he did not agree with an assertion made by the *Daily Mail* editor Paul Dacre to the same inquiry that the standards of the British press had improved over the past 20 years:

> We've got a situation in which newspapers are employing private detectives! We used to employ reporters, trained reporters whose job it was to find the facts. and the idea that the press has now come to the fringes of the criminal underworld, I'm totally appalled by what I see. So I have to part company from Mr Dacre in that regard, while paying tribute to the general standards, the quality of papers in Britain, the *Guardian*, the *Telegraph* and *The Times* remain pretty good. (Leveson 2012b)

However, not all support the dumbing down thesis. Temple (2006) argues that

> Concerns that dumbing down is responsible for the rise in public apathy about politics ignore the need for public spheres that will engage the politically illiterate or disenchanted in a way that will encourage them to participate in public debate . . . A less elite-driven news agenda—one driven by the interests of the audience rather than by a small core of political journalists—offers the opportunity for engagement with political issues by those (the vast majority) uninterested in the minutiae of policy or the internal differences of the Conservative Party . . . The task of providing accessible, entertaining yet authoritative 'ground-level' introduction to political and social issues is essential if the mass of citizens are to remain connected in any meaningful way to the public sphere. (258)

Others have argued that while there is clearly a change of tone in the contents of our so-called quality newspaper, it does not reflect a fall in quality, just that there is something different going on. As *Guardian* editor Alan Rusbridger (1999) puts it,

[dumbing down] is a plausible way of describing the disenchantment of the people who either were, or missed out on being the 'old elite', with this new difficult world in which high culture and so-called low culture meet, in which classes blur and different voices are heard. Dumbing down is a dumb word to describe something far more complex at work in society today and every alarm bell ought to ring every time you hear it.

However, there is more than social change at work here. Davies (2008) labels the development 'churnalism', a type of journalism in which reporters rewrite press releases and agency copy without checking or follow-up in order to meet pressures of time and cost imposed by managements. Supporting his case, researchers at Cardiff University found that 80% of stories in the quality press in Britain were not original and that only 12% were based on original material generated by journalists, with obvious implications for quality and accuracy (Davies 2008, 94–96). Similar over-use of public relations material has been found in local and regional newspapers (Fenton et al. 2010, 14). The point was emphasised by the documentary *Starsuckers*, in which fake stories were generated. Several British newspapers published the fake stories without checking, and they went on to be reported as fact by numerous publications around the world (Atkins 2007).

Similar trends can be found at the local and regional level, alongside a democratic deficit as the routine reporting of courts, councils and other local decision-making bodies has been reduced. This is happening at a time when journalistic scrutiny is needed more than ever, as new decision-making powers are devolved to the local level (Hunt 2010; Ofcom 2009, 16; House of Commons Culture, Media and Sport Committee 2010, 25). Yet Ofcom found "little evidence of deteriorating quality of news coverage" in the provincial press. They commissioned a 2009 content analysis of 13 local and regional titles (Oliver & Ohlbaum Advisory 2009a), which found wide variation in editorial content in the previous five years, with news content increasing in three papers and reducing in two; investigative journalism also increased in three titles and decreased in two. Overall, across all titles surveyed, editorial content changed little. The seeming contradiction was explained by editors and publishers who told Ofcom that newspaper content was changing, rather than deteriorating, by responding to more public interest in lifestyle and leisure topics and by complementing breaking news on other platforms through increased analysis and comment (Ofcom 2009, 81). Readers may not want detailed coverage of local courts and councils—but as citizens, perhaps they need it.

RISE OF THE CELEBRITY CULTURE

A by-product of the 'churnalism' industry has been a growing infatuation with celebrity, often feeding off television soap operas and reality shows. Celebrity journalism, with its reliance on the PR industry, is cheaper to produce and sometimes benefits other shared business interests. For example, Richard Desmond's *Daily Star* was filled with the activities of the cast of *Celebrity Big Brother* while it was showing on Channel 5, also owned by Desmond. Such is the draw of celebrity journalism that the travel sections of some papers, such as the *Mail on Sunday*, insist that the lead travel article should be written by a recognisable celebrity, no matter the quality of their copy or whether they have anything interesting to say. While celebrity culture is a reflection of the wider obsession of society as a whole, it has been absorbed on an industrial scale by the 'red-top' press, with columns such as the *Sun*'s Bizarre and the *Mirror*'s 3am Girls, with their ancillary industries of intrusive paparazzi and lucrative tip-offs. It was the pressures of this culture that led to the misdeeds revealed by the Leveson inquiry as journalists competed, not only among themselves but with celebrity web sites, to uncover the latest gossip scandal.

The celebrity obsession extends wider than the tabloids or the middle-market papers. The Duchess of Cambridge, along with the abduction victim Madeleine McCann, was the most frequently depicted woman on a British newspaper front page over a period of four weeks, including qualities (Women in Journalism 2012). One of the front pages on which the duchess most regularly appears (as well as her sister Pippa) is that of the 'quality' *Daily Telegraph*. The *Independent* has not been slow to embrace the cult of celebrity, inviting such diverse figures as the rock star Bono and the comedian David Walliams to guest-edit editions of the paper. However, the celebrity obsession has not been mostly harmless, as some have claimed. In 2012, it emerged that the disc-jockey Jimmy Savile had been an abusive paedophile for most of his career at the BBC and that the Corporation's flagship serial news programme, *Newsnight*, had scrapped an investigation into his behaviour, while a tribute went ahead on another BBC channel. It is also true that no newspaper investigative team exposed Savile's actions, either—although several newspapers reported prominently that the BBC had dropped its own *Newsnight* investigation. As the columnist Deborah Orr wrote in the *Guardian*, "The cult of celebrity abetted Savile in both his exploitation and his ability to get away with it" (Orr, 2012).

LEVESON AND THE CRISIS IN ETHICS

Although the Leveson Inquiry into the ethics of the British press did not come about because of a failure of quality journalism in the sense that it is defined in this book, the inquiry was set up, in essence, to address a failure of quality in the way ethics are applied to newsgathering. Lord Justice Leveson, a senior High Court judge, was appointed by the Prime Minister David Cameron in July 2011 after it had been revealed that journalists from Rupert Murdoch's Sunday newspaper, the *News of the World*, had hacked into the mobile phone of a murdered teenager, Milly Dowler. It was the biggest examination of the operations of the British press since the Calcutt inquiry of 1990, when journalists were told by the then culture secretary David Mellor that "they were drinking in the last chance saloon" (Greenslade 2004, 539). A parade of witnesses revealed that abuse by journalists was widespread—not just phone-hacking, but intrusion, doorstepping, 'blagging', distortion of fact and other nefarious practices. Most of it involved the red-top and middle market press, but the traditional quality titles did not escape unscathed. In contrast, Leveson praised the working practices, culture and ethics of the local press (Leveson 2012a, executive summary), while police evidence illustrated how the greater accountability of the local press can encourage higher quality journalism. Anne Campbell, head of corporate communications at Suffolk Constabulary, told the inquiry that local journalists tended to provide a balanced and "rounded view", whereas the national media were "not so worried about putting our side of the story; in other words, that balanced view" (Leveson 2012a, 758).

INTERNET ADVERTISING DIVERTS THE 'RIVER OF GOLD'

By the end of the 1990s, as newspapers struggled against the migration to the web of what was once known as the 'river of gold' of traditional classified advertising, it was clear that they were never going to recover their supremacy in the medium. The regional press, with its greater reliance on classified advertising, was hit even harder than the nationals (Leveson 2012a, 149). No longer would advertising and news, like the proverbial horse and carriage, be inseparable as they had been in the days when *The Times* thought advertising so important that it covered its front page with classifieds, which it deemed more important than news, a practice that came to an end only as recently as 1966. Now most classified ads in the main newspaper are restricted to the Court page or dating section. As Murdoch stated, "This is a generational thing . . . I don't know anyone under 30 who has ever looked at a classified advertisement in a newspaper" (Reeves 2005). As the *Economist* pointed out,

A newspaper is a package of content—politics, sport, share prices, weather and so forth—which exists to attract eyeballs to advertisements. Unfortunately for newspapers, the internet is better at delivering some of that than paper is. It is easier to search through job and property listings on the web, so classified advertising and its associated revenue is migrating onto the internet—news and share prices can be more easily updated, weather can be more geographically specific—so readers are migrating, too. The package is thus being picked apart. (*Economist* 2009)

Many blamed recessionary times following the collapse of Lehman Brothers in 2007. But the extent of the problem was more serious. Three years into the financial crisis, internet and TV revenues had begun to recover, but the line on the revenues for most quality newspapers in 2010 were either static or down, with the *Guardian* dropping by 5% compared with five years earlier and even News International, including revenues from the *Sun*, Britain's best-selling newspaper, down by 2% (Enders Analysis 2011). Gulyas (2012, 28) identifies another structural change besides the internet—a shift in marketing practices away from advertising and towards market research, PR, events and sales promotions. While these changes have affected most newspaper markets in western Europe and North America, UK advertising, circulation and revenues have fallen significantly faster than the European average (Chisholm 2012, 9–10). Chisholm believes this is largely due to the insularity and conservatism of UK publishers and journalists.

MONETISING THE MEDIA IN A DIGITAL WORLD

After a halting start, many print organisations have fought back with high-quality online operations of their own. On the face of it, the figures look impressive. Some 39m unique UK users visited news and information web sites in August 2011. However, they spent only an average of 2 mins 20 seconds a day (compared with the estimated average time of up to 40 minutes spent on reading a national quality paper). A pioneer in quality content in this area has been the *Guardian/Observer,* which, in July 2012, was claimed to be the world's third most popular newspaper web site (after *Mail Online* and the *New York Times;* Enders Analysis 2011). Impressive though this might sound, digital news supply is a further cost burden to traditional print-based media. Enders Analysis points out that for a quality title, a paywall subscriber is worth, at best, a quarter to a third of a print buyer. Costs of digital news supply are on top of the costs of print, leading to dual costs in any print to digital transition.

So, with a perfect storm of recession, the flight of advertising, declining circulations and the lack of a viable model to monetise the product, media organisations have flirted with a number of different strategies.

i. Paywalls. The most widely deployed—and controversial—model has been to erect a 'paywall' or subscription, whereby users are charged for accessing online content. Three British daily quality newspapers—*The Times* and the *Financial Times* and the *Telegraph* titles—now charge for accessing content online, although the *Telegraph*'s model provides a generous 20 free views, in a similar model to the *New York Times.* However, there is no evidence that this provides an enduring means of monetising quality news for the future, and regional newspaper publishers such as Johnston Press have now abandoned their unsuccessful attempts (Gulyas 2012, 31). Online readerships, if they are not accompanied by a print subscription, can 'cannibalise' the print edition, eroding circulation and reducing the rates for advertising, which are much lower online. Nor is there evidence that paywall revenues will ever make up for the continuing collapse in print advertising. Ingram (2011) neatly encapsulates the problem, declaring that paywalls are "by definition a stopgap strategy . . . newspapers that rely on a paywall to save their bacon are likely doomed". He goes on:

> While it's true that publications like the Wall Street Journal, the Financial Times and the Economist have managed it, this isn't a strategy that every newspaper is going to be able to duplicate, since these outlets have a very targeted readership (and therefore higher value advertising). Even the New York Times arguably falls into a separate category, since it is a leading brand, not just for national news but for international news. It is worth noting that even the New York Times's paywall which has been hailed a success for signing up about 300,000 paying customers . . . has not improved the fortunes of the newspaper in a significant way.

In a British context, the same applies to the *Times*'s paywall, which offers far less access than the relatively relaxed model adopted by the *Daily Telegraph* in Britain and the *New York Times* in the United States. Another possibility is micro-payments for time-sensitive news such as live sports reports (Ofcom 2009, 126).

Ingram asserts,

> An API-based platform strategy is a gamble, just as erecting a paywall is. But one of these is a gamble aimed at profiting from the open exchange of information and other aspects of an online media world, while the other is an attempt to create the artificial information scarcity that newspapers used to enjoy.

Some of the problems—and solutions—are matters of culture and perception. The UK is unusual in its low level of newspaper subscriptions, which may have discouraged the take-up of online subscriptions. A precedent has now been set for giving away high-quality online news, with the added difficulty of the BBC 'skewing' the UK online news market with its publicly funded free content. Yet consumers seem to accept the principle of subscriptions for tablets and e-readers, and payment for apps.

ii. Free newspapers. In some niche markets, print has experienced a limited revival through the distribution of free copies. The free daily newspaper *Metro*, with 1.38m copies handed out in London and 10 other regional centres, made more than £20m profit in 2011. It describes its formula as "facts, not spin, sound-bitey expresso-shot rather than long-form content, use of images, use of white space and with frictionless access" (Greenslade 2012b). Another success has been the free London *Evening Standard*. When the ailing paper went free in October 2009, it was failing to sell at a cover price of 50p and on the point of closure. In 2012, it reported a profit of £1m. The *Manchester Evening News* began free distribution in the city centre in 2006, in tandem with paid-for sales in the suburbs, and believes this has protected sales and advertising revenue (Wood 2012, 76). However, free newspapers need a critical mass of relatively affluent readers in compact urban centres—preferably commuters at railway stations. The model does not easily translate. An interesting 'halfway house' has been the *i* newspaper, launched in October 2010, consisting of pared down copy derived from its sister paper *The Independent*, presented in accessible 'bites' and selling at the reduced price of 20p.

iii. The web-only newspaper. In the United States, the online and left-leaning *Huffington Post*, a news web site, aggregator and blog, has achieved success, winning a Pulitzer Prize and achieving sufficient worth that it was bought out in 2011 by AOL. However, it has been criticised for a paucity of quality original content. Another online newspaper to achieve some reputational success in the United States is *The Daily Beast*, founded by the British journalist Tina Brown in 2008, although it is not known whether it makes money. Another online-only paper called *The Daily* was launched by Rupert Murdoch in New York in February 2011, differing from his other online platforms in that it took the form of an app for a tablet computer. But it was a flop, publishing its last edition in December 2012, having run up losses of $60m (Sweney 2012). Although it was the world's first iPad-only newspaper, it was never likely to work in a world where consumers expected to get their news on the internet for free. No such enterprises have gained traction in the UK. More successful, in terms of rivalling quality news output by the British print press, have been political blogs, such as Guido Fawkes and Conservative Home. The blogger Paul Staines, behind the 'Guido Fawkes' site, has broken a number of 'scoops', such as his 2009 story on the covert smear campaign against senior Conservative politicians by Gordon Brown's Director of Communications, Damian McBride, which led to McBride's resignation. The site currently has more people access it than read the traditional political weekly, the *New Statesman*.

iv. Subsidies, levies and tax breaks. Although there are periodic calls for some kind of state funding to support the survival of quality newspaper journalism, particularly in the regional press, such calls seem destined to fail given that Parliament already protects a hard core of quality journalism via the BBC licence fee. An alternative model is a suggested £2 levy on the monthly bills of UK broadband providers (Leigh 2012). The money would then be distributed to news providers in proportion to their online readerships. However, there are many pitfalls, such as persuading ISPs to become, effectively, tax collectors. And how would news organisations be made accountable for what they do with the money? Conversely, Nel and others have suggested targeted tax breaks, aimed at encouraging editorial training (Ofcom 2009, 132), although this has received little support.

v. Philanthropic, externally funded journalism. As shrinking news budgets have curtailed the ability of newspapers to fund expensive investigations, they have turned to other sources. One such has been the not-for-profit Bureau of Investigative Journalism, established at the City University in London and funded by such bodies as Save the Children and the philanthropic Potter Foundation. However, its reputation was seriously tarnished when it was associated with a story on BBC's *Newsnight* on 2 November 2012 that wrongly implied the former Conservative Party chairman Lord McAlpine was a paedophile. The report led to the resignation of the BBC chairman George Entwistle and a crisis of confidence at the BBC.

vi. Crowdfunded journalism. Although the idea of public donations funding quality journalism may seem far-fetched, a digital project in San Francisco called 'Matter' raised $128,000 from 2,400 members of the public in 2012 for a fund to publish high-quality, in-depth journalism about science and technology (Greenslade 2012a), although there have not been any similar projects in the UK.

vii. NGOs fill a gap. With funding limited for big investigations, reputable pressure groups and charities have filled a gap with investigations of their own. Whether it is the Children's Society providing data on young runaways or Greenpeace highlighting environmental concerns, properly researched data has added to the armoury of quality newspapers. For instance, in November 2012, the *Guardian* led the newspaper on a Greenpeace investigation in which a Conservative Party candidate had been secretly filmed supporting an anti-wind turbine rival in a parliamentary by-election (Greenpeace 2012).

viii. Collaboration and consolidation. There is particular scope for collaboration among publishers, for example, in sharing 'back-office' functions, but more importantly in offering joined-up advertising across print and online to cover entire regions or even nations (Chisholm 2012; Oliver & Ohlbaum Advisory 2009b). This has traditionally been done through consolidation among newspaper publishers, sometimes leading to the improvement of under-resourced titles, and sometimes leading to decline as decisions are made many miles from the communities served by the papers. In 2012 the 92 newspapers and 63 associated web sites of Northcliffe Media and Iliffe News and Media were sold to a new company, Local World, headed by former Mirror Group boss David Montgomery. Northcliffe, Iliffe and a third regional publisher, Trinity Mirror, own 80% of the new company, which promises to apply new methods to the challenging local market (Local World 2012).

ix. Diversification. Oakley urges newspaper publishers to use their trusted brands to diversify into other businesses not subject to the same cycles of advertising boom and bust (Oakley 2012b). Examples include non-news products such as e-books and events that draw readers to "real-world" get-togethers. Ingram (2011) adds that another promising strategy is to

> look at your newspaper not as a thing you need to charge people for, but as a platform for data and information that you can generate value from in other ways—including by licensing it to developers and other parties via an open application programming interface [app or API].

Both these approaches seem to be favoured by the *Guardian* in Britain, which has had some success in extending its brand through an ambitious events programme, including its Masterclasses, in a range of areas from fiction-writing weekends to cookery classes. Similarly, regional publisher the KM Group gathers information from searches conducted on its *What's On* web site, for targeted advertising. The KM Group has also expanded into local radio (Carter 2012, 69–70), although its attempted purchase of newspapers from a rival was thwarted in 2011 after it was referred to the Competition Commission. There is political support for a relaxation of rules on consolidation and cross-media ownership; supporters say this will allow cross-platform provision of quality journalism, while opponents believe that profit-driven public companies will simply asset-strip anything they touch (Ofcom 2009, 126; House of Commons Culture, Media and Sport Committee 2010, 21). Bradshaw believes that diversification is the hallmark of successful online business:

> People never bought news, they bought a newspaper which was a package which had certain functions: it was portable, it was high resolution, it was serendipitous. Online they are not selling any kind of package that I can see and if you look again at successful business models online, it is about selling packages. (House of Commons Culture, Media and Sport Committee, 2010, 65)

Other strategies are appropriate only to the regional and local press, highlighting the fact that these titles are qualitatively different from national newspapers, with distinctive functions, operating in distinctive markets, and should not be seen merely as miniature versions of national newspapers:

x. Hyper-local web sites and publications. These platforms serve small towns and villages, or discrete districts of larger towns and cities. They follow the traditional advertising-led business model on the basis that 'narrowcast' print advertising is cheaper and more effective than 'broadcast' online advertising. Traditional local newspaper publishers such as Tindle continue to launch new weekly newspapers on this model, such as the *Pembroke and Pembroke Dock Observer* in south Wales, which offer quality journalism alongside the promotion of local identity (Adamson 2012). Sir Ray Tindle believes that "the future for local papers is rosy—and the more local the paper the better that future will be" (Tindle 2012, 2). Hyper-local web sites, some run by trained journalists, others by business people or members of the public, have had mixed fortunes. *Filton Voice* in Bristol is profitable and provides a living for its journalist founder Richard Coulter (personal communication 17 December 2012), while the *Saddleworth News* site straddling the Lancashire-Yorkshire border was a journalistic success but a commercial failure (Jones 2012). Regional commercial publishers such as the Guardian Media Group and Northcliffe have also tried their hands at hyperlocal sites, with limited success; the *Guardian* abandoned its sites in 2011.

   xi. A return to local ownership. Many commentators believe that most of the problems of the regional press have been caused by excessive profit-taking from publicly quoted companies whose shareholders demand short-term gains. Circulation figures bear this out—seven of the ten worst performing weekly papers between 2007 and 2010 were owned by public companies, while seven of the ten *best* performing papers were independently owned (Hobbs 2011). Indeed, Fowler has called for large regional publishers to be allowed an 'orderly default' on their huge debts in return for selling their titles to local owners who understand their markets, are committed to the social benefits of a thriving local press (Fowler 2012, 266) and are able to make long-term investments in innovation (Chisholm 2012, 15; Oakley 2012, 64).

HARNESSING NEW TECHNOLOGIES—DO THEY ADD TO QUALITY?

Many have suggested that instead of eroding or dumbing down quality, new ways of 'telling stories', especially through blogging and social media, can enhance and invigorate quality in the newsgathering process. Blogging by journalists in the print and traditional broadcast media has been a powerful new tool for those who might have found their voices limited by constraints of space or controls by editors. One of the biggest stories of the world banking crisis that developed after the collapse of Lehman Brothers in 2007 was broken by a print journalist who had joined the BBC as a business editor. Robert Peston chose to reveal his knowledge that the British bank, Northern Rock, was about to collapse, not through traditional media, but through his daily blog on the BBC's web site. It was effective since it was filed early in the morning as the markets were opening—too late for the newspapers and with too informal a source to make the main broadcast news bulletins. The consequences were far-reaching as customers queued around the block to withdraw their money as a result of the first British bank collapse for 150 years, and the government was forced to set up a compensation scheme. For the most part, journalists have shifted traditional working methods from print to online, but new techniques could potentially improve the democratic function of journalism, such as the live blog. This is used by the *Manchester Evening News* and other local papers when reporting important local government meetings, attracting sizeable audiences (Wood 2012, 75).

Amid the uncertainty, the Telegraph Media Group, owned by the Barclay brothers—Scottish entrepreneurs most of whose outside interests are in property—stands out as the last quality, non-specialist, print news organisation in the UK still confidently making a profit without cross-subsidy. *Daily Telegraph* executive editor Mark Skipworth refutes notions that somehow the transition from print to digital has led to a diminution in quality and that the commitment to quality specialist journalism was somehow less. "The way we achieve quality is through flexibility," says Skipworth. He continues,

No longer are there fiefdoms. There are very small numbers of people who are section-specific, compared with those producing the whole of the product. The 'hub' structure is the key to this flexibility. All this works well because the structure is so informal.

Some have argued that the demands of the 24-hour news cycle have diluted quality. But the great resource we have are our offices around the world, so when we go to sleep, we hand over the editing function to our offices in Australia, which cover for us in our downtime.

The Telegraph has invested in the expensive end of journalism—now we have a very successful Investigations Unit. Contrary to some assertions, great news stories do sell newspapers. We are operating in the way that the best newspapers have operated for generations. We've made sensible economies aided by new technologies, such as outsourcing the production of some of our supplements. Before the desks do the final editing they are sent out of house for what you might call rough-subbing. This enables our desk chiefs to polish them up. It used to be in Australia, but it's now in Chiswick. the sub-editors are nearly all former Fleet Street subs, vastly experienced, they're just working in a different way.

Skipworth believes that knowing the readers well has also contributed to the success of the *Telegraph*. This enables the paper to earn income from other sources such as escorted tours and events. The *Telegraph* recently took over sponsorship of the Hay Festival, Britain's biggest literary festival, previously sponsored by the *Guardian*. "The partnership had pushed ticket sales up 20%. This is the way forward for quality print journalism—building communities of like-minded people. How do we still make money? The answer is because we are managing the change process, from print to digital, better."

A DOOMED FUTURE FOR QUALITY PRINT?

Given the inexorable decline of both circulations and revenues, it is unsurprising there have been many doomsayers for quality print. Claire Enders of Enders Analysis predicted in 2009 that up to half of all regional and local papers would close by 2014 (House of Commons Culture, Media and Sport Committee 2010, 12), while Bell has spoken of 'carnage', with five or six British newspaper titles disappearing or consolidating with others. "Who is most at risk?" she speculated in 2008:

> When I met a senior news executive from another news organisation two years ago he foresaw something worse. He privately opined that in the long term the News International titles would survive because of the robust focus and funding of Rupert Murdoch's parent company, that the Associated titles—the *Mail* and *Mail on Sunday* were likewise on firm ground, and that the *Guardian* titles, because of the Scott Trust purpose and funding of the parent company would all live on, as would the *FT* because of its brand equity and focus. But the medium to long-term future for all other titles would be questionable. (Brook 2008)

Whether this prediction is right or not, the demographics are not on the side of newspaper publishers. Newspaper reading habits have come under huge pressure from the increasing choice UK adults have about how to spend their leisure time. According to a 2010 Ofcom survey, TV is the favourite medium of choice for adults with 45% of time spent, followed by the internet, with 22% of time spent. Print media consume just 7% of time. Young adults spent more time on the internet (30%) and less time on TV (32%) than adults as a whole and multitask as well. Only 4% of 16 to 24 year olds regularly consume print media. The survey showed that buyers and readers of print media are aging, while the digitally engaged lose interest in print media. Although it has been argued by some that as younger readers mature, they will migrate to newspapers from social media in what is known as the Radio 2 effect—whereby a dying older audience has been successfully replaced by a maturing younger one, acquiring the same tastes. However, the flaw with this theory is that radio listeners are constantly 'sampling' the product as their tastes change and mature, while those growing up in households where a daily newspaper is no longer bought cease to have exposure to print media and thus do not replicate the reading habits of the previous generation. A 2011 sample mini-survey of 150 UK undergraduate journalism students on well-respected courses found that only 10% admitted to reading a newspaper at all—although most of these were 'quality' papers such as the *Guardian* (Williams 2011).

However, this takes no account of technical advances, further pursuit of which may produce new solutions in a similar way to that in which tablet devices and apps have revolutionised the way we use computers. One exciting possibility are experiments with so-called 'interactive newsprint', involving the development of a new kind of paper that would give access to content through 'touch' in a similar fashion to tablet screens. One such research project is being developed by a team at School of Journalism in the University of Central Lancashire, along with the University of Surrey and other institutions. Beckett (2012) believes that rather than dying, quality journalism is simply changing:

> There has always been an oversupply of material that most people did not want. The on-demand world tells us precisely what people will really consume. The days of hundreds of hacks all attending the same press conferences and churning out very similar stories is over. Every platform has to add something: quality, quantity, speed, intelligence, amorality, campaigning, investigation, wit. This means that new jobs and organisations are emerging and journalism is increasingly being created beyond the media profession. The citizen does not want to become a journalist. They have other things to do. But they are contributing a vast amount of deliberate and "accidental" journalism. Much of this is done interactively with mainstream media but there's also a vast amount of reporting, comment and analysis happening to social networks and other non-professional platforms that counts as a kind of journalism. Much of it is trivial but some of it is also highly serious and expert.

Other commentators believe that the best traditions of newspaper journalism will live on in other media, as print titles attempt to move their 'brands' online. Meehan (2012, 103) believes that "the platform is not important—the content is", while Shirky (2009) asserts that "society doesn't need newspapers. What we need is journalism". At the regional level, too, "it is local journalism, rather than local newspapers, that needs saving" (House of Commons Culture, Media and Sport Committee 2010, 68).

Some are more optimistic, however. Barnett (2006, 9) says,

> Our research suggests that newspapers may have a longer shelf life than many believed possible and that the model of the cinema—adapting to the television age but not being overwhelmed by it—may be the more appropriate analogy . . . There will certainly be continued circulation decline. But the evidence suggests that just as cinema-going declined until the 1980s and then bottomed out and rose again, newspapers will find their plateau. In cultural and consumer terms, as long as the newspaper industry can continue to offer something of real journalistic

substance, out data suggests that it will continue to find a willing and substantial readership.

It's a view supported by the world's most powerful newspaper owner, Rupert Murdoch, who says,

Great journalism will always be needed but the product of their work may not always be on paper it may ultimately just be electronically. But for many, many, many years to come it will be disseminated on both. There will always be room for good journalism and good reporting. And a need for it to get the truth out. (Murdoch 2008)

Cole and Harcup (2010, 192) comment wryly on the doomsayers: "Philip Meyer in his book *The Vanishing Newspaper* predicts that the last newspaper will be dead in 2043. By that time he is likely not only to be dead, but also wrong."

REFERENCES

Adamson, Andrew. 2012. "Towards a Newspaper for Every Street." In *What Do We Mean By Local?*, edited by John Mair, Neil Fowler, and Ian Reeves, 79-82. Bury St Edmunds: Arima.

Anderson, Chris. 2007. *The Long Tail*. London: Random House.

Atkins, Chris, writer and director. 2007. *Starsuckers*. Metfilm. http://www.starsuckersmovie.com.

Barnett, Steven. 2006. "Reasons to Be Cheerful." *British Journalism Review* 17: 7–14.

Beckett, Charlie. 2012. "The Citizen Does Not Want to Become a Journalist." 24 September. http://blogs.lse.ac.uk/polis/2012/09/24/how-do-we-save-journalism.

Brook, Stephen. 2008. "'Media Facing Carnage,' Warns Emily Bell." *Guardian*, 15 October. http://www.guardian.co.uk/media/2008/oct/15/downturn-pressand publishing.

Carter, Ian. 2012. "Rethinking What Local Means to the Audience." In *What Do We Mean By Local?*, edited by John Mair, Neil Fowler, and Ian Reeves, 67–71. Bury St Edmunds: Arima.

Chalaby, Jean. 1998. *The Invention of Journalism*. Macmillan: Basingstoke.

Chisholm, Jim. 2012. "The Industry in Context—and How We Can Rediscover it." In *What Do We Mean By Local?*, edited by John Mair, Neil Fowler, and Ian Reeves, 8–17. Bury St Edmunds: Arima.

Cole, Peter, and Tony Harcup. 2010. *Newspaper Journalism*. London: Sage.

Curran, James. 1978. "The Press as an Agency of Social Control." In *Newspaper History from the Seventeenth Century to the Present Day*, edited by David George Boyce, James Curran, and Pauline Wingate, 51–75. London: Constable.

Davies, Nick. 2008. *Flat Earth News*. London: Chatto & Windus.

Economist. 2009. "The Rebirth of News." 16 May.

Enders Analysis. 2011. "Competitive Pressures on the Press." Presentation to Leveson Inquiry. http://www.levesoninquiry.org.uk/wp-content/uploads/2011/11/Presentation-by-Claire-Enders1.pdf.

Fenton, Natalie, Monika Mtykova, Justin Schlosberg, and Des Freedman. 2010. *Meeting the News Needs of Local Communities*. London: Media Trust.

Fowler, Neil. 2012. "The Future Needs Radical Action." In *What Do We Mean By Local?*, edited by John Mair, Neil Fowler, and Ian Reeves, 262–268. Bury St Edmunds: Arima.

Franklin, Bob. 1986. "Public Relations, the Local Press and the Coverage of Local Government." *Local Government Studies* 12: 25–33.

Franklin, Bob. 2009. "The Local and Regional Press; Organisational Change, Editorial Independence and Political Reporting." Report submitted to the Broadcasting Sub-Committee. National Assembly of Wales No. BSC(3)-03–09: Paper 2, Evidence gathering on the current state of the Welsh newspaper industry. Cardiff: National Assembly of Wales.

Greenpeace. 2012. "Tory Candidate Admits Bragging About Windfarm Role." http://www.greenpeace.org.uk/newsdesk/energy/news/conservative-election-wind-plot-revealed.

Greenslade, Roy. 2004. *Press Gang*. London: Pan Macmillan.

Greenslade, Roy. 2008. "The Digital Challenge." *Guardian*, 7 January. http://www.guardian.co.uk/media/2008/jan/07/pressandpublishing.digitalmedia.

Greenslade, Roy. 2012a. "New Crowdfunding Models Provoke Either Delight or Dismay." *Guardian*, 22 March. http://www.guardian.co.uk/media/greenslade/2012/mar/22/digital-media-investigative-journalism.

Greenslade, Roy. 2012b. "Linda Grant: Metro is 'Facts Not Spin, Sound-Bitey Espresso-Shot'." *Guardian*, 3 June. http://www.guardian.co.uk/media/2012/jun/03/metro-linda-grant-facts-spin.

Guardian Media Group. 2010. "The Scott Trust Is a Unique Form of Media Ownership in the UK." Accessed 25 February 2013. http://www.gmgplc.co.uk/the-scott-trust.

Gulyas, Agnes. 2012. "Changing Business Models and Adaptation Strategies of Local Newspapers." In *What Do We Mean By Local?*, edited by John Mair, Neil Fowler, and Ian Reeves, 27–33. Bury St Edmunds: Arima.

Hall, Ben. 2012. "Independent's Monthly Unique Users Pass 14.5m." *Media Week*, 26 April. http://www.mediaweek.co.uk/news/1128994/Independents-monthly-unique-users-pass-145m/

Hall, Jim. 2008. "Online Editions: Newspapers and the 'New' News." In *Pulling Newspapers Apart*, edited by Bob Franklin, 204–11. London: Routledge.

Hobbs, Andrew. 2011. "Lessons from History: Why Readers Preferred the Local Paper in the Second Half of the Nineteenth Century." Paper presented at the Future of Journalism conference, Cardiff University, 8–9 September.

House of Commons Culture, Media and Sport Committee. 2010. *Future for Local and Regional Media*: Vol. 1, report, together with formal minutes. No. HC 43-I. London: Stationery Office.

Hunt, Jeremy. 2010. "Measures to Boost Local Media." Accessed 25 January 2013. http://www.culture.gov.uk/news/news_stories/7135.aspx.

Ingram, Matthew. 2011. "If a Paywall is Your Only Strategy, You Are Doomed." 31 October 2011. http://gigaom.com/2011/10/31/if-a-paywall-is-your-only-strategy-then-you-are-doomed/.

Jones, Richard. 2012. "Interviewing the PM with Toddler in Tow: An Experiment in Hyperlocal Journalism." In *What Do We Mean By Local?*, edited by John Mair, Neil Fowler, and Ian Reeves. Bury St Edmunds: Arima.

Koss, Stephen. 1981. *The Rise and Fall of the Political Press in Britain*, Vol.1, *The Nineteenth Century*. London: Hamish Hamilton.

Leigh, David. 2012. "A £2 Broadband Levy Could Save Our Newspapers." *Guardian*, 23 September. http://www.guardian.co.uk/media/2012/sep/23/broadband-levy-save-newspapers.

Leveson, Brian. 2012a. *An Inquiry into the Culture, Practices and Ethics of the Press: Report*. London: Stationery Office.

Leveson, Brian. 2012b. *An Inquiry into the Culture, Practices and Ethics of the Press:* Transcript of hearing, 17 May, 2pm, Sir Harold Evans. Accessed 5 March 2013. http://fullfact.org/leveson/hearings/120517-pm.

Local World. 2012. "Local World to Re-invigorate UK Regional Media Sector." 21 November 2012. http://local-world.co.uk/news%20releases/newsrelease.html?page=newsrelease1.html.

MacArthur, Brian. 1988. *Eddy Shah and the Newspaper Revolution.* Newton Abbot: David & Charles.

Meehan, John. 2012. "Innovative Ways to Sustain Community Journalism." In *What Do We Mean By Local?,* edited by John Mair, Neil Fowler, and Ian Reeves, 103–108. Bury St Edmunds: Arima.

Murdoch, Rupert. 2008. "The Future of Newspapers: Moving Beyond Dead Trees." Boyer Lecture, ABC Radio, 16 November. http://www.abc.net.au/m/boyer lectures/stories/2008/2397940.htm.

Newspaper Society. 2012. "Regional Press Structure." Accessed 31 October 2012. http://www.newspapersoc.org.uk/regional-press-structure.

Oakley, Chris. 2012a. Speech to Society of Editors conference, 10 May. Accessed 31 October 2012. http://www.holdthefrontpage.co.uk/2012/news/five-minutes-to-midnight-chris-oakleys-speech-in-full.

Oakley, Chris. 2012b. "The Men Who Killed the Regional Newspaper Industry." In *What Do We Mean By Local?,* edited by John Mair, Neil Fowler, and Ian Reeves, 51–66. Bury St Edmunds: Arima.

Ofcom. 2009. *Local and Regional Media in the UK: Discussion Document.* London: Ofcom.

Ofcom. 2010. "TV, Phones and Internet Take Up Almost Half Our Waking Hours." http://consumers.ofcom.org.uk/2010/08/tv-phones-and-internet-take-up-almost-half-our-waking-hours/

Oliver & Ohlbaum Advisory. 2009a. *An Analysis of the Content of Local and Regional Newspapers: A Report Prepared for Ofcom.* London: Ofcom.

Oliver & Ohlbaum Advisory. 2009b. *A Macro-Economic Review of the UK Local Media Sector: A Report Prepared for Ofcom.* London: Ofcom.

Orr, D. 2012. "Jimmy Savile Was an Emperor with No Clothes—and a Celebrity Cloak." *The Guardian,* 2 November. http://www.guardian.co.uk/commentisfree/2012/nov/02/jimmy-savile-emperors-new-clothes

Reeves, Ian. 2005. "Rupert Murdoch Tells All." *Press Gazette,* 1 December. http://www.pressgazette.co.uk/node/32634.

Rusbridger, Alan. 1999. "Dumbing Down." Cobden Lecture, Manchester Metropolitan University, 17 April.

Sabbagh, Dan. 2012. "The Truth Behind Murdoch's Economics." *Guardian,* 1 July. http://www.guardian.co.uk/media/2012/jul/01/truth-behind-murdoch-economics.

Schlosberg, Justin. 2012. Co-opting the Discourse of Crisis: Re-assessing Market Failure in the Local News Sector. In *What Do We Mean By Local?,* edited by John Mair, Neil Fowler, and Ian Reeves, 51–66. Bury St Edmunds: Arima.

Shirky, Clay. 2009. "Stop Press—And Then What?" *Guardian,* 13 April. http://www.guardian.co.uk/commentisfree/cifamerica/2009/apr/13/internet-newspapers-clay-shirky.

Sweney, Mark. 2012. "News Corp to Close iPad Newspaper The Daily." *Guardian,* 3 December 2012. http://www.guardian.co.uk/media/2012/dec/03/news-corp-close-ipad-the-daily.

Temple, Mick. 2006. " Dumbing Down is Good for You." *British Politics* 1: 257–273.

Tindle, Sir Ray. 2012. Preface to *What Do We Mean By Local?,* edited by John Mair, Neil Fowler, and Ian Reeves, 1-2. Bury St Edmunds: Arima.

Wiener, Joel H. 2011. *The Americanization of the British Press, 1830s–1914: Speed in the Age of Transatlantic Journalism.* Basingstoke: Palgrave Macmillan.

Williams, Michael. 2011. "I've Seen the Future and It's Crap." *British Journalism Review* 22: 37–45

Women in Journalism. 2012. *Seen But Not Heard: How Women Make Front Page News.* http://womeninjournalism.co.uk/wp-content/uploads/2012/10/Seen_but_ not_heard.pdf

Wood, Ian. 2012. "Innovation on the Streets of Manchester." In *What Do We Mean By Local?*, edited by John Mair, Neil Fowler, and Ian Reeves, 8–17. Bury St Edmunds: Arima.

7 One Newsroom, Many Possibilities

How the Merging of Digital and Print Journalism in American Newsrooms is Shaping the Future of U.S. News Media

Alex Ortolani

The pressing question in U.S. newsrooms in recent years has not focused on when digital journalism will dominate the print sector, but which model will be most effective (Anderson, Bell, and Shirky 2012). This is not necessarily a declaration of the death of print publications, which are still relatively widespread despite drastic declines (Edmonds, Guskin, Rosenstiel, and Mitchell 2012), but an admission that every relevant newsroom must have a strong digital presence to capture readers and advertisers increasingly shifting to computers, smart phones and tablets (Edmonds et al. 2012; Pew Research Center). One of the most challenging questions facing U.S. journalists is how to successfully make this shift without losing the quality and impact of a media sector that has historically been a fundamental player in almost every sector of U.S. life.

The shift to digital journalism and consumption has taken many forms over the past decade—including less formal, but increasingly important venues such as Twitter—but it is useful for the discussions that follow to consider three clear strains of news production coming out of full-time, dedicated newsrooms. One comes in the form of solely digital players that have started with a blank slate in terms of how content can be used and distributed. Examples range from *The Huffington Post*, which combines original content with aggregation, and *ProPublica*, which focuses on original, investigative journalism funded through a nonprofit model. The second strain comes from those so-called 'legacy' newsrooms that may have been around for more than 100 years, but have become major players in the digital world by transferring their editorial missions and goals to the online and digital space. *The Atlantic* magazine, which embarked on an ambitious online strategy early in the web's development, has turned a monthly magazine known for long-form journalism into a lively and well-trafficked current events web site (Peter 2011). Meanwhile, large metropolitan dailies, struggling to survive in a world of fewer advertisements and money from classifieds, have seen the internet as a last bastion for content, with newspapers such as the *Christian Science Monitor* (Slattery 2008) going solely online and the *Detroit Free Press* turning its focus to digital (Perez-Pena 2009). Finally, newspaper giants such as *The Wall Street Journal* and *The New*

York Times have embraced online journalism as a key part of strategy despite having the first and third largest circulation in the country, respectively (Lulofs 2012). The third strain can be found in those more traditional news outlets naturally suited for the web, such as CNN or Fox News, which cover breaking events in a fashion that—especially with the increased capacity for video online—seems a natural fit with their coverage. Newswires such as Bloomberg News and Reuters may also be counted in this category due to their focus on speed, though much of their content is distributed through syndication or, in the case of Bloomberg, on terminals.

Whichever type of media outlet you look at, this relatively fast shift to digital content raises fundamental questions on the state, future and quality of the news being produced. While the internet provides a chance to offer much more to consumers—in terms of space, multimedia, direct access to data and reader response (Kawamoto 2004)—it doesn't necessarily mean all that extra content will be as impactful or influential as a simple morning read of the newspaper. On the other hand, there's no reason these new forms of journalism cannot be as impactful, if not more so, with the most difficult question being around how to pay for these new models. This chapter does not seek to make any definitive claims about this shift from a print to digital world. Rather, its purpose is to present the reader with some insider accounts of how these challenges are playing out on the ground in U.S. newsrooms at storied institutions such as *The Wall Street Journal*, or young upstarts like *The Atlantic*'s new digital business magazine, *Quartz*.

In February 2012, **Raju Narisetti** *was named as Managing Editor of* The Wall Street Journal *Digital Network and a Deputy Managing Editor of* The Wall Street Journal. *This marked his return to WSJ, where he had spent 13 years in the United States and Europe from 1994–2006 in positions including the Editor of* The Wall Street Journal Europe *and a Deputy Managing Editor of* The Wall Street Journal, *with overall responsibility for Europe, Middle East and Africa. In 2009, Raju joined the* Washington Post *as managing editor. As one of two Managing Editors, he was responsible for all content, staff and digital content strategy for Washingtonpost.com as well as the Post's mobile and tablet platforms. Narisetti was also the founding editor of* Mint, *India's only Berliner format business newspaper, from 2006–2009, and launched the livemint.com web site in 2007 for HT Media Ltd, the New Delhi-based publisher of the Hindustan Times.*

Q: How does the contemporary newsroom—in which we assume almost every editor and reporter has at least some interaction with digital media—differ from the newsroom of five or ten years ago?[1]

A: Historically, the pattern has been that almost every single major newsroom has set up a separate entity for online content with its own staff. [But] It's only in the last half-a-dozen years that the focus has been about integrating these two businesses or newsrooms. Just the idea that the same newsroom will supply content for multiple platforms is still relatively nascent at most media outlets.

The big difference now obviously is that the more advanced newsrooms like *The Wall Street Journal* or *The Washington Post* have single content-creation teams that produce content for multiple platforms. It is evolving to the point where you provide your content, or brand experience, to readers no matter where they consume you. At the *Journal* it's called "WSJ Everywhere," and the idea is that if you have a subscription, then no matter where you access it you ought to have the same experience and the same content. So while the content may be adjusted for different platforms, it can't be of a different quality or provide an uneven experience of your brand.

One of the biggest changes that has not been fully embraced, especially in legacy newsrooms, is that customers in actual real time are telling you what they think of your content. Most newsrooms grew up with this happy illusion that everything you write, especially if it appears on the front page, is read by every single reader. Digital has upended that because you can actually tell how much people are reading and how often. I think that has been a tough adjustment for a lot of journalists. The initial reaction has been to say that when you pay attention to those metrics you are pandering to page views and things like that, but at the end of the day your audience is sending you a pretty overt signal about how valuable, engaging and useful your journalism is, and newsrooms are starting to deal with that knowledge in different ways. At the *Journal* we have established daily metrics in the form of a report that goes out to 200 people in the newsroom. What's emerging from that data is a plan to actually ask if we can aspire to improve performance in this area and set some goals.

Q: Does looking at page views in this way risk hurting the quality of the content?
A: That's a false choice to be honest. Newsrooms sometimes treat metrics with derision. But at the end of every pair of eyeballs is a reader who could go anywhere in the world of digital journalism to consume content from any other brand or any other newsroom. Wanting to attract them, engage them, and keep them is not something that flies in the face of any conflict with the quality of journalism. I think metrics have a role to play in informing you about why something is not working, and the onus is on you to figure out how to make your journalism choices more engaging. If you use metrics to change your journalistic priorities is that a problem? Sure. But that's not a problem of metrics, that's a problem of your decision-making.

Today, for example, if you spent a lot of energy and time on President Obama's gun-control policies, and you're finding through metrics that nobody is reading the story on your homepage, the problem is not with metrics. The problem is you're not doing something engaging with your content, your packaging and your presentation, so people are bypassing you and getting that information somewhere else. You have to figure out what you want to do because you know journalistically that it's the highest priority story today, but at the same time you want to make sure that audiences are consuming it.

Technology is allowing our readers to be more promiscuous than they have ever been because at the click of a finger, or increasingly through a phone, they can go somewhere else. In the newspaper world you had a fairly captive audience due to the inertia of getting a different newspaper from the one that dropped into your driveway. Technology has removed that inertia and as a result audiences will be more and more promiscuous. Your challenge as a newsroom and as a journalist is to say: 'how do I attract, engage, and bring back more readers to my journalism?' I'm of the belief that in 2013 the definition of journalism has to expand to the point where the journalist says 'it's my job to try and find ways to bring more people to my journalism'.

Q: Where do you see some of the opportunities to take advantage of digital content to improve the quality of journalism?
A: One of the biggest trends, especially at *The Wall Street Journal*, is the emergence of video as a form of storytelling. We take it for granted, but it's only started happening recently. We now produce about 1,500 videos a month out of a newsroom that is primarily a print newsroom. We do this for two reasons. Increasingly audiences seem to want to consume journalism in multimedia formats. But the business model of video is also helping because advertising rates are pretty high for video. More important, and this is pretty significant, is that our business model travels without journalism. Meaning that if you watch *Wall Street Journal* video on YouTube, the advertisement you see on it is an advertisement that has been sold by the *WSJ*. That is not the case with articles or blogs because there's no advertising that is inherently traveling with that piece. If you think of the evolution of digital media, we first began by doing what we knew best, which was to take printed text and put it up on our web site. Then just as journalism itself added black and white pictures, then color pictures, we added pictures. Then we added charts. Then over time we discovered that with digital you could actually make the chart more interactive than static. Then we discovered that instead of just giving a chart of a piece of data you can actually put the database up and allow readers to engage with that. Then video has been added. Now the big thing

is to make it a two-way conversation. This ranges from comments to the ability to upload your Instagram pictures, to things like sharing haikus on the fiscal cliff—you name it. You can do fun stuff and serious stuff. So it's become about more than just providing the ten stories of the day. It's become more of an equal system where you are some part of content creation, some part of content sharing, some part of content absorbing, and all of these are enabled by the technology.

Q: One of the biggest challenges for news outlets in the digital age is to get readers to continue to pay for news when so much is available for free. The *Journal* has famously stuck by its subscription-based model and has been followed by *The New York Times* and others. Can this model survive in the long term?

A: I fundamentally believe that for journalism to thrive and continue to do well we have to go back to a model that we knew very well, which is: both readers and advertisers pay for our services. For some reason, as an industry, we decided just as we moved to digital that we could just rely on advertisers. So instead of having a dual-track we went to a single track. What's happening is that we are discovering that was a mistake, and in some cases, like *The Wall Street Journal*, we never made that mistake. We've always charged. Those who have made the mistake are discovering that the dual model is actually pretty good, and a lot of them are coming back.

If the question is will paywalls or pay models fix our broken business model? The answer is probably–No. Would they make it more sustainable for us and give us more time to figure out a more sustainable business model? Absolutely. For some, it's going to be $100 million in new revenue, like *The New York Times* seems to have done over the last couple of years. For others it's going to protect their newspaper if you price it in such a way that you're better off buying the newspaper to get the full range of content. I think everybody is going to experiment, and some will find that just having a paywall will not be salvation. But the notion that it's okay for our readers and advertisers to pay is what works for us. There's no reason not to expect that to work in the future.

I understand the concern that in a world of sharing it's hard to make such a business model work. But remember, by and large Facebook, Google, YouTube, Twitter, Linked-In, and almost all of those organizations don't create content on their own. They're amazing platforms for sharing, but they're not actually creating content. So in that sense if you're in the business of creating content, and not necessarily in the business of newspapers or web sites or apps, I do think you have a pretty bright future.

Despite all the gloom and doom about the so-called death of journalism, there have never been more consumers of journalism since the invention of the Gutenberg press as of this moment. The problem is not that we have a problem with journalism, but that we have a problem with the business of journalism. And that's a shared problem to solve. It's not a challenge just for a newsroom or a journalist to figure out. It is for us to work much more closely with our business-side colleagues.

My job is a newsroom job. But in my mind I have a simple mission: get more people to consume more *Journal* content profitability. If you break it down, the first 'more' is just bringing more people, the second 'more' is engagement, and profitability has to underscore everything that we do. If you think of it that way, metrics fall into place, the idea of bringing more people in falls into place, and thinking of innovative ways to charge for new things or reinforcing the value of things you're already charging for by creating innovation comes into play. All these things have to be part of how you define journalism these days.

Q: Do you envision a day when all news will be on electronic devices, and if this shift occurs will the newsroom change because of it, or is the newsroom essentially there already?

A: We have to be where our audiences want us to be. As of last month 32% of my visitors on my digital content came from either a mobile phone or a tablet. That number is probably going to go to 50, probably 60, probably 70, and if that happens, *Wall Street Journal* journalism ought to be there. I think there's nothing wrong in thinking that way.

Radio still is pretty widespread. It's a niche, it no longer has the over-sized influence and impact as it used to have pre-television, but it's there. I have a feeling that print will be somewhat similar. It will be influential and perhaps even be profitable for a lot of people. It will be smaller, it will be a niche, but it will be a force to be reckoned with for a long time to come, because there is a serendipity value that will exist even if we expect content to be wherever we want it to be. You could see some businesses evolve into weekend only. Some could evolve into a very tight digest rather than a multiple section paper. Printing on demand, the way things are going, could become a viable option. Imagine you being able to say: 'Great, I'm looking at six stories,' and going to your computer and saying 'download these six and print them out for me at home'. I think there are going to be a lot of interesting possibilities, and I think print as a form will probably be there for a long time.

Hamilton Boardman *was a homepage producer for more than three years at* The New York Times *before becoming an assistant news editor in 2011. He previously ran the production department at* Women.com, *worked in the online magazine division of Condé Nast, and spent time at a political web consulting company called Plus Three. He was also Editor in Chief of* Columbia University's Journal of International Affairs.

Q: **The New York Times is often seen not just as the pinnacle of print journalism in the United States, but globally. As an outsider this might suggest a rough transition from print—which the paper has mastered—to digital and online content. How have the *NYT*'s efforts to become one of the premier online news web sites developed in your time there?**[2]

A: We now have more or less completely eliminated any of the distinctions that used to exist between the print and web operations. When I started, the web newsroom was a separate organization with its own leadership and its own ranks of editors. Jim Roberts, the top editor at that time for the web, reported to the executive editor of the paper, but essentially from there downwards, the web was its own operation. A couple of years ago they started the process of erasing those distinctions and making each desk within the newsroom responsible for its reports both on the web and in print.

I think a big part of this change was the recognition that the long term future of the *NYT* is on the web and on various digital platforms. I think the print product still remains incredibly important, and I think it has a really long future ahead of it. But they wanted to make it clear that everyone involved in the reporting and editing shouldn't see the web as an afterthought, and in order to do that they had to get rid of those distinctions.

Q: **Has everyone bought into the merging of the departments?**

A: I definitely see a huge amount of progress, which is not to say it hasn't been without its hiccups in terms of getting the mindset changed. Part of it is that there are a lot of people who have been at the *NYT* and in journalism for a long time that have taken time to adjust to new realities. The *NYT* is an organization that is deeply steeped in tradition, and the ways that that manifests itself are both in respect to that tradition but then sometimes, among some people, creates a resistance to change.

Q: **What is your mandate in terms of getting great print content to be great online content that truly takes advantage of the medium?**

A: I think one of the biggest things in leveraging the abilities of online for the reader is showing documents and primary materials to the reader. You point to documents, you point to links to videos, and essentially you try to turn an article from a walled-off description of something to an entryway where if someone is interested they can go a lot deeper by following those sources.

Q: What challenges does the online focus bring for the newspaper?
A: I'll qualify this by saying that I'm primarily involved in the very last stages of stories and working on putting on the finishing touches and presenting them. I do know that particularly for a breaking news event it's a challenge for our reporters not only to be filing very quickly to the web, but also writing a deeper and broader story for print the next day. There's a comprehensiveness and sweep that we expect of the stories that make it into the newspaper the next day, and it's hard to do all of these things at once. To certain degrees on really big stories what we often do now is use more of a team-based approach. We might have one person who is writing for the web throughout the day, and another who is simultaneously doing the more in-depth reporting and putting together a version that will appear later. I also recognize that at a place like the *NYT* we have a great luxury in being able to use this model. There are a lot of news organizations that can't throw that many people at a story, and even for us it can be a challenge sometimes.

Q: If tomorrow print played the lesser role to digital and online content, do you think the newsroom is ready?
A: I wouldn't say that we're quite there yet. But it's hard to say that, because in the end 'necessity is the mother of invention'. If print went away tomorrow I think we'd adapt very quickly. I think today some things we do online take cues from the print edition. The deadlines that we have for print, and the scarcity of space, and the necessity of prioritizing resources and effort and attention that are inherent in print drive a lot of decisions we make online. An example of this is that every night I work with the producers who work on the foreign desk or the national desk and they get the stories up onto the site and organize things on their section front, and that is still driven by how things appear in the print edition. If a story is on the front page it goes on the top of the section front. That's a useful decision-making process, but if things changed we could change that process.

Adam Pasick, *currently Senior Asia Correspondent at Quartz, was managing editor of* NYMag.com *at the time of this interview. He previously spent nearly 10 years at Reuters in New York and London, covering the media industry, launching a virtual Second Life bureau, and serving as U.S. editor of Reuters.com.*

Q: A write-up of *NYMag.com* I found describes the web site as a 'counterpart' to the magazine. Is there a divide between your weekly print magazine and your web site?[3]

A: We don't think of NYMag.com as being the online counterpart to the magazine. The number of people who read the so-called magazine articles online vastly dwarfs the number of people who read it on paper. When the print stories are being conceived of and executed the journalists keep online in mind, and after they run we look at the online reaction.

That is not to say there aren't people whose jobs aren't to write mostly for one or the other. It's more of a differentiation of the kind of stories that we do for both forms—they both generally end up in the same bucket. But it's much more long form in the magazine, and the tempo of the features and the news that they do are different because they are putting them out once a week, and the blogs on the web site are more or less 24/7. So there is differentiation, but it's not that one is a counterpart or compliment to the other. You can get everything from an up-to-the-second news update to a long-form piece of investigative journalism or a critical essay. Clearly we're not 100% integrated, but I think we've done a good job of shrinking the distance, and it's shrinking more and more all the time.

Q: Why is it important to shrink the distance?

A: We have a lot of great reporters and writers throughout the company, and it doesn't make sense to keep people siloed as a blogger or a reporter. People here are interested in writing in different formats for the most part, and there's no reason to limit them. I also think that's a reflection of where journalism is going. The differences are becoming more and more arbitrary. They are a legacy of how things used to be. The world that those divisions reflect doesn't really exist anymore.

Q: In what ways do you think the online content can offer a higher-quality experience to readers?

A: I don't know about 'higher-quality', but there are certain circumstances where online vastly trumps the paper experience, and I think it mostly has to do with time. Something like the Newtown shooting comes out and you have an incredibly fast developing story where every minute you're learning something new. When you think about that happening, could you ever imagine waiting until the next morning to find out what happened? That seems inconceivable now. People don't tolerate that kind of lag anymore. It used to be that you would go to CNN for that kind of thing. Now I think that's no longer the best way to keep up with the latest with what's happening—clearly Twitter is where it's at, and we all live in that ecosystem now. Now the CNN producers are looking at Twitter along with everyone else.

Q: What is your role at *NYMag.com* with a fast-breaking story like Newtown?

A: We don't see our role as breaking the latest development. Our role is much more about being an intelligent filter, or curator, in the heat of the moment. We can tell people what is going on by using our judgment and experience to piece all of this crazy, chaotic material together into some kind of reliable narrative. The real sweet spot for us as a web site is that within an hour of something big happening we try and come in with a new, fresh angle, analysis, or idea about what's happening that is the first layer of context or analysis. I think that's really where we shine. There's a whole media food chain now, and everyone has to participate in all parts of it, but certain institutions are stronger at doing different things. I feel like that one-hour window is when people know they can go to *New York Mag* and we will tell them something about the event that will be interesting and useful.

Q: What challenges does the digital form present in terms of the journalism? Are there downsides?

A: There are challenges that you didn't really have to deal with as a journalist five or 10 years ago. There has always been a challenge to be original and not derivative and to say something different. But now the field is so wide-open—you have so many people trying to be original so quickly that the pace is really punishing. I think it just has become exponentially more difficult to come up with a new idea or be first with an idea. It's Darwinian competitiveness on fast-forward. Twitter is like a crazy petri-dish where everyone is battling to the death to come up with something new and interesting to say, and it can produce a really chaotic mess of people shouting out things and hoping that they stick. But you can't really complain about it because that is just the way things are these days, and ultimately I think the result is the best stuff rises up to the top. You don't get your opinion noticed just because you write for *The New York Times*. You don't automatically get credibility just because of who you write for. Certainly it matters, but it's not enough on its own.

Q: But do you worry that sensational stories, headlines or tweets are the ones that get the most attention, and not necessarily the smartest ideas?

A: I really don't worry about that. I think the market decides what it wants. Just take the recent Manti Te'o case. That was a very sensational story, but it also required investigative journalism, so I have no problem with Gawker getting 10 million clicks on that. Just to use another example, the long-form stuff from our magazine does extremely well, and that stuff is journalistically very solid, is fact-checked to death, and is held to every kind of journalistic standard that you would want to apply to quality journalism. There's no way to predict what is going to do well. Sometimes what you think will do amazing just sinks below the surface without making a ripple. Sometimes the story you least expect to work rises up. Sometimes you just know you've got the goods and it upholds your expectations. It would be one thing if really uninteresting copycat stuff did well. But I don't see that happening as much anymore. There was a time a couple of years ago when you had content farms churning out SEO (search engine optimized) headlines that had nothing to say. But I feel like the ecosystem self-corrected, and those sites don't do well anymore. It's a constantly evolving thing, but I don't worry about sensationalism or people chasing pageviews. The system tends to compensate for those tricks over time. In some ways I think there's never been a better time for long-form journalism. The business model may be difficult, but if you write something great right now it doesn't really matter where you work, it will rise to the top.

Q: Would *NYMag.com* be ready right now for a world without print?
A: Everything that we do right now goes up online. However, if print was outlawed tomorrow and we all had to live through online, the money isn't there to pay for it all. Print advertising is still way above digital advertising. So if print disappeared tomorrow we would see every single publication that currently uses dead trees take a huge hit and not be able to afford the editorial staff that they have today. But digital is where the trend line is going. I don't know if we'll ever get there completely—you still have people that make LP's, right? But it's going to probably result in a slowly shrinking number of paid journalists unless someone figures out a different revenue model to make all this work.

In the end I don't think moving to digital is an editorial issue. Is there anybody outside of a couple magazines that isn't publishing their stuff online? It just doesn't seem like a problem. Writing for online versus writing for print, there are a couple small differences, but really, speaking as someone who has never worked for a dead tree publication, I don't really see how that would change things. It's how you pay for it that presents the problem.

S. Mitra Kalita is Ideas Editor at Quartz, *and previously worked at* The Wall Street Journal, *where she oversaw coverage of the Great Recession,*

*launched a local news section for New York City and, most recently, re-
ported on the housing crisis. She also launched* Mint, *a business paper in
New Delhi, and has previously worked for* The Washington Post, Newsday
and The Associated Press. *She is the author of three books related to migration and globalization, is an adjunct professor of journalism at St. John and
Columbia universities and previously served as president of the South Asian
Journalists Association.*

Q: *Quartz* is one of many upstart digital media enterprises, but unlike
many of those upstarts has the backing of a major print and online publication, *The Atlantic.* What is *Quartz's* model, and why
did *The Atlantic* decide to launch this product?[4]

A: The model comes from an existing philosophy that *The Atlantic*
adapted a few years ago, which was essentially to go digital first.
That means when something happens you think about your web
site before your monthly magazine. It sounds very obvious given
the age in which we're in, but ten years ago this was very revolutionary for a magazine to put such an emphasis on its web site,
and also say the ethos of the web site is going to embody the
magazine, meaning it's still an analysis or a side-angle into a story,
not '10 people died today in an X, Y, or Z incident'. This model
did very well in terms of traffic. *The Atlantic* was actually getting
more traffic from overseas than *The Economist* and *The Financial
Times* combined. When looking at that global footprint in both
the pre-financial and post-financial crisis world, it was clear how
much the world's economies rely on each other for better or worse
and that we could design a product focused on that space. That
left us with a clear market, a clear business strategy, and a much
higher-end advertising base for business coverage. The idea of
Quartz was kicked around for about three years, and then in 2012
the editor was hired. When you're launching a digital business it's
possible to be fairly lean, see where things go, and then scale up
accordingly, and that's where we are now.

Q: How is the environment different from an outlet that has a print
element along with online?

A: *Quartz* is a pretty pure start-up. There are about 25 of us in a
room, and every morning we ask the question: 'how can we do
this differently?' We have our musings and we have approaches,
but there isn't really a template per se, which is incredibly liber-
ating. We're not encumbered by two things in particular. One,
the physical output of a newspaper every day, which doesn't
allow you to be lean and nimble because you're manufacturing
a product every day that requires a certain assembly-line style

of journalism that is capital intensive, manpower intensive, and doesn't allow you to be up-to-the-minute and nimble as readers need and want you to be. The second is just that newspapers have a lot of legacy. A lot of the reason newspapers have sections such as Marketplace, Lifestyle, or Politics, and coverage in a somewhat more silo-formation is because they're driven by the pages of the newspaper and where articles might go. So in a way the newspaper dictates how the newsroom is organized, which might not be the best way to approach coverage.

We can, for instance, dictate coverage around a moment such as the 'fiscal cliff'. Or we can say you cover economics and markets, because those two things have everything to do with each other right now. Or we can say you cover economics and you cover technology, but the iPhone is really affecting the U.S. trade imbalance, so let's take a step back and try to understand this a little bit more. Those kinds of conversations in a traditional newspaper can be very difficult because the focus might be on filling a hole as opposed to taking that step back and asking the question.

There are also differences that we don't benefit from. For instance, *The Wall Street Journal* is a massive operation that is a paper of record, and there's a lot of power in a paper of record. People turn to you first, and they'll then turn to you for the analysis. There's a necessity of that read every day, whereas something that is more analytical doesn't start out as a must read, and as a business model that can be pretty deadly. So our challenge is to make sure that people view the coverage we do on something like the 'fiscal cliff' as something they need to read every day. Because it is breaking news, but we're doing it in a conceptual way that goes beyond what just happened.

Q: I realize you're in a start-up situation so there are challenges there. But are there other challenges or limitations in terms of content and story creation for a solely online format?
A: One challenge is that we have to be updated all the time. The hunger is constant for news and information. Our reporters are sometimes scrambling and can feel like they're feeding the beast. The other thing is that aggregation becomes a crutch, and smart aggregation is very hard to do. Often aggregation is taking a crappy story that buries the lead and putting the most important aspect of the story out there. But is that the role of digital journalism, to just take what's out there and spin it for you? I would argue it's not. I think original reporting is important and key to what we do, but because of the demand you have to balance aggregation with original reporting.

One advantage with our model is that you don't have to publish a newspaper every day. So you don't have the same demands of the newspaper, the editing process is a lot more streamlined, and you can choose your goals for what you want to do. In some ways it's the same issues we faced before digital journalism appeared. As a reporter you say: 'here are the things I want to do this week, and at the end of the week I better have some things I'm really proud of'. In that sense it's the same model we've had all along. It just requires a lot more discipline, because it would be easy to just do aggregation all the time.

CONCLUSION

The dominant theme that emerges in these interviews is that although breaking down any remaining divides between print and digital teams at newsrooms is fairly recent and still an ongoing process, there is agreement that it is an essential need for competitive media outlets going forward. Encouraging reporters and editors to conceive every story with both print and digital mediums in mind, as one interviewee notes, is crucial for preparing for a future in which many more consumers will be reading on tablets and smart phones. This, however, is not the only point of overlap between the speakers. All seem to see potential in the digital age of journalism and what is possible in a time when journalists can reach more people in more places with ever more inventive and creative means of presentation. Furthermore, they do not fear investigative or hard-hitting journalism dying out with a decline in long-form print magazines in part because 'digital' does not always have to mean 'short'. The fear among the interviewees, rather, is whether online models can produce the necessary revenue to keep investigative teams employed and with enough resources to do their work. This leads to what may be the final and most vexing theme of the discussions, which is that no one has the answer to how to run robust newsrooms off much smaller advertising revenue for digital content.

Each interviewer had their own specific areas of interest in terms of producing quality journalism in an age of digital media. Raju Narisetti, who spearheads *The Wall Street Journal*'s digital network of products, believes making page views less of an anathema to journalists and instead an important gauge of reader interest can help improve the quality of digital media. As long as looking at page views doesn't somehow distort your journalistic ethics and standards, he argues, it can be a force to improve an organization's content. Hamilton Boardman, an assistant editor at *The New York Times*, speaks to that newspaper's recent melding of the print and online desks to create a more integrated production line. When it succeeds, Boardman says, the results can be astonishing stories in both print and digital formats. Meanwhile, the managing editor of online content for *New York Magazine* makes the case that the digital world has pushed media toward meritocracy, in which readers and users can raise the profile of a good story regardless of which publication or writer produced it. Finally, S. Mitra Kalita of *Quartz* speaks to working at a publication geared toward the most cutting edge of users—smartphone and tablet readers—but steeped in the traditions and journalistic goals of one of the most storied U.S. print magazines, *The Atlantic*. While producing 'must-read' journalism at a relatively small outlet with an untested model can be taxing, she says it can also produce great results that can outshine content from larger media organizations.

In sum, these interviews present some interesting experiences from within some of the most successful news organizations in the country. The trend of combining online and print teams has come a long way in the past five years and now seems an inevitability for all news organizations. Another theme that emerges is that journalists can no longer hide from the fact that they must produce stories for a digital world that can live and thrive in that world. That does not mean that long, investigative stories with narrative pacing and inventive writing won't thrive in a digital age, but rather, that the journalist should also consider how such a piece might best be presented to readers using a tablet or smartphone to view the story. Should there be photos? Video? Documents for the reader to access and an interactive way the reader can respond to the story? All the interviewees agreed that the journalism happening in the United States is as vibrant, powerful and important as ever, and the shift to digital seems to provide more opportunity than encumbrance to the craft. The problem is how news outlets can continue to be paid for their work, and as Raju Narisetti says, that's an issue no one media outlet is going to solve, but must be a shared burden in the industry.

NOTES

1. Raju Narisetti, telephone interview with author, 16 January 2013.
2. Hamilton Boardman, telephone interview with author, 20 January 2013.
3. Adam Pasick, telephone interview with author, 15 January 2013.
4. S. Mitra Kalita, telephone interview with author, 12 January 2013.

REFERENCES

Anderson, Chanders, Emily Bell, and Clay Shirky. 2012. "Post-Industrial Journalism: Adapting to the Present." *Tow Center for Digital Journalism*. http://towcenter .org/research/post-industrial-journalism.

Edmonds, Rick, Emily Guskin, Tom Rosenstiel, and Amy Mitchell. 2012. "Newspapers: Building Digital Revenues Proves Painfully Slow." In *The State of the News Media 2012*. Pew Research Center's Project for Excellence in Journalism. Accessed 28 January 2013. http://stateofthemedia.org/2012/newspapers-building-digital-revenues-proves-painfully-slow.

Kawamoto, Kevin, ed. 2004. *Digital Journalism: Emerging Media & the Changing Horizon of Journalism*. Lanham, MD: Rowman & Littlefield.

Lulofs, Neal. 2012. "The Top U.S. Newspapers for September 2012." Alliance for Audited Media. Accessed 7 February 2013. http://accessabc.wordpress.com/2012/05/01/the-top-u-s-newspapers-for-march-2012.

Perez-Pena, Richard. 2009. "Detroit's Daily Papers Are Now Not So Daily." *New York Times*, 30 March.

Peter, Jeremy. 2011. "At 154, a Digital Milestone." *New York Times*, 20 November.

Pew Research Center's Project for Excellence in Journalism. 2012. "Changing News Landscape, Even Television is Vulnerable: Trends in News Consumption: 1991–2012." Accessed 7 February 2013. http://www.people-press.org/files/legacy-pdf/2012%20News%20Consumption%20Report.pdf

Slattery, Brennon. 2008. "Christian Science Monitor Goes Online-Only." *Washington Post*, 31 October.

8   American Broadcast News and the Future

Robert Beers

INTRODUCTION

This chapter will survey the current and emerging situation across the American television and radio news sectors and on the basis of that analysis assess the prospects for the future. In doing this it will evaluate also the extent to which American broadcast news currently is meeting the quality standards set down in chapter one and the extent to which they look likely to do so within the foreseeable future.

NATIONAL TELEVISION NEWS IN THE UNITED STATES

In January 1989 a major story in Havana demanded that Cuba make a rare departure from its reluctance to admit Western reporters and issue hundreds of news media visas to journalists around the world. America's three over-the-air networks and several cable networks moved their main bulletins and dozens of support staff to originate days of broadcasts from Havana presented by their main anchormen to cover the first visit of Pope John Paul II to Cuba. But just as ABC *World News Tonight*, CBS *Evening News* and NBC *Nightly News* were set to cover the three-day visit of the anti-Communist Pope in one of the last bastions of Communism, the news cycle in the United States changed dramatically. Monica Lewinsky's name appeared on the wire services as possibly linked to a sex scandal with President Bill Clinton, causing a massive exodus of the major network players back to New York (Foerstel 1998, 122).

This, and the whole subsequent focus on the affair, was the pinnacle of modern tabloid journalism (Foerstel 1998, 122). It was a profound sign of the times in American television as long-time CBS foreign correspondent Tom Fenton (2005) sees it.

The networks used the end of the Cold War to justify their drastic reduction of foreign correspondents in the 1990s, together with a purely cost-driven argument that foreign news does not sell, i.e., attract viewers. A comprehensive CBS story on Sarajevo was dropped after Eric Sorensen, Executive Producer of the CBS Evening News, found the war in the Balkans depressing. Fenton in 1996 went to great lengths to set up an interview with an Islamic extremist but was told it was of no interest to viewers. The subject of the interview was to have been Osama bin Laden (Fenton 2005, 31–36). For network news, the glory days of the big name anchors and huge audiences, when Murrow invented CBS News and Walter Cronkite became it, have long gone in a process of slow decline. In 1980 the dinner-hour network news attracted 53 million views, combining the audience of ABC News, CBS News and NBC News. That was almost one in every four Americans tuning into the half-hour news bulletins on one of those networks, which were all broadcast live on the east coast of America at 6:30 pm and then across the other western zones on tape at the same hour, or an hour earlier, but always head-to-head (Academy of Television Arts and Sciences 2012). Thirty years later, with an increase of more than 88 million Americans, only 22.5 million watched the network news bulletins (Pew Research Center's Project for Excellence in Journalism [Pew] 2012). According to Pew's Network News portion of its annual report on American Journalism, that means viewership of the old big three bulletins in 2011 was down 54.5% since 1980. Actually, there was a slight spike in 2011 due to such major stories as the Arab Spring, the death of Osama bin Laden, the shooting of Congresswoman Gabrielle Giffords in Tucson, the royal wedding in Britain and the tsunami in Japan. The increase was 4.5% over the previous year, but major on-going stories, such as the attack on the Twin Towers and the Pentagon in 2001, or the early stages of the Iraq War, produced similar peaks, only to go back toward the 30-year increasing decline of the programmes (Nielsen 2012). It does show that when a major story breaks, some viewers return to one of the big three rather than cable news.

The reason for the decline in the network audience is easy to identify. The big three—ABC, CBS and NBC—have gone from an environment with very little competition to today's satellite world of thousands of channels for entertainment and dozens for news on some stations and non-TV, mobile platforms. Nonetheless, the average 22.5 million viewers the network news attracts is considerable when Nielsen says the median viewership of the major cable news channels is 3.3 million in primetime in the same year. The highest rated news programme on cable news is Fox News's *The O'Reilly Factor*, which has the largest audience, but which in turn has only half the audience of the CBS *Evening News*, which is the least watched of the evening networks (Nielsen 2011).

The network audience leader is NBC *Nightly News* with an average of 8.75 million viewers, while 7.82 million watched ABC *World News* and 5.97 million watched the CBS *Evening News* (Nielsen 2012). But with more than half of their audiences lost in the last 30 years, these network broadcasts are expensive. There have been sweeping staff cuts over the last 20 years. In 2010 ABC News fired 400 staff members, a quarter of its news staff, and CBS News cut 70 jobs. Yet these are only the latest reductions as both have had repeated staff culls in recent years (Stelter 2010).

NBC News is the only network news that is profitable, due to its cable channels. MSNBC, which began in 1996 and which was for years trailing CNN and Fox, has passed CNN in the ratings in recent years, with Fox News still by far the market leader. Cable subsidiary MSNBC supplies revenue from its advertising, but also from the cable subscriber fees, which make up half of its income (Stelter 2010).

With Fox News showing healthy profits, there have been concerted efforts by both ABC and CBS to forge a relationship with CNN over the years. Kurtz writes that CBS President Les Moonves felt especially handicapped without a cable news channel and repeatedly approached Richard Parsons, the former Chief Executive Officer of Time Warner, parent company of CNN, with an offer to buy CNN. Parsons insisted the channel was not for sale. Then CBS entered into negotiations with CNN for a joint newsgathering agreement that was unsuccessful because neither could agree over issues of editorial control (Kurtz 2007).

ABC has the news and lifestyle channel ABC News Now, which is available on broadband, some digital television systems and on streaming video. It has two news segments, but focuses on daily living programmes about financial tips and good health advice along with features on film and music celebrities. For any major breaking stories, it switches to BBC World News.

However, in early May of 2012 ABC announced that it had indeed found a partner for a true cable news channel. ABC News and Univision News were creating a multiplatform news channel aimed at U.S. Hispanics. Univision is the leading Spanish language network in America, with 73% of the Spanish-speaking audience in prime evening viewing hours. It will cater for the 50 million Hispanic Americans, focusing on news, especially from Latin America, as well as lifestyle and cultural programming. Staff will be a mix of ABC News and Univision News journalists.

Both organizations promised in a statement to provide "uncompromising coverage of current events with a unique perspective" on an around-the-clock, English-language television network and digital platform. The cable channel would be launched in 2013. The target audience is 16% of the U.S. population but is growing at a faster rate than any other segment of the United States and is likely to reach 30% of the population by 2050 (Stewart and Campo-Flores 2012).

Meanwhile, the new channel will leave CBS News as the only one of the old big three without a cable channel. CBS News remains the network with a heritage unmatched by any other American broadcast news organization. Cronkite was a great admirer of CNN and like Chief CBS Foreign Correspondent Tom Fenton had hoped that CNN founder Ted Turner's bid to take over CBS in 1986 would succeed. It did not, and Fenton thought it was a great missed opportunity (Fenton 2005). CNN was founded in 1980 by American philanthropist Ted Turner, providing the first 24-hour television news coverage in broadcast history from its headquarters in Atlanta, Georgia. The author received instructions from CBS News shortly after CNN began broadcasting not to let them into any pool situation and, in essence, to ignore them, as they would not be around in another six months. The other older networks felt much the same way (Whittemore 1990). Yet, on 1 January 1982 they launched CNN2, which was then largely a series of half-hour news summaries. Then, on the first of January 1985 they launched CNN International. Throughout the 1980s there were start-up rough spots, and some referred to the initials as the Chicken Noodle Network (Whittemore 1990). That all ended on 16 January 1991. The first Persian Gulf War saw CNN beat and soar past all competition in its coverage. It alone stayed to cover Operation Desert Storm when the other American channels left Baghdad. The sensational coverage of the bombing through to the tank blitz that was the final battle was all live on CNN. Even the Pentagon admitted it was watching and gaining information from CNN. It now had prestige it had never possessed before. While virtually all the rest of the world's press had left Baghdad, CNN decided to stay with reporters Peter Arnett, Bernard Shaw, and John Holliman on the air, with camera crews capturing bombs and in-coming rockets plummeting onto the city, all live and only on CNN (Arnett 1994).

More than two decades later, however, CNN in the United States is in last place among the three major all-news channels. In a 26 June 2012 Nielsen Survey, Fox News was in first place, MSNBC in second and CNN in third, with a quarter of Fox's audience. These figures are consistent with ratings throughout 2012 (Bibel 2012). HLN, formerly CNN2, has dropped its half-hour news bulletins and now airs long-form popular culture programmes, along with legal and opinion programming. It was in a distant fourth place in the aforementioned ratings (Pew 2012).

But while U.S. publications are bemoaning the fact that CNN has its lowest ratings since before that first Gulf War—when there was a considerably smaller cable or satellite U.S. audience—and while certainly its parent company would like to see it more competitive in America, CNN is an international company whose operations outside the US are far more profitable than its domestic network (Steel 2012). CNN International is available in more than 265 million households in excess of 200 countries, with record growth in audience and revenue. CNN International accounts for more than twice the revenue of U.S. primetime advertisements. And despite many new and old international rivals, it topped Sky News in Europe for monthly reach according to Europe's Marketing and Media Survey and attracts 50% more viewers than its closest rival in Asia, BBC World News, according to Pan Asia Pacific Cross-Media survey (Steel and Edgecliffe-Johnson 2012).

As for its U.S. problems, one former executive says CNN faces what amounts to an identity crisis. There is, according to Politico, a struggle to make CNN interesting because of the rival allure of MSNBC, a liberal opinion/news channel and Fox News, a conservative opinion/news channel. While competitors capture the partisan audience, CNN, with its nonpartisan approach, according to Washington Bureau Chief Sam Feist, should not be compared to opinion channels MSNBC and Fox. They both have much less reporting and much more talking, debating and arguing. And Americans appear to prefer opinion rather than facts, so, in effect, like is not being compared with like (Cohen 2006).

Because it is the only dedicated 'news channel' in the United States, CNN will always be a hostage to the news year. In 2011 CNN's primetime ratings in America increased by 16%. It was the year of the Japanese tsunami, the beginning of the Arab Spring leading to the Egyptian Revolution, the killing of Osama bin Laden, the British royal wedding and the death of Gaddafi. Viewers tend to turn to serious news outlets when there are serious news events underway (Rather 2012).

Still, despite CNN's global success, with 10 specialized channels around the world, including Chile, India, Turkey, Japan and Germany, an all-Spanish service and its popular and highly profitable CNN International Channel with 30 foreign bureaux, it remains in third and thus last place in the ratings in the United States (Patten 2012).

The Fox News Channel is the highest rated of the three cable news channels in America (Pew 2012). Fox was launched in 1996, nine years after the Reagan Administration pushed the Federal Communications Commission to drop the Fairness Doctrine requiring balanced reporting, which would have never allowed the Fox News Channel to exist. Republican operative Roger Ailes was named News Chairman to run the new channel in 1996 and has been its only president. He at first seemed an odd choice, having no background in journalism. Cohen (2006, 53) observed that Ailes was the perfect choice to operate "a partisan propaganda outlet". He had engineered Nixon's two presidential victories as well as Reagan's and Bush Senior's. A senior Republican guru and Ailes business partner said that Ailes had two speeds, namely, attack and destroy (Cohen 2006).

Fox has recently signed its two biggest stars, with their number one and two primetime ratings on cable news, Bill O'Reilly and Sean Hannity, to new multiyear contracts that will take them through the 2016 elections. Fox boss Roger Ailes also has been re-signed for four more years (Stelter 2012a).

To much of the world, the "Foxification" of the news would not be controversial. In India, 81 all-news TV channels are aligned with a political party; in Italy, the three state TV channels often have partisan approaches; and the same practice is common in South America and in some European countries. But Americans grew up with a newspaper culture that tried to be objective and not to alienate advertisers, as did radio and television stations and networks. Plus, until it was axed, the Fairness Doctrine assured equal treatment of candidates. In Britain, the BBC has licence-fee holders from every political persuasion and yet it is still criticized by some for being allegedly too left-leaning. On the internet impartiality is the exception not the common practice. Still, Americans (and the British) have a long history of expecting balance and fairness and not partisan coverage in broadcast news. They still get that on the three major U.S. networks, with news programmes that must be non-partisan by tradition and with staffs dedicated to objectivity.

According to a 2012 Fairleigh Dickinson University study, the people who watch Fox News did much worse answering questions about domestic current events than people who watch no news at all. Those who watch MSNBC and CNN exclusively did better, and in both domestic and international coverage National Public Radio listeners had the highest number of correct answers (Beaujon 2012).

MSNBC started out intending to be neither an opinion channel nor to embrace a liberal agenda. It was launched on the fifteenth of July 1996. MSNBC was a partnership with Microsoft (hence the 'MS'), which invested $221 million for 50% ownership of the cable channel, with the other half owned by NBC. The two corporations would share the cost of a $200 million newsroom in Secaucus, New Jersey, for msnbc.com. NBC supplied the studio space with America's Talking, another NBC cable channel (Cohen 2006).

It was the first cable news channel owned and operated by one of the three original American television networks, each with their own news divisions. The programming was to be a mixture of news and opinions, with the latter ring-fenced from the news coverage. The channel went through a series of identity crises after its foundation, but eventually the Pew Project for Excellence in Journalism determined in 2007, after a special seven-year survey of cable news, that MSNBC had found its brand: politics (Pew 2007). In 2006 and 2007, MSNBC's political-centric and liberal news formula resulted in a 61% ratings increase. Key to its new popularity was Keith Olbermann. Jeff Cohen, whom he asked to join him in 2002 on a new evening issues-oriented programme on MSNBC, considered Olbermann to be America's best-liked liberal. The programme was scheduled to go head-to-head with Bill O'Reilly, Fox's highest rated show. The show would be partisan and fiery, but from the opposite viewpoint of Fox. By 2007, *The New York Times, Politico* and the *Washington Post* all ran articles noting that MSNBC was left-leaning and that Olbermann was the leading figure on the channel and known for his liberalism. Subsequently, Rachel Maddow's became the hottest show, at least for one night on cable news, beating Fox and CNN in the third week of September 2012. The Pew survey shows that MSNBC is a solid second in the ratings, well ahead of CNN (Pew 2011, 2012).

Former Democrat President Bill Clinton told *Esquire Magazine* in January 2012 that MSNBC has become "our Fox". MSNBC provides some solid journalism and has seasoned NBC correspondents to provide independent reporting. It does not report outright falsehoods to underpin its liberal agenda. It still has a long way to go to match Fox's concept that you do not let the facts get in the way of a good story if that helps the American right wing, or the Republican Party. Nonetheless, increasingly MSNBC sees the news through good and evil left lenses. The Democrats-good and the Republicans-bad. MSNBC's most recent hire, the Reverend Al Sharpton, a long-time civil rights leader, has been a radio talk show host but never a journalist, and in an interview on CBS's *60 Minutes*, Sharpton said he had decided on his new television programme not to criticize the president about anything (Greenwald 2012).

Solid broadcast journalism still exists in America: on *60 Minutes* on CBS, PBS won nine Emmys for documentaries in 2012; ABC and CBS won seven Emmys each and NBC three, while CNN won two (Weprin 2012). There are insightful, sometimes courageous reports on several of these American networks or channels every week.

But, especially on cable news, the bulk of the time, they often seem to have missed the guidance offered by one of the most accomplished reporters in the last half century, Robert Woodward: "When you practice reporting for as long as I have, you keep yourself at a distance from True Believers—either conservatives or liberals or Democrats or Republicans" (Woodward 2005).

This is the aim of one daily news bulletin in America. It is also one of the most award-winning news broadcasts in the United States, known now as the Newshour on PBS. This is presented today by a variety of journalists, primarily Gwen Ifill and Judy Woodruff and also Hari Sreenivasan, Ray Suarez and Margaret Warner. Unlike its commercial competition, it is an hour long, and stories are not compressed into 90 seconds but run the length they require, which also means there are not the three-second soundbites often seen on commercial TV news. The programme is a part of Jim Lehrer Productions, and Lehrer still appears occasionally on Newshour. The format is different than the other American news broadcasts, too. The lead story is covered in depth, followed by a news summary of the headlines around the world, then several longer news segments each running 6–12 minutes. Nielsen ratings indicate that about 2.7 million viewers tune in nightly (WETA 2013).

Over the years, like all newscasts, PBS's hour of news has been accused of bias. However, Dr Tim Groseclose, UCLA professor of political science, has evaluated many news programmes and how they fall on a liberal-conservative continuum, and he concluded that PBS's *NewsHour* is the most centrist and objective news bulletin on U.S. television (Groseclose 2012).

LOCAL TELEVISION NEWS IN THE UNITED STATES

The 1970s saw an unfortunate convergence of commercially persuasive local news consultants' advocacy of an emphasis on softer news with the emergence of new technological developments that greatly facilitated this. Videotape replaced film in the early 1970s, and then came transmission vans from which stories could be microwaved back to the stations. Hours were saved from the old routine of driving back to the television newsroom and waiting for film to be developed. Sony developed 3/4-inch tape in 20-minute cassettes. RCA and Ikegami had shoulder-borne video cameras, and video editing machines became ever more sophisticated. ENG, electronic news-gathering, had arrived. By 1975, 65% of the local stations in the United States had shifted to ENG (Paterson 2012). The advent of tape, reusable and with sharper pictures, made stations want enhanced visual stories. Now the cost of shooting after the equipment was purchased was negligible. Grue-some car accidents, or major fires, provided eye-popping visuals and could be shown live during a news bulletin. "The more visual the better" became the mindset of many American assignment editors (Kurtz 2007).

While many local stations still were doing half-hour evening news bul-letins in the early 1970s, by the 1980s an hour was common, and then in large markets that spread to two hours. In the next decade, some local news departments were doing six hours a day (Paterson 2012).

The new expanded news hours and the ability to cover many more sto-ries more quickly began a slow but steady process of trivialisation of what constituted a news story. Critics blame the consultants that first appeared in the early 1970s, and some station managers praise them, for spreading the dumbing down of news, or increasing the ratings. McHugh & Hoffman in McLean, Virginia, Frank Magid Associates in Marion, Iowa and Audience Research & Development in Dallas had clients in most major and middle-sized markets in America (Paterson 2012). They do not accept the dumbing-down premise. However, Frank Graham of McHugh & Hoffman admits that in the 1970s there was a formulaic approach to many consultants' re-vamping of news programmes, as they considered what they recommended was what people truly wanted as TV news (Paterson 2012).

When compared with other news media, print or even radio, local televi-sion news was once a constant, entrenched in Americans' daily lives. It was highly competitive and viewers had strong opinions on their most trusted news presenters. The ownership was either local or a group with a long-standing reputation in the community. Today, whatever the consultants may say, they have brought sameness to a lot of news from station to station and from city to city.

In turn, ENG and its ability to quickly get video on the air changed the news values of television news, most severely at the local level in America. Quality journalism was replaced all too often with quantity journalism. Minor fires or accidents trumped a thoughtful piece on the death of a city centre's commerce. One took 15 minutes to shoot and a reporter a few min-utes to jot some notes on a pad and then deliver an account, live, of a grease fire at a franchise food outlet before it had opened for business. The other story, however, would involve 'legwork', such as shooting video of closed shops, tracking down the owners for an interview about their uncertain fu-ture and vanished incomes, along with talking to shopping centre managers and city council members about their plans to counter the malls that had taken their customers. Then a reporter would have to go over the tape with an editor, select the soundbites and then carefully write a complicated story that wound in the current local and national economic conditions. More likely now a full day ends instead with a half-dozen short, highly visual secondary events in the community that are 'snappy' and are often taken for far greater significance than they deserve (Paterson 2012).

Most stations with hours to fill rely on what Paterson (2012) calls 'passive discovery' to fill their news day. Someone constantly listening to police and fire department scanners, wire service supplied stories, press conferences and rewriting press releases to pictures is much more time-filling and productive on the local news assembly line than allocating too many reporters to actively discover or uncover news. Plus, there is now SNG—Satellite News Gathering—with the proliferation of communications satellites and new efficient frequency bands, stories can be fed by satellite back to the stations, creating regional newsgathering capabilities. In many instances, in large markets this can be extremely useful. But it is also another supplier of a plethora of video that crowds out traditional 'grunt reporting' that involves getting well-embedded in a community you are supposed to be serving (Paterson 2012).

Other stations own, or have easy access to, a helicopter and will use them for hours of breaking news, or within a news bulletin to follow a runaway vehicle pursued by the police down motorways, side streets and then perhaps even in the wrong direction back to a main highway.

In many cases stations have gone to the VJ model, as well—the 'one-man-band' where the reporter shoots and reports the story. It saves money, is better than having no coverage, but again can encourage visual rather than editorial content. However, some VJs are very good at both and will no doubt be playing an increasing role in broadcast news (Paterson 2012).

The most ominous current development is a rapidly growing phenomenon of news sharing—stations providing content with their competitors. According to a Radio and Television and Digital News/Hofstra University survey, more than one-quarter of all U.S. TV stations provide news for another local station, or one nearby. This is rationalised on the grounds that stations need to pool their resources because they have increased the amount of news time presented daily. Yet the expectation originally was that the extra hours, be they 4–10 in the morning, or 4–6:30 in the evening, would allow for the provision of more original content. A study by the University of Delaware found that stations in eight markets with shared services agreements did not deliver unique content, and instead, two stations even have overlapping content, which is script and video. The amount of sharing has been going up steadily since 2009. At the same time, almost a quarter of all local stations air no news at all (Pew 2012, 19).

The year before, when a record was set for mergers and acquisitions, NBC and Fox, two ardent cable news channel foes, announced a local television news-sharing agreement aimed at reducing the number of reporters, trucks and helicopters assigned to cover major events. This announcement in November 2008 followed a test in May of the two networks' stations in

Philadelphia, which resulted in an agreement to run a joint assignment desk for the NBC and Fox local stations in the fifth largest metropolitan area in the United States. The agreement only covered video—the stations were to prepare their own stories. Then it would be implemented in Los Angeles, Chicago, New York and Washington. It was, after all, 2008, when the world economy was in a spiral toward recession or worse. More than a third of the stations in the 150 largest markets had cut their staffs in the first quarter of the year (Papper 2008).

Four years later, *New York Times* reporter Brian Stelter went to visit San Angelo, Texas, population 93,000. He found that if you call a reporter at the CBS station in town, the anchorman from the NBC station may return your call. While separately owned, they share one newsroom, the same news video and the exact same scripts for their nightly presenters going head-to-head at the same time on two different channels. The programmes are presented from two side-by-side studios. The same kind of sharing goes on, Stelter found, in dozens of other cities. In Honolulu the NBC and CBS stations broadcast the same morning show. In Burlington, Vermont, the Fox and ABC stations sometimes share anchors. Critics in these areas and elsewhere charge that there are fewer and fewer reporters covering the news (Stelter 2012b).

This phenomenon receives very little national attention. The Federal Communications Commission (FCC) claims to be interested, but has in recent years agreed to tear up most of the rules that encouraged diversity in the broadcast sector. Meanwhile, news staffs have been greatly reduced by the corporate ownerships, news-sharing is growing in popularity as a means of covering for this and revenue and audience share are dwindling. There was a time when most Americans could tell you the names of the major anchors on the three or more local evening news programmes. That is far less likely today (Kurtz 2007).

U.S. local news bulletins in the twenty-first century have suffered 30 years of decline in audience and revenue, which in 2011 was very close to a 15-year low. In 1980 a top local station could get a 12 rating and a 20 share, meaning that 20% of viewers watching television were watching that newscast. In 2011 a top rated local station in some markets would have 7% of the viewers. These numbers are much the same for the network news that follows local news (Pew 2012).

Surveys often report that local news is a primary source of news to viewers in some markets (Pew 2012). Yet there are in America three all-news, 24-hour news channels, the Weather Channel and a variety of sports networks to supply much of the information that would also be on the local news, especially any major local news story, any threatening weather and sports scores. In essence, any major local news in middle to large markets is now available 24 hours a day elsewhere (Paterson 2012).

Meanwhile, the overall viewing competition is daunting, with 90% of American households subscribing to cable or satellite systems (Nielsen

2011). There are often hundreds of channels on cable, and the new Verizon FiOS has more than 2,000 channels.

Local stations suffer financially from the fact that network-affiliated local channels must give a goodly portion of their share of the cable or satellite subscription fee back to their network. According to Nexstar Broadcasting, the local stations get 40% of the viewers (watching network or syndicated programming) and end up with 5% of the revenue (Pew 2012).

At the same time local television in America, with few exceptions, has not been successful in the multiplatform journalism world of today. Only 6% of the American public say they rely on a station's web site for weather, while 5% said they look at the local station web site for breaking news and only 3% for local or political news (Pew 2012, 5).

Another decisive factor in the fortunes of local television news has been significant changes by the FCC, which have relaxed ownership rules for television stations (FCC 2011). Today, the deregulation of broadcasting begun under the Reagan administration has reached a point where there is no limit on the number of TV stations any company can own in the United States, so long as the "national audience reach" is not more than 39% of all American TV households (Sophos 1990; FCC 2011). This has opened the door wide for the further expansion of corporate dominance of the U.S. television market.

The company with the largest advertising revenue of television stations in the United States in 2012 is Fox, which owns 27 local stations in 18 cities, including more than 1 in 9 of those markets reaching 36.7% of the households in the country. Second is CBS, with 30 stations with more than 1 station in 10 cities and with just under the maximum coverage of 38.5%. It is followed by NBC, which owns 26.6%, 10 of which are in the same city, and then ABC is in fourth place with 8 stations in 8 cities covering 22%. The fifth largest, Tribune Broadcasting, owns 23 stations in 18 cities with 35.5% coverage. Its largest network connections are the 13 affiliates of the CW Network, a joint venture of CBS, Paramount and Warner Brothers that specialises in programmes for viewers aged 18–34. Seven are affiliated with Fox, one with ABC and one is independent (McAvoy 2012).

Stations owned by the four major networks in the United States, then, are the four largest stations in terms of advertising revenue. NBC also owns the Spanish language network Telemondo, which is 21st on the list of the 30 largest station owners' groups, with 15 stations in 15 cities and advertising revenue of $245 million. Because of the language differentiation, it is not included in the overall NBC Universal total. If it was it would beat CBS by a slim margin and then make NBC the second largest broadcaster in the country. However, Telemondo trails America's dominant Spanish network: Univision is by far the leader among the two U.S. Spanish language networks. It owns 62 stations—more than one in 13 markets. It is owned by a variety of financial capital and entertainment firms (McAvoy 2012).

The Spanish news programmes aside, stations now owned by large media conglomerates have changed local television profoundly, with the previously outlined switches to news sharing arrangements, downsizings, loss of local focus, a continuing preference for the snappy and the visual over serious quality hard news content and (arguably) and at least partially consequent loss of audience and revenue. The year 2006 was the high point for acquisitions and mergers, where various largely mega-media conglomerates spent $518 million buying stations or companies that owned groups of stations (Pew 2012, 13; Paterson 2012). In terms of plurality, diversity of viewpoints and original hard news material, this has not been a good era for American local television, and the public are being poorly served in terms of the needs of a participatory democracy set out in chapter one.

RADIO NEWS IN THE UNITED STATES

As radio stations approach their 100th anniversary in the United States, the industry has gone from scratchy, primitive signals to crisp reception from signals sent by satellites orbiting the earth.

There are around 14,000 AM and FM radio stations in the country, with Clear Channel Communications being the largest single owner, with 1,200 stations. CBS Radio owns 127 stations, but these include most of the all-news stations in the United States (BBC Monitoring 2012).

Each radio station is licensed to a community, but the public service obligations required to serve those cities and towns have been drastically reduced over the years. Also, while at one point the number of radio stations any one company could own was limited to five in some areas, it is now unlimited in the smallest local markets, as long as one company does not own enough stations to amount to 50% of the audience of the market area (FCC 2011).

The most popular radio format in the United States is country music, followed closely by what is called news/talk, which is mainly talk with perhaps news on the hour for five minutes from the AP, CBS, ABC, ARN, Fox, amongst others, including, in many large cities, the BBC. Larger cities also augment these networks with some local news during the day (Radio Advertising Bureau 2012).

The all-news format was first tried in 1959 on KFAX San Francisco. However, it did not last long and was considered a failure. Several other attempts were tried, but the format only really became successful on Westinghouse's 1010 WINS New York, beginning in April 1965. It worked on half-hour cycles, mixing local with national and world news. It had an array of field reporters, and as the company switched its stations KYW in Philadelphia and KFWB in Los Angeles to the format, they opened their own Washington bureau. CBS copied the concept in New York, Chicago and Los Angeles.

CBS purchased the Westinghouse stations so, in New York, the company now has two all-news stations operating in one market (Stout 1995).

The highly respected NPR, formerly called National Public Radio, is non-commercial. Without advertisements, it is privately and publicly funded and creates and distributes news and cultural programmes to a network of 975 stations. Member stations must be non-commercial, have at least five employees and not be designed solely to further religious broadcasting philosophy, or for distance learning programming (NPR 2013a). Its funding comes from foundations or business entities, contributions and sponsorships. Its two daily news programmes are *Morning Edition* and in the afternoon *All Things Considered* (NPR 2013b, 2013c).

According to the Washington Post, while NPR does not subscribe to the Arbitron ratings service, public stations do show up in their diary and meter ratings, and in 2009 almost 21 million listeners tuned in to NPR each week (Farhi 2009). NPR claims a weekly audience of 26 million in 2013 (NPR 2013d). In a Harris survey in 2005, NPR was considered the most trusted source of news in America (Eggerton 2005).

For 22 million Americans the old radio in the kitchen or car is a thing of the past. They tune in to commercial-free satellite radio SiriusXM, with its more than 140 channels of music, sports, entertainment, comedy, talk, weather and news in its premier package (SiriusXM 2013). In the early 1990s Sirius and XM began programming as separate satellite radio services and then merged in 2008. Sirius hired former CEO of CBS Mel Karmazin in 2004 to turn around the management of the company, which was losing $670 million a year. Karmazin oversaw the merger and, in April 2012, said he was expecting $700 million profit with annual revenue growing in eight years to $3 billion (Bercovici 2012a). Then, six months later, as Liberty Media had been steadily increasing its stake in the ownership of SiriusXM Radio, the company announced that Karmazin would step down as CEO on 1 February 2013, at the expiration of his contract. He once claimed he was one of the most underpaid executives in America, but *Forbes Magazine* concluded that, despite the company's rapid growth, Karmazin's compensation was too high compared to the value added to the shareholders during his reign (Bercovici 2012b). Nonetheless, the growth in SiriusXM is still expected to be three-quarters of new sets/listeners a year.

At the same time as radio from space, standard radio and television are as easily portable on tablets and smart phones. Add to that digital newspaper and magazine editions, and millions of Americans have daily access to more news media on their person daily in the digital age than they would ever have purchased perhaps in months in analogue times. How much news they actually read, watch or listen to may or may not have changed. The quality may have diminished across a large range of outlets, yet, its availability is now truly virtually everywhere in the USA. As American actress Grace Kelly once told Frank Sinatra, the freedom of the press works in such a way that there is not much freedom from it (as recounted to the author by Burt Lancaster in 1988).

THE FUTURE AND NEWS QUALITY ACROSS
AMERICAN TELEVISION AND RADIO

At the level of television network news, the worrying headline is that, in a corporatised, profit-driven media market, only NBC news is profitable. While the overall news audience for the networks remains considerable at more than 22 million, they have lost in excess of half of their viewers over the last 30 years. Furthermore, the decline has not halted—current evidence shows that the younger audience is watching less television news than their predecessors (Paterson 2007), and if that habit feeds through into their middle age and beyond and is passed on to their children, it is unlikely that all three networks will remain in business for hard news. Even if they do, the question remains, what will be the quality level of the hard news? There has already been a serious decline. In 1977 CBS News was the only one of the three networks that chose not to lead its broadcast with the death of Elvis Presley. The management at the time was very proud of that decision. Today it would be unthinkable.

As demonstrated earlier, American TV began to go toward more soft news when large national consultancy firms gained success in the 1970s with local stations, offering formulaic remedies for ratings woes. "In the '70s and '80s there was a generalization by a lot of consultants about what people wanted as TV news" (Prato 1993). The consultants recommended less hard news by requiring more coverage of consumer and 'Joe-6 Pack' news-you-can-use.

At the network level, ownership had changed hands from founding families to international corporations. Network news was no longer an acceptable loss leader. 'News light' was working locally, so it was inevitable it would creep into the national bulletins as well. At the same time the national audience was fragmented first by cable and then by satellite TV and, ultimately and perhaps fatally, by the internet. The saving grace in quality terms is that the three networks remain committed to non-partisan news programmes as a traditional part of their brands. However, in news content terms they now perform relatively poorly overall compared to public service news, as will be seen in the following discussion. The worry for the future must be that if they continue to lose audience share, they will employ the same corporate response as in previous years—further 'downsizings' of the news staff—and that their quality levels and the range of coverage will decline further in consequence—unless, as seems very unlikely, the regulatory framework is changed in a way that mitigates corporate fixation on the bottom line and the tendency to regard news as a "product" that ultimately must pay its way like everything else.

Another worrying development for some has been the growth of the opinion news channels in the form of Fox and MSNBC and the disturbing figures about the awareness levels of Fox viewers reported earlier. On the basis of these, then in terms of the journalism quality requirements set out in chapter one, Fox is failing significantly with regard to the quality of news provision required for a participatory democracy. For the future, should the role of opinion news channels continue to grow and television remain the primary source of news for the U.S. audience, the implications from a democratic point of view are highly negative.

At the local level, the loss of much unique original local content, particularly with regard to governance and politics, is again highly negative from the viewpoint of the requirements of a participatory democracy.

Having raised all of these concerns, however, it is necessary to bear in mind also that American quality television hard news provision is underpinned by PBS and, on cable, by CNN. While CNN is only third in popularity among the cable channels and PBS remains a minority interest, they do provide more high quality news content than any of the other channels for those who want to access them. The PBS *NewsHour*, for example, provided over a third more coverage of international news proportionally in 2011 than "the rest of the media overall, including all other forms of television news (cable, morning and evening network news). In all, 40% of the time on *NewsHour* was devoted to foreign events and U.S. foreign policy compared with 28% of the media sample generally: 23% on cable news, 24% on network morning news, and 24% on network evening broadcasts" (Guskin and Rosenstiel 2012). Proportionally, *NewsHour* devoted a third more of its time covering government than the evening newscasts on the commercial networks (Guskin and Rosentiel 2012). PBS's statement of Editorial Standards and Policies (PBS 2012) dovetails with most of the requirements for high quality hard news set down in chapter one.

But, to return to a previous point, this is coverage that is provided for those who want to access it. If people choose not to take advantage of the service provided, then ultimately that is their responsibility. The same is true for CNN. It attempts to provide the balance and the detail that its two cable competitors do not. If people choose to use Fox instead of CNN, then, in terms of the requirements for a participatory democracy, they are in effect disadvantaging themselves, although greatly contributing to the financial health of Rupert Murdoch's media empire in the process.

So, in summary, the extent to which high-quality television hard news provision is likely to be available to the American public of the future is dependent on two things. First, the presence or absence of a regulatory framework that legislates for quality in, for example, the manner suggested previously with regard to the networks. The current balance of political attitudes in Washington and the deregulatory trend of recent years makes 'absence' more likely than 'presence'. Second: audience choice. High quality television news is available to the American audience and will remain so for as long as its current funding structures remain in place and its audience is of at least the minimal level necessary to justify them doing so. If viewers choose not to access it then that ultimately is their democratic right, although many would question the level of citizen responsibility demonstrated by such a choice.

Space allows only a brief analysis of quality U.S. radio news provision. First, there is good news. By 2014 it is estimated that total radio revenues will return to the 6% annual growth rate seen in 2010. "Broadcast stations will still dominate, but most of that growth will come from new technology in online and mobile services" (Santhanam, Mitchell, and Rosenstiel 2012). However, outside that silver lining there are several clouds. As pointed out earlier, there has been a loss of some of the depth of public service provision as regulations affecting, for example, local news provision, have been loosened significantly. Less locally produced local news is available than used to be the case, although the situation improves in the larger cities. With more than 14,000 stations across the country, it is impossible to generalise about the quality of commercial radio in the United States, but, as pointed out previously, the most popular news format is within news/talk formats and with, in many cases, short, five minute hourly bulletins, does not have the provision for in-depth news that the kind of participatory democracy outlined in chapter one requires. However, on the upside, as in the case of television, high-quality news provision is available on radio for those who want it, for example, via NPR. On the basis of the statistics cited previously, around 26 million Americans take advantage of this weekly. Furthermore, the UK high-quality news provider, the BBC, is also available in many cities.

So, ultimately, the extent to which high-quality radio hard news is likely to be available to the American public of the future is dependent on the same two factors as for television. There is no reason for the U.S. public not to have high quality radio news available to them now, or within the foreseeable future, other than their own choice. As long as NPR retains respectable audience levels, it is unlikely that its funders and sponsors will go away. It will retain the status of a public good that is worth supporting, or being associated with for image purposes, or whatever. At the moment, while there is evidence, cited previously, that many young people are accessing hard news less, there is no visible basis within that for assuming that the audience for radio is going to 'fall off a cliff'. So, for the moment at least, the future of high quality American hard news remains firmly in the hands of the American public. If they want it, it is there and looks likely to remain so. The only reason for them not having it is their own choice. For those who want them there are very fine television and radio news services available to everyone in the United States. In this sense at least, news provision within these two formats meets the requirements of the kind of participatory democracy set down in chapter one. The commercial news sector, however, despite pockets of continuing quality provision within outlets such as CBS, is a much less impressive picture overall, and that is the worrying part of the equation.

REFERENCES

Academy of Television Arts and Sciences. 2012. "TV History." Accessed 27 January 2013. http://www.emmytvlegends.org/resources/tv-history.

Arnett, Peter. 1994. *Live from the Battlefield: From Vietnam to Baghdad, 35 Years in the World's War Zones.* New York: Simon & Schuster.

BBC Monitoring. 2012. "United States Media." Accessed 1 December 2012. http://www.bbc.co.uk/news/world-us-canada-16757497.

Beaujon, Andrew. 2012. "Survey: NPR's Listeners Best-Informed, Fox Viewers Worst-Informed." Poynter Institute, 23 May. http://www.poynter.org/latest-news/mediawire/174826/survey-nprs-listeners-best-informed-fox-news-viewers-worst-informed/.

Bercovici, Jeff. 2012a. "SiriusXM's Mel Karmazin: I'm One of the Most Under-paid Executives in the History of Executive Payment." *Forbes Magazine*, 2 April.

Bercovici, Jeff. 2012b. "Mel Karmazin Stepping Down As SiriusXM CEO." *Forbes Magazine*, September 23.

Bibel, Sara. 2012. "Cable News Ratings for Saturday–Sunday, June 23–24 2012." *TV By The Numbers*, 26 June. http://tvbythenumbers.zap2it.com/2012/06/26/cable-news-ratings-for-saturday-sunday-june-23–24–2012/139303/.

Cohen, Jeff. 2006. *Cable News Confidential: My Misadventures in Corporate Media.* Sausalito: Polipoint.

Eggerton, John. 2005. "Survey Says: Noncom News Most Trusted." *Broadcasting & Cable Magazine*, 10 November.

Farhi, Paul. 2009. "Good News for NPR: Its Most Listeners Ever." *Washington Post*, 24 March.

Federal Communications Commission. 2011. *Review of the Broadcast Ownership Rules*, 9 May. http://www.fcc.gov/guides/review-broadcast-ownership-rules.

Fenton, Tom. 2005. *Bad News: The Decline of Reporting, the Business of News and the Danger to Us All.* New York: Harper Collins.

Foerstel, Herbert N. 1998. *From Watergate to Monicagate: Ten Controversies in Modern Journalism and Media.* Westport, CT: Greenwood.

Greenwald, Glenn. 2012. "MSNBC Hosts Mimics Fox News' Bullying Jingoism." *Guardian*: Comment is Free blog, 24 August. http://www.guardian.co.uk/commentisfree/2012/aug/24/msnbc-host-mimics-fox-news.

Groseclose, Tim. 2012. *Left Turn: How Liberal Media Bias Distorts the American Mind.* New York: St Martin's Press.

Guskin, Emily, and Tom Rosenstiel. 2012. "Network News: The Pace of Change Accelerates." In *The State of the News Media 2012*, Pew Research Center's Project for Excellence in Journalism. Accessed 28 January 2013. http://stateofthemedia.org/2012/network-news-the-pace-of-change-accelerates/.

Kurtz, Howard. 2007. *Reality Show: Inside the Last Great Television News War.* New York: Free Press.

McAvoy, Kim. 2012. "Fox is TV's New Station Group Leader." *TVNewscheck.com*, 15 April. http://www.tvnewscheck.com/article/58737/fox-is-tvs-new-station-group-leader.

Nielsen. 2012. "Cross-Platform Report Q3 2011." http://www.nielsen.com/us/en/insights/reports-downloads/2012/cross-platform-report-q3–2011.html

NPR. 2013a. "About NPR: Our Mission, Vision, and Goals." Accessed 28 January 2013. http://www.npr.org/about/aboutnpr/mission.html.

NPR. 2013b. "Programs: Morning Edition." Accessed 29 January 2013. http://www.npr.org/programs/morning-edition/.

NPR. 2013c. "Programs: All Things Considered." Accessed 29 January 2013. http://www.npr.org/programs/all-things-considered/.

NPR. 2013d. "About NPR: Audience." Accessed 28 January 2013. http://www.npr
.org/about/aboutnpr/audience.html.

Papper, Bob. 2008. "The Real Story of TV News Staffing and Other Numbers for
TV and Radio in 2008: RTNDA/Hofstra University Survey 2008." Accessed 29
January 2013. www.rtdna.org/uploads/files/08survey.pdf.

Paterson, Chris. 2012. "News, Local and Regional." In *Encyclopedia of TV*.
Museum of Broadcast Communications. Accessed 28 January 2013. http://www
.museum.tv/eotvsection.php?entrycode=newslocala.

Paterson, Thomas E. 2007. *Young People and News*. Cambridge, MA: Joan
Shorenstein Center on the Press, Politics and Public Policy.

Patten, Dominic. 2012. "Fox News Tops 2012 Cable News Network Ratings;
MSNBC Up Big." *Deadline.com*, 13 December. http://www.deadline.com/2012/12/
fox-news-2012-cable-news-networks-tv-ratings-msnbc-cnn/.

PBS. 2012. "PBS Editorial Standards and Policies." Accessed 29 January 2013.
http://www-tc.pbs.org/about/media/about/cms_page_media/35/PBS%20Editorial%
20Standards%20and%20Policies.pdf

Pew Research Center's Project for Excellence in Journalism. 2007. "Cable TV:
Introduction, Public Attitudes." In *The State of the News Media 2007*. http://
stateofthemedia.org/2007/cable-tv-intro/public-attitude/.

Pew Research Center's Project for Excellence in Journalism. 2011. *The State of the
News Media 2011*. http://stateofthemedia.org/overview-2011/.

Pew Research Center's Project for Excellence in Journalism. 2012. *The State of the
News Media 2012*. http://stateofthemedia.org/.

Prato, Lou. 1993. "Don't Bash Consultants For Tabloid TV News." *American Journalism Review*, November.

Radio Advertising Bureau. 2012. "Why Radio Fact Sheet: Radio Format Analysis." Accessed 28 January 2013. http://www.rab.com/public/marketingGuide/
DataSheet.cfm?id=6.

Rather, Dan. 2012. *Rather Outspoken: My Life in the News*. New York: Grand
Central.

Santhanam, Laura Houston, Amy Mitchell, and Tom Rosenstiel. 2012. "Audio:
How Far Will Digital Go?" In *The State of the News Media 2012*. Accessed 28
January 2013. http://stateofthemedia.org/2012/audio-how-far-will-digital-go/.

SiriusXM. 2013. "What is SiriusXM?" Accessed 29 January 2013. http://www
.siriusxm.com/whatissiriusxm.

Sophos, Marc. 1990. "The Public Interest, Convenience or Necessity: A Dead Standard in the Era of Broadcast Deregulation?" *Pace Law Review* 10: 691–695.

Steel, Emily. 2012. "Former NBC Chief to Head CNN." *Financial Times*, 29 November.
http://www.ft.com/cms/s/0/ebb153fa-3a46-11e2-baac-00144feabdc0.html
#axzz2TSgiwpv9.

Stelter, Brian. 2010. "Job Cuts at ABC Leave Workers Stunned and Downcast."
New York Times, 30 April.

Stelter, Brian. 2012a. "Fox News is Set to Renew O'Reilly and Hannity Through
2016 Elections." *New York Times*, 19 April.

Stelter, Brian. 2012b. "You Can Change the Channel, Local News is the Same."
New York Times, 28 May.

Stewart, Christopher S., and Arian Campo-Flores. 2012. "Univision, ABC to Start
News Channel—in English." *Wall Street Journal*, 7 May.

Stout, David. 1995. "The Media Business: The Radio Market; Merger Not Expected
to End a Sharp New York Rivalry." *New York Times*, 2 August.

Weprin, Alex. 2012. "CBS News Leads the Way in 2012 News and Doc Emmy
Nominations." *MediaBistro*, 12 July. http://www.mediabistro.com/tvnewser/
cbs-news-leads-the-way-in-2012-news-and-doc-emmy-nominations_b137347.

WETA. 2013. "PBS NewsHour: Backgrounder." Accessed 28 January 2013. http:// www.weta.org/about/press/kits/627/additional/39425.

Whittemore, Hank. 1990. *CNN, The Inside Story: How a Band of Mavericks Changed the Face of Television News.* New York: Little Brown.

Woodward, Bob. 2005. "PBS: Frontline: Why America Hates the Press: Interview with Bob Woodward." Accessed 28 January 2013. http://www.pbs.org/wgbh/ pages/frontline/shows/press/interviews/woody2.html.

9 How the Audience Saved UK Broadcast Journalism

Deborah Robinson and Andrew Hobbs

INTRODUCTION

This chapter argues that UK TV news and current affairs are currently in rude health, with sound prospects for the short to medium term. The situation for radio is more mixed. As far as TV is concerned, a new respect for the audience has led to high-quality, imaginatively crafted output, still watched by millions, despite a growing choice of TV channels and other media devices—TV is the main source of news for 74% of the UK population; the internet is the main source for only 7% (Foster 2011, 15). We use three case studies to demonstrate how weighty issues such as regulation of private health care and globalisation can be intelligently presented in ways that are still attractive to mass audiences and in line with the understanding of quality set down in chapter one. Our conclusions are based on a review of the academic literature, interviews with seven senior broadcasters across TV and radio, BBC, ITN and Sky News and our own focus group research.

Before introducing the case studies, it is useful to sketch the broad picture of UK news and current affairs output, to quantify its audiences, and to demonstrate how broadcasters have become more responsive to their audience.

Millions continue to participate in the "appointment viewing" of the national and regional news bulletins broadcast by the five main TV channels: BBC1, BBC2, ITV1, Channel 4 and Channel 5. The quantity of national news and current affairs output on television has remained stable since 2000 and is now increasing (Ofcom 2011a). In addition, there are two 24-hour news channels: the BBC News Channel and Sky News. However, multichannel news output fell by almost a third (31%) between 2010 and 2011 (Ofcom 2011a, 142). Radio news is dominated by the BBC, which produces more than 160 bulletins per day across its national networks (Luscombe 2009, 115), plus a significant amount of local news on its six stations in Scotland, Wales and Northern Ireland and 40 local stations. The 301 commercial radio stations (three national, the remainder local), with a few exceptions, provide much less news than BBC stations, broadcasting an average weekly total of 180 minutes of local news and 120 minutes of national news (Radio Centre 2011, 9), with an emphasis on "soft" entertainment and celebrity stories (House of Lords 2008, 28). All commercial stations, which have greatly reduced their news teams over the last decade, receive their national and international news from Independent Radio News, currently supplied by Sky News Radio. However, a minority of local commercial stations maintain a commitment to high-quality news and continue to win Sony Awards (the most prestigious radio industry awards) for news and documentaries, and to go beyond their public service commitments, as when Lakeland Radio suspended normal programming in June 2010 to report on the Derrick Bird shootings and advise listeners on their safety (Radio Centre 2011, 44). Commercial radio news is regulated by Ofcom, and varying commitments to news are included in each station's licence.

Broadcasters express surprise that viewing figures have either remained steady or declined only slightly on the five main television channels, despite growing competition from the internet and new devices such as tablets and smartphones. "We are getting mass audiences for television news in a way we didn't expect", said Helen Boaden, BBC Director of News, in an interview for the book. Viewing trends across all news bulletins on the five main channels are either stable or slightly down (see Table 9.1). Audiences for the two 24-hour channels are small but growing: audience share for the BBC News

Table 9.1 Average audiences to news programmes 2011/2021, millions

	2010–11	2011–12
	Breakfast news	
BBC1	1.5	1.5
ITV1/Daybreak	0.7	0.7
	Lunchtime news	
BBC1	2.6	2.6
ITV	1	0.9
	Early evening network news	
BBC1	4.4	4.3
ITV1	3.3	3.2
Channel 4	0.8	0.7
Channel 5	0.7	0.7
	Early evening regional news	
BBC1	5.5	5.4
ITV1	3.2	3.2
	Late night news (10pm)	
BBC1	4.4	4.4
ITV1	2.3	2.2

Source: BBC Trust 2012: pt 2: 2-15.

Channel doubled between 2004 and 2011, from 0.6% to 1.2%, overtaking Sky News, whose share rose more modestly from 0.6% to 0.7% (Ofcom 2012a, 163, 167). Audiences for the BBC Parliament channel are also growing so that it now reaches more than 1% of viewers (BBC Trust 2012a).

Radio news remains popular. Of the adult population, 66% listen to BBC stations, with commercial radio not far behind at 63% (RAJAR September 2012). Radio 4's *Today* peaked at 7.2 million listeners a week in 2011/12, a million more than five years earlier (BBC 2012c, pt 1, 15)—but slightly less than the 8 million listeners to the 8am weekday bulletin on commercial radio (Ryley interview 2012). Audiences for the BBC's 40 local radio stations, which carry a great deal of local news, have been growing since 2009 after a long period of decline. Some 7.4 million people in England tune in to BBC local radio each week, or 17.3% of adults (BBC Trust 2012b, 3).

Increased choice has led to less audience fragmentation than broadcasters such as Boaden feared. "We never thought that at this point we'd be getting the kind of audiences that we get for the ten o'clock news 4–5 million. We thought that we'd be down to one or two million by now" (Boaden interview 2012). The main TV channels have seen only small declines in their news audiences, while 24-hour news channels attract relatively few viewers, and even online, consumers tend to use three or fewer trusted news brands per week (Newman 2012, 16). Yet, as Egglestone noted in an earlier chapter, broadcasters are still concerned that this fragmentation will continue, particularly among young audiences. "The long-term and still-to-be-answered question is whether the current young heavy users of digital media and rejecters of TV news will, like the generations before them, learn to love catching up on the day's events in front of the TV or will they become life-long rejecters of TV news" (Purvis 2010). Only one of our interviewees was more positive, Andrew Hawken of Sky, whose "analytics" tell him that the same individuals use Sky News across different platforms during the day. It may be that his measurement methods are more accurate, or perhaps the Sky News audience are atypical "news junkies" (Barnett, Ramsay, and Gaber 2012, 34).

Equally, the availability of new media devices such as smartphones and tablets has made news audience behaviour volatile. "Nobody knows where audiences, particularly the digitally savvy audiences, are going next", says Boaden. "That's the interesting bit of where we are at the moment" (interview 2012). While some consumer research finds that more devices lead to more news consumption, others find the opposite. Among tablet users, 57% had downloaded news applications (apps or APIs), making them the fourth most popular type of app; yet 34% of smartphone users say they access less news on radio and TV since they acquired their new phones (Ofcom 2012a). Second and third screens are becoming increasingly common, as young people, in particular, sit in front of the television while using a smartphone and/or a laptop, enabling them to cram nine and a half hours of media use into six and a half hours of "real time" (Postgate 2011). In a related development, viewers are increasingly encountering news via social media. Two members of our focus group first heard about the death of Osama Bin Laden in May 2011 via Facebook.

A striking theme throughout our interviews with senior British broadcast journalists was awareness of the audience. This is in marked contrast to previous studies such as Schlesinger (1987), who detected a "missing link" between journalists and their audience (see also Scollon 1998). Not so, nowadays, according to Richard Frediani, editor of ITV's 6.30pm bulletin:

> In the 20 years I have been in the business, that is something you are more acutely aware of now than you were in the late '80s, early '90s. You think more about who are your audience at set points of the day, therefore how do you produce the news, structure your programmes to try and relate to that audience?

Senior journalists and managers today know their audience intimately. Sky News can track them from when they wake up to when they go to bed:

> We have a commuting wake-up spike on the iPhone and Android, people are just getting their news on the move. Then a lunchtime spike on the PC and laptop, a lunchtime-at-work audience. There's another commuting spike on our smartphones as we go home, and then the iPad is all about in the evening catching up on the sofa. (Hawken interview 2012)

Broadcasters devote time and energy to understanding their audience and shaping their output accordingly, as Rod McKenzie, editor of Newsbeat, BBC Radio 1's news department, explains:

> If you walk around our newsrooms, people have got their text consoles open or minimized, our Facebook page open or minimized and our presenter who leads our Twitter discussions very often has the Twitter page up with feedback coming back. Then in addition I do focus groups, I unpick everything I can out of RAJAR [an industry ratings survey] every quarter. It's terribly, terribly important, and it's a very significant part of my day, my week, my year.

Across the BBC, "metrics" such as the Appreciation Index, which measures "to what extent people enjoy and appreciate BBC programmes", a daily "Pulse survey," asking what people want more of, and overnight viewing figures are combined with

> your own much more subjective sense of was it good or was it not good? Was it clear? But you have to always start from the audience really. Journalism can be self-referential. (Boaden interview 2012)

At ITV, the number of web site 'hits' per story are discussed at editorial meetings for the early evening TV bulletin and can influence decisions on running order, says Frediani. "It doesn't dictate what you do but you do take an interest in what people are and aren't talking about" (interview 2012). The immediacy of web site hits, Twitter and Facebook contrast with the feedback for TV, which arrives the day after transmission from BARB.

Several commentators find some of this worrying. Barnett (2011) acknowledges that "the more diverse agenda of British current affairs journalism . . . suggests a culture of production driven less by journalistic diktat and more by the interests of viewers" (162), but a common theme in his interviews with senior journalists was "the replacement of journalistic or editorial instinct with an unhealthy focus on ratings targets and consumer research" (163). "Others talked of the pressure to bring pace and 'edge' to every story which inevitably led to techniques such as hidden camera work with an emphasis on the emotional and dramatic rather than the narrative" (164). "This is not, in other words, about presenting serious or provocative issues in a more populist way but about privileging presentation and storytelling above content" (164–165).

This view feeds into a central question of the moment when the news quality necessary to enable a participatory democracy is considered: is the news dumbing down? Barnett (2011, 169) believes that the "golden age" of television journalism lasted from the 1960s to the 1980s, when varied and challenging news and current affairs programmes, plus the innovations of Channel 4, attracted mass audiences. But now current affairs, and to a lesser extent news, is under threat from "tabloidization".

However, Barnett's anonymous interview evidence is problematic. Reporters, however senior, who eschew management jobs may lack a broad view of their organisation or industry (Altmeppen 2008, 52). Further, older journalists have been asserting that the golden age is past since the nineteenth century. As the policemen get younger, the journalism gets worse (see also Luscombe 2009).

Barnett's second type of evidence, content analysis, is of higher quality, but unfortunately undermines his case. It is an analysis of more than 1,000 evening TV news bulletins from 1975 to 2009, including BBC1, ITV, Channel 4 and Channel 5 (Barnett 2011; Barnett et al. 2012). Between 1975 and 1999, Barnett found a decline in the proportion of "broadsheet", i.e., serious news stories carried on early evening news bulletins, and a corresponding increase in "tabloid" style stories, particularly on ITV (146–147). However, foreign coverage, classified as "broadsheet," increased (see Figure 9.1). And content analysis in 2004 and 2009 found that the proportion of broadsheet stories on BBC bulletins had almost returned to the 1977 level, while ITV's quality decline had been arrested, and even reversed in the case of the Ten O'Clock News (149). Channel 4, meanwhile, maintained a consistently high level of news quality from its launch in 1982, with "around half its bulletins devoted to domestic broadsheet issues, around

% foreign news 1975–2009

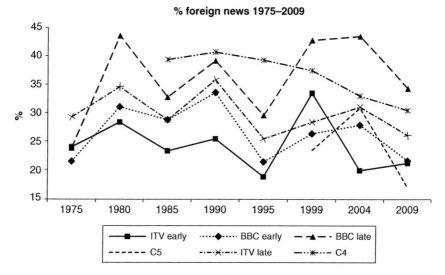

Figure 9.1   Foreign news as proportion of bulletin, main UK channels, 1975–2009 (Barnett et al., 2012)

40% to foreign issues and around 10% to tabloid issues" (with a slight recent increase of tabloid content to 18%, at the expense of foreign news, 150). Indeed, Barnett et al.'s conclusion is that, despite the "ec-tech squeeze" (Anderson 2007, 51) of the last 10 years, "we have found no evidence of a significant shift towards a more tabloid news agenda" (2).

We accept that the quality of news has varied over time, as seen in a slight decline between the 1970s and the 1990s, but there has been a more recent improvement, due in part to a renewed emphasis on context and explanation in BBC reporting under John Birt's management (Barnett et al. 2012, 18) and a renewed commitment to the very principle of broadcasting news and current affairs on ITV since Adam Crozier's appointment as chief executive officer in 2010. Further, as Barnett accepts, news coverage changes according to the news, and the economic downturn has led to greater interest in quality news.

Barnett has stronger evidence for a decline in current affairs, although even here his findings are equivocal. There was a steep decline on ITV after *World in Action, This Week* and *First Tuesday* were cancelled, but he notes an increase in BBC current affairs between 1977 and 1997, albeit shifting from foreign topics to more popular subjects such as crime, consumer affairs and individual ethical issues including abortion and animal rights (Barnett et al. 2012, 160). He underplays the importance of Channel 4's current affairs output, including *Dispatches, Unreported World*, short films within *Channel 4 News* and a significant number of single documentaries. Since Barnett's book was published, ITV has increased its output, with the *Exposure* documentary strand (launched 2011), the *Perspectives* arts documentary series (2011) and *The Agenda* discussion show (2012), plus single documentaries and the softer *Tonight* (launched 1999). He also ignores the insertion of current affairs material and investigations into routine news bulletins, "piecemeal" across a week, as for example in ITN's series on MRSA in hospitals. To talk of "the demise of hard-hitting, well-resourced current affairs journalism on British commercial television" (252) is to overstate the case.

If there is now an obsession with ratings and a disregard for professional journalistic judgment, one would expect that the juries who give out industry awards to their peers would detect such a development. But the judges for the news and current affairs award categories of the British Academy of Film and Television Arts (BAFTA) and Royal Television Society (RTS) have made no public comment on declining standards. Neither can we can find any evidence that the Hutton Inquiry and subsequent Neil Report have had a chilling effect on BBC journalism (McQueen 2008, 51). One of our interviewees suggested that the lack of a BBC winner in the BAFTA news coverage category for the past six years was significant; yet the BBC has won that category twice (in 2004 and 2005) since the publication of the Neil Report in 2004, and won it only three times—before Neil—between 1986 and 2003. BBC current affairs programmes and documentaries have won recent BAFTA awards. In the other major British TV awards, those given by the RTS, BBC journalism has also been well represented, winning eight awards in 2008, for example.

The following three case studies examine award-winning examples representative of the current strengths of UK broadcast journalism.

"UNDERCOVER CARE: THE ABUSE EXPOSED". *PANORAMA*, BBC1, 2011

This one-hour documentary on care workers' abuse of adults with learning difficulties in a private health facility is an example of how 'playing it by the book' and following the BBC's allegedly bureaucratic editorial decision-making and compliance procedures can assist high-quality hard news journalism. The programme was tipped off by a former nurse at Winterbourne View near Bristol, a private facility contracted to the National Health Service (NHS), where staff were systematically abusing vulnerable adults. The "whistleblower" had complained repeatedly to the hospital's owners and to the sector's regulator, the Care Quality Commission (CQC), but had been ignored. A young reporter, Joe Casey, used deception to gain a job at Winterbourne View and spent five weeks filming with hidden cameras. The bulk of the programme is the violent footage of carers inflicting pain on patients, interspersed with Casey's "video diary" pieces to camera, comments from the whistleblower, two sources of expert opinion, reactions from the parents of patients, and right-of-reply comments from the head of the company running the hospital and from a CQC official. It makes gripping if disturbing viewing, as rising viewing figures throughout the hour of transmission attest (Kanter 2011). Audiences for *Panorama*, which celebrates its sixtieth anniversary this year (2013), have been increasing since Tom Giles became editor in 2010, and figures for that edition, of 3.1 million, were about the average for the programme in 2011 (BBC Annual Report 2011/12).

Like most factual programmes, this edition of *Panorama* used techniques borrowed from Hollywood and from reality TV—grainy, sinister black-and-white freeze-frames of the perpetrators; flashbacks; the reporter's video diary; emotional reactions of experts and parents as they watch the abuse footage. The necessary context—of increasing privatisation of health and social care, lack of regulation, low pay, good practice in dealing with difficult patients, group dynamics and historical background—was worn lightly and carefully distributed among different speakers, to allow the secretly filmed footage to tell the most important part of the story: the violence and suffering. New technology, in the form of lightweight, easily concealed equipment, also played its part.

The film engaged the emotions, indeed one could argue that an emotional response was the only ethical one to such cruelty. As Barnett (2011, 142) acknowledges, "affective involvement, properly employed, can be one of the most powerful manifestations of great television journalism". Any discussion of storytelling in broadcast news must distinguish between topic and treatment; one can, and indeed should, treat the same topic in many different ways, according to the audience, and even Lord Reith included the need to entertain in his three-fold credo for broadcasting. The current fad for documentaries and reality shows on physical disability, popular on Channel 4 and BBC3, such as *The Undateables, Britain's Missing Top Model* and *Beauty and the Beast: The Ugly Face of Prejudice* are marketed as freak-shows, but the programmes themselves, sometimes produced with the aid of disability charities, present disabled people as human beings and qualify as quality current affairs TV. *Wife Swap* and *Supernanny* address current concerns about 'parenting' in accessible, helpful, ways. Celebrity presenters lead viewers into topics where they would not otherwise venture, such as X Factor judge Tulisa Contostavlos on young carers (*Tulisa: My Mum and Me*, 2010). Broader social structures such as class, wealth, race, disability and government policy "leak" even from trite reality formats such as *Secret Millionaire,* in which a millionaire lives undercover in an impoverished community and chooses deserving recipients for his (rarely her) largesse in the climactic "reveal" (Oullette 2010, 69–71). Popular culture "needs to be acknowledged as a relevant resource for political citizenship" (Van Zoonen 2005, 151). An appeal to the emotions can stimulate political participation (Örnebring and Jönsson 2004, 284), creating an "emotional public sphere" (Dahlgren 2005, cited in Hill 2007, 14).

The *Panorama* programme was relevant to the lives of its audience because so many people know of someone in care, either elderly or disabled.

"Relevance" has been decried as another cause of dumbing down, yet the need to convince an audience of the significance of a story in their lives is not a new idea; the *Daily Mail* has been doing it with skill for decades. Rod McKenzie of *Newsbeat* explains:

> We talk to audiences and we say "Are you interested in politics?" They say "No." We say "Are you interested in your school closing down or your hospital ward shutting?" and they say "Oh God yes." Well that's politics. Connecting political events with an outcome that affects people is the key to telling the story. (McKenzie interview 2012)

John Birt's directive to employ more specialist BBC correspondents has also improved storytelling, thanks to the skill of specialists such as business editor Robert Peston, economics editor Stephanie Flanders and security correspondent Frank Gardner. "A really good specialist knows exactly how to hone down something complicated without caricaturing it", says Boaden. "You need specialists to tell most people why this story matters" (Boaden interview 2012).

Panorama's close adherence to BBC editorial guidelines meant that they could go into difficult ethical territory with a clear purpose and full managerial support. Casey, the reporter, lied to get the job, used hidden cameras, continued filming rather than prevent other care workers committing assaults, and held back information from parents and the police. Editors made difficult decisions about what and how much material to broadcast. The BBC paid for Casey to receive private training in the care of people with learning disabilities (Casey 2011). Editor Tom Giles said,

> I could never have done a film like the Winterbourne View film unless I had been able to go through, with editorial policy, and make sure that at every stage and every step we had a plan laid out and a framework laid out for what we were trying to do, and . . . it had been clearly defined by both myself and by others in the BBC as being of significant public interest. (House of Lords [HoL] 2011, 16)

The evidence was gathered meticulously to assist any police investigation and to protect the BBC from complaints. These take up a great deal of time and money for the BBC and other news organisations, as Channel 4's Dorothy Byrne told a 2011 Select Committee:

> Complainants will not just try to threaten us with libel actions, they will launch worldwide PR exercises against us—there is one going on now against us about our investigation into Sri Lankan war crimes—and they will try to make complaints to our bosses, they will leak stories against us to newspaper diaries, they will go to our regulator and they will make potentially scores of complaints against us. (HoL 2011, 3)

Only days after "Undercover Care" was broadcast, the BBC Trust highlighted a counter-example of what happens when journalists do not follow the rules, publishing their 51-page investigation of a complaint against a 2008 *Panorama* edition in which footage of child labour linked to Primark may have been faked by a freelance journalist (BBC Trust 2011b). *Panorama* reporter John Ware may have been referring to this case when he claimed that the cost of investigating a complaint against one *Panorama* programme "was significantly more than the actual transmission itself" (HoL 2011, 57). This level of governance, uncommon in the commercial sector, helps to maintain the reputation of BBC journalism.

The Primark case was a rare exception, as was the smearing of Lord McAlpine in a 2012 edition of BBC2's *Newsnight*. The vast majority of BBC journalism adheres to the five traditional principles of journalism, "essentially matters of ethics and values" (Starkey and Crisell 2009, 55), outlined by Ronald Neil in 2004: truth and accuracy, serving the public interest, impartiality and diversity of opinion, independence, and accountability. Neil, a former BBC Director of News and Current Affairs, had been commissioned to report on the Hutton Inquiry's criticism of BBC journalism. This crisis was turned into an opportunity as the BBC invested millions in improving in-house training and setting up the BBC College of Journalism in 2005, now part of a BBC Academy. The college guards the BBC way of doing journalism through a mandatory journalism foundation course for journalists new to the BBC, a mandatory 'safeguarding trust' course for all staff, a 'safeguarding BBC values' course for selected staff and external contractors, and a huge range of other courses, most now available via a public web site. In 2011/12, the BBC spent £5.8 million on journalism training, excluding journalism trainee schemes (Baker interview 2012). However, the BBC Academy must make cuts of 35% over the next three years (BBC Trust 2011a).

Those savings are part of a 20% cut across the BBC to deal with its frozen licence fee settlement (the first cut in real-terms income in the BBC's history). The £6.5 million budget for *Panorama* (average cost per hour £225,000) has been protected (Brown 2012a), along with other current affairs and investigations, but not news, where journalism redundancies will be compensated for by covering fewer stories (Boaden interview 2012) and by using output more widely across different outlets; there is a commitment, however, to improve local radio news (BBC Trust 2011c). "Part of it is about doing less and part of it is about sharing what we do more", says Boaden. "But I'm not going to sit here and wring my hands, because we've still got far more money than most of our competitors". Channel 4 and Sky News are also bullish about resources for news. Dorothy Byrne, C4's Head of News and Current Affairs, says her budget has been maintained at a "very good" level (HoL 2011, 20), while John Ryley, head of Sky News, says they are "well-resourced". Funds at ITV are less certain, but there is a new commitment to news and current affairs, says Frediani (see also Foster 2011, 31):

ITV's commitment to it a decade ago was under the spotlight. In the last few years ITV has declared a commitment and interest in it from the very top, which does offer a brighter future than there has been in recent years.

FALL OF TRIPOLI, SKY NEWS, 2011

On Sunday 21 August 2011, Alex Crawford, Sky News Special Correspondent, rode into Tripoli on the back of a rebel convoy truck, the first journalist to report live on the liberation of Libya's capital city from Muammar Gaddafi's regime. Her commentary and eyewitness interviews amidst chaotic celebrations in Green Square were broadcast to the world via a manually operated satellite signal and a camera plugged into their pick-up truck's cigarette lighter socket (Foster 2011). Crawford's courageous reporting and her team's creative use of broadcast technology allowed Sky to scoop rival news organisations and won Crawford a clutch of awards.

John Ryley, Sky's head of news, believes the Tripoli coverage epitomises his channel's distinctive approach to journalism:

> News now *is* now, what's happening *now*. It's not something that is saved up for six o'clock or six-thirty on ITV or ten o'clock on the BBC. It's happening *now*. The BBC didn't have any of that coverage in part because their first-class reporters on the ground were filing for the Ten O'clock BBC Sunday evening bulletin rather than being out there getting the news. (interview 2012)

BBC resources devoted to foreign news will reduce in coming years, although Boaden believes that collaboration and technology will protect quality. Lap-top editing, smart phone apps and the portable, rugged, satellite technology used by the BBC and Sky News in Libya make reporting foreign news cheaper, as well as faster and easier. Significantly, technology also has the potential to improve quality, freeing reporters to spend more time gathering news and less time processing and presenting it.

Technology has assisted another trend, "user-generated content" (UGC)— video and other news material supplied by members of the audience—with its potential to improve the quality of storytelling and broaden the range of voices heard. Many events during the 2011 "Arab Spring" were recounted through tweets and mobile phone video footage, but this material must be verified, collated and structured, all of which requires journalists. The BBC's User-Generated Content Hub within BBC News operates seven days a week, 24 hours a day and has a team of more than 20 staff who often work with the BBC's various language services to verify UGC material (Wardle and Williams 2010). In November 2012 ITN launched Truthloader, a citizen journalism channel on YouTube, showcasing the work of citizen journalists around the world but 'curated' by ITN journalists (*Press Gazette* 2012).

The need for journalists to curate (i.e., to select, arrange, provide context, organise and update material from many sources, using expertise to research and check the information: McAdams 2008) suggests that the craft of journalism is less threatened by citizen journalism and UGC than thought. Former BBC Radio 4 *Today Programme* editor Kevin Marsh claimed in 2009 that "the story is dead" (Marsh 2009), but no one told the audience, who still prefer carefully constructed narratives produced by skilled journalists. To return to the Sky Tripoli case study, the BBC's Rupert Wingfield-Hayes was scooped by Sky because he was crafting a traditional journalistic story for a fixed-point bulletin, the Ten O'Clock News, watched by five million viewers, while only 142,000 British viewers saw Crawford on Sky News (according to BBC World News Editor Jon Williams, speaking on the *Media Show* 2011).1

Audiences turn to 24-hour news for big, breaking stories such as the Arab Spring or the August 2011 riots in England. The BBC News Channel attracted a record daily audience of 13.1 million during the riots, while Sky News had 9.28 million (*Guardian* 2011), but viewers value the programmes of record, the BBC and ITV early evening bulletins, more highly than rolling news channels, despite their emphasis on speed, breaking news and extensive use of UGC. Audiences still want the products offered by professional broadcast journalists—the balanced, well-crafted, accurately sourced and checked stories that explain what happened and why in a clear narrative. Boaden believes that the Birtian values of "context and significance" are still in demand.

GRANADA REPORTS: MORECAMBE BAY, 2006

Our third case study is an example of the most popular type of news programme on UK TV, the early-evening regional news bulletin, in particular Granada's coverage of the 2004 Morecambe Bay cockle-picking disaster, in which 23 illegal Chinese immigrants drowned in the freezing waters of the Irish Sea when they were cut off by the tide. *Granada Reports*, the ITV regional news programme for the North West of England, featured the story prominently as it unfolded over several days. Two years later, at the close of the manslaughter case against the gang-masters who had sent the Chinese workers to their deaths, *Granada Reports* scrapped its usual early-evening mix of regional news and features to devote a full 30 minutes to the story. This included a court report, an investigation into the inadequate regulation of the shellfish industry, a re-telling of events on the day of the tragedy and a film shot illegally in China by Granada reporter Elaine Willcox, exploring why the victims had emigrated, how they had been smuggled into the UK and the impact on their families. A separate 30-minute documentary using more of Willcox's exclusive footage was broadcast in the Granada 10.35pm regional opt-out slot. The bold decision to track the story for 18 months and devote considerable resources to it was taken by Granada's then head of news, Richard Frediani.

The coverage won the only BAFTA news award ever given to a regional TV programme. Although the story had sensational elements—death, people-smuggling, criminal gangs and the manslaughter trial—it dealt with the larger issues of globalisation, immigration, Chinese rural poverty, treatment of migrant workers and government regulation. Granada's storytelling was compelling and of high quality in terms of production and narrative. Dramatic reconstruction and eye witness accounts were used to explain the sequence of events clearly and accurately. Harrowing recordings of dying workers' 999 phone-calls and interviews with grieving relatives shot in close-up appealed to the "emotional intelligence" of the viewer (Barnett 2011, 142). The imagery and editing were creative and, with evocative music and natural sound, were designed to draw the viewer into the story.

Frediani argues that what he and his team achieved, in working on one story for more than 18 months, can be done by any news organisation with strong leadership and the ability to manage a budget. No extra funding was provided by ITV Granada. Frediani released money and reporters from the daily rota to investigate and film the story, as he had done on other big stories.

> We only achieved those results because we put the resource into it, we put the time into it, the journalistic effort. You can show ambition even with the most limited resources. As an editor, you know the budget you have signed up to, it's about being creative, making it work, stretching it where you can, focusing it where you feel it needs focusing. (Frediani interview 2012)

He says that high-quality regional TV news is not unique to his programme.

> ITV regularly wins critical acclaim for its regional coverage, as evidenced by those national RTS wins over the last six years. I could go round every part of the country and name very good, strong examples of quality journalism.

Most regional news bulletins are a mix of hard news, features, soft news and sport. In-depth investigation is rare, although programmes may broadcast 'one-off' specials on stories like the Manchester riots or run a series of reports on a single subject across a week's bulletins. ITV provides nine regional news services in England, the Borders and Wales (with STV, UTV and Channel Television providing bulletins for Scotland, Northern Ireland and the Channel islands respectively), competing with 12 BBC regional services (Foster 2011, 4). The BBC transmits significantly more regional news and current affairs than ITV (Table 9.2).

Table 9.2   Hours of regionalised output, all UK, 2009

BBC news	5024
ITV/stv/UTV news	3450
BBC current affairs	499
ITV/stv/UTV current affairs	176

Source: Ofcom 2011b, Fig 2.7

While ITV is committed to providing regional news, it may reduce the quantity in coming years. The company's licence to broadcast national and regional news across its 11 channels will be renewed from the end of 2014 until 2024, but, at the time of writing, ITV was negotiating with Ofcom on the exact level of regional news provision. The broadcaster has proposed cutting its early-evening regional bulletins from 30 to 20 minutes and transmitting more aggregated output across several regions. However, it has also proposed increasing the number of regionally differentiated news programmes from 9 back to the 17 it offered before 2009 (Brown 2012b). Whatever is agreed, news budgets are unlikely to grow for ITV, which is unusual in devoting most of its resources to regional rather than network news, spending about £67 million and employing 300 journalists in the regions, compared to £40m for network news, produced by some 140 journalists (Foster 2011, 29).

In contrast, the BBC's 12 regional TV centres benefit from being part of a much larger regional, national and international newsgathering operation, although it has to deliver savings across its regional TV and local radio networks under "Delivering Quality First" recommendations. ITV, under the leadership of Michael Grade, restructured its regional operation, reducing the network's 17 regional news services to the present 9 (Lay and O'Neill 2009). Of the ITV regional news workforce, 40%, amounting to some 430 jobs, was cut to make savings of £40 million between 2006 and 2011 (Foster 2011, 30).

ITV was launched in the 1950s with a regional structure to counteract the perceived London bias of the BBC; but since the original 15 ITV companies reduced to the current 4, they have thinned their regional output, including news and current affairs. The only regional current affairs programme is a monthly political slot, branded as *Party People* in the Granada region, airing at 11.35pm on a Thursday. The weekly BBC regional current affairs series *Inside Out* broadcasts at 7.30pm in competition with ITV's *Coronation Street*, attracting an average audience of 3.1 million. Stories have included a region-by-region study of the effects of increased university tuition fees, an investigation of the 2011 Bonfire Night M5 crash and analysis of hospital reorganisation plans. The programme's reach varies, at its highest in southern regions and lowest in the North-West. However, the content and tone of these programmes has changed over the past decade.

Inside Out carries strong, well-produced regional stories, but the programme now features three stories rather than one, allowing less context and depth. As Barnett found with national current affairs (2011, 160), at regional level there has also been a shift from harder to softer topics. *Inside Out* is now almost a hybrid of regional news and old style regional current affairs.

The most significant development in regional TV is the approval of 21 *local* TV broadcasting licences, granted in March 2012 and due to launch in 2013. The initiative came from then Culture Secretary Jeremy Hunt, who questioned why Birmingham, Alabama had eight TV stations and Birmingham, England had none (Hewlett 2011). While there are strong arguments in favour of local TV, from the perspective of local democracy (filling the gap left by the declining regional press) and audience demand (the most common complaint about regional TV news is that it is not local enough—Lay and O'Neill 2009, 4), there are grave doubts over its commercial viability and capacity to deliver quality news. "You're only going to watch it if it regularly produces a quality news service", says Frediani. "If it doesn't, it will go the same way as every other attempt to do local TV".

However, TV-like services over the internet may have more potential for quality journalism (Shott 2010), and Sky News is piloting just such a service in North-East England. Sky Tyne and Wear is a regional news web site, launched in February 2012, offering text and video content across news and sport. Andrew Hawken, Head of Digital Media for Sky News, said response to the site had "exceeded our expectations by a long way". The web site had 180,000 unique visitors in March 2012 (*Press Gazette* 2012), 300,000 individual hits in May 2012 when flash flooding hit Tyneside, and recorded its biggest-ever audience of 35,000 unique hits in one day in June (RTS). Sky see it as a pilot project but are unwilling to reveal further plans in this area.

Journalists generally have a poor opinion of regional TV, but this perception is not shared by audiences. Total viewing hours of early evening regional TV news has remained stable since 2006 (Ofcom 2012b, 83), the BBC's combined 6.30pm regional news programmes still command the highest average news audience in the UK, at 5.4 million in 2011, with ITV's early evening regional news drawing 3.2 million (see Fig 9.1). The BBC's audiences are larger than ITV's across all regions except Border and Northern Ireland. Regional news may be the most popular type of broadcast news (Ofcom 2012a, 106) because it is clearly relevant to viewers' lives. "People want to see their communities and places they know" (Lay and O'Neill 2009) and have the culture of their region validated.

THE FUTURE

News and current affairs broadcasting in the UK is currently in a healthy state in a broad sense, as these case studies and other evidence show. The quality of *much of* the journalism easily available to TV and radio audiences is as high, if not higher, than it has ever been. However, this is not to claim that news and current affairs broadcast journalism always meets this book's definition of quality hard news, i.e., journalism that enables consumers to act as truly participative citizens within their democracy. Too much news is based on official or PR sources (Davies 2009; Cushion and Lewis 2009, 138), lacks context (Cushion and Lewis 2009, 144–146), and is overly focused on London and South-East England (BBC Trust 2008), while investigations focus more on the dwindling public sector rather than the expanding but less transparent private sector. However, our case studies demonstrate how talented individual journalists, supported by skilful and committed management and the latest technology, can still report and explain significant stories in a way that engages the public—and how they can, in some of the biggest stories, reach the standards for quality news journalism set out in chapter one.

The internet's disruption of British journalism—including broadcast journalism—continues, but the situation is not as volatile in 2013 as it was in 2007. There is some stability in the slowing decline in viewing figures for news and current affairs on the main TV channels. "Television is an amazingly resilient media", says Boaden. "Most people get most of their news from the television, still" (interview 2012). There is also stability in the financial commitment to journalism among television broadcasters. The 2012 *Newsnight* debacle is unlikely to inflict any long-term damage on the BBC because the current government is largely pro-BBC (Cameron 2008), and the corporation's most powerful enemy, Rupert Murdoch, is unable to capitalise on the BBC's problems because of his own difficulties after the *News of the World* phone hacking scandal. The regulations preventing UK TV journalism from following the Fox News path (Cushion and Lewis 2009, 149; Barnett 2011) are unlikely to be weakened in the short to medium term. So some of the most important conditions for quality journalism are currently stable.

However, other factors are less predictable. On the demand side, as Egglestone pointed out in an earlier chapter, news audiences are changing their behaviour so quickly that broadcasters are struggling to keep up with them. "Your audience may suddenly consume or want something very different from what you're currently offering. That's what happened with newspapers, and you can get left behind", says Boaden (interview 2012). Rapid take-up of smartphones and tablets, and the ease of use of YouTube and news aggregators such as Google, may create media habits, particularly among young people, that lead the audience away from news to other content.

> Thirteen- and fourteen-year-olds have got a dizzying array of digital media. Why would they go to the radio? They don't, they've got YouTube, they've got smartphones. If you're not doing visual stuff you're not in the game with young people, so we must be able to

visualize Radio 1. And that really means on a smartphone. If we get it wrong both on Radio 1 and on Newsbeat the future is very grim indeed for a youth-facing Radio 1, what we'd be left with is an ageing audience. (McKenzie interview 2012)

Both McKenzie and Hawken of Sky News believe that smartphones and tablets are the way forward in the short term. Boaden and Frediani highlight the problems for democracy if young people cannot be weaned on to news:

People can pre-select what they want to watch. My fear is they may therefore sometimes avoid stories that actually have got a serious impact on their lives. Are we potentially going to lose—particularly— young people where there are stories and issues of significant interest to them that they should know about but they are choosing not to engage in? (Frediani interview)

On the supply side, there are more imponderables. Broadcasters are chasing their audiences across platforms, aiming to offer 'pervasive' news, while the wider news ecology will change as newspapers continue to decline and local TV channels are launched. BBC Radio 1's Newsbeat, for example, plans to follow its audience on to YouTube and social networking sites, with apps tailored to smartphones. Frediani hopes for a 'both/and' future of promiscuous news consumers, rather than an 'either/or' choice between old and new media:

The challenge for broadcasters is to ensure that we are communicating with people across as many platforms in as many ways as possible. It's about using those platforms to your benefit to engage with all the different types of audiences that there are, so that eventually they come back to your brand.

The alternative could be calamitous for non-subscription commercial TV channels such as ITV, who are wholly dependent on advertising.

The suppliers of news are responding to their audiences by using technology to present the news as attractively as possible. Matthew Postgate, head of BBC research and development, believes that detailed shot-by-shot audience feedback will enable journalists to craft their stories in more arresting ways. Journalists are adapting creatively to the haiku-like discipline of presenting news intelligently for mobile phones. Audiences like user-generated content, but its democratic, creative promise has yet to be realised; Wardle and Williams (2010, 789, 792) believe that collaborative content has the potential to 'revolutionise' journalism if only journalists would cede some control. Channel 4 have experimented with this approach, inviting the public to share in their investigative journalism via social media, to the extent of broadcasting two films based on ideas from the public (Byrne in HoL 2011, 20, 23–24): "Landlords from hell" and "Train journeys from hell" (the latter using significant amounts of audience material). Beyond technology, more awareness of audiences is revealing under-served groups. Only 67% of British women, for example, access news every day, a lower proportion than in Germany, Denmark, France or the United States (Newman, 19), demonstrating that there are parts of the UK "news market" whose demands have yet to be met by journalism in its current form.

The decline of newspapers will have more complex effects. As circulations fall and more journalists are made redundant, fewer stories will be originated by the press. The UK news agenda is led disproportionately by national newspapers, but this may change; while understaffing on local newspapers now prevents them from originating the stories that were once the lowest part of the news food chain, feeding into local radio and national media. BBC local radio and the new local TV channels, even if successful, can only partially fill the gap.

CONCLUSIONS

In the mid-1950s ITN made British television news more entertaining by introducing innovations from U.S. commercial TV such as vox pops and interrogative interviewing. Its new approach was intentionally downmarket of the stuffy BBC, who quickly updated their style (Day 1961, cited in Schlesinger 1987, 14). Few would now claim that this was dumbing down. In the same way, a renewed concern for the audience, and the use of new technology to understand the audience better and to offer them news in more accessible, culturally democratic ways, holds great promise. Multi-channel TV has not only brought more choice, but more quality, with the BBC News Channel, Sky News and the Parliament Channel freely available, to mention only British channels. Relatively strict regulation and the presence of the BBC, a publicly funded news broadcaster, skews the market in favour of high-quality journalism—Sky is not Fox (Cushion and Lewis, 146; Barnett 2011, 155).

Current UK broadcast journalism is far from perfect, and as the detail of our analysis has shown, the situation in radio is much weaker than in television, with only a few of the commercial stations now aspiring to produce quality hard news and the burden of doing this largely falling on the BBC. But, where television and the finest radio journalism are concerned at least, there is some evidence for Ryley's assertion that "the best days of British journalism are ahead of us" (Ryley interview 2012). And if he is proved right, then this will be due, in no small part, to journalists' growing respect for, and understanding of, their audiences. As Newsbeat's Rod McKenzie says, "When I first joined Newsbeat people used to laugh at the audience. Nobody laughs at the audience now".

INTERVIEWS

All interviews were conducted by Deborah Robinson.
Baker, Jonathan, Head of the BBC College of Journalism. 15.00, 2 August 2012.
Boaden, Helen, Director of BBC News Group. 13.30, 2 August 2012.
Frediani, Richard, Programme Editor, ITV 6.30pm News. 09.30, 10 August and 15.30, 27 November 2012.
Hawken, Andrew, Head of Digital Media, Sky News. 16.00, 5 October 2012.
McKenzie, Rod, Editor, BBC Radio 1 Newsbeat and 1Xtra News. 31 October 2012.
Postgate, Matthew, Controller, BBC Research and Development. 14.00, 3 October and 16.50, 7 November 2012.
Ryley, John, Head of News, Sky News. 15.30, 5 October and 17.00, 11 October 2012.

REFERENCES

Altmeppen, Klaus-Dieter. 2008. "The Structure of News Production: The Organizational Approach to Journalism Research." In *Global Journalism Research: Theories, Methods, Findings, Future*, edited by Martin Löffelholz and David H. Weaver, 52–64. Malden, MA: Blackwell.
Anderson, Peter J. 2007. "Challenges for Journalism." In *The Future of Journalism in the Advanced Democracies*, edited by Peter J. Anderson and Geoff Ward, 51–69. London: Ashgate.
Barnett, Steven. 2011. *The Rise and Fall of Television Journalism: Just Wires and Lights in a Box?* London: A&C Black.
Barnett, Steven, Gordon Neil Ramsay, and Ivor Gaber. 2012. *From Callaghan to Credit Crunch: Changing Trends in British Television News 1975–2009*. London: University of Westminster. http://www.westminster.ac.uk/__data/assets/pdf_file/0009/124785/From-Callaghan-To-Credit-Crunch-Final-Report.pdf.
BBC. 2011. *Media Show*, BBC Radio 4, 24 August. http://www.bbc.co.uk/programmes/b013fj1m.
BBC. 2008. "Impartiality Report: BBC Network News and Current Affairs Coverage of the Four UK Nations, including an independent assessment by Professor Anthony King and research from Cardiff University and BMRB." http://downloads.bbc.co.uk/northernireland/archive/chronicle/pdf/2000s_archival/2_king_report.txt.
BBC Trust. 2011a. "BBC Training: Observations on the Current Operation and Effectiveness of the BBC's Arrangements for the Training and Retraining of BBC Staff." http://downloads.bbc.co.uk/bbctrust/assets/files/pdf/regulatory_framework/other_activities/staff_training_2011.pdf.
BBC Trust. 2011b. "Finding of the Editorial Standards Committee of the BBC Trust: *Panorama*: Primark—On the Rack." http://downloads.bbc.co.uk/bbctrust/assets/files/pdf/appeals/esc_bulletins/2011/panorama.pdf.
BBC Trust. 2011c. *Delivering Quality First: News and English Regions*. http://downloads.bbc.co.uk/aboutthebbc/reports/pdf/dqf_newsandenglishregions.pdf.

BBC Trust. 2012a. *Service Review: BBC Parliament and BBC News Channel.* http://
www.bbc.co.uk/bbctrust/our_work/services/television/service_reviews/news_
parliament.html.

BBC Trust. 2012b. *Service Review: BBC Local Radio.* http://www.bbc.co.uk/
bbctrust/our_work/services/radio/service_reviews/local_radio.html

BBC Trust. 2012c. *BBC Annual Report and Accounts 2011/12.* http://downloads.
bbc.co.uk/annualreport/pdf/bbc_trust_2011_12.pdf

Broadcast. 2012. "Broadcast Awards 2012: Best Documentary Programme." 3 February.
http://www.broadcastnow.co.uk/about-us/awards/best-documentary-programme /
5037370.article.

Brown, Maggie. 2012a. "Tom Giles: 'There Is Nothing Off-Limits.' " *Guardian,* 4 March.
http://www.guardian.co.uk/media/2012/mar/04/tom-giles-panorama-editor.

Brown, Maggie. 2012b. "ITV to Get Licence Renewal." *Guardian,* 17 September.
http://www.guardian.co.uk/media/2012/sep/18/itv-to-get-licence-renewal

Cameron, David. 2008. "Bloated BBC Out of Touch with the Viewers." *The Sun,*
3 November. http://www.thesun.co.uk/sol/homepage/news/1884401/Bloated-
BBC-out-of-tough-with-the-viewers-says-Tory-chief-David-Cameron.html.

Casey, Joseph. 2011. "Undercover Reporter 'Haunted' by Abuse of Patients."
Panorama website, BBC, 31 May. http://news.bbc.co.uk/panorama/hi/front_
page/newsid_9501000/9501531.stm.

Cushion, Stephen, and Justin Lewis. 2009. "Towards a 'Foxification' of 24-hour
News Channels in Britain? An Analysis of Market-driven and Publicly Funded
News Coverage." *Journalism* 10: 131–153. doi:10.1177/1464884908100598.

Davies, Nick. 2009. *Flat Earth News: An Award-winning Reporter Exposes
Falsehood, Distortion and Propaganda in the Global Media.* London: Vintage.

Day, Robin. 1961. *Television: A Personal Report.* London: Hutchinson.

Foerstel, Herbert N. 2001. *From Watergate to Monicagate: Ten Controversies in
Modern Journalism and Media.* Westport: Greenwood Press.

Foster, Patrick. 2011. "Libya Coverage: Sky's Alex Crawford Scoops Her Rivals."
Guardian, 22 August. http://www.guardian.co.uk/world/2011/aug/22/libya-sky-
alex-crawford

Guardian. 2011. "Sky and BBC News Attract Record Audiences During UK
Riots." 10 August. http://www.guardian.co.uk/media/2011/aug/10/sky-bbc-record-
audience

Hewlett, Steve. 2011. "Local TV Is Happening, but It Bears No Relation to Jeremy
Hunt's Big Vision." *Guardian,* 21 August. http://www.guardian.co.uk/politics/
2011/aug/21/local-tv-jeremy-hunt-big-vision.

Hill, Annette. 2007. *Restyling Factual TV: Audiences and News, Documentary and
Reality Genres.* London: Taylor & Francis.

House of Lords (HoL). 2008. Select Committee on Communications. *The Ownership of the News.* First Report of Session 2007–08. http://www.publications
.parliament.uk/pa/ld200708/ldselect/ldcomuni/122/12202.ht.

House of Lords (HoL). 2011. Select Committee on Communications. *Inquiry on the
Future of Investigative Journalism,* unrevised transcript of evidence, session 3,
18 October. http://www.parliament.uk/documents/lords-committees/communications/
Investigativejournalism/IJev.pdf.

Kanter, Jake. 2011. "Panorama Patient Abuse Probe Draws 3m." *Broadcast,* 1 June.
http://www.broadcastnow.co.uk/ratings/panorama-patient-abuse-probe-draws-
3m/5028285.article.

Lay, Samantha, and Deirdre O'Neill. 2009. "Informing the Regions or News by
Numbers: Regional Television News, Audiences and Producers." Paper delivered
at Future of Journalism conference, 9 September, Cardiff University. http://www
.caerdydd.ac.uk/jomec/resources/foj2009/foj2009Lay-ONeill.pdf.

Luscombe, Anya. 2009. "The Future of Radio News: BBC Radio Journalists on the Brave New World in Which They Work." *Radio Journal:International Studies in Broadcast & Audio Media* 7:111–122.

Marsh, Kevin. 2009. "Death of the Story." In *The Future of Journalism: Papers from a conference organised by the BBC College of Journalism*, edited by Charles Miller, 70–88. London: Cojo Publications, BBC College of Journalism. www.bbc .co.uk/blogs/theeditors/future_of_journalism.pdf.

McAdams, Mindy. 2008. " 'Curation' and Journalists as Curators." *Teaching Online Journalism*. Accessed 28 January 2013. http://mindymcadams.com/tojou/2008/curation-and-journalists-as-curators/.

McQueen, David. 2008. "BBC's Panorama, War Coverage and the 'Westminster Consensus.' " *Westminster Papers in Culture and Communication* 5: 47–68.

Neil, Ron. 2004. "Report of the Neil Review Team." *BBC*. http://downloads.bbc .co.uk/aboutthebbc/insidethebbc/howwework/reports/pdf/neil_report.pdf.

Newman, Nic, ed. 2012. *Reuters Institute Digital News Report 2012: Tracking the Future of News*. Oxford: Reuters Institute for the Study of Journalism. http:// reutersinstitute.politics.ox.ac.uk/fileadmin/documents/Publications/Other_ publications/Reuters_Institute_Digital_Report.pdf

Ofcom. 2011a. UK Communications Market Report data. http://stakeholders .ofcom.org.uk/binaries/research/cmr/cmr11/UK_all.csv.

Ofcom 2011b. UK Communications Market Report 2011: Scottish TV and Audio-Visual Content data. http://stakeholders.ofcom.org.uk/binaries/research/cmr/ cmr11/Scotland_TV_and_AV.csv.

Ofcom. 2012a. *UK Communications Market Report*. http://stakeholders.ofcom.org .uk/binaries/research/cmr/cmr12/CMR_UK_2012.pdf.

Ofcom 2012b. Part C. PSB viewing: reporting BARB data on PSB viewing. http:// stakeholders.ofcom.org.uk/binaries/broadcast/reviews-investigations/psb-review/ psb2012/section-c.pdf

Örnebring, Henrik and Anna Maria Jönsson. 2004. "Tabloid Journalism and the Public Sphere: a Historical Perspective on Tabloid Journalism." *Journalism Studies* 5:283–295.

Oullette, Laurie. 2010. "Reality TV Gives Back: On the Civic Functions of Reality Entertainment." *Journal of Popular Film and Television* 38:66-71.

Panorama. 2011. "Undercover Care: The Abuse Exposed." 31 May.

Postgate, Matthew. 2011. "Being the BBC in the Information Age: Towards a New Broadcasting System." Barlow memorial lecture, University College London, 25 March. http://downloads.bbc.co.uk/rd/pubs/presentations/pdffiles/Barlow_ memorial_lecture_25_03_2011.pdf.

Press Gazette. 2012. "ITN Launches Youtube Channel Hosting Amateur Journalism from Around the World." 26 November. http://www.pressgazette.co.uk/content/ itn-launches-youtube-channel-hosting-amateur-journalism-around-world.

Purvis, Stewart. 2010. Highlights of speech by Stewart Purvis, Ofcom Partner, Content & Standards, 30 June. http://media.ofcom.org.uk/2010/06/30/halt-in-decline-of-flagship-tv-news-programmes/.

Radio Centre. 2011. "Action Stations! The Output and Impact of Commercial Radio." http://www.radiocentre.org/files/2011_radiocentre_action_stations.pdf.

RAJAR Quarterly Listening Figures, quarter ending 30 September. 2012. http:// www.rajar.co.uk/listening/quarterly_listening.php.

Schlesinger, Philip. 1987. *Putting 'Reality' Together?: BBC News*. London: Methuen.

Scollon, Ron. 1998. *Mediated Discourse as Social Interaction: A Study of News Discourse*. Harlow: Longman.

Shott, Nicholas. 2010. "Commercially viable local television in the UK: A review by Nicholas Shott for the Secretary of State for Culture, Olympics, Media and

Sport." http://www.culture.gov.uk/images/publications/Local-TV-Report-Dec10_
FullReport.pdf.
Starkey, Guy and Andrew Crisell. 2009. *Radio Journalism*. London: Sage.
Van Zoonen, Liesbet. 2005. *Entertaining The Citizen: When Politics And Popular
Culture Converge*. New York: Rowman & Littlefield.
Wardle, Claire, and Andrew Williams. 2010. "Beyond User-generated Content:
A Production Study Examining the Ways in Which UGC Is Used at the BBC."
Media, Culture & Society 32:781–799. doi:10.1177/0163443710373953.

10 U.S. Citizen Journalism and Alternative Online News Sites

Clyde Bentley

INTRODUCTION

Americans did not invent citizen journalism. There is a strong argument, however, that citizen journalism invented Americans.

A unique set of historical, political and cultural factors give citizen journalism a special place in American life that has only recently been fodder for headlines. For more than two centuries, publishing news, social information and political commentary submitted by members of the public was a normal part of New World journalism.

Normal, but not universally appreciated. Since long before there was a United States, both citizens and professional communicators have wrestled over their interpretations of accuracy, fairness and propriety.

'Citizen journalism' as a commonly applied term with the specific usage that it has today is something that was popularized a half-decade into the twenty-first century. The phrase popped up in the headlines in the winter of 2004–2005 as the U.S. mainstream press struggled to describe the amateur-written but professionally edited *OhmyNews* in Korea. Oh Yeon-ho started the site in 2000 as a reaction to the conservative oligarchy of the Korean press and proclaimed his mantra "Every citizen is a reporter"(Oh 2004).

Earlier American interpretations of Oh's idea were 'open source journalism', 'participatory journalism' (Bentley et al. 2005) and 'grassroots journalism' (Gillmor 2004). After endless newsroom arguments over what constitutes a 'citizen', the terms 'user generated content' (UGC) and 'participatory journalism' seem to be the currently favoured descriptions for content created by people who have no intent to launch a professional journalism career.

All of those terms, however, were just titles of the latest incarnation of a long tradition in American journalism.

EARLY HISTORY

Europe's journalism history reflected the long and relatively stable history of Europe itself. European cities developed hundreds of years before Gutenberg began to print with moveable type. By the sixteenth century, printing shops in those cities were substantial businesses whose owners were often members of guilds. The newspaper was invented by these civilized craftsmen (Leth 1993).

For at least the first century of its existence, however, America was just a shadow of European culture. It had neither the people nor the resources to duplicate the great cities of Europe and their centuries-old infrastructures, though its economic elite tried their best to follow European fashions and customs.

America's founders also were Protestants—in more than the religious sense. They left Europe to be free of religious constraints, but became known for their protests against government authority and even disagreements among each other (Kaminski 2002). Political discourse in the form of pamphlets and later newspapers was common. But like their European forebears, it was the leather-aproned printers who produced these written protests, not professional journalists.

Printers made their money producing commercial papers and similar documents, not from their news publications. Like their European forbearers who profited by reprinting Luther's 95 Theses without his permission, the Colonial printers focused more on publishing and selling popular material than on authoring it themselves (Brown 1992). Even when printers began to produce newspapers, they had no staff journalists, so they supplemented their own writings with items borrowed from other publications, with letters and with submissions from their readers.

One of these early examples of citizen journalism played a pivotal role in the separation of the American Colonies from Great Britain. In 1787 and 1788, several New York newspapers published a series of essays under the nom de plume "Publius". The 85 essays were later collected into the Federalist Papers extolling the virtues of the new U.S. Constitution and urging voters in New York to ratify it. The essays were actually written by founding fathers Alexander Hamilton, James Madison and John Jay. Though anonymous (the identity of Publius was revealed after Hamilton's death), the articles had enormous impact throughout the young country and are still referred to as sage interpretations of the Constitution (Knautz 2007).

Following its angry separation from the British Crown, much of the focus and energy of the United States was on expansion. The original 13 Colonies represented just a fraction of the vast continent. From 1800 to 1900, the United States grew from less than 1 million square miles (2.6 million square kilometers) to about 3 million square miles (7.7 square kilometers)—almost twice the size of Germany, France and the UK combined.

Into that vastness poured 60 million immigrants from Europe, taking with them the literacy and culture of information that had developed in Europe (Vandenbroucke 2008). As historian Robert Althearn quipped,

> Whenever two Westerners lived within hailing distance of each other they began to regard themselves as urbanites. If they lived along a railroad, they usually decided that their location might be an entrepôt of

trade and a distributing center for the surrounding region. If a third Westerner joined them, they had a Chamber of Commerce and a booster spirit. (Stelter 1973, 190)

It is fair to add that if a fourth Westerner joined the pioneers, he would start a newspaper. The young country was awash in itinerant printers. The character of the tramp printer with "a shirt tail full of type" is legendary in America. More accurately, however, the traveller was a literate businessman equipped with a small Washington or Ramage hand press and a sturdy wagon. Towns meant business and business meant a demand for cards, forms, handbills and signs (Cloud and Simpson 2008).

Commercial printing paid the bills, but newspapers gave the printers position in the frontier society. The literary skill of some travelling printers—notably Walt Whitman and Samuel Clemens—brought them fame in the greater world. But most focused on building their towns and their businesses. Very often the publisher/editor/printer was the sole employee of the operation (Cloud 1992, 111).

In the pre-typewriter, pre-Linotype era, publishing even a four-page weekly newspaper was a considerable chore. Few editors could write all the content by themselves. Instead, the major sources of content were letters, magazines, books—and amateur writers (Reilly 2010). Much early western journalism was accomplished without the editor leaving the newspaper office by using "the news that townsfolk brought to him and clipping stories from other newspapers" (Cloud 1992, 112).

As the country grew and matured into a more civilized nation, traditional journalism flourished. But the practice of amateur journalism was still common. Walter Williams, who founded the world's first journalism school at the University of Missouri in 1908, spoke fondly of these folksy contributors who "often worked for stamps, stationery and recognition among their neighbors" (Taft 1992).

AN AMERICAN RIGHT

The concept that every citizen may be a journalist became so firmly ingrained in the American spirit that it prompted the first great political debate of the new United States of America.

The American Revolution was as much a war of words as it was a war of muskets. Thomas Paine, James Madison, Patrick Henry and Alexander Hamilton inflamed the colonists with their anti-Crown essays in newspapers and handbills. Loyalists fired back with their own pamphlets—but also through the British sedition and libel laws.

The attempts by the government to stifle dissent were rallying points for the Patriots, who continued to fear government censorship even after the war. It took 12 years for the new nation to come up with a viable Constitution, and even then it was only accepted by the states with the promise of an immediate set of amendments. First among these was,

> Congress shall make no law respecting an establishment of religion, or prohibiting the free exercise thereof; or abridging the freedom of speech, or of the press; or the right of the people peaceably to assemble, and to petition the government for a redress of grievances. (U.S. Constitution 1789)

The ability of citizens to speak or write their own minds is more than a tradition in the United States. It is a right—an absolute right. Neither government nor fellow citizen can block publication, nor force an author to change the content. With the exception of a period of martial law during the Civil War, Americans have never had the need to 'sneak' their words to the public, as have many beleaguered citizens around the world. As First Amendment expert Ken Paulson noted, freedom of expression is wired into the American psyche: "Nations all over the world have emulated freedom, but we believe it" (Paulson 2012).

FORWARD TO CITIZEN JOURNALISM

While the combination of publishers unrestrained by guild rules or culture, an audience well used to hearing its own voice and a legal system that treats truth, lies and criticism equally would seem untenable, it worked. The moderating factor was the competitive media market. By 1900, it was not unusual for a small town to have two or more newspapers. Even in the frontier years, newspaper owners knew that another itinerant printer could move in to appease unhappy readers.

Many papers in the nineteenth century also catered for audiences less interested in the absolute truth than in the truth interpreted by their own political party. Though the party press is gone in the United States, the legacy of this is the dozens of newspapers with 'Democrat', 'Republican' or 'Whig' in their titles.

Credibility was and is a powerful marketing niche. Editors frequently passed along reader-generated content with the caveat that they had not checked the facts personally. It was also common to offer information as a quote from a letter (Cloud and Simpson 2008). The newspaper industry's mantle of credibility took on folkloric status with the popular idiom, "It's there in black and white" and is still guarded by the mainstream press. As a market factor, it also works. Wanta and Hu (1994) demonstrated that credibility is a fundamental driver of newspaper readership.

Views about accuracy and who best could ensure it began to change as the United States filled with daily newspapers staffed by rooms full of professional journalists who looked askance at anyone without their training:

The reader-generated stories were mostly relegated to the inside pages. Editors and reporters figured readers were not blessed with news judgment. Journalists were information elites. Readers and citizens didn't know the handshake; no one let them in on the code. Reporters figured anyone who called with a story idea was in the self-serving business, only trying to get pictures of their kids, businesses, causes, or pets in the paper. (Weldon 2008)

Nevertheless, notices from community correspondents and folksy local columns remained popular in non-metropolitan papers until the early 1970s. A series of paper mill strikes caused the price of newsprint to skyrocket and, in 1973, forced suppliers to ration paper to publications. Newspaper owners took drastic measures to maintain enough advertising to remain profitable. Comic strips shrank to a fraction of the page width, even some ads were restricted and most of the 'non-essential' content—particularly those local columns—was pulled (*The New York Times* 1973).

When the newsprint market stabilized, only the ads came back. After four decades, there are few editors and newsroom managers who remember the popularity of correspondents' folksy stories about community social life. By the turn of the twenty-first century, reader-generated stories were a curiosity.

BLOGGING CHANGES THE MEDIA ENVIRONMENT

What we now call citizen journalism was both preceded by and enabled by a world-rocking phenomenon: blogging.

The internet first granted wide access to the ordinary readers through newsgroups and later personal Web pages. The ability to chat with people of similar minds around the world made newsgroups especially popular in the 1990s with disenfranchised segments of the population, such as members of the gay community and political radicals.

The development of the World Wide Web by Tim Berners-Lee allowed a relatively easy combination of text and graphics. Programming complexity, however, kept it in the domain of the technically adept, who often logged their programming progress on small diaries called weblogs.

Like many internet developments, the functional weblog workhorse soon became a recreational Web fixture. When entrepreneurial companies offered free software and hosting in 1999, the technical world took notice. *Wired* reported that the upstart Pyra company had an amazing 3,000 subscribers on its year-old Blogger platform in February 2000 (Kahney 2000).

The Blogger program and its many emulators made publishing simple enough to attract pre-teens and senior citizens alike. Suddenly, millions of people became publishers, if not journalists.

The reaction from the traditional press in the United States was not just critical, but cynical. The very notion that untrained, unedited and uncontrolled amateurs could compete with real journalists for the eyes and minds of the American public was unfathomable.

Two factors were at work here. First, like their earlier peers who lamented that hometown correspondents "didn't know the handshake", journalists facing the rise in blogs were offended that amateurs so easily could emulate professional skills that took them years to learn.

The more important second factor is that blogging followed few of the rules and procedures that journalism had developed to ensure credibility. Quality newspaper journalism in the twentieth century required a reporter trained not only in observation and writing, but also in the libel laws imposed by civil courts and the ethics the profession imposed on itself. The work of that reporter was vetted by one or more editors who checked facts, spelling and grammar, topped it with a clear headline and placed it on the 'appropriate' page.

Bloggers of the twentieth century simply wrote whatever they wanted, tagged it with a headline that may or may not make sense, and pushed the 'post' key.

The frustration was palpable. As Jonathan Klein, a former CBS news executive, said in 2004, "You couldn't have a starker contrast between the multiple layers of checks and balances, and a guy sitting in his living room in his pyjamas writing what he thinks" (Klein 2004).

Ironically, Klein was commenting on a standoff between the old and the new that would shortly overturn the American media equation: Rathergate.

In May 2004, CBS anchor Dan Rather narrated an investigative story challenging the military service record of President George W. Bush, who was running for re-election. The report suggested that as a Texas Air National Guard lieutenant in the 1970s, Bush received preferential treatment that kept him from being posted to Vietnam. Four documents allegedly from the period were offered as proof.

Within hours of the newscast, bloggers were questioning the validity of the documents, suggesting that the type on the memos was computer generated. Bloggers noted that the proportional fonts in the memos were unavailable on 1970s-era typewriters.

Scott Johnson, editor of the *Powerline* public policy blog, read the early reports and posted about them on the blog during the morning after the broadcast.

I put that up at 7:50 a.m. and left for work. And I thought, "Gee, if that's a mistake, I'll hear from a few readers who will set us right. And I'll post that information. And if we're right, we'll hear from a few readers who will supply some additional information. We'll post that".

Well, by the time I got to work, we had 50 e-mails from experts of all kind around the country, supplying additional information. (Hume 2004)

The world had just seen the new face of "credibility". Journalism, in both its traditional and citizen forms, would never be the same.

Blogging introduced 'truth' by mass judgment. Newspaper reporters turned each story over to at most a handful of editors who held it, manipulated it and only released it when it was 'perfect'. These puzzling bloggers released their stories to the world raw. They counted on their readers in the blogosphere to catch any errors.

The key to this new type of editing was the 'comment'. Although newspapers had long printed "letters to the editor" as a forum for readers to express their opinions, the comment function of blogging software offered something truly new in text publishing: two-way communication. Response to a post could be almost instantaneous—or it could be a belated observation offered months after the original post. In either case, the original author's work is corrected, supplemented, applauded or simply noted by the readers.

American newspapers were slow to appreciate the power of comments. At first, newspapers either banned comments from their Web editions or posted only select, edited comments—much as they had letters to the editor in the print edition. Reporters complained of rude, often anonymous remarks about their work or the reporters themselves. In 2007, only a third of the top 100 newspapers in the United States included comments in some form on their web sites (Santana 2011).

The *Washington Post* was one of the first large newspapers to open its journalism to the cyber comments of citizens, reporting 4,600 posts daily in 2007. Although two staff members pored through the comments looking for blatant abuse, enough 'marginal' commentary got through to irritate some readers. One reader called the comment section "an open sewer", and another was shocked that the Post would allow "racist and bigoted attacks on a regular basis". Jim Brady, *Washingtonpost.com*'s executive editor, conceded that the new online commentary system is "much more of a free-for-all". And, he added, the editor's role in this new world is challenging: "It's obviously subjective", Brady said. "We have to make judgment calls about what's an attack and what isn't. It's kind of like the old line about pornography: You know it when you see it" (Howell 2007).

Today almost no news site could survive without a robust comments section. Reporters have learned both to turn a cheek to digital insults and to use the comments to expand their work. Santana (2011) found that 98% of the reporters he surveyed read comments at some level, and about a quarter said they get story ideas from the comments. Perhaps more importantly, 70% said the comments have changed their thinking on the newsworthiness of a topic.

FROM BLOG TO CITIZEN JOURNALISM

The fundamental difference between blogging and citizen journalism is intent. Blogging is first a software format: templated design, easy access and posts stacked latest upon oldest. But more importantly, blogs are expressions of personality.

Because blogs are largely the work of single authors, their content varies as widely as the people who write them. While some blogs are news-oriented, most are not. Technorati said 60% of bloggers are hobbyists who blog for fun. They write about their families, sports, collecting, poetry and similar topics. 'Mommy blogging'—women writing tips, observations and support for other women—is one of the fastest growing sectors. Approximately 14% of American mothers either write or turn to one of the 3.9 million mommy blogs for advice (Laird 2012).

Citizen journalists, on the other hand, have the overt intent of informing the public in a news-like manner. While much of both blogging and citizen journalism in the United States is about 'soft' subjects, the general tone of what is generally considered citizen journalism is "this is new, you should know about it". Research shows that citizen journalism site owners most often want to provide an alternative to traditional media—though they have little interest in running a media business (Lacy, Duffy, Riffe, Thorson, and Fleming, 2010).

Blogging was already a formidable phenomenon when Oh Yeon-ho developed the benchmark *OhmyNews* web site. Oh's focus was very political. As a liberal, he was forced to stay on the fringes of the conservative mainstream South Korean press. So he resorted to what he called the "guerilla methods" of using volunteer reporters and posting the material on the internet to avoid the costs of printing a traditional newspaper.

> I wanted to open a place of fair competition where people who wanted to share news with one another could do so through the Internet. I wanted to establish a culture where the quality of news determined whether it won or lost. I wanted to start a tradition free of newspaper company elitism were news was evaluated based on quality, regardless of whether it came from a major newspaper, a local reporter, an educated journalist or a neighborhood housewife. I wanted to realize through the Internet the motto "Every citizen is a reporter," something that couldn't be done through printed newspapers. So I decided to make the plunge into the sea of the Internet, even though I feared that which was different from what I was accustomed. (Oh, 2005)

What differentiated *OhmyNews* from other blogs and other user-generated content is that it consolidated material from a variety of writers and published it on a platform with much greater distribution than a single blog or personal web site. It used a variant of the traditional newspaper circulation strategy to compete against traditional newspapers.

The history of accepting non-professional content in American newspapers did little to assuage the unease that Oh's words created amongst U.S.

journalists. News organizations and journalism researchers alike watched as the original 727 *OhmyNews* citizen reporters grew to 60,000 volunteers and 75 professional journalists.

The growing political power of *OhmyNews* was an eye-opener, but professional interest grew in an unexpected evolution of the site's content. Nonpolitical submissions written in a folksy, non-journalistic style began to attract a substantial readership. A December 2003 story that simply began "The first snow fell in our neighborhood, too" inspired Oh to re-examine the need to emulate newspapers in the web site's writing style and content mix. "If the time had come for every citizen to be a reporter, why was it necessary to continue to follow the same article writing formula set by the professional journalists?" (Oh, 2005).

It was this aspect of the Korean experiment that finally brought citizen journalism to the United States. Where Oh initially found his success in politics, Mary Lou Fulton found success in horses. Saddle horses and their hobbyist riders in the hinterlands of California, to be precise.

Fulton was founder of *The Northwest Voice*, the first practical U.S. experiment in substantially internet-based citizen journalism. Located far from the icons of American journalism, *The Northwest Voice* was an entrepreneurial adjunct to the daily newspaper in the small California agricultural city of Bakersfield. Fulton was an experienced newspaper reporter who moved into the digital world first as editor of *Washingtonpost.com* and later as senior manager of *America Online*. Tired of the East Coast, she moved back to California to be a member of the independent *Bakersfield Californian* board of directors.

Fulton persuaded the paper's management to let her experiment with a suburban section under development for an affluent area northwest of Bakersfield. She surprised most of the newspaper industry by reversing the normal publication order of online and print. She developed a web site filled with locally contributed articles, photos and columns, then she printed the copy from the site in a biweekly newspaper.

Even veteran online journalist Fulton was taken aback by the reaction to *The Northwest Voice* by readers. "The emotion has taken me by surprise. People love this paper". She attributed that emotion to the fact that people saw themselves on the site and "it is written by people in this community" (Bentley 2013).

The subject matter of the content was entirely up to the reader/writers. But they tended to stay away from political issues and instead chronicle everyday life in a semi-rural suburb of 'ranchettes'. Columns and stories giving tips and information about horses were enormously popular, Fulton said. The same applied to hot rods, religion and youth sports—all subjects spurned by the traditional newspaper.

Fulton had discovered another key that would feed the success of citizen journalism in the United States, something she termed the "lack of authenticity" in traditional journalism. "Reporters cover education, not schools, healthcare, not clinics. Not writing about you, but about an abstraction" (Fulton 2004).

Both Oh and Fulton were closely watched by the University of Missouri School of Journalism. As the first journalism school in the United States, the Missouri School of Journalism is something of an academy for traditional journalism. It publishes a daily newspaper, operates a commercial network television station and produces a host of web sites—not for the university's students, but for the residents of its host city of Columbia, Missouri.

A team of faculty and graduate students took on the task of determining whether this new variant could co-exist with traditional newspaper journalism. The project turned its focus on the question of how a product written by untrained authors could provide the assurances of accuracy, fairness and credibility that American newspapers—and the journalism school—held dear.

Discussions with journalists in the field and media researchers produced four key concerns about publishing user-generated material—even before facing the accuracy question:

1. Decency: Would the writers violate journalism's norms of good taste with profanity, anti-social content or unwarranted attacks?
2. Commercialism: Would businesses or organizations turn the citizen journalism format into a free public relations outlet?
3. Literacy: How much editing and rewriting should be done before items are published?
4. Banalism: Is anything just too stupid to appear on the citizen journalism site? If so, how dumb is dumb?

Like Oh Yeon-ho, the Missouri researchers concluded that the norms of traditional journalism were unjustifiable in this new media world. He had realized this when non-news feature submissions gained popularity in *OhmyNews*. That said, maintaining a relationship with a traditional newspaper—even if the citizen journalism content was relegated to a separate web site—gave the new medium's designers a tested framework in which they could build credibility.

The key was moderation. While blogs are usually the unedited product of their authors, citizen journalism might be more successful if a few trained journalists worked as partners with the non-professional authors. The researchers found that many of the concerns disappeared if editors abandoned the meat-axe approach of old-style copy desks, offered just a few simple pre-publication rules, reviewed the copy for readability rather than arbitrary style and then worked on the final version via an email conversation with the authors,

The rules were brief and simple: no profanity, no nudity, no personal attacks and no attacks purely on race, religion, gender, origin or sexual orientation. Those were the bounds of decency that both newspapers and their readers had followed for generations. Commercialism, the researchers decided, was a chimera. Editors could ask writers to avoid promoting sales or replicating ads, but material that showed the honest pride of a business owner or organization member was merely the reflection of a citizen's life.

Concerns for literacy were equally unwarranted. Computers with spell checkers and grammar checkers kept most of the copy clean and a 'gentle' edit for readability rather than style retained the voice of the author.

After considerable soul-searching, the researchers realized that journalists are in no position to decide what is too stupid for the audience. Besides, with the infinite room of the internet, the truly unusual could be placed on the site under 'oddities' or 'other' headings.

The attempt to resolve the other-than-accuracy concerns about citizen journalism eventually also opened a new window on credibility for the Missouri researchers. The editor/moderators assigned to read citizen copy for taste and readability would also have the opportunity to look for signs of factual errors and libel—an everyday skill for trained newspaper editors. Most citizen copy at *OhmyNews* and *The Northwest Voice* was not time critical, so editors who suspected a problem would have time to discuss it with the author before posting.

That was borne out when *MyMissourian.com* launched in October 2004 as the citizen journalism affiliate of the *Columbia Missourian* daily newspaper. Errors were very minimal. When they did appear, the online readers were quick to point them out. The self-correcting nature of citizen journalism seemed to work. The simple submission rules were meant to bring an air of civility to the content, but not to control the volume of content as in many print papers (Bentley et al. 2005).

CITIZEN JOURNALISM BLOSSOMS

While the University of Missouri experiment in citizen journalism was deliberately methodical, the new genre quickly spread in the non-academic journalism world. Scores of web sites sprang up across the country in a wide variety of formats.

Most citizen journalism efforts, however, fell into one of two categories. Some sites were affiliated with traditional news outlets, as was both *The Northwest Voice* and *MyMissourian.com*. Many more were independent and positioned as an alternative to the traditional press.

The United States was primed for alternatives to traditional media. An annual poll by the Gallup organization showed that trust by the public in the U.S. media fell steadily from above 70% in the late 1960s to less than 50% in the early 2000s (Gallup 2012). But as the century closed, new technologies increasingly put the power of publication in the hands of amateurs. The nation was enthralled when in March 1991 a Los Angeles resident used his home video camera to record police beating Rodney King, an unarmed black man. The attacks on New York's World Trade Center on 11 September 2001 overwhelmed traditional media web sites. But as Halavais (2002) noted, the ubiquitous video camera in the hands of "the boulevardiers" captured the disaster. Blogs and other non-news web sites "were turned into conduits for information, commentary, and action related to 9/11 events" (Halavais 2002).

The government itself became the conduit for another early but huge citizen journalism event in 2003. The explosion of the shuttle Columbia on 1 February sent NASA engineers and researchers scrambling to explain what caused the catastrophe. The space agency solicited home videos and photographs of the explosion taken by private citizens. With the 12,000 images and videos submitted, the investigators pieced together the accident and stitched the best video clips into a video narrative of the flight (Barringer 1999).

It is of little surprise, then, that quick on the heels of the citizen journalism experiments in Bakersfield and at the University of Missouri, citizen journalism exploded across the United States. There were soon so many variants that media watchers argued over which qualified as citizen journalism. The Poynter Institute's Steve Outing took a shot at it outlining "the 11 layers of citizen journalism", a hierarchy running from simply allowing public comment in traditional media, to MyMissourian-like units of newspaper or television organizations, to free-standing independent citizen journalism sites or community blogs, to integrating citizen journalism and professional journalism under one roof (Outing 2005). The introduction of Facebook in 2004 and Twitter in 2006 gave almost anyone the ability to post 'news' to their cyber friends. Press critic and New York University professor Jay Rosen reduced the definitions to one sentence: "When the people formerly known as the audience employ the press tools they have in their possession to inform one another, *that's* citizen journalism" (Rosen 2004).

The mobile phone has arguably become the most potent of those laymen's tools, putting a camera in almost every pocket. The power of the mobile phone goes far beyond its ready access, however. Writing coherently takes talent. But anyone can capture some sort of image or video with a camera phone. Perhaps more importantly, anyone can transmit that image or video to almost anywhere in the world instantly. The first public images of fires, floods, demonstrations and almost any gathering of two or more people are now invariably the work of 'amateurs' armed with cell phones. The sheer number of photos and videos taken by eye witnesses ensures that at least *some* will be memorable and of sufficient quality to attract an audience.

Today citizen journalism is ubiquitous in the United States. Nearly every traditional media source has some means of allowing its audience to participate. Even "The Gray Lady" of the newspaper world, *The New York Times*, allows submissions to reader photo galleries, full stories from readers, terse one-line comments, reader recipe columns and several other features (Rabaino 2012).

For newspapers and television stations, citizen journalism is becoming a routine part of daily journalism. A key sign of that was when the pioneering *MyMissourian.com* merged into its parent *Columbia Missourian* in 2012 (Bentley 2012).

Freestanding neighbourhood blogs and alternative news sites also abound, though they have had a more difficult time with financial sustainability. Volunteer writers are easier to find than volunteer advertising sales people, and the NGO grants that launched many sites are running out (McLellen 2011).

WHO DEFINES THE TRUTH?

American culture has combined with digital technology to fulfil the colonial patriot's dream of a free and unfettered press. The challenge now is separating the truth from the chaff in that unfettered flood.

Many traditional media organizations employ professional journalists to moderate submissions to their citizen journalism adjuncts. On busy national sites, those professionals become the new gatekeepers. The volume of traffic on the site can be the determinant of how much material is checked and posted to the readers and how much is rejected.

CNN's *iReport*, one of the most globally visible American citizen journalism sites, counts heavily on the skill of the professional journalists who monitor the approximately 500 daily submissions. Only about 8% of the submissions are selected for further vetting by CNN staff, who double-check with CNN field reporters, subject-matter experts, affiliate networks and local media. It is as much art as science, according to CNN's Lila King:

> It's an emerging craft, one that combines an eye for a good story with a flair for connecting the dots and, above all, a human touch. Vetting is the heart of *iReport*, CNN's platform for citizen journalism. You won't see *iReports* on television or on *CNN.com* (outside the special *iReport* section, that is) before they've been fact checked and cleared. (King 2012)

A more common form of quality control is blogging's truth by mass judgment. Many citizen journalism sites count on the interactivity of the Web to provide accuracy: Readers post comments correcting the errors. Reaction from readers dates back to the earliest newspapers, but digital technology allows it to be both instantaneous and continuous. 'Truth' in this format is an organic being that evolves with the story.

Perhaps the most overlooked effect of citizen journalism is this reframing of the concept 'truth'. For most of the history of mass media, what is alleged to be 'true' has been defined by the information provider. With millions of providers now pumping content into the Web, nothing short of a law could guarantee that they maintain accuracy.

No such law can exist in the United States.

Americans built their country and their culture on the First Amendment–assured right to say what they will without government control. This has always allowed for lies to live alongside gospel, but never before has there been less reliability in the information stream.

That stream is a bottomless source of facts, but as Pierce (2008) said, facts are merely the available data, simple and incomplete snapshots of events. "Truth is the reality behind the facts"(Pierce 2008).

Recalling chapter one and the requirements set out there for a journalism that meets the needs of a participatory democracy, the requisite skill for informed citizenship in the twenty-first century is triangulation. While the internet can overwhelm readers with its volume, that same trait also gives citizens the unequalled opportunity to personally find their own version of 'the truth' (the caution here is occasioned by the fact that what is 'true' is defined, of course, within the inherent limitations of subjectivity common to all citizens).

By vastly increasing the variance in the reports available to the public, citizen journalists have given life to a success strategy long employed by traditional scholars. Triangulation requires the reader to pore through two or more reports, to critically compare their content and to make an independent assessment of which report or which pieces of either report appear to bear 'the truth'.

Triangulated assessments of what is true offer a future for citizen and traditional journalist alike. The millions of 'amateurs' feed an increasingly insatiable appetite for free facts—some of which are accurate and representative of 'the truth' of often complex situations. The professionals, with their training and traditions, provide a marketable shortcut to a reasonable approximation of 'the truth' for those too impatient to find it themselves. It's a media system rife with uncertainty, but peculiarly at home in the United States.

Americans have taken to a personal level the rejection of the information control that drove them to create a new nation.

THE FUTURE

The question of how journalistic quality and credibility can be established vis-à-vis the contributions of 'citizens' has now been addressed via a discussion of the process of triangulation, and, in so doing, the chapter has shown how the reputation of good citizen journalism can be ensured within the future. However, there are other 'future issues' that need to be addressed with regard to citizen journalism also.

It is of course easier to lay out the path that has taken citizen journalism to where it is and to examine the implications of that than it is to decipher the future for journalism as a whole that its development is helping to create. In its modern, internet carried form, citizen journalism is by definition part of the problem for traditional mainstream journalism, insofar as its *independent* manifestations have increased the competition for the audience's attention on the communication platform of the moment and the foreseeable future. It is a temptation to cost-cutting media companies and their owners insofar as its incorporation within traditional news providers' offerings can be seen as a way of saving on the salary budget for professional journalists. But equally, as has been shown in the discussion, it can develop new enthusiasms and new audiences and help re-engage those that have been lost to mainstream news brands when housed under their roof, or in close-related proximity to the main operation, as in the case of the *Northwest Voice*.

Thinking back to chapter one, in giving its audience and writers a feeling that they are genuinely engaged in an interactive relationship with other citizens, journalists, etc., that is an essential part of a participatory democracy; citizen journalism, as part of a conventional news provider, can help preserve, restore or promote the position of its host as a part of the community that people want to access. What it can't do as yet is contribute very much to the financial position of newspapers that host it, for example, and who have found their revenues shrinking as a result of the difficulty of creating an online business model that compensates adequately for the loss of print revenues as reader interest switches increasingly to the internet. That is another story altogether, and the question of how online news providers for whom a paywall or advertising won't pay enough of the bills are to survive over the longer term is one to which citizen journalism doesn't in itself have any real answers. What it is, undoubtedly, is part of the answer as to how local and community news gaps can be filled if traditional providers vanish, or cease to be able to fund sufficient staffing levels to keep a decent level of provision in place. Nevertheless, if something like *The New York Times* succumbs to the problems of online economics and shrinking print sales, as could yet happen, it is difficult to conceive of citizen journalism filling the gap left by the quality of writing, the scale of focussed expertise and still considerable (if not always justified) brand trust that the *NYT* represents, with its reliably available and constantly updated news on a daily basis. It is that kind of example, perhaps, that helps keep the scale of what citizen journalism has achieved so far and what it might achieve in the future in proportion. It should be remembered *that OhmyNews* was created in a Korea that very definitely was lacking a *NYT* or a *Washington Post*.

So, on one level, American citizen journalism is the re-birth of the past within a format of the present and the future. It gives a new meaning and vitality to the participative traditions that were at the heart of the republic at its foundation. But, while being potentially a means of helping keep the mainstream media in touch with its audience, even where it is incorporated within the news sites of traditional news providers, it has little to offer in terms of assisting with the financial sustainability of expensive quality news operations—the exception is that, when its offering is sufficiently attractive, it can help achieve the number of site visits that are necessary to keep in place the modest payments that online advertisers pay for news site space. As pointed out previously, it can also help to fill the gap when those news operations that are losing out to internet news economics most severely 'downsize' their newsrooms, but many critics would argue that this is just to 'plug the gap' with a frequently 'second rate' amateur news source—news on the cheap.

Equally, it is difficult to see a business model for independent citizen journalism that will help it achieve the financial base necessary for long term sustainability. For example, while *OhmyNews* was something of a trailblazer, as pointed out earlier, its financial position has been quite shaky in recent years, and its Japanese offshoot effectively went bankrupt in 2008 (Tran 2009). Qualitatively good citizen journalism enriches and helps enable participatory democracy as defined in chapter one, but even in its collectivity it cannot match the scope of the biggest and the best of the American professional journalism providers that in many cases are crumbling around it. Means such as crowd-sourcing, the OhMyNews model, etc., can boost its impact, but, as pointed out previously, what they do not do is provide a *NYT* equivalent.

Citizen journalism, as it has been described within this chapter, looks to be here to stay as part of the American newsscape, but the scale of news operation that is required to report on, analyse and monitor the political elephant that is the United States is so large that, certainly at the core of Washington level politics and administration, a healthy, high quality, pluralistic mainstream needs to be in place if the government is to be held to full account by its citizens. An equally healthy citizen journalism presence is essential to report on those things the mainstream ignores, to criticise what it does badly and to present the views of ordinary citizens that might otherwise be invisible, but it needs the professional core to do the key bits that it is not well resourced enough to handle. Ultimately, citizen journalism is an important part of the answer to the question of how best to provide news that meets the needs of participatory democracy within the United States, but it has little to offer in terms of assisting with the long term financial viability of high quality hard news. For the most part its contribution to the American newsscape is political and social rather than economic and on the basis of existing evidence will continue to be so into the future.

REFERENCES

Barringer, Felicity. 1999. "Publications Are Trying New Techniques to Win Over Loyal Readers." *New York Times,* 4 January.

Bentley, Clyde. 2012. "MyMissourian to become a new section, From Readers." *MyMissourian.com,* 9 February. http://mymissourian.com/.

Bentley, Clyde. 2013. "Citizen Journalism: The American Migration." In *Citizen Journalism: Back to the Future?,* edited by Clyde Bentley. Knight Community

News Network. Accessed 30 January 2013. http://www.kcnn.org/research/citizen_journalism_migration/.

Bentley, Clyde, Jeremy Littau, Brian Hamman, Hans K. Meyer, Beth Welsh, and Brendan Watson. 2005. "The Citizen Journalism Movement: MyMissourian as a Case Study." Paper presented at the Association for Education in Journalism and Mass Communication conference, San Antonio, TX, 10–13 August.

Brown, Perry. 1992. "Preaching from the Print Shop." *Christian History* 11: 34–35.

Cloud, Barbara L. 1992. *The Business of Newspapers on the Western Frontier.* Reno: University of Nevada Press.

Cloud, Barbara L., and Alan K. Simpson. 2008. *The Coming of the Frontier Press: How the West Was Really Won.* Evanston, IL: Northwestern University Press.

Fulton, M. L. (2004, June 31). [Telephone Conversation: Explanation of the Northwest Voice project].

Gallup. 2012. Media Use and Evaluation. Accessed 27 October 2012. http://www.gallup.com/poll/143267/distrust-media-edges-record-high.aspx

Gillmor, Dan. 2004. *We the Media: Grassroots Journalism by the People, for the People.* Sebastopol, CA: O'Reilly Media.

Halavais, Alex. 2002. "The Rise of Do-it-yourself Journalism After September 11." In *One Year Later: September 11 and the Internet,* edited by Susannah Fox, Lee Rainie, and Mary Madden. Pew Internet & American Life Project. http://www.pewinternet.org/Reports/2002/One-year-later-September-11-and-the-Internet/04-The-Rise-of-Do-it-yourself-Journalism-After-September-11/01-Key-Findings.aspx

Howell, Deborah. 2007. "Online Venom or Vibrant Speech?" *Washington Post,* 6 May.

Hume, B. (Writer). (2004). How the Blogosphere Took on CBS' Docs [Transcript of television show]. In Fox News (Producer), *Special Report With Brit Hume.* New York City: Fox News.

Kahney, Leander 2000. "The Web the Way it Was." *Wired,* 23 February. http://www.wired.com/culture/lifestyle/news/2000/02/34006?currentPage=1

Kaminski, John P. 2002. "Religion and the Founding Fathers." *Annotation* (March): 1, 4, 19. http://www.archives.gov/nhprc/annotation/2002/2002-mar.pdf

King, Lila. 2012. "Vetting Citizen Journalism." *Nieman Reports* 66: 17–19.

Klein, Jonathan. 2004. Quoted in *Special Report With Brit Hume*: "How the Blogosphere Took on CBS' Docs." Fox News. Partial transcript. 17 September. http://www.foxnews.com/story/0,2933,132494,00.html.

Knautz, Rob. 2007. Introduction, *The Federalist Papers.* Accessed 24 May 2008. http://www.foundingfathers.info/federalistpapers

Lacy, Stephen, Margaret Duffy, Daniel Riffe, Esther Thorson, and Ken Fleming. 2010. "Citizen Journalism Sites Complement Newspapers." *Newspaper Research Journal* 31: 34–46.

Laird, Sam. 2012. "The Rise of the Mommy Blogger." *Mashable,* 8 May. http://mashable.com/2012/05/08/mommy-blogger-infographic/

Leth, Goran. 1993. "A Protestant Public Sphere: The Early European Newspaper Press." *Studies in Newspaper and Periodical History* 1: 67–90. doi: 10.1080/13688809309357887.

McLellen, Michele. 2011. "Emerging Economics of Community News." In *The State of the News Media 2011.* Pew Research Center's Project for Excellence in Journalism. http://stateofthemedia.org/2011/mobile-survey/economics-of-community-news/.

The New York Times. 1973. "Newsprint Shortage Likely to Continue for Months; Some Features Suspended." 2 September.

Oh, Yeon-Ho. 2004. "New Book: 'OhmyNews Story' OhmyNews founder Oh Yeon Ho Recounts Four Years of His New Media Venture in His News Book." OhMyNews, 12 August. http://english.ohmynews.com/articleview/article_view.asp?article_class=8&no=181975&rel_no=1.

Oh, Yeon-Ho. 2005. "OhmyNews: A Unique Product of Korea." Cited in Ronda Hauben, "OhmyNews and 21st Century Journalism." 9 September. http://english.ohmynews.com/articleview/article_view.asp?at_code=279015.

Outing, Steve. 2005. "The 11 Layers of Citizen Journalism." Poynter Institute. 31 May, updated 2 March 2011. http://www.poynter.org/uncategorized/69328/the-11-layers-of-citizen-journalism/.

Paulson, Ken. 2012. "The Digital First Amendment: Free Speech in the Age of Social Media." Master class given at Missouri School of Journalism, 15 October.

Pierce, Roger. 2008. *Research Methods in Politics: A Practical Guide*. Los Angeles: Sage.

Rabaino, Lauren. 2012. "10 Ways *The New York Times* Tells Stories Through Reader Content." *MediaBistro*, 10 February. http://www.mediabistro.com/10000words/10-ways-the-new-york-times-tells-stories-through-its-readers_b10700

Reilly, Hugh J. 2010. *The Frontier Newspapers and the Coverage of the Plains Indian Wars*. Santa Barbara, CA: Praeger.

Rosen, Jay. 2004. "Journalism is Itself a Religion." Accessed 24 May 2008. http://www.therevealer.org/archives/timeless_000149.php

Santana, Arthur D. 2011. "Online Readers' Comments Represent News Opinion Pipeline." *Newspaper Research Journal* 32: 66–81.

Stelter, Gilbert. 1973. "The City and Westward Expansion: A Western Case Study." *Western Historical Quarterly* 4: 187–202.

Taft, William Howard. 1992. *Missouri Newspapers and the Missouri Press Association: 125 Years of Service*. Marceline, MO: Heritage House.

Tran, Mark. 2009. "OhmyNews Appeals to Readers for Cash." *Guardian*, 8 July. http://www.guardian.co.uk/media/2009/jul/08/ohmynews-appeals-for-cash.

U.S. Constitution. 1789. Amendment 1.

Vandenbroucke, Guillaume. 2008. "The U.S. Westward Expansion." *International Economic Review* 49: 81–110. doi: 10.1111/j.1468–2354.2008.00474.x.

Wanta, Wayne, and Yu-Wei Hu. 1994. "The Effects of Credibility, Reliance, and Exposure on Media Agenda-Setting: A Path Analysis Model." *Journalism & Mass Communication Quarterly* 71: 90–98.

Weldon, Michele. 2008. *Everyman News: The Changing American Front Page*. Columbia, MO: University of Missouri Press.

11 UK Social Media, Citizen Journalism and Alternative News

Clare Cook and Andrew Dickinson

INTRODUCTION

The drawing of boundaries between citizen journalism, alternative media and mainstream media is easier said than done and often represents more an effort in defining battle lines. For some, even including citizen journalism will be problematic. The term as a description is not only seen as discredited but also anachronistic. BBC journalist Andrew Marr declared that "the so-called citizen journalism is the spewings and rantings of very drunk people late at night" (Plunkett 2010). Their distaste for it is, in part, a reaction to how the concept was first introduced around 10 years ago. Suddenly, it was claimed, anyone and everyone could be a journalist, and citizen journalists were charged with deskilling a profession. Where were the editing, the analysis, the professional codes and ethics? Shirky claimed that "everyone is a media outlet" in a process of mass amateurization (2009, 55–80). But far from being the domain of ranting drunks, social media has fast become an accepted platform for news and debate, and despite the attitude of some in the media, those who might practise or by random acts (Lasica 2003) create citizen journalism have become part of the mainstream discourse. The acceptance of the medium as a suitable platform for mainstream media, despite uncertainty around the economic models, indicates they recognise its broad engagement and appeal. Yet the mainstream media have been grappling with how to incorporate a wider proliferation of voices and story-telling mechanics into their own production and how to understand the challenges of the social media ecology.

For the most part, mainstream media remain sceptical as to how best to incorporate alternative narratives into their own traditionally focused requirement of quality. In many ways, their definition of quality is defined against the inherent subjectivity of the profession (Gaber 2009) and underpinned by an unwritten but accepted role for journalism within the democratic process that has meant the process that purports to uphold a measure of quality is rarely questioned (Gans 2003). However, the definition of quality, as this chapter will argue, could and should be a fluid concept, incorporating methodologies devised by users and social platforms. If we consider part of the ideological purpose of journalism is to contribute to and inform meaningful democratic debate, the element of comparativeness is particularly important as a measure of quality—the idea that key issues are poorly covered if they are reported within only one "ideological prism" when others of a practical, logical and well-constructed nature are available that could offer alternative ways of viewing the matters at the heart of the report (see chapter one). The concept of comparativeness could be one of the fundamental ways in which alternative narratives contribute to a robust definition of quality news. The question of how to reconcile these various possible interpretations of quality with those inherited from professional practices can create a developmental paradigm. Indeed, as chapter one showed also, parts of the mainstream do from time to time meet in the same territory as some alternative providers and use 'comparativeness' within their own hard news output and analysis. However, this chapter suggests that this behaviour is the exception rather than the norm, and the continuing requirement to frame any interaction within the internal practices of traditional media is a fundamental stumbling block to the process of building better relationships with an engaged and informed public, which, in turn, would help address the broader issue of comparativeness.

This chapter will show how difficult it is to pin down the impact of citizen journalism and alternative narratives on the quality of news. This is not simply because of the different practical and ideological approaches used to underpin the notion of quality in the mainstream and alternative press; in that respect any attempt to define the developments within the social media space purely through this representation of the profession of journalism and its institutions is destined to fail. We argue that the dynamic and inclusive nature of the growing social media ecosystem outside the traditional media challenges the process and ideological underpinning of a measure of quality. This is, to a greater extent, a reflection of the mainstream media's failures to build relationships that allow their institutional requirements of quality to be effectively communicated, critiqued and developed. The fragmented nature of the mainstream media and its legion problems has resulted in a lack of a coherent response to the challenges and opportunities of the social media space—but on a more fundamental level, it challenges their capacity to fulfil their role in the democratic discourse by failing to contribute to a multiperspectival news environment (Gans 2005).

DEFINING PARTICIPATION

Attempts to categorise user involvement in the news reporting process have become ever more complex due to the dynamic definition of the user and their role in the process of consuming and creating news. In this section we identify and develop the key terms that frame our central line of inquiry relating to quality news provision.

We take mainstream media to be organisations with an established brand and audience that work within traditional editorial frameworks that dictate the collection and presentation of content. These frameworks take balance, verification and (in some but not all cases) objectivity as the benchmarks of quality.

A definition of citizen journalism is harder to pin down. The development of the term, as we use it, owes much to the use of blogs. As a free and easy-to-use publishing platform, blogs offer individuals a robust way to present, organise and promote content outside of the traditional media cycle. Whilst it could be argued that blogs facilitate citizen journalism, it would be a mistake to conflate the two. The motivations for blogging can range from a political commitment (political bloggers) to the spreading of full and free information, a simple desire or just to do well a job that attracts and entertains them even if that is simply a desire to communicate information to friends and families.

The increased visibility of content facilitated by blogs places the work of individuals and organisations in the same space as the traditional media. It could be argued that this simply made visible the relationship that already existed between informed individuals and the mainstream, but it also offered an opportunity for individuals to by-pass traditional media processes and actively build their own. The mainstream media's response to this transformation of "the people formerly known as the audience" (Rosen 2006) has been mixed, and it is telling that though many of those who may be called citizen journalists do not seek or demand the title, attempts by the mainstream media to describe this activity have studiously tried to avoid journalist or journalism. The National Union of Journalists (NUJ) talked about "witness contributors", not citizen journalists (and said news organisations should strive to use alternative material from NUJ members, if available). Deuze, Bruns, and Neuberger (2007) characterise citizen journalists as news-producing consumers, but also see them as being in opposition to professional journalists, as competitor-colleagues, also called "information providers" (Strömbäck 2005).

In the context of this chapter we take as the core of our definition of citizen journalism the idea of *intent*, to reflect the ideological motivations rather than the structural practice of journalism. This could be a practical commitment to contribute to the range of content available on a specific subject, to adopting a gatewatching role (Gans 2005; Bruns 2005). A citizen journalist is thus someone who is not a trained, professional journalist working for salaried or freelance payment within the media and who is motivated to use the communication and research tools (what Rosen [2008] calls the Press tools) at their disposal to contribute to the telling of the story of an event, or the explaining of an issue to the benefit of an audience.

The explosion in availability of accessible creation and distribution platforms (like blogs) has brought the phrase *social media* into common use. For this chapter we present *social media* as being the space outside of the recognised structures of the mainstream and "alternative" media where people interact and create content. This builds on the three qualities of the web, namely web 1.0 as a web of cognition, web 2.0 as a web of human communication and web 3.0 as a web of co-operation (Fuchs et al. 2010).

The accessible and individual nature of production using social media has given rise to the term User Generated Content (UGC). Although its meaning is well defined (Vickery and Wunsch-Vincent 2007), as with citizen journalism the mainstream media struggles with the term. Within the mainstream, the phrase *user-generated content* has evolved to describe material appearing on mainstream media news web sites that was originated by the public. Foust (2011) frames that transformation in terms of participation along a continuum of increased audience involvement from sources, user feedback, UGC, crowdsourcing through to citizen journalism. Wardle and Williams (2010) propose instead the term *audience material*. They evidence five different types of audience material used within BBC news output. UGC can be seen simply as part of a broader range of material generated by the audience, facilitated by an explosion in the availability and usability of production tools and the normalisation of applications such as Facebook, Twitter and YouTube.

We take 'alternative media' to be organisations or individuals with dynamic brands and audiences, with individual editorial frameworks that, in contrast to the mainstream, take transparency and the interplay with social media as their benchmark for quality. This reliance on transparency as opposed to the mainstream's structural representation of objectivity is an important distinction and one that lies at the heart of the challenge of mainstream media's engagement with alternative voices. We propose that mainstream and alternative media exist at opposite ends of the same spectrum, with the measure of quality determined by the reach their own frameworks and editorial processes will allow. Later in the chapter we briefly explore the example of WikiLeaks and what can happen when these frameworks do meet and are found to be incompatible.

In setting out these key definitions we will examine the extent to which understandings of quality news, both in theory and in practice, are shifting against a background of a complex and rich media ecosystem. The methodology here is to review the provision of UGC during key sample UK news events selected from the last 10 years. We will explore the extent to which an alternative narrative can emerge through social media with independent and credible definitions of quality. We will explore whether mainstream media is missing the opportunity to embrace these alternative narratives as part of the requirement for comparativeness, and in doing so losing its place in the setting of the parameters of quality due to a lack of flexibility in its own processes.

THE UGC FLOODGATES

A watershed day came in 2005 when grainy mobile phone images of victims of the London tube bombing were flashed across the world, the most dramatic proof yet of the power of citizens as eyewitness to events. No one could deny that, whatever you wished to call it, a new force in journalism had arrived. Mainstream media struggled to cope with the dynamic reporting of an event in which users, armed with mobile phones and portable devices, were actively participating. How could such work by 'the general public' encompass the breadth and complexity of the existing order of professional journalism? Could it—whatever 'it' was—become a true alternative or contributor to quality news journalism in answer to shrinking newsrooms and institutional problems already plaguing the industry?

Most mainstream media accepted some user content as a way of including a wider variety of voices into their news provision, incorporating social media in the basic journalistic process. During the 7/7 attacks, several sites created spaces for firsthand accounts from eyewitnesses to the attacks, thus creating a more open interface. The BBC, for example, received 22,000 emails and text messages about the London tube and bus bombings. There were 300 photos—50 within an hour of the first bomb going off—and several video sequences (Allan 2007). Mainstream media learnt the need to provide a range of opportunities to participate, with site space that included topical polls, 'most read', chat rooms, post-moderated message boards, live debates, blogs and comment sites. These allow for the possibility, in principle at least, of interactivity, providing different perspectives, modes of address and story selection (Goode 2009). One thing is clear, during the July 2005 terrorist bombings in London, alternative narratives confirmed a capacity to recast the conventions of on-the-ground news reporting. According to BBC journalist Torrin Douglas, 7/7 "was the day the phenomenon of user-generated content or citizens' journalism came into its own in Britain, as members of the public took over the roles of photographers and news correspondents" (Douglas 2006b). While newspaper early editions were focussed on the jubilation of Olympic success following London being awarded the 2012 games, the public's photos of events were helping to decipher what was going on: the blown-up bus, for example, confirming this was a bomb and not a power surge, as London Underground had first suggested. According to analysis of citizen journalism within the reporting of the London bombings by Allan (2007), members of London's blogging community mobilised whatever news and information they possessed by way of statements, clips, survivor diaries, roll-calls and more. While it is not possible to assess these individually as part of this analysis, there can be little doubt that collectively these posts, along with chat room messaging, forum discussions and other independent message boards, amplified the range of voices available as part of the wider information provision. Atton and Hamilton (2008, 86) argue that this role part-counterbalanced mainstream media, allowing for the devotion of attention to the issues ignored by the mainstream press and in so doing inverted "the hierarchy of access to the news" in a way that foregrounded the viewpoints of ordinary people. At a conceptual level, Robinson and DeShano (2011, 963) cite how bloggers and local reporters develop influence over each other to "redefine the aims, standards and ideology of journalism".

Of particular news value was the bloggers' capacity to articulate the sorts of personal experience that typically fall outside journalistic boundaries. The former *Guardian* editor-in-chief Emily Bell cited how bloggers and the "the engagement of the public in disseminating and surrendering news footage" added to the news reporting of the day. She argues that the contribution of citizen storytellers marked "the earliest stages of a revolutionary relationship" (Bell 2005).

Users caught up in the event had a particularly poignant role to play, given how mainstream camera crews were unable to access the aftermath of the London Underground stations due to tight security. Several newsworthy images were taken by individuals acting as witnesses to the event, with many of the resultant images resonating with a particularly raw edge that would have been difficult to replicate with the third-person objectivity of a tactically positioned news team. The images helped formulate a new understanding of what it means to report the immediate aftermath of a catastrophe, suggesting that social media, with its lack of resourcing and deployment issues, is better suited by construction to reporting events as they happen.

There is no shortage of belief that the event showed that involving citizens fully in the news process is a move towards the creation of quality news content. In his reflection on user-generated content from the 7/7 bombings, former BBC journalist and news executive Richard Sambrook notes, "Our reporting on this story was a genuine collaboration, enabled by consumer technology—the camera phone in particular—and supported by trust between broadcaster and audience. And the result was transformational in its impact: We know now that when major events occur, the public can offer us as much new information as we are able to broadcast to them. From now on, news coverage is a partnership" (Sambrook 2005; see also Harrison 2010).

However, the interplay and inter-reliance between mainstream media and citizen-produced content involves a complex relationship. There are issues of timing. Nicola Bruno's study found, for example, that although news organisations rely on user-generated content at first, they tend to move to professionally sourced material as the story unfolds (2011). There are also considerations of reach. Part of the limitations of citizen journalism in the UK in 2013 is that it lacks the perception of being of *mainstream* quality unless it makes its output point to a mainstream legacy site or news output. As we have seen in preceding discussions, it is not without meaning. However, whilst the statistics show that the mainstream media still retain a level of brand loyalty, citizen journalism (outside of audience generated content) would lack a recognisable level impact if it were never to become available as part of a quality news agenda. Alexander Chadwick's camera phone picture became so iconic because of the technological determinant of its output destination: the image, selected from among thousands, became a headline story in the days following the London bombings and was published in many news outlets, including *The Times* and the BBC. Had it been exclusively shared among close friends or alternative sites, its impact as part of quality news may have been limited.

For the most part, while the inclusion of this type of user-generated content within the mainstream helped in softening the image of news organisations as monolithic structures and highlighted the value of the relationship between mainstream and social media, attempts continued to place this activity within the context of the existing professional order. Inside the traditional media, the value of citizen journalism was seen to be limited outside of its still strictly controlled presence within professional news providers' outputs. Mainstream UK news web sites want to retain control, particularly over users' submissions, to meet the standards of professionally produced output (Thurman 2008) and to distance this activity from the core terms of journalism and journalist. As Dvorak put it, "you can't play professional baseball just because you think the Seattle Mariners stink" (2006). Dvorak's view echoes a common amateur versus professional rhetoric within traditional journalism that alludes to a broader concern over the identity of a journalist in a shifting media landscape. In a number of ways, 7/7 highlights a missed opportunity for a fuller and more productive relationship. But it also reveals a much more complex set of debates within the traditional media that are as much about the challenges to the role and identity of journalists as they are about measures of quality.

THE PROMISE OF PARTICIPATORY JOURNALISM

In December 2005, the Buncefield oil fire at Hemel Hempstead was the UK's biggest peacetime blaze and highlighted a further shift in the dynamic between citizen storytelling and mainstream media. Having sensed the capacity for raw storytelling through eye witness content in 7/7, the audience started to actively seek to be part of the journalistic process. This enhanced the tensions with mainstream media as to what, if anything, users had to contribute in the provision of quality news journalism. Discussions turned to participatory journalism (for example, Singer et al. 2011) and the extent to which citizen participation progresses the journalistic process, incorporates a wider range of voices (Rosen 1993) and necessitates new, more reciprocal, interpretations of quality in a dynamic relationship with mainstream media. Was there still a boundary affecting user participation as witnesses to events that existed in the same way that it always had? Could citizen content still only predominantly be accepted for use by the mainstream media according to their editorial judgement alone?

According to the BBC, the first picture of the blaze was received within 13 minutes of the explosion, followed soon after by video footage. On the one hand, raw amateur video footage brought an alternative voice to the storytelling (Douglas 2006a). Users were aware from the experiences of 7/7 that their footage might make headlines in the mainstream. This corresponds with conclusions by Bock (2012) identifying emerging strategies used by citizen video journalists to establish authority in their reports. But there was also an alternative voice emerging, taking on the role of gatewatcher, when one considers the blog posts relating to the event. Brixton-based non-profit blog Urban75, for example, critiqued the American channel Fox News for several inaccuracies in their reports, not least for one news item under the headline "Britain ablaze" (Urban75 2005).

The British public was also developing a growing awareness of how to organize their content into an alternative narrative of events. Photo-sharing sites, such as Flickr, allow for individual photographs and photographers to be tagged into groups by key words, thus facilitating search and categorisation. These practices allow for photographs to be viewed thousands of times within hours of posting, through linking and sharing.

Fast-forward four years to the G20 protests in April 2009 in London. Users, increasingly active on UGC platforms, were familiar with the acts of rating, commenting, tagging or reposting their content. Here the user demonstrates not just the ability to act as content producer or information provider, but as content disseminator. It adds a dimension of metajournalism (Dvorak 2006). Bruns (2003) articulates this by distinguishing between gatewatchers as those who publicise news (by pointing to sources) and those who publish it (by compiling an apparently complete report from the available sources). Further studies have evidenced upward trends in the quantity of distributed news via social networks and the complexities of delineating narratives in these spaces (Hermida 2010; Johnson and Wiedenbeck 2009; Newman 2011; Willemsen, Neijens, Bronner, and Ridder 2011). These build on the idea that social media is evolving its own structures and processes to contribute to quality news provision through information dissemination.

Tools for user participation had become more sophisticated by April 2009, with audio and video recording taking centre stage. There was a rise in the use of social media as part of a response to legacy media coverage and to the actions of the police and government. Sites such as Flickr were being used to store images when cameras were confiscated, for example. iPhone recording tool Audioboo was used for on-the-spot interviews with demonstrators, and many people broadcast live to the web with services such as Qik. It is interesting to note that the *awareness* of Audioboo as a reporting tool was prompted by its use by the *Guardian*'s reporter Matthew Weaver. After he started linking to it, the site had 20,000 requests in 14 minutes. Other web users evidenced their growing awareness of tools by creating maps and mashups, which combine data (Beaumont 2009).

The London riots in 2011, sparked by the fatal shooting of 29-year-old Mark Duggan by the police, were a seminal moment for Twitter—and the need for mainstream media to understand the ways in which social media could become the story. As legacy news providers often struggled to keep up with the unpredictable, dynamic story on the ground, the social networking site became the go-to place to track events. There was panic among the authorities. The then Acting Commissioner of the Metropolitan Police Tim Godwin concluded that the site was fanning the contagion and being used to coordinate the unrest (Procter 2011, quoted in Ball and Lewis 2011). Closer examination evidenced how a free mobile phone messaging service on Blackberry Messenger proved to be the pivotal communications network (Wasik 2012). A separate analysis of how rumours circulated on Twitter during the riots revealed how the network was used by people to collectively clarify and dispel false information (Ball and Lewis 2011). Social media was something that not only needed greater understanding and engagement, but also represented an element of the storytelling narrative that required investment from the beginning.

It was only through a genuine relationship with social media that the true potential for producing quality hard news reports on the riots could be exploited by the mainstream. There was then and still is evidence in the UK to suggest the potential for much more significant citizen journalist and social media interactions with professional journalists. Citizens collaborated extensively with reporters in the middle of the London riots, for example, on Twitter and social networks, often advising on and helping refine the coverage. A new place for readers and journalists to connect with one another more intimately was waiting to be found beyond the blurred boundaries of blogging (Domingo and Heinonen 2008) in to social media. Indeed, many mainstream journalists had already seen the benefit of blogging—both by themselves and by citizens—as a way to further improve the depth and range of quality news. "I see our relationship with bloggers and citizen journalists as being complementary on a story", stated Neil McIntosh, Assistant Editor of *Guardian Unlimited* (Allan 2007). But without true collaboration extending beyond the duration of the riots and other major incidents, most of the mainstream media have been continuing on a closed-gate approach and, it could be argued, risk being bypassed by an alternative and growing body of social media with its own definitions of quality.

To counter this, the *Guardian* is one mainstream media organisation that has pioneered an approach designed to encourage the public to play a much bigger role in the production of news. It has run an Open News weekend and makes the newspaper's news agenda open to the public ahead of publication (Guardian 2011). An interactive Riots Guardian map was also produced in 2012 for anyone wanting to know what was happening and where. Journalists compiled a list of every incident where there were verified reports and mapped it with Google Fusion tables, allowing people to download the data behind it. The *Guardian's* detailed and impressive "Reading the Riots" research project, set up after the event in partnership with the London School of Economics, summarised the 'clout' that professional journalism can provide, with large numbers of interviews with rioters and detailed analyses of how Twitter and BBM were used during the unrest (*Guardian* 2012).

The *Guardian* is widely perceived as being successful in putting user content on a quality level parallel to the criteria applied to the rest of the journalistic provision. It could be argued that some mainstream newsrooms are acknowledging the relative permanence of citizen journalism as part of quality news production in creating roles and positions with a specific remit for user-generated content. Apps exist now purporting to allow mainstream media to assign citizen journalists to reports (for example, the app 'Rawporter'). National and regional newspaper editors have appointed social media editors, community news editors, digital community editors and heads of communities, to name but a few. There is not space within the confines of this chapter to discuss the remit of these roles in terms of their impact on quality news. It is however worth considering the extent to which these roles exist to manage user relations in order to preserve and promote the traditionally focused interpretations of mainstream quality alluded to throughout this chapter. It could be argued that mainstream media have a lack of trust and certainty in dealing with social media, which needs to be managed in order to preserve the parameters of quality distinguishing professional journalism from them.

Mainstream media would perhaps find a justification for a certain distancing between themselves and social media when the content produced by citizen contributors is subjected to further scrutiny. The sheer volume and diversity of content created and easily distributed through social media creates major operational issues if it is to be filtered to fit into a fixed quality and operational frameworks. Equally, not everyone is joining in. Studies have shown the Pareto principle to be applicable to social media (Poell and Borra 2012; Procter 2011, quoted in Ball and Lewis 2011). This states that 80% of the effects come from 20% of the causes. As such, the creation of content through the processes of citizen journalism is not a majority practice on social media platforms. Studies have shown that 'easy' participation—sharing of existing material, such as links and media that often originate from traditional media sources (although the content may be user/audience generated)—enabled by new technology is the norm (Goodier 2012) Academic studies reinforce this mode of participation, demonstrating, for example, that the most influential Twitter activity is dominated by the mainstream media (for example, Murthy 2011).

ALTERNATIVE MEDIA. ALTERNATIVE VOICES

The previous case studies have evidenced how mainstream media can, enabled by social media, interact with individual users and benefit from the content they produce. The coverage of the G20 protests represented a turning point in the media ecology at large, as the alternative media emerged as an increasingly credible platform for UGC and citizen content. On one level, this showed how alternative narratives and modes of expression have emerged in a way that would be impossible for mainstream media to achieve (ruled by stringent quality parameters and rigid structures). And on another, alternative media also engaged with users and moved beyond community-based organisations into formats that more resembled newsrooms, with editorial structures that embraced (perhaps because of their community and forum-based roots) social media in a way the mainstream media had failed to do. In terms of who, and what, had a role to play in defining quality news, the traditional media was seen by some as now just one force among many competing influences (Meraz 2009).

There is a range of alternative news sites dealing with UK hard news stories, and it would be useful here to focus on them in a little more detail. They are so called because they offer an alternative perspective to the mainstream media, or use different reporting methods. Given their numbers, varied raisons d'etre and approaches, one might expect alternative news sites to be different to one another in both form and function. In fact, there are a number of similarities between groups of them, which arguably, as with the traditional media, serve to reduce the diversity and spread of their overall coverage. There is also evidence that the opportunity these sites present for increased plurality is diminished by the fact that a number of them appear to have a similar worldview (a negative perception of the established order, and how it is reflected and supported by the mainstream media). Some sites, such as Indymedia UK and Schnews, overtly align themselves with the activist movement. Others, such as Media Lens and Spinwatch, concentrate on scrutinising existing mainstream media for bias or spin, adopting a 'watchmen' role, which will be explained later.

Other sites adopt alternative ways of news reporting, most notably Wikinews, where members of the public can write articles that are moderated and approved before being posted. The method may be different, but frequently the articles do not appear to represent a radical departure from the mainstream news agenda, nor do they appeal to mainstream audiences. Similar observations can be made about the *Huffington Post* UK, which, for example, offers extensive coverage of UK crime news through standard reportage of serious criminal events.

Taking these factors into account, when observing the totality of alternative news sites in the UK, it would seem hard to argue that they provide a comprehensive alternative to the range and quantity of mainstream national news output and thus cannot be measured by the same markers. Many, by their chosen focus or role, do not aspire to such an ambition; and most do not have the resource, run as they are by committed individuals or small teams and financed by public donation. This is particularly true of the 'alternative' reporting in places that are increasingly devoid of a mainstream media presence. However, they clearly contribute to an 'alternative perspective', and it should be remembered that all retain the potential, amplified by social media, to make a significant impact on both the wider public consciousness and established news agenda by breaking a major national story.

Ironically, once a story is 'in the system' of mainstream news, the affiliation with alternative is less acceptable.

This is a fluid interplay, however, and can be progressed with two main lines of inquiry: firstly, how is mainstream news provision influenced by social and alternative media and, secondly, to what extent does the definition of alternative lie in opposition to the traditional structures (this may be more centred on calling into question existing definitions of quality rather than framing anything new)? Primarily, this moves social media beyond information provider and more fully into the news ecosystem: in direct tension with the mainstream.

There is an increasing recognition of the interplay between mainstream and social media in driving quality news agendas. The forced resignations of UK Radio 2 presenters Russell Brand and Jonathan Ross is one such example, after a furore over a radio show that was aired on the BBC that included an exchange that insulted actor Andrew Sachs. More than 34,000 complaints were received by the BBC as reaction grew across social and alternative media sites, trending on Twitter. In the mainstream, the *Daily Mail* played a "leading role . . . in articulating public anxiety about the episode" (Greenslade 2008)—in effect, amplifying the existing social media discourse. The positive nature of that symbiotic relationship was illustrated in the case of an injunction relating to Trafigura, brought by libel lawyers Messrs Carter-Ruck. One "suitably gnomic post saying we had been gagged" on Twitter from *Guardian* editor Alan Rusbridger was enough to prompt furious activity (Rusbridger 2010). Twitterers sleuthed out MP Paul Farrelly's parliamentary questions, published the relevant links and pushed Trafigura to be one of the most searched terms in Europe, a collective activity that resulted in the injunction being dropped. These cases go some way in demonstrating how the news agenda is driven through a new intimacy of commentary that exists between it and mainstream media. The implications here are considerable as it would suggest the capacity for the public voice to prompt action and contribute to the process through the collective, not because of any one singular participant. "[M]ass collaboration of strangers had achieved something it would have taken huge amounts of time and money to achieve through conventional journalism or law" (Rusbridger 2010). The level of this interplay can become highly sophisticated and is becoming more common. While there is not space to develop this here, academic work in this field draws on theories relating to the power and wisdom of crowds (Surowiecki 2005), but both examples suggest the potential for creating influence through collaboration.

As much as mainstream media benefit from these new exchanges, so do the alternative (despite their oppositional stance). This is highlighted by the case of the "Smeargate" affair involving bloggers Derek Draper of LabourList.org and Paul Staines, aka Guido Fawkes (on Order-Order .com), which culminated in the resignation of a political adviser. Both operated as bloggers, commanding daily readerships of 50,000 (robust alternative media), with the aim of breaking the stories the supposedly docile Westminster press pack dared not go near. "Cowardice and cronyism run right through the lobby, who are fearful of being taken off the teat of pre-packaged stories served to them. That is not journalism; that is copytaking . . . As an outsider, my blog . . . has been campaigning for them to get some backbone and stand up to the spin machine" (Staines 2009). The success of the Smeargate exposé could be cited as an example of the rising influence of the alternative media. Yet Staines recognised that it was in providing co-pies of information regarding "Smeargate" to the *News of the World* and the *Sunday Times*—the mainstream media—that he leveraged enough of an audience to continue his campaign for a more engaged Fourth Estate.

This position of actively testing the efficacy of the mainstream media's process is not just limited to the political sphere. In 2011 the journalis-tic practices of the *Independent*'s award-winning Johann Hari came under scrutiny. Ultra-left bloggers Deterritorial Support Group and editor Brian Whelan highlighted his plagiarism by comparing Hari's interviews with pre-vious interviews by journalists of his interview subjects, such as Gideon Levy. In 2011, Hari was suspended following accusations of plagiarism and making malicious edits to Wikipedia pages under a pseudonym. Both exam-ples show how the alternative media have taken to the role of gatewatcher. But the Hari case, in a similar way to the Trafigura case discussed previ-ously, also shows a capacity (and benefit) for mainstream media journalists working in conjunction with the alternative press to effectively police the activities of the media.

PROTECTING NEWS QUALITY OR PROTECTIONISM?

Growing in the gap between mainstream and alternative media is the dy-namic churn of users and activity that make up social media. It is difficult to draw definitional consistencies within social media such is the range of groups, communities and forums—and corresponding narratives—which emerge. However, as was seen earlier, it can be seen to coalesce around events and issues, often influenced by traditional media output. It could be argued that whilst this critical mass may be temporary and unpredictable, it gives social media a position that, unlike the oppositional alternative media, can, in its apparent scale and immediacy, effect a positive level of influence on mainstream media, rather than undermining their position.

However, the open, reciprocal nature of social media often means en-gagement in the active pursuit of reciprocity and transparency—an open partnership with users: giving not just taking. This is a dynamic that is often understood and expertly managed by individual journalists, but, at an in-stitutional level, the mainstream seems less comfortable in connecting di-rectly with the dialogues and accommodating them within the quality news framework.

Part of the root cause of this is the shifting definition of quality that exists in these social spaces. Facilitated by elements of user sharing and tagging, voting or rating, users help to decide what content comes to the fore. Users on citizen journalism site Blottr with its strapline "letting people talk" have more influence and kudos the more they contribute through a system of points, user ranking, credibility scores and "like" functionality. Slashdot .org has a moderation system designed to sort comments from the steady stream of information that flows through the site and "tries to make the readers of the site take on the responsibility" of moderating them (Slashdot .org 2012). This is a judgment of quality that is shared through the network, but the thresholds and criteria are unlikely to be the same as those inherited from the mainstream (see, for example, Christakis and Fowler 2011; Weinberger 2008; Van Dijk 2006).

As was shown earlier, not all mainstream news producers are reluctant to involve their audience in genuine and productive ways. The *Guardian* used the valuable resource of contributions by interested members of its audience to directly impact on the quality of their reporting in deciphering former Prime Minister Tony Blair's financial portfolio. Despite attempts to source coherent information from experts, it was the collaborative input from users by way of a competition that helped unravel the story (*Guardian* 2009). This approach supports public connection theory, which argues that the relevance of journalism for its readers is embedded in the social fabric of their everyday lives (Heikkilä, Kunelius, and Ahva 2010) to form what is seen as a more personalized "service journalism" (Usher 2012). Despite this and other examples, in general, the complexity of more players contributing to the process and the challenges of holding those outside the organisation to the same values and standards as those inside results in much of the mainstream media having a tendency to withdraw from the space, to further ringfence their notions and processes of quality.

Studies have consistently found that journalists favour professional sources (Singer 2005), with editorial staff maintaining their domination and control over the news territory (Chung 2007; Mitchelstein and Boczkowski 2009) and facing difficulties in engaging with non-professional expression and its role as part of the ideological predictions of web 2.0 (Rebillard and Touboul 2010). Reese, Rutigliano, Hyun, and Jeong (2007) found that bloggers often rely on professional news reports as prompters for their activity, but their work is often not recognised when stories that use their content are developed by the mainstream. It is interesting to note that some mainstream sites may be attempting to tame the 'black market journalism' aspects of blogging by bringing it within journalistic norms and practices (Wall 2004), but with limited success. Indeed, as Hermida notes in his study of blogging at the BBC (2009), "if [blogging] is considered as a process that involves both the author and the audience in an exchange of ideas, then BBC news blogs fall short". The rise of sites like the *Huffington Post*, who have attracted a number of 'bloggers' and journalists to their roster in a way that alludes to mainstream news production, suggests that this is an opportunity that has passed for the mainstream media. But this internalising and controlling of the modes of citizen discourse by the mainstream is not just limited to blogging. A study of the tabloid press in the UK and Sweden revealed UGC was being kept limited in scope to generate popular culture-oriented content and personal/everyday life-oriented content, but given little or no opportunity to generate news/information-oriented content (Örnebring 2008). The news desk at the *North West Evening Mail*, a newspaper in North-West England, for example, employed social media to decipher a local stabbing, but it was used in a way that served to highlight the value of the traditional process. "No one on social media knew what was going on, so we could counter the rumour mill" (Jonathan Lee, personal interview with Clare Cook, 2011).

This lack of the "exchange of ideas" is further evidenced by the outward linking policy of news organisations. The BBC linking strategy, for example, promotes internal linking unless outward links are "clearly editorially justifiable", much to the frustration of alternative sites and some commentators (BBC 2012).

It is interesting to explore an emerging trend for structured sites to act as amplifiers of social media towards the mainstream in the form of citizen news wires in this context. Acting as intermediaries, they play by the rules of social media but can package and filter content in a way to make it fit within the quality definitions of their mainstream media clients. Tweetminster, for example, curates news and opinion around topics on Twitter in order to identify what and who is important. Originally focused on politics, aggregated subject feeds are now available for free, but they also charge for aggregated and curated feeds of Twitter activity at the request of mainstream media. Demotix is an online platform that allows anyone anywhere to upload their news, videos and images. The staff vet that material and license it on to mainstream news producers. Turi Munthe, founder and CEO cites a mission to connect the work of citizen journalists to global news outlets. The company has high profile partners, such as the *Guardian* and the *Daily Telegraph*. Essentially, it acts as a citizen journalism press agency and splits the revenue 50/50 with its contributors, who can achieve Demotix accreditation. Similarly, Storyful sells verification of social content from the social web onto mainstream media.

At the conceptual level, at least, these sites represent a shift towards including user-generated content in the supply chain of news production—a space that was previously occupied by local newspapers, press agencies and freelancers. Their existence, however, is a tacit admission by mainstream media that they cannot find a way to incorporate such content into their news production processes in a structured way without outside assistance. This is not a lack of recognition of the value of the content. It is clear that there is only so much capacity for the mainstream media to change; there is only so much elasticity in their definition of quality. It certainly cannot be stretched to incorporate the quality measures of alternative media or the morass of UGC and the alternative narratives that emerge in the crowd. This desire to control the direction of the dialogue is often justified as part of the quality process—at some point the experts have to be left to do their job. However the problem is articulated, the pressure on resources that originally tempted the mainstream media to open its gates to UGC leaves it in a difficult position.

THE SHARED RESPONSIBILITY FOR QUALITY

Mainstream media work within traditional editorial frameworks that dictate the collection and presentation of content. These frameworks take balance, verification and (often) objectivity as the benchmarks of quality, benchmarks often ignored and derided by alternative media. Yet mainstream media recognise the benefits of engaging with the richness of representative narrative from the public at large, particularly as eye witnesses to events. Given the problematic background against which they work, the relative ease with which technology allows them to monitor and collect this content is appealing enough. Under the right conditions, involvement with independent and social media has clear benefits for the quality of journalism. It produces journalism that is more inclusive and engaging and that speaks at an emotional level that engenders commitment from an engaged public.

However, as our examples show, the mainstream media is the member within the changing media ecology struggling to keep up. The structures and frameworks on which it has relied in the past to define quality are now proving to be insufficiently elastic to cope with the expanding opportunities to connect with a diverse range of sources. Whilst the appointment of community managers and the increased use of social media interaction show a clear intent to engage, a resistance to open up the editorial process puts pressure on resources that hinders the level and value of engagement that the mainstream can facilitate.

Tensions arise when attempting to unpick where alternative definitions of quality may emerge. Mainstream media still have a steering role in guiding what is and isn't quality, helping to be the springboard for communities to form and filter content, offering editorial judgements on content and being motivated for the most part to sustain the accountability functions consistent with traditional professional journalism. But there is no guarantee of that situation remaining unchanged.

In the absence of a coherent engagement from the mainstream, users are applying a growing confidence in new technologies to produce cogent alternative narratives. The sophistication of what they produce alone—and collaboratively—is trending upwards. As Jeff Jarvis claims, "live, distributed news gathering and sharing will change the news more radically than we can yet imagine" (Jarvis 2007).

Confidence in the power of the network to provide alternative news provision in the terms Jarvis (2007) describes for live reporting is not universal and is certainly a way off maturity. But those sites growing up more organically around citizen content (ohmynews, nowpublic, demotix, storify) are developing their own parameters and methods for defining quality. It remains to be seen whether social media will ever be able to create or even absorb a coherent and lasting measure of quality that is a true representation of the dynamic and organic nature of its content, or whether alternative media will develop beyond imitating or being defined by its opposition to the mainstream definition. Whether this will make a significant contribution to what constitutes quality journalism, as an addition to mainstream media, is more difficult to evidence. But in some respects that is not the point.

Any measure of quality is influenced by the conversation amongst the members of the new media ecosystem. Our examples show the role of social media in driving the news agenda, and the use of user-generated content by the traditional media means some engagement with what the audience decides is suitable—by making the decision about what to submit, the audience are making decisions on its newsworthiness. It's a conversation the mainstream has proved unwilling or unable to get to grips with, but the conversation continues. A strategy of opposition, whether structural or philosophical, to the idea of opening up their own processes and definitions of quality to debate and development simply serves to reduce their relevance in that conversation.

CONCLUSIONS: THE FUTURE

In short, the fluid and dynamic nature of all of this makes it impossible to try and predict with any precision "the future" in terms of the relationship between those many and amorphous groups, facilitated by social media, that form what we might loosely define as social media—a deceptive term, perhaps, that challenges traditional ideas of coherence and identity—and the mainstream and its alternatives. The one thing that can be said with certainty is that the need to understand and develop the relationship continues to grow as the long-term stability and some of the business models of key parts of the mainstream come more into question. They in turn still possess things that the alternative media do not, such as brand trust and access to the 'corridors of power' that often remain closed to those outside of traditional media 'magic circles'.

However, this unique access is no longer guaranteed, and the alternative media, through the web, are an increasingly common platform for material that once would have gone to mainstream journalists. The spectacular breakdown of the partnership between the mainstream media in the form of several national and international newspapers and WikiLeaks over the redaction of details from documents relating to Iraq and Afghanistan (Ellison 2011) is as instructive of the different approaches and issues to be resolved as they are examples of the common purpose and mutual benefit that can be generated when the traditional and alternative media work together.

Whilst the news media in countries like the United Kingdom or the United States might measure up to the needs of indicators such as accuracy, comprehensibility and context, they still struggle to successfully and consistently embrace the range and depth of content available through the network. Social media has created an opportunity for 'the audience' to be more than just passive readers; they can now be active voices in the debate. In terms of participatory democracy, the struggle that the mainstream media have to find consistent ways in which to engage with the sources of alternative narratives could be seen, at best, as a missed opportunity. At worst it constitutes a failure to fulfil their part in the broader democratic process.

It is that mutual benefit coupled with a dynamic and challenging environment for the mainstream that will most likely provide a continuing incentive for them to find a means of developing their concept of what quality hard news should be. The challenge, in the social media age, comes in identifying with whom to negotiate.

It is varying levels of commitment to the idea of quality, as we may understand it in a traditional context, by those in the social media space, that make building relationships difficult for the mainstream. A participatory democracy requires a mainstream media that can more openly communicate and develop its notion of quality, and can recognise and embrace the range of alternative voices, in order to offer multiperspectival, comparative high-quality news. This would go some way to providing "the bottom-up corrective for the mostly top-down perspectives of the news media" (Gans 2003, 103).

REFERENCES

Allan, Stuart. 2007. "Citizen Journalism and the Rise of 'Mass Self-Communication': Reporting the London Bombings." *Global Media Journal, Australian Edition* 1: 1–20.
Atton, Chris, and James F. Hamilton. 2008. *Alternative Journalism*. London: Sage.
Ball, James, and Paul Lewis. 2011. "Twitter and the Riots: How the News Spread." *The Guardian*, 7 December. http://www.guardian.co.uk/uk/2011/dec/07/twitter-riots-how-news-spread.
BBC. 2012. "Editorial Guidelines: Guidance: Social Networking, Microblogs and other Third Party Websites: BBC Use: Guidance in Full." Accessed 31 October 2012. http://www.bbc.co.uk/editorialguidelines/page/guidance-blogs-bbc-full#linking-strategy.
Beaumont, Claudine. 2009. "G20: Protesters Use Twitter, Facebook and Social Media Tools to Organise Demonstrations." *Telegraph.co.uk*, 1 April. http://www.telegraph.co.uk/finance/g20-summit/5090003/G20-summit-Protesters-use-Twitter-Facebook-and-social-media-tools-to-organise-demonstrations.html.

Bell, Emily. 2005. "London's Citizen Reporters Prove Their Worth with Their Coverage of Bombing." *Guardian*, 11 July. http://www.guardian.co.uk/technology/2005/jul/11/media.mondaymediasection.

Bock, Mary Angela. 2012. "Citizen Video Journalists and Authority in Narrative: Reviving the Role of the Witness." *Journalism* 13: 639–653. doi:10.1177/1464884911421703.

Bruno, Nicola. 2011. "Tweet First, Verify Later? How Real-Time Information Is Changing the Coverage of Worldwide Crisis Events." Reuters Institute Fellowship Paper. Oxford: Reuters Institute for the Study of Journalism. http://reutersinstitute.politics.ox.ac.uk/fileadmin/documents/Publications/fellows__papers/2010-2011/TWEET_FIRST_VERIFY_LATER.pdf

Bruns, Axel. 2003. "Gatewatching, Not Gatekeeping: Collaborative Online News."*Media International Australia Incorporating Culture and Policy* 107: 31–44.

Bruns, Axel. 2005. *Gatewatching: Collaborative Online News Production*. Oxford: Peter Lang.

Christakis, Nicholas, and James Fowler. 2011. *Connected: The Amazing Power of Social Networks and How They Shape Our Lives*. London: HarperPress.

Chung, Deborah Soun. 2007. "Profits and Perils: Online News Producers' Perceptions of Interactivity and Uses of Interactive Features." *Convergence* 13: 43–61. doi:10.1177/1354856507072856.

Deuze, Mark, Axel Bruns, and Christoph Neuberger. 2007. "Preparing for an Age of Participatory News." *Journalism Practice* 1: 322–338. doi:10.1080/17512780701504864.

Domingo, David, and Ari Heinonen. 2008. "Weblogs and Journalism: A Typology to Explore the Blurring Boundaries." *Nordicom Review* 29: 3–15. http://jclass.umd.edu/classes/jour698m/domingoblogs.pdf

Douglas, Torin. 2006a. "'Citizen Journalism' Moving Mainstream." BBC News Newswatch, 25 January. http://news.bbc.co.uk/newswatch/ifs/hi/newsid_4640000/newsid_4647000/4647096.stm.

Douglas, Torin. 2006b. "How 7/7 'Democratised' the Media." BBC News Channel website, 4 July. http://news.bbc.co.uk/1/hi/uk/5142702.stm.

Dvorak, John C. 2006. "The Folly of Citizen Journalism." *PC Magazine*, 27 September. http://www.pcmag.com/article2/0,2817,2018636,00.asp.

Ellison, Sarah. 2011. "The Man Who Spilled the Secrets." *Vanity Fair*, February.

Foust, James C. 2011. *Online Journalism: Principles and Practices of News for the Web*. Scottsdale, AZ: Holcomb Hathaway.

Fuchs, Christian, Wolfgang Hofkirchner, Matthias Schafranek, Celina Raffl, Marisol Sandoval, and Robert Bichler. 2010. "Theoretical Foundations of the Web: Cognition, Communication, and Co-Operation. Towards an Understanding of Web 1.0, 2.0, 3.0." *Future Internet* 2: 41–59. doi:10.3390/fi2010041.

Gaber, Ivor. 2009. "Them and Us: Is There a Difference?" *British Journalism Review* 20: 41–46.

Gans, Herbert J. 2003. *Democracy and the News*. New York: Oxford University Press.

Gans, Herbert J. 2005. *Deciding What's News: A Study of CBS Evening News, NBC Nightly News, Newsweek, and Time*. Evanston, IL: Northwestern University Press.

Goode, Luke. 2009. "Social News, Citizen Journalism and Democracy." *New Media & Society* 11: 1287–1305. doi:10.1177/1461444809341393.

Goodier, Holly. 2012. "BBC Online Briefing Spring 2012: The Participation Choice." *BBC Internet Blog*. Accessed 29 January 2013. http://www.bbc.co.uk/blogs/bbcinternet/2012/05/bbc_online_briefing_spring_201_1.html.

Greenslade, Roy. 2008. "Daily Mail Leads Middle England Against Ross, Brand and the BBC." *Guardian*, 29 October. http://www.guardian.co.uk/media/greenslade/2008/oct/29/dailymail-jonathan-ross.

Guardian. 2009. "The Blair Mystery." 1 December. http://www.guardian.co.uk/politics/series/blair-mystery.

Guardian. 2011. "An Experiment in Opening up the Guardian's News Coverage." 10 October. http://www.guardian.co.uk/help/insideguardian/2011/oct/10/guardian-newslist.

Guardian. 2012. "Reading the Riots: Investigating England's Summer of Disorder." Accessed 27 January 2013. http://www.guardian.co.uk/uk/series/reading-the-riots.

Harrison, Jackie. 2010. "User-Generated Content and Gatekeeping at the BBC Hub." *Journalism Studies* 11: 243–256. doi:10.1080/14616700903290593.

Heikkilä, Heikki, Risto Kunelius, and Laura Ahva. 2010. "From Credibility to Relevance." *Journalism Practice* 4: 274–284. doi:10.1080/17512781003640547.

Hermida, Alfred. 2009. "The Blogging BBC: Journalism Blogs at 'the World's Most Trusted News Organisation.'" *Journalism Practice* 3: 268–284. doi:10.1080/17512780902869082.

Hermida, Alfred. 2010. "Twittering the News: The Emergence of Ambient Journalism." *Journalism Practice* 4: 297–308. doi:10.1080/17512781003640703.

Jarvis, Jeff. 2007. "When the [News] Comes from the People—Live. A New Architecture of News." *Buzzmachine*, 17 April. http://buzzmachine.com/tag/livenews/.

Johnson, K. & Wiedenbeck, S. 2009. "Enhancing Perceived Credibility of Citizen Journalism Web Sites." *Journalism & Mass Communication Quarterly* 86: 332–348.

Lasica, J.D. 2003. "Blogs and Journalism Need Each Other." *JD's Blog: New Media Musings*, 12 March. Accessed 7 February 2013. http://www.jdlasica.com/2003/09/08/blogs-and-journalism-need-each-other.

Meraz, Sharon. 2009. "Is There an Elite Hold? Traditional Media to Social Media Agenda Setting Influence in Blog Networks." *Journal of Computer-Mediated Communication* 14: 682–707. doi:10.1111/j.1083–6101.2009.01458.x.

Mitchelstein, Eugenia, and Pablo J. Boczkowski. 2009. "Between Tradition and Change: A Review of Recent Research on Online News Production." *Journalism* 10: 562–586. doi:10.1177/1464884909106533.

Murthy, Dhiraj. 2011. "Twitter: Microphone for the Masses?" *Media, Culture & Society* 33: 779–789. DOI: 10.1177/01634437114047442011

Newman, Nic. 2011. "Mainstream Media and the Distribution of News in the Age of Social Discovery." Report. Oxford: Reuters Institute for the Study of Journalism. http://bit.ly/rbERRJ.

Örnebring, Henrik. 2008. "The Consumer as Producer of What? User-Generated Tabloid Content in *The Sun* (UK) and *Aftonbladet* (Sweden)." *Journalism Studies* 9: 771–785.

Plunkett, John. 2010. "Andrew Marr Says Bloggers Are 'Inadequate, Pimpled and Single.'" *Guardian*, 11 October. http://www.guardian.co.uk/media/2010/oct/11/andrew-marr-bloggers.

Poell, Thomas, and Erik Borra. 2012. "Twitter, YouTube, and Flickr as Platforms of Alternative Journalism: The Social Media Account of the 2010 Toronto G20 Protests." *Journalism* 13: 695–713. doi:10.1177/1464884911431533.

Rebillard, Franck, and Annelise Touboul. 2010. "Promises Unfulfilled? 'Journalism 2.0', User Participation and Editorial Policy on Newspaper Websites." *Media, Culture & Society* 32: 323–334. doi:10.1177/0163443709356142.

Reese, Stephen D., Lou Rutigliano, Kideuk Hyun, and Jaekwan Jeong. 2007. "Mapping the Blogosphere: Professional and Citizen-based Media in the Global News Arena." *Journalism* 8: 235–261. doi:10.1177/1464884907076459.

Richards, Jonathan, and Paul Lewis. 2011. "How Twitter Was Used to Spread—and Knock down—Rumours During the Riots." *Guardian*, 7 December. http://www .guardian.co.uk/uk/2011/dec/07/how-twitter-spread-rumours-riots.
Robinson, Sue, and Cathy DeShano. 2011. "'Anyone Can Know': Citizen Journalism and the Interpretive Community of the Mainstream Press." *Journalism* 12: 963–982. doi:10.1177/1464884911415973.
Rosen, Jay. 1993. "Beyond Objectivity." *Nieman Reports* 47: 48–53.
Rosen, Jay. 2006. "The People Formerly Known as the Audience." *PressThink*, 27 June. http://archive.pressthink.org/2006/06/27/ppl_frmr.html.
Rosen, Jay. 2008. "PressThink: A Most Useful Definition of Citizen Journalism." *PressThink*, 14 July. Accessed 29 January 2013. http://archive.pressthink. org/2008/07/14/a_most_useful_d.html.
Rusbridger, Alan. 2010. "Does Journalism Exist?" Hugh Cudlipp Lecture, 25 January. Accessed 7 February 2013. http://www.guardian.co.uk/media/2010/jan/25/ cudlipp-lecture-alan-rusbridger.
Sambrook, Richard. 2005. "Citizen Journalism and the BBC." *Nieman Reports*. http://www.nieman.harvard.edu/reports/article/100542/Citizen-Journalism-and- the-BBC.aspx.
Shirky, Clay. 2009. *Here Comes Everybody: How Change Happens When People Come Together*. New York: Penguin Press.
Singer, Jane B. 2005. "The Political J-blogger 'Normalizing' a New Media Form to Fit Old Norms and Practices." *Journalism* 6: 173–198. doi:10.1177/1464884905051009.
Singer, Jane B., Alfred Hermida, David Domingo, Ari Heinonen, Steve Paulussen, Thorsten Quandt, Zvi Reich, and Marina Vujnovic. 2011. *Participatory Journalism: Guarding Open Gates at Online Newspapers*. Malden, MA: Wiley-Blackwell.
Slashdot.org. 2012. "Slashdot Moderation." http://slashdot.org/moderation.shtml.
Staines, Paul [Guido Fawkes]. 2009. "Why Did So Few Stand Up to the Spin Machine?" *Times*, 17 April.
Strömbäck, Jesper. 2005. "In Search of a Standard: Four Models of Democracy and Their Normative Implications for Journalism." *Journalism Studies* 6: 331–345. doi:10.1080/14616700500131950.
Surowiecki, James. 2005. *The Wisdom of Crowds: Why the Many Are Smarter Than the Few*. London: Abacus.
Thurman, Neil J. 2008. "Forums for Citizen Journalists? Adoption of User Generated Content Initiatives by Online News Media." *New Media & Society* 10: 139–157. doi:10.1177/1461444807085325.
Urban75. 2005. "Buncefield: The Fuckwittedness of Fox News." http://www .urban75.org/blog/625/.
Usher, Nikki. 2012. "Service Journalism as Community Experience." *Journalism Practice* 6: 107–121. doi:10.1080/17512786.2011.628782.
Van Dijk, Jan A. G. M. 2006. *The Network Society*. London: Sage.
Vickery, Graham, and Sacha Wunsch-Vincent. 2007. *Participative Web and User-Created Content: Web 2.0 Wikis and Social Networking*. Paris: Organization for Economic Cooperation and Development (OECD).
Wall, Melissa. 2004. "Blogs as Black Market Journalism: A New Paradigm for News." *Interface* 4 (2). http://bcis.pacificu.edu/journal/2004/02/wall.php.
Wardle, Claire, and Andrew Williams. 2010. "Beyond User-Generated Content: A Production Study Examining the Ways in Which UGC Is Used at the BBC." *Media, Culture & Society* 32: 781–799. doi:10.1177/0163443710373953.
Wasik, Bill. 2012. "Crowd Control: How Today's Protests, Revolts and Riots Are Self-Organising." *Wired*, 27 January. http://www.wired.co.uk/magazine/ archive/2012/02/features/crowd-control?page=all.

Weinberger, David. 2008. *Everything Is Miscellaneous: The Power of the New Digital Disorder*. New York: Henry Holt.
Willemsen, Lotte M., Peter C. Neijens, Fred Bronner, and Jan A. de Ridder. 2011. " 'Highly Recommended!' The Content Characteristics and Perceived Usefulness of Online Consumer Reviews." *Journal of Computer-Mediated Communication* 17: 19–38. doi: 10.1111/j.1083–6101.2011.01551.x.

Current Quality Levels in the Journalism of South Africa and Kenya, and What Needs to Be Done to Maintain or Improve Them

12 The Future of Quality News Journalism and Media Accountability in South Africa and Kenya

George Ogola and Ylva Rodny-Gumede

The debate about quality news in the developing world necessarily raises fundamental conceptual and practical challenges. While the very idea of quality often assumes a universal understanding, that position is potentially misleading, for we can arguably conceive of it as contextually relative and generally contingent upon the factors against which it is measured. Where those factors are neither obvious nor uniform, the task demands that we remain open to much more complex, even contradictory nuances inherent in the term. The news media in Africa, for example, emerges from a history fundamentally informed and shaped by the continent's experiences with the colonial project. Those experiences were, however, just as varied as the project itself. Even if we argue that Africa's media was implicated in the institutionalisation of the colonial project but also in its repudiation, these roles were both obvious and ambiguous, with implications on what constituted and still constitute quality journalism. Assessing this history enables us to contextually locate quality in and of African journalism and therefore stretch its meaning to be able to understand its various textures as a subject of both historical and contextual agency.

This chapter looks at South Africa and Kenya's print and broadcast media, which are not only foundational in understanding the various histories and traditions that have shaped journalism in these countries, but also key to our reading of the future of quality journalism in the broader Southern and Eastern African regions. We are aware of the two countries' varied experiences with the colonial project—itself complicated by South Africa's experience with a related and distinct political project: apartheid. While these varied histories defined and shaped the growth of fairly different media systems, to examine the two offers us an opportunity to locate quality journalism beyond the ideological confines of liberal internationalism. We stretch our use of the term to capture and explain traditions unique to these two regions. This approach helps us start a conversation that questions, critiques and affirms but also disputes received narratives that have dominated debates about quality journalism.

HISTORICIZING KENYA AND SOUTH AFRICA'S PRINT AND BROADCAST MEDIA

The 1960s remain especially epochal in the history of Kenya's media. It is this period that lends the sector some of its most enduring characteristics and traditions. At independence in 1963, Kenya had a small but relatively vibrant media, serving various political and largely racial constituencies. Broadly, the English settler press served the white colonial administration, while the African press, a term we use to refer mainly to local language media, served the indigenous black population. The latter were generally unified in their opposition to colonial rule, while the former's position insofar as the colonial project was concerned was fairly ambiguous. At independence, however, uncertain about the new political dispensation, the settler press, primarily the *Daily Nation* and the *East African Standard,* shifted allegiance to the new Kenyatta government. This support grew stronger when Roland Rowland's Lonrho Plc acquired the *East African Standard* in 1967. For the new government, however, the appropriation of these newspapers was important for two main reasons. First, the newspapers had become important spaces for public communication. Their support would therefore be used to validate the new political order and enhance the legitimacy of the Kenyatta state. Secondly, co-operation with the newspapers meant they could also be used to promote the government's programmes.

It is instructive to note that the formative phase of Jomo Kenyatta's presidency was severely disrupted by a major political fall-out between the president and some of his erstwhile supporters, led by his then vice president Jaramogi Oginga Odinga. It was a fall-out that laid bare a symbolic but important project that the Kenyatta regime had circulated as necessary and unequivocal immediately after independence–the idea of nation-building. While not unique to Kenya, it was nonetheless one of the various instrumentalities of order (Atieno-Odhiambo 1987) that the Kenyatta regime found necessary for its political survival. It was used as a way of bringing together varied competing political and economic interests that the state perceived as a threat to its legitimacy. The successful institutionalisation of the nation-building project was important for the government because it subsequently validated acts of coercion and force on the regime's opponents at a time when there was an apparent lack of political consensus on the new post-independence political order. The institutionalization of this project also fundamentally defined the prevailing attitudes towards what constituted quality journalism. Quality news, for example, was broadly meant to refer to news that supported 'nation building' and that was by implication largely supportive of the government. Accordingly, stories about the president or the vice-president were not directly reported by the private news media; instead, they relied on the Presidential Press Unit (PPU), the Vice-Presidential Press Unit (VPPU) and the Kenya News Agency (KNA). *The Daily Nation* and *The East African Standard* thus became, almost by default, an informal publicity arm of the state. While it is true that there were instances of criticism of the government in the newspapers, this was often more symbolic than real (Herman and Chomsky 2002).

To be sure, nation-building was part of a broader ideological argument that dominated most of Africa's news media in the 1960s through the 1970s. It was especially validated by UNESCO's endorsement of 'development journalism', which was particularly central in the arguments in favour of a New World Information and Communication Order (NWICO). Informed largely by the critical tradition, 'development journalism' was positioned as a direct challenge to the expansion of the Western liberal media (Bougalt 1995; Nyamnjoh 2005). Supported by most African countries, it was appropriated by governments to ensure that the news media was used to "promote national unity", an idea that was fiercely promoted as necessary for national development (Barton 1979). Kenyatta found development journalism particularly consistent with his nation-building project, which had become a euphemism for the state's regime-building strategy. It is also important to note that the political realities of independence saw the collapse of most of the oppositional news media that had thrived just before independence. As such, the Kenyan print media remained dominated by the *Daily Nation* and the *East African Standard*, while the broadcast media was state-owned, with the public having access only to one TV station, Kenya Broadcasting Corporation (KBC), and to KBC radio and its various sister channels that broadcast in local languages.

Unlike Kenya, South Africa already had a well developed media system when it held its first free elections in 1994. Since the end of legal apartheid when the African National Congress (ANC) was voted into power, the media landscape in South Africa has changed dramatically. The new democratic dispensation has meant that South Africa has been re-accepted into the world community, has re-established trade relations all over the world, has established itself as a political leader on the African continent and, most importantly, has embraced a culture of democracy in terms of universal franchise, human rights, non-racialism, non-sexism, equal opportunities and freedom of expression, including freedom of the press.

However, while it could be argued that South Africa is in many ways a stable democracy with all vital democratic institutions in place, it is still a country in transition from autocracy to democracy, and the history and legacy of apartheid still permeate all facets of life, including the media. This is reflected in the patterns of media ownership and control (Duncan 2010a, 2011), the shortage of skills and the juniorisation of newsrooms (Steyn & deBeer 2002), prevailing racist attitudes both in the newsroom and in the contents of the media (Mtwana and Bird 2006; South African Human Rights Commission 2000) and the absence of a deeper understanding of non-racialism (Everatt 2009, 2010), the lack of access to the media for many marginalised communities (Berger 2001, 2005; Duncan 2001, 2004, 2010a, 2011), the lack of space for a diversity of opinions to interrogate governance and reform (Berger 2001, 2005), and in the continuing antagonistic relationship between the media and the government (Berger 2010; Hadland 2012; Harber 2006, 2007, 2008; Wigston 2007; Wasserman 2010; Wasserman and de Beer 2006).

At the top of debates post-apartheid have been how best to transform the news media. Transforming the media means querying what role the media should play in the new democratic South Africa and also querying the links between media and political power. The debate has focused on whether or not the media should, as is often argued mainly by the news media themselves, retain its watchdog stance against the government, or whether they should, as is often heard from government, focus less on what is wrong in society and instead report on the progress being made in many areas. The argument from Government is that the media should serve the "national interest" as opposed to the "public interest" and collaborate towards development ideals and nation-building (Hadland 2007; Netshitenzhe 2002a, 2002b; Wasserman and de Beer 2006). Furthermore, a common criticism from Government has been that the South African media are racist and unpatriotic and that media agendas are set by those who wish to see the new South Africa fail (Ibelema and Bosch 2004, 307). As a result, some critics argue that the new democratic government is coercing the media into a developmental approach along the same lines as the previous government under the Nationalist Party (NP), especially when it comes to black journalists, who have come under pressure to side with the government that liberated them (Fourie 2001, 276; Hadland 2007).

THE CHALLENGES OF MEDIA LIBERALIZATION

Under apartheid South Africa, newspapers were essentially controlled by four companies, and little has changed. Today, two out of the four companies dominate South Africa's newspaper scene: Independent Newspapers (formerly the Argus group) and Media24 (formerly Naspers), which together control approximately two-thirds of the market (*All Media Product Survey* 2012). Independent Newspapers is now foreign-owned since it was bought in the mid-1990s by Irish media magnate Tony O'Reilly. Media24 is an Afrikaner capital dominated media conglomerate that has developed into a multinational media business with interests far beyond the print media and is the market leader in the news industry in South Africa. It publishes the highly successful tabloid the *Daily Sun*, along with major dailies and weeklies. It also publishes a range of community newspapers and magazines and has established itself on the internet through several online ventures. The web site news24.com has quickly become South Africa's most popular news site.

The Independent Group owns several national and regional newspapers, publishing newspapers in most of the major cities. The group also publishes the Zulu-language daily *Isolezwe*, whose huge growth is part of South Africa's tabloid newspaper explosion. The paper has also launched the world's first Zulu-language web site. The Independent Group also own the web site iol.com, which carries news, classifieds and information syndicated from all its newspapers.

The largest black owned company, Times Media (formerly Avusa) owns South Africa's bestselling Sunday newspaper, the *Sunday Times,* one of the country's largest papers overall. The fourth company dominating the print media market in South Africa is Caxton Publishers. Caxton's interests are mainly in community newspapers and magazines, although it has some dailies and weeklies in its stable as well as the free paper *Metro Citizen,* which is available on Metro buses in the major city of Johannesburg.

At the end of official apartheid, there was an initial fast change of ownership as the new government liberalized the publicly owned media, and black groups made inroads into media ownership in organisations such as Times Media. Since the end of apartheid, quite a lot of the local media have fallen into foreign hands. This is not a trend unique to South Africa, but one that follows global trends in which ownership is increasingly in the hands of fewer and fewer large international groups as well as news agencies (Baker 2007; Boyd-Barrett and Rantanen 1998; Herman and McChesney 1997). Post-apartheid, a new trend in foreign ownership has emerged, namely that of ownership of newspapers by African owners. The well-established weekly and only alternative paper that has survived post-apartheid, the *Mail&Guardian,* is owned by a Zimbabwean consortium, and the now defunct *ThisDay* was owned by a Nigerian businessman.

The concentration in ownership post-apartheid has translated into healthy profits for the owners, but journalism has been suffering. The Independent Newspapers Group, for example, has continued to downsize newsrooms. It has introduced the concept of syndication, in which one parliamentary team produces copy for all the newspapers in the group, and sports copy has gone the same way. In Durban, one newsroom produces copy for three newspapers. In Cape Town, one newsroom produces the copy for two newspapers within the Independent group. This has meant that editorial duties are shared between different publications by the same editor.

The effects of syndication between newspapers is by no means unique to South Africa; the same trend can be seen all around the world. Smaller regional or city newspapers have been swallowed up by big groups, sharing the same central pool of writers and technical resources. Local papers that used to compete have been taken over by the bigger newspapers (Baker 2007; Boyd-Barrett and Rantanen 1998; Herman and McChesney 1997). At the heart of the consolidation of the South African newspaper market are rising costs and a decline in readership. The Independent Newspaper Group has been the most zealous in cutting costs and the *Sunday*

Independent—launched in 1994 as a quality read—has seen its resources and personnel heavily cut, and the paper is now put together solely from syndicated wire copy. The cost-cutting in the Independent Newspaper Group over the past years has surely made it more profitable, but it will come at a great cost to the quality of journalism and diversity in the country (Freedom of Expression Institute [FXI] 2008). The decline in newspaper readership is mainly put down to the rise of the internet and internet publishing, as well as to the death of alternative newspapers after the fall of apartheid. Young readers are also deserting newspapers.

In terms of the African language media, three major newspapers now fight for market space. There is the bi-weekly *Ilanga*, a newspaper with a 100-year old history, owned by the Inkatha Freedom Party, which is up against its more commercial and hugely successful competitor, *Isolezwe*. There is also *UmAfrika*, a smaller weekly paper that focuses on in-depth reporting. While the established newspapers have seen declining circulation, there has been a growth in black readership and South Africa has seen the successful emergence of cheap, racy tabloids, thriving on sex and scandal. Black readership has increased overall, and new publications have appeared geared towards the black middle classes. Taken as a whole, however, the African language press remains underdeveloped.

In the case of Kenya, the developmental tradition of the country's news media did not end with the death of Kenyatta in 1978 and Daniel Moi's constitutional take-over of the government. Moi inherited a state with fundamentally weak governance structures. Political survival still required the very instrumentalities of order that his predecessor had utilized, such as a co-opted news media. In fact, the media's support for the government became even more important as a legitimating institution as the elite political class that Kenyatta had managed to sustain mainly through clientelism and patronage began to crumble in the 1980s (Cheeseman 2008). The latter part of the 1980s through the early 1990s was dominated by serious political turmoil and rapid economic decline. Unable to placate the political class due to a flagging economy, the Moi government gradually began to use force to ensure dissent was contained. This, coupled with the increased informalization of the state, further eroded the government's legitimacy, providing conditions for the emergence of various forms of oppositional cultures. This period thus witnessed what Angelique Haugerud has described as "the shattering of previously held silences as an opposition culture stormed the public domain" (1995, 15). Oppositional discourses, mobilized around political, religious, and cultural groups, emerged and began to find voice in the existing media and other spaces of public expression. The news media found itself immersed in a new political discourse of which it gradually became an important driver. Quality news became news that was primarily oppositional and that located itself within the discourse of the reform agenda. As Tettey (2006) observes of most media organizations in the emergent Africa's pluralist political dispensation starting in the early 1990s, the mass media became "an integral and necessary part of the process of democratization" (229). As a result of the new dispensation, new titles emerged, many disparagingly described as 'gutter press'. These were notoriously abrasive guerrilla news media, largely funded by opposition politicians to discredit Moi's government. They were brash, unprofessionally written and most often without any known addresses. Although fundamentally self-serving, the gutter press nonetheless expanded the bounds of the expressible. Gradually, journalists working for the mainstream newspapers also became emboldened by the emergent political aesthetic around political pluralism, an aesthetic loudly voiced by various interest groups including civil society, sections of the Church, the international community and motley pressure groups. What became especially significant in the early years of multipartyism was the arbitrariness with which "freedom of expression" was exercised by the press. It was unfettered 'freedom' with little in the form of media accountability.

In the mainstream news media, the mid-1990s saw a small but notable shift away from the development model of journalism. Organizations such as the Nation Media Group (NMG) became notably adversarial in their relationship with the state. Quality news was not only political but also oppositional. The emerging political order created a new economic order in which news organizations no longer depended primarily on state patronage for survival. New private investments into the media sector also gave news organizations some nominal freedom by offering alternative revenue streams. The economy, newly liberalized, continued to deteriorate, but it also allowed for the injection of more private capital into the media sector. The NMG, for instance, saw a massive growth in its portfolio because of new private capital, allowing it to make major acquisitions of media groups in Uganda and Tanzania. Its new financial clout gradually made it less reliant on state patronage, relative to its competitors, partly allowing it to become particularly abrasive in its political reporting in the 1990s.

But as Ansah (1991) observes, while political pluralism and the adoption of neo-liberal policies undermined the power of the state in Africa, news organizations still faced major constraints. Governments devised new ways of frustrating these media by, for instance, strengthening privacy and libel laws, most of which worked to undermine executive probity. Meanwhile, the ailing economies within this period meant that media organizations still relied, even if not primarily, on the state for ad revenue, compromising the media's independence. While private advertising may have freed the press from direct political control, it introduced its own form of constraints (Negrine 1994, 70–85). In 2007, for example, the Kenyan government instructed government bodies to stop or withdraw any adverts put in the *Standard* newspapers. This followed a war of words between the newspaper and the Kibaki administration following a news story published by the newspaper "claiming that a government minister had approached Armenian organised crime members with a view to having former President Daniel arap Moi's son murdered" (Reporters Without Borders 2007). The *ancien régime* of the old communication infrastructure survived political pluralism and thus continued to affect media practice.

THE BROADCAST MEDIA AND THE CRISIS OF LIBERALISATION

The challenges above notwithstanding, emerging private news media slowly became wary of the nation-building discourse as the new pluralist discourse and transnational narratives began to filter into and define journalistic practices in the 1990s. In Kenya, the broadcast sector has witnessed arguably the most significant changes since the re-introduction of political pluralism. But it is also the sector that revealed most acutely the challenges that liberalization introduced. For example, there was an apparent failure in the new dispensation to reconcile the rights to freedom of expression and of the press with accountable journalism (Tettey 2006). Quite often, these two seemed and still appear to exist in tension with direct impact on quality journalism.

In general, while most scholars agree to the positive role the media has played in trying to institutionalise democratic processes in Africa since the 1990s, several point to this media's failure or in many cases struggles to operationalize their own accountability (Berger 1998; Nyamnjoh 2005). The expansion of Kenya's media sector was not attended by appropriate legislation to nurture its growth. As a consequence, rogue media and rogue journalistic practices emerged. For example, it became commonplace for some publications to be paid to pull stories or publish libellous material. The so-called gutter press became a press for hire. They published rumours as truth, innuendo as fact and in the process maligned and destroyed people's reputations, especially at election time. Until the turn of the century, there was no agreed code of conduct for journalists, much less an understanding of media ethics.

The exponential growth of the local-language FM radio especially revealed this professional lacuna as a significant problem with serious implications for quality journalism. In 2000 a Nairobi businesswoman, Jane Kimotho, started the first urban FM local language station, Kameme FM. Broadcasting in Kikuyu, the station quickly established itself as one of the most popular FM radio stations in Nairobi and its catchment area. The station had a readymade audience, willed together, in part, by a common language. Although primarily a commercial enterprise, the station had the backing of the government, which had hoped it could eventually be used as a new gateway to reaching an important political constituency, the Gikuyu Meru Embu Association (GEMA) community. The station was only licensed to broadcast cultural and social programmes, but as it grew, it began to experiment with new formats, particularly talkshows and phone-in programmes where discussions on culture and politics often overlapped as to become inseparable. These programmes helped the station draw huge audiences, high ratings, and therefore advertisements. The talkshow format was especially successful because listeners found an accessible platform to discuss issues that directly affected them but that were ignored by the mainstream media, and in a language the state "did not understand".

Kameme FM's success, though eliciting heated debate over its potential risks in light of prevailing ethnic political tensions, prompted the emergence of other vernacular stations, including Ramogi FM (Luo), Kass FM (Kalenjin), Musyi FM (Kamba), Mulembe FM (Luhya), Eggesa (Kisii), and many others. These stations targeted specific ethnopolitical constituencies, with morning talkshows especially attracting big audiences. The state's seeming reluctance, even brief encouragement, of these stations was strategic. They were to help destroy trans-ethnic political alliances seen as a threat to the incumbent administration. The intention, in part, was to reawaken ethnic consciousness and suspicions to weaken or discourage the formation of such alliances.

These local-language FM stations grew rapidly in part because of the widespread disillusionment with the urban FM radio stations. The latter seemed to privilege entertainment programmes rather than engage with serious civic and social issues, and more so at a time when democratic reform and accountable governance dominated public debate. And yet most of the stations were staffed with presenters without any formal journalism training and could not, therefore, for example, adequately moderate talk shows. These radio stations were openly partisan, routinely broadcasting vitriol, exciting and animating ethnic and political tensions and through coded vernacular phrases calling upon ethnic groups to rise against those perceived as opponents at the height of the 2007–2008 post-election crisis. One such presenter, Joshua Arap Sang of Kass FM, a Kalenjin language station, was one of the four Kenyans later indicted by the International Criminal Court at the Hague for committing crimes against humanity as a result of some of his broadcasts.

Apart from the professional lacuna, there was a legislative one as well. The Government did not develop appropriate legislation to regulate media ownership, and, therefore, the allocation of broadcast licences was largely arbitrary. Politicians with close links to the state were easily awarded broadcast licences, often at the expense of the more professional media players. For example, Samuel Kamau Macharia of Royal Media Services was awarded several broadcast licences at a time when the Nation Media Group had been denied the same. When Macharia began to associate with then Opposition leader Mwai Kibaki, his licences were temporarily withdrawn: when he renounced his ties with Kibaki and formed a "development group" in Central Kenya with senior KANU functionaries, he got his licences back.

In spite of these problems, the broadcast sector in Kenya has continued to grow. Recent studies indicate that Kenya now has nearly 23 regular newspaper titles (not all are national newspapers), 20 TV stations and more than 116 radio stations (Baseline Survey on Citizens Perception of the Media Report 2011, 20). These include the first FM radio station, Capital FM in 1996; Kenya's first private TV station, the Kenya Television Network

(KTN), both owned by the Standard Group through a subsidiary, Baraza Limited; Stellavision owned by Hillary Ng'weno; and Macharia's Royal Media Group, whose media portfolio includes Citizen Radio, Citizen TV, and several FM stations, most of them local-language radio stations broadcasting across the country. Intense lobbying and criticism of the government's position on media liberalization has seen it reluctantly license new players. However, until recently, most of the broadcast licensees have only been awarded to politicians, their proxies or businessmen with close ties to the state. While the number of media outlets does not always necessarily act as a measure of media diversity, the number now available in the country does suggest at the very least that the public has a range of media outlets from which to choose.

The post-apartheid era in South Africa has similarly seen a rapid liberalisation of the broadcasting arena, and broadcasting is, by contrast to the print media, much more diversified in terms of ownership. By granting new licences and by selling off state-owned stations, the South African government has tried to foster diversity in ownership in broadcasting, a sector that used to be directly controlled by the state. In order to ensure diversity, the new democratic government set out to create new black media owners. However, many new black media owners have complained that liberalisation has not gone far enough and argue that cross-media ownership makes it impossible for them to enter into print media and build big companies that can compete with those already established (Reuters 2003).

The main broadcaster, the South African Broadcasting Corporation (SABC), is still mainly funded by government and has for the past decade been trying hard to transform itself from an apartheid organ into a modern public broadcaster. The SABC has adopted a rapid programme of transformation, including a new vision statement that spells out its commitment to deliver services to all South Africans in all 11 official languages. The transformation of the public broadcaster has, however, had mixed fortunes. For example, SABC radio news is produced and broadcast in 13 languages (the 11 official languages plus 2 San languages), which generates a whole set of problems that journalists elsewhere who produce in one language, often their mother tongue, do not encounter. Furthermore, the reliance on advertising has led to an increase in entertainment programming in the form of soap operas, sitcoms and game shows at the expense of current affairs, news and educational programming. To combat this, quotas for local programming are set by the Independent Communications Authority of South Africa (ICASA). Furthermore, with the argument that the SABC could no longer afford the luxury of having separate journalists covering the same event, the organisation started a bi-media experiment between 1999 and 2001 whereby journalists were expected to cover events for both radio and television. The project has for now been put on ice, following complaints from journalists (Duncan 2008).

In 2009 it became clear that the SABC had run into severe financial difficulties. It is as yet unclear whether government will bail the organisation out, and a clear turn-around strategy is still missing. The democratic government has been reluctant to put more state money into the SABC, arguing that they must find their own road to sustainability. This has meant that the SABC has increasingly had to become more commercial, and is likely to become even more so, as it tries to become profitable. In its quest to become more commercially viable, critics have argued that it has jettisoned more and more of its public service responsibilities (Duncan 2010b). Budgets for locally produced productions have been slashed as the SABC buys cheaper, American productions, and non-profitable rural and indigenous language operations have been shut down (FXI 2008). Most of the SABC's revenue comes from advertising with a small percentage coming from licences and government funding.

The post-apartheid era has also seen increased competition in the broadcast sector. In 1995 Media24 introduced a satellite service, DSTV, that broadcast in South Africa and across the African continent. South Africa's first free-to-air television channel, e-tv, was started in 1999, and can be received in all major urban areas as well as many rural areas. e-tv was started by mostly black economic empowerment groups with money sourced from, among others, trade union pension funds. After initial hiccups, the television channel's audience has now soared to make it the second most popular station in the country.

In terms of bidding for programming, e-tv has outmanoeuvred the SABC on several key occasions. It outbid the SABC for the broadcasting of the 2002 Soccer World Cup. It also took on the SABC and won the war over the evening news. e-tv's 7pm news slot proved so attractive that it forced the SABC to change their news time, from 8pm, where it has been since the introduction of television in South Africa in 1976, to 7pm. In order to do this e-tv used clever marketing strategies, such as the slogan, "Watch the news at 7, because by 8 it's old news!" As much as the SABC tried to claim that the main news time slot shift had nothing to do with e-tv, it probably had. In spite of e-tv's successes, the station is still not financially secure, and its senior managers, all former leading trade unionists, are fighting hard to make the station profitable in order to prevent the station from changing hands. Moreover, in spite of e-tv's progressive roots, it has not offered much new in terms of quality programmes or public service television. It mainly shows soap operas, cheap American action movies and wrestling shows.

QUALITY JOURNALISM IN THE EMERGING
NEW SPACES AND VOICES

The approbation that has attended the liberalisation of and expansion of the media sector in Africa has in the same vein invited questions about the quality of its performance. The response from governments and media organisations have varied. Indeed, according to Tettey (2006), "in response to growing concerns about the quality of the press in Africa, media organizations are themselves [now] initiating measures to address the shortcomings of their profession" (230).

Similar to other liberalised media economies in Africa and beyond, the expansion of the media sector led to increased commercialisation. This shift often provokes questions about the place of quality news in the emergent media structures as organizations race to cash in on mass advertising and audiences. Expensive quality programming such as investigative journalism is often cut down in favour of cheaper but more commercially lucrative advertisement-driven programming, such as reality shows.

The expansion of the media sector was not attended by a similar development of training opportunities for journalists. As a result, a recurring public criticism of South African journalists has been that they do not have the necessary skills to cover the complexities of the South African transition, and, therefore, the South African National Editor's Forum (SANEF) undertook a two-stage skills audit of journalists and media managers in South Africa (Steyn and de Beer 2002; Steyn, de Beer, and Steyn 2005). The first step in this audit was to look at reporters with between two to five years of experience in the country's newsrooms who were identified as the future leaders of the profession (Steyn and de Beer 2002; Steyn et al. 2005). Key weaknesses identified in the South African journalism make-up ranged from lack of accuracy, weak knowledge of ethics and poor writing skills to poor general, historical and contextual knowledge. SANEF felt that the report was so serious that critical interventions were needed as a matter of urgency (Steyn and de Beer 2002; Steyn et al. 2005). The second stage of the audit looked at managerial skills within the South African media industry, and, even here, the audit found major skills gaps in terms of how journalism managers are prepared to lead teams of journalists, take informed and ethical decisions in the newsroom and mentor young journalists (Steyn et al. 2005). These are findings that all have implications for the role and conduct of the news media and for levels of professionalism in the South African news media. However, despite attempts at working more closely with different media stakeholders, as well as academic institutions, change is slow, and it will not be until a proper follow-up study has been carried out that any assessments can be made to show how much things have actually changed.

All in all, the print media scene post-apartheid has transformed from a narrow and highly segmented media market into a broader, more mainstream market characterised by higher ownership concentration and commercialism. To a certain extent, racial transformation has happened, and so-called Black Economic Empowerment deals have seen at least ownership become somewhat more equitable in terms of race, post-apartheid. Foreign ownership is a new feature of the post-apartheid print media landscape, including ownership from other African countries. The new tabloids are here to stay and have caused a debate around whether or not they contribute to the building and strengthening of the new democracy. Sales and circulation figures are looking good, and they have given the older, more established papers in the country a real run for their money. Whether journalism will improve is a matter of considerable debate.

In Kenya, since 2007, there has been an increasing focus on the professionalization of the sector. There is an emerging awareness of the need for journalists to work within broadly agreed professional norms informed, in part, by formal journalism training, what Tettey (2006) describes as the media's "self-imposed accountability" (242). This is a form of accountability "based on voluntary acceptance of certain standards and codes of behaviour that govern membership of a professional body or employment in a particular media organization" (242). All the major news organizations in the country have now signed up to a uniform code of conduct written by local news organizations jointly with the Kenya Union of Journalists (KUJ) and the Media Council of Kenya (MCK). There has also been a notable increase in the number of journalism schools in the country. Nearly 23 institutions, including 6 universities, are now offering standardized journalism training courses. Meanwhile, journalists now have formal representation in associations such as the KUJ, Kenya Correspondents Association (KCA) and the Association of Media Women in Kenya (AMWIK), among others. AMWIK focuses on and aims to improve working conditions for women journalists in the country. These associations also organise regular training courses and workshops for practising journalists and correspondents around the country. The creation of the MCK alongside other bodies such as the Editors' Guild and the emergence of and strengthening of other associations such as the KUJ and AMWIK provides some indication that the professionalization of journalism in Kenya is gradually taking root.

This trend is further supported by the formal recognition of the independence of the media in the constitution. While Kenya was still ranked 84th in the 2011–2012 *Press Freedom Index* by Reporters Without Borders, there have been a number of progressive laws enacted over the last 10 years aimed at creating a more conducive environment for journalism. Even then, critics still complain that the fragmentation of the country's media laws, and the fact that they "exist in different sections of civil and criminal laws" (Oriare 2010, 28) undermine the extent to which this media can perform its normative roles. Kenya's media laws are variously contained in the country's constitution in statutory law and common law. While the constitution guarantees freedom of expression, this is largely constrained by certain provisions within statutory law, which have in the past been used punitively by the state. These provisions include the Penal Code, the Preservation of Public Security Act, Film and Stage Plays Act and Official Secrets Act among others. The Penal Code gives the government inordinate powers that it often uses to control the news media. This control has historically been exercised in two ways: through direct intimidation, as when the government ordered a raid on the Standard Group in 2006, or through litigation. In 2006, the SG's head office was broken into by masked gunmen who shut down the group's TV studios, confiscated several computers from the newsroom, disabled printers and destroyed copies of the following day's newspapers. The government had previously expressed indignation at the group's criticism of the Mwai Kibaki administration.

There have been controversial attempts in the recent past to harmonise these laws. For instance, in 2008, the government enacted the Kenya Information and Communications (Amendment) Bill, also known as the ICT bill. The law generated heated public debate, including protests by journalists, media owners and civil society. Some of the Bill's provisions were regarded as punitive, including, for example, hefty penalties for breaches and the powers given to the Minister of Information to regulate broadcast content allegedly to ensure "good taste". The legislation would also force media organisations to store content for up to three years. Curiously, it remained silent on fundamental problem areas such as cross-media ownership, a critical issue that has continued to undermine the growth of the print sector in the country. The public outcry and protests that forced the government to temporarily shelve the Bill and initiate a consultation process does indicate that, increasingly, press freedom is now considered especially important by the state and the public as an important driver in the consolidation of the country's democratic process.

In South Africa, the ANC has proposed a new statutory Media Appeals Tribunal (MAT) under the auspices of safeguarding pluralism in the media. This is based on the argument that media self-regulation is not enough to ensure diversity and the protection of minority rights and interests in the media. However, critics argue that the suggested tribunal is not so much about the protection of rights as about an attempt to muzzle a print media that so far have been difficult to co-opt, and that have kept up the pressure on government to deliver, by scrutinising corruption and issues of non-performance (Berger 2010). The ANC has also proposed a new Protection of State Information Bill. If passed, this bill, which has become known as the "Secrecy Bill", has the potential to make even the most inauspicious piece of government and state information classified and would have the power to impose heavy fines as well as prison sentences of up to 25 years.

In Kenya, more progressive legislation, on the other hand, includes the Media Act 2007, which established the Media Council of Kenya, an organization created to regulate the media industry and the conduct of journalists. The council is funded by the state but is shielded from political interference by the same Act. Access to information, especially from the state, has also been made possible following the enactment of the Freedom of Information Bill 2007. At least in theory, this Act should make it easier for journalists to access information they were previously denied. Still, certain provisions within statutory law, such as the Official Secrets Act, are sometimes used to frustrate attempts by journalists to access state information. Indeed, in

2006, the Finance Ministry denied the *Standard* newspaper an interview following the newspaper's publication of a story the Finance Minister argued was negative. While the implementation of these laws remains a challenge, their enactment provides encouraging signs for quality journalism in the future.

With the enactment of the Kenya Communications (Amendment) Bill 2008, there is also an acknowledgement, however tentative, that digital media is and will become an important part of the broader Kenyan media infrastructure. Relative to other African countries in sub-Saharan Africa, with the exception of South Africa and Nigeria, internet penetration in Kenya is notable and has been growing year on year. In the first quarter of 2012, the number of internet users was estimated at 11.8 million, which, according to the Communications Commission of Kenya (CCK 2012), represented a 63% increase year on year. This is likely to grow even faster with the rolling out of broadband technology and the falling cost of smartphones. While it is true that the newspaper still holds a fairly important place in the popular imagination as a record of the "truth" in Kenya, and while it also the case that newspaper readers in Kenya may not be declining, a new generation of digital natives is also growing. A 2011 survey notes that social media and the internet have become a media choice for growing numbers of people (Strategic Public Relations and Research Limited [SPRRL] 2011, 24).

Indeed, at the height of the country's post-election crisis in 2007–2008, Kenya's online media—largely comprising citizen journalists and bloggers—played a particularly important role in reporting incidents of violence and debating the election crisis at a time when the government had imposed a live news blackout on mainstream media (Makinen and Kuira 2008; Zuckerman 2009). The opportunities and challenges that digital media have created are now acknowledged by policy makers in the country. For instance, the conditions of relative anonymity and lack of a regulatory framework within which bloggers operate is being checked by organizations such as the National Cohesion and Integration Commission (NCIC), which is mandated to investigate and prosecute hate crimes in the country. However, such cases of 'assigned accountability' can be 'proscriptive' precisely because of their ambiguity. Because there is still no internet-specific legislation, there is fear that the state can exploit that absence to clamp down on dissent online easily.

There have also been some steps, albeit tentative, by mainstream media organizations to develop their online presence even if major investments in these platforms remain to be seen. All the major newspapers now have some online presence. Both the NMG and the SG have Managing Editors for their Digital/Convergence platforms. They have also started using material across the platforms. It is now common to find journalists working on stories for the various platforms including, audio, video and print. Convergence is already creating new efficiencies, but it has also led to an increase in the re-purposing of news. This is having implications for the range of voices being 'heard' in news, at the same time that the digital media platform is creating new spaces for consumers to access news. However, it is unlikely the internet platform will replace the more traditional media of radio and television. Media consumption habits remain relatively firm in Kenya with the newspaper and radio still regarded as the pre-eminent news providers.

The growth of mobile telephony is, however, likely to invite some investment and experiments, especially in the distribution of news. It is now safe to say that the mobile phone is relatively ubiquitous in Kenya. Mobile phone penetration in the first quarter of 2012 stood at 74%, according to the CCK (2012). *The Standard* and *The Daily Nation* both have mobile sites, but these remain relatively underdeveloped with the focus mainly put on the occasional breaking news story and text messages. *The Star,* on the other hand, has an app for citizen reporters on its web site, but it is unclear how many use it or how many of the user-generated stories are actually picked up by the newspaper. Still, a number of new media technologies have been appropriated by various news organisations, making it easier to gather news and occasionally distribute it. But as Opubor (2000) observes, new media technologies tend to succeed only if they strengthen, not necessarily alter, existing communication systems.

Post-apartheid South Africa has also seen more technological convergence and digitisation of information. Convergence has been the motor behind the mushrooming of media web sites post-apartheid, most of them coupled to older established media operations. However, the global dot.com downturn severely hit South Africa's web operations, and worst hit were the stand-alone web operations. The leading news site, Woza, was hit hard and forced to close. Only those web sites that were based on old established media organisations survived as they were cushioned by their parent company. However, they all saw large-scale retrenchments and downsizing. Convergence using mobile phone platforms has been more successful. Editorial content is re-purposed for mobile phone reception and delivered to subscribers for a fee. The SABC, for example, has a partnership with South African cellular network Vodacom. Its Newsbreak service allows a small team to tap into the computer network that carries the corporation's internal news items for radio and TV and to repurpose this information for mobile phones. The service has expanded into the African market by offering African language audio.

The ushering in of democracy in South Africa also saw the mushrooming of new community radio stations in the mid-1990s, where local communities actively could participate in the affairs of the station. However, many of the new radio stations soon collapsed because they could not secure enough advertising revenue to be sustainable. In 2002, the Media Development and Diversity Agency (MDDA) was established (see MDDA Act 2002). The Agency is tasked with encouraging ownership and control of, as well as access to, media by historically disadvantaged communities, historically diminished indigenous languages and cultural groups, as well as encouraging the channelling of resources to community and small commercial media. The MDDA has huge potential to add to the diversity of the media scene in South Africa. So far, however, the agency's developments have been slow and few.

Although new media outlets have contributed to the broadening of the sector, in terms of content, it is questionable whether these new channels have contributed substantially to the diversification of media content in the broadcasting sector. Post-1994, the public broadcaster, the SABC, has taken substantial steps towards becoming a fully-fledged public broadcaster rather than a state broadcaster. However, events in which the ANC government has interfered directly in programming as well as in the appointment of the SABC Board and CEO have raised questions about the state of freedom of expression in South Africa. On the side of community media, much seemed to happen with the coming of democracy in South Africa, but the lack of funding and advertising revenues have seen many of the newer media outlets collapse. Even though progress has been slow, the formation of the MDDA, which was set up to provide financial and technical support to smaller media outlets, has the potential to change this situation if properly managed and funded.

In Kenya, of the 116 radio stations, for example, there is no single talk radio dedicated to serious political, social and economic issues like South Africa's Talk Radio 702 or SAFM. Instead, the radio stations are predominantly music entertainment stations. Indeed, in the 2011 audience survey, only 28% of respondents surveyed said they were happy with the coverage of national issues by the media (SPRRL 2011, 36). Many feared that the media's normative functions were being undermined by their disproportionate focus on entertainment. But while radio has been much criticized for a general dumbing down, the television sector provides a mixed picture. The three main national stations, NTV, Citizen TV and KTN, with a viewership of between 38% and 80% of the local audience (SPRRL 2011), seem to be developing a new public service ethos. Their programming has also been relatively diverse.

CONCLUSION

The new political dispensations in both South Africa and Kenya have enabled much progress and have transformed former authoritarian institutions into emerging democratic ones. Civil liberties are protected in the two countries' constitutions, including freedom of speech and the freedom of the press. There is also evidence of a growing professionalization of journalism in both countries. Rogue practices and rogue journalists are increasingly frowned upon, and associations such as SANEF in South Africa and the MCK in Kenya are slowly institutionalizing specific codes of conduct for journalists, more so for the latter where such codes were only casually adhered to. The expansion of the media sector in general has also presented the public with more choice. This also comes through in content and language policies, where programming and news media are becoming available in indigenous languages and where there is a growing focus on providing news media for previously disadvantaged groups.

However, media ownership remains a significant challenge. Media concentration is high, and even though the post-apartheid era has seen the introduction of new titles into the print market, especially through the introduction of a number of new tabloids, real diversification of the media market is yet to happen. Emerging news outlets have found it difficult to establish themselves, and increased commercialisation in the sector has put pressures on the broadsheet newspapers to keep up with the new racy tabloids. In Kenya, due to the lack of cross-media legislation, the print sector, for example, is still dominated by two of the biggest media organizations in the country: the NMG and the SG. With already well-developed publishing and distribution networks, public profiles, and a powerful relationship with the political class, it has become virtually impossible for new media players to break this duopoly. Meanwhile, licensing of broadcast media remains controversial with politicians and state operatives still having access to licences. There is also an enduring authoritarian culture lodged within the political systems that has been carried over and internalised by the new liberal democratic political dispensations in their dealings with the media and their efforts to control the media. The way in which the ANC as well as the successive administrations in Kenya have tried to tighten their grip over the media, through new media legislations, is indicative of this. This will have implications for the quality of journalism and the role that journalism can play in the consolidation of democratic processes in the two countries.

REFERENCES

All Media Product Survey (AMPS). 2012. Johannesburg: South African Advertising Research Foundation. Accessed 19 October 2012. http://www.saarf.co.za.

Ansah, Paul. 1991. "Blueprint for Freedom." *Index on Censorship* 209: 3–8.

Atieno-Odhiambo, Elisha. 1987. "Democracy and the Ideology of Order in Kenya." In *The Political Economy of Kenya*, edited by Michael Schatzberg,177–201. New York: Praeger.

Baker, Edwin C. 2007. *Media Concentration and Democracy: Why Ownership Matters*. Cambridge: Cambridge University Press.

Barton, Frank. 1979. *The Press in Africa: Persecution and Perseverance*. New York: African Publishing Company.

Strategic Public Relations and Research Limited. 2011. Baseline Survey on Citizens' Perception of the Media Report. Nairobi: Kenya Media Programme.

Berger, Guy. 1998. "Media and Democracy in Southern Africa." *Review of African Political Economy* 78: 599–610.

Berger, Guy. 2001. "De-Racialization, Democracy and Development: Transformation of the South African Media 1994–2000." In *Media, Democracy and Renewal in Southern Africa*, edited by Keyan Tomaselli and Hopeton Dunn, 151–180. Colorado Springs: International Academic Publishers.

Berger, Guy. 2005. "Current Challenges." In *Changing the Fourth Estate, Essays on South African Journalism*, edited by Adrian Hadland, 19–26. Cape Town: HSRC Press.

Berger, Guy. 2010. "Drop the Media Tribunal if You Want a Debate about the Press." *Thought Leader*, 16 August. http://www.thoughtleader.co.za/guyberger/2010/08/16/drop-the-media-tribunal-if-you-want-debate-about-the-press.

Bougalt, Louise. 1995. *Mass Media in Sub-Saharan Africa*. Bloomington: Indiana University Press.

Boyd-Barrett, Oliver, and Terhi Rantanen. 1998. "The Globalization of News." In *The Globalization of News*, edited by Oliver Boyd-Barrett and Terhi Rantanen, 1–18. London: Sage.

Cheeseman, Nic. 2008. "The Kenyan Elections of 2007: An Introduction." *Journal of Eastern African Studies* 2: 166–184.

Communications Commission of Kenya (CCK). 2012. *Quarterly Sector Statistics Report: Third Quarter of the Financial Year 2011/12 (January–March 2012)*. http://cck.go.ke/resc/downloads/SECTOR_STATISTICS_REPORT_Q3_11–12.pdf.

Duncan, Jane. 2001. "Talk Left, Act Right? What Constitutes Transformation in Southern African Media?" In *Media, Democracy and Renewal in Southern Africa*, edited by Keyan Tomaselli and Hopeton Dunn, 25–40. Colorado Springs: International Academic Publishers.

Duncan, Jane. 2004. "Stability or New Freedom of Repression." *Rhodes Journalism Review* 24: 27–28.

Duncan, Jane. 2008. "SABC's Bi-Media Operation in Urgent Need of Review." Freedom of Expression Institute. Accessed 17 October 2012. http://www.fxi.org.za/archive/Linked/Public%20Broadcasting%20e-archive/PB_SABC%20bi-media.html.

Duncan, Jane. 2010a. "The ANC's poverty of strategy on media accountability." Presentation delivered at the Colloquium on Media, Democracy and Transformation Since 1994, Rhodes University, Grahamstown, 16–17 October.

Duncan, Jane. 2010b. "Public Services Broadcasting Bill an Exercise in Maldevelopment." South African Civil Society Information Service, 11 January. Accessed 21 October 2012. http://www.sacsis.org.za/site/article/406.1.

Duncan, Jane. 2011. "South Africa: The Print Media Transformation Dilemma." AllAfrica, 3 March. Accessed 15 October 2012. http://allafrica.com/stories/201103030841.html.

Everatt, David. 2009. *The Origins of Non-Racialism: White Opposition to Apartheid in the 1950s*. Johannesburg: Wits University Press.

Everatt, David. 2010. "State & Meaning(s) of Non-Racialism: What is Non Racialism—Past & Current Debates." In *Non-Racialism: An Unbreakable or Very Fragile Thread of South Africa's Democracy?* 5–7. Ahmed Kathrada Foundation. Accessed 22 October 2012. http://www.kathradafoundation.org/stories/akf_workshop_booklet.pdf.

Fourie, Pieter J. 2001. "The Role and Functions of the Media: Functionalism." In *Media Studies: Institutions, Theories and Issues*, edited by Pieter J. Fourie, 264–289. Cape Town: Juta.

Freedom of Expression Institute (FXI). 2008. Submissions on Protection and Viability of Public Broadcasting Services. Accessed 19 October 2012. http://www.fxi.org.za/archive/Linked/Public%20Broadcasting%20e-archive/PB_subm4.html.

Hadland, Adrian. 2007. "The South African Print Media 1994–2004: An Application and Critique of Comparative Media Systems Theory." PhD diss., University of Cape Town.

Hadland, Adrian. 2012. "Africanizing Three Models of Media and Politics: The South African Experience." In *Comparing Media Systems Beyond the Western World*, edited by Daniel Hallin and Paolo Mancini, 96–118. Cambridge: Cambridge University Press.

Harber, Anton. 2006. "Defamation: The New Frontline of Media Freedom." *Business Day*, 4 July.

Harber, Anton. 2007. "ANC's New Views on the Media." *The Harbinger*, 17 June. Accessed 16 October 2012. http://www.theharbinger.co.za/wordpress/2007/06/17/ancs-new-views-on-the-media.

Harber, Anton. 2008. "2007 Overview." *The Harbinger*, 5 January. Accessed 16 October 2012. http://www.theharbinger.co.za/wordpress/2008/01/05/2007-overview.

Haugerud, Angelique. 1995. *The Culture of Politics in Modern Kenya*. Cambridge: Cambridge University Press.

Herman, Edward S., and Noam Chomsky. 2002. *Manufacturing Consent: The Political Economy of Mass Media*. New York: Pantheon.

Herman, Edward S., and Robert McChesney. 1997. *The Global Media: The New Missionaries of Corporate Capitalism*. Washington, D.C.: Cassell.

Ibelema, Minabere, and Tanja Bosch. 2004. "Sub-Saharan Africa (East, West, and South)". In *Global Journalism, Topical Issues and Media Systems*, edited by Arnold de Beer and John Merrill, 299–341. Boston: Pearsons Educational.

Makinen, Maarit, and Mary Kuira. 2008. "Social Media and Postelection Crisis in Kenya." *International Journal of Press/Politics* 13: 328–335.

Media Development and Diversity Agency (MDDA) Act. 2002. http://www.mdda.org.za/gifs/MDDA%20Act.pdf.

Mtwana, Nonceba, and William Bird. 2006. *Revealing Race: An Analysis of the Coverage of Race and Xenophobia in the South African Print Media*. Johannesburg: Media Monitoring Project.

Negrine, Ralph. 1994. *Politics and the Mass Media in Britain*. London: Routledge.

Netshitenzhe, J. 2002a. *Should Media Serve the National Interest or the Public Interest?* Accessed 14 May 2013. http://www.gcis.gov.za

Netshitenzhe, J. 2002b. *The Role of the Media in Building the National Interest*. Accessed 14 May 2013. http://www.gcis.gov.za

Nyamnjoh, Francis. 2005. *Africa's Media: Democracy and the Politics of Belonging*. London and Pretoria: Zed Press and Unisa.

Opubor, Alfred. 2000. "If Community Media is the Answer, What is the Question?" In *Promoting Community Media in Africa*, edited by Kwame Boafo, 11–24. Paris: UNESCO.

Oriare, Peter. 2010. *Media Practice in Kenya: Systems and Practice*. Nairobi: Jomo Kenyatta Foundation.

Reporters Without Borders. 2007. "Government Orders State Sector to Withdraw Advertising from Standard Group Media." 19 April. Accessed 13 February 2013. http://en.rsf.org/kenya-government-orders-state-sector-to-19–04–2007,21804.html.

Reuters. 2003. "NAIL bidding for Johnnic assets—paper." Accessed 14 May 2013. http://business.iafrica.com/news/202349.htm

South African Human Rights Commission (SAHRC). 2000. *Fault Lines: Inquiry into Racism in the Media*. Accessed 13 February 2013. http://www.info.gov.za/view/DownloadFileAction?id=70341.

Steyn, Elanie, and Arnold S. de Beer. 2002. *Sanef's "2002 South African National Journalism Skills Audit": Final Report*. South African National Editors' Forum. Accessed 13 February 2013. http://www.sanef.org.za/images/uploads/Sanef_2002_Skills_Audit_1.pdf.

Steyn, Elanie, Arnold S. de Beer, and T.F.J. Steyn. 2005. *Sanef Skills Audit Phase 2: Managerial Competencies Among First-Line News Managers in South Africa's Mainstream Media Newsrooms: Final report*. South African National Editors' Forum. Accessed 13 February 2013. http://www.sanef.org.za/images/uploads/Sanef_Skills_Audit_2005_1.pdf

Strategic Public Relations and Research Limited (SPRRL). 2011. *Baseline Survey on Citizen's Perception of the Media Report*. September 2011. Nairobi: Hivos. http://www

.kmp.or.ke/wp-content/uploads/2011/10/Hivos-Baseline-Survey-on-Citizens-Perception-of-the-Media-Final-Report1.pdf.

Tettey, Wisdom. 2006. "The Politics of Media Accountability in Africa: An Examination of Mechanisms and Institutions." *International Communication Gazette* 68: 229–248.

Wasserman, Herman, ed. 2010. *Taking It To The Streets: Popular Media, Democracy and Development in Africa*. London: Routledge.

Wasserman, Herman, and Arnold S. de Beer. 2006. "Conflicts of Interest? Debating the Media's Role in Post-Apartheid South Africa." In *Mass Media and New Democracies*, edited by Katrin Voltmer, 59–75. London: Routledge.

Wigston, David. 2007. "A History of the South African Media." In *Media Studies: Media History, Media and Society*, edited by Pieter J. Fourie, 4–58. Cape Town: Juta.

Zuckerman, Ethan. 2009. "Citizen Media and the Kenyan Electoral Crisis." In *Citizen Journalism: Global Perspectives*, edited by Stuart Allan and Einar Thorsen, 190–196. New York: Peter Lang.

13 Citizen Journalism in South Africa and Kenya

The Quandary of Quality and the Prospects for Growth

Harry Dugmore and Dina Ligaga

Any discussion about the worth and quality of citizen journalism should consider at least four elements: voice, veracity, reach and sustainability. Voice is critical because the whole premise of *citizen journalism* is to allow those marginalized from the mainstream media to be heard, and to be heard in a manner that articulates their worldview, and not the mores, ethos and tones of the dominant media and dominating elites. Veracity is also vital, because even for the most partisan media, if care is not taken to be truthful and accurate, credibility is compromised. Being able to reach a target audience and build audiences over time is both premised on the power of the available and accessible dissemination technology but also on elements such as marketing, reputation and credibility. It is axiomatic that the highest quality citizen journalism, articulating authentic voices, telling truths, but unseen, is useless. Sustainability builds on all these elements, but is concerned with renewability of finances and of purpose, as well as content/practitioner sustainability. Much of what is named as citizen journalism is housed in projects that come and go, often rapidly, or sustained by individual enterprise that wanes and waxes. In an era when commercial media, particularly print, are facing a deep sustainability crisis, the systemic viability of any citizen journalism project is an important element of a discussion of quality. This chapter looks at citizen journalism in South Africa and Kenya, two countries in which it manifests itself in remarkably different ways. But the chapter is also specifically interested in locating the place of quality in what has rightly and wrongly been variously described as a form of 'alternative' journalism, both in the generic sense of the word but also to emphasize its implied association with the 'margins' and investment with, mainly, political agency.

Citizen journalism in South Africa has evolved rapidly over the past decade. It is currently being further transformed by sharp rises in internet use, and particularly by the speedy uptake of social media and by related shifts in both media consumption patterns and newsroom journalism production practices. The promise of the digital age is enormous reach at low cost. The boundaries of journalism, in terms of conceptions of what it is and what it is not, are being disrupted even more by both new technologies and by a deep ethical and even existential crisis within journalism in developed countries that has played out, in different ways, in South Africa as well. Different projects and people have tried different strategies to promote a diversity of voices, to link storytellers and journalists to audiences, in a sustainable way. Three projects, representative of both the historical trajectory and the evolving conceptualization of citizen journalism in South Africa, are examined in this chapter, with respect to their approaches to voice, veracity, reach and sustainability.

In Kenya on the other hand, citizen journalism has tended to follow an eminently political trajectory. Fundamentally emphasizing the weaknesses inherent in mainstream media and its various institutional practices, citizen journalism in the country has at the same time attempted to assert its own voice, quite often unambiguously a political one.

While the debate on quality journalism in Kenya is complicated by factors such as poor policy and legal regimes, weak regulatory media frameworks and so on (Ogola 2009), this chapter seeks to argue that citizen journalism further complicates that debate by questioning existing paradigms within which quality journalism is often measured in Kenya. As illustrative examples, the chapter uses selected online discussion forums and blogs that engage variously with news items in Kenya. When it comes to these new media platforms, questions of transparency, participation and subjectivity (agency) arguably displace more traditional yardsticks for measuring quality journalism. These factors are particularly important in a context where the state and a small but powerful political elite have historically dominated the public sphere.

THE SPECIFICITY OF CITIZEN JOURNALISM IN SOUTH AFRICA: CONCEPTS AND CONTEXT

Prior to 1994, South African media and South African journalists could be roughly grouped into either an apartheid supporting camp, a liberal (mostly English-speaking print newspaper) camp that opposed elements of apartheid, and a radical 'alternative' camp that supported liberation (and often liberation movements) and sought to be part of the struggle for full democracy (Wasserman and de Beer 2006). Ideas rooted in the oppositional and alternative media that drew heavily on enthusiastic amateurs and attempted to practice 'participatory journalism' would feature prominently in later South African conceptions of citizen journalism (Berger 1999). This alternative press (as it was mostly print-focused) had, "a value orientation towards partisanship in favor of justice and liberation (loosely defined) and a championing of the disempowered against the powerful" (Berger 1996). This activist tradition within alternative media had ambitions to what was quaintly described as "POEM: Popularize, Organize, Educate, and Mobilize" (Kessel 2000, 284) so as to move away from commercial media's 'one-way street' monologues towards a media that could "interact with their readership and to help shape, rather than only report, events" (Kessel 2000, 283). These kinds of notions would animate many later citizen journalism projects, including some of those examined in this section (Hyde-Clarke 2010, 41–42).

In addition to this dynamic of helping 'citizens' claim the rights and exercise the responsibilities of citizenship through participation in the media, and, to a certain extent, to build social capital and senses of local community (and perhaps even national cohesiveness), there was a second strand of citizen journalism that was (and remains) much less political. This strand is built on the idea of allowing people to report and share information and opinions, visuals and audio, as an end in itself. People domesticate available technology (Schoon 2011; Silverstone and Hirsch 2002), and the power of the internet and the capacity of the mobile phone to capture and rapidly transmit audio, video, photos and words quickly attracted platforms for this content to be shared. Some of this content can be seen as journalism, or as acts of journalism, or a contribution that can be used in journalism, but much of it is perhaps better described as just random content. In January 2012, YouTube loudly celebrated passing the 'one hour per second' mark: for example, every second, an hour of video is uploaded to the global site, or some 72,000 hours per day (Reisinger 2012). Perhaps equally interesting is that four billion videos are viewed *per day*, just on the YouTube site (Reisinger 2012). At a global level, the integrating of still and video citizen journalism into mainstream media took off with the September 11 attacks in the USA and, three years after this conflagration, with the December 2004 tsunami in Southeast Asia. For many commentators, this was a coming of age for citizen journalism, where cell phone footage was widely used by TV networks for the first time, and thousands of eyewitness were able to do more than merely relate their story to reporters: they were able to generate usable audio, photos and video and, through this, tell their own stories (Allan 2009; Bentley 2008).

Perhaps more appropriately termed 'open source journalism', or 'citizen reporting', or just 'user generated content' (UGC), this accidental, incidental content production also rapidly fell under the rubric of citizen journalism.[1] So did online diary keeping and blogging, regardless of the intent of the bloggers, only some of whom aspired to journalism. Indeed, the capacity of new technology to enhance "ordinary people's ability to bear witness" (Allan 2009, 18) got conflated, and remains conflated, with a more deliberate intent to do journalism. Being able to capture a photo of a burning house and transmit that to the world is certainly witness bearing, but it is only a *potential* act of journalism, qualitatively different to also composing a story (or filming elements) that also tell the viewer/reader *whose* house is burning (and finding that out), where it is located, and when and why it caught fire, for example. Going further and reporting on how the householders, neighbours and the authorities reacted, for example, and even reporting on how future fires might be prevented, are also acts of journalism.

Much of the difference can be discerned in the *intent* of the content creators. Mark Glaser's often cited definition of citizen journalism clearly sways towards the idea of intentional civic-minded, public-sphere enhancing citizen journalism: "people without professional journalism training can use the tools of modern technology and the global distribution of the Internet to create, augment or fact-check media on their own or in collaboration with others. For example, you might write about a city council meeting on your blog or in an online forum" (Glaser 2006). Jay Rosen's equally seminal definition hinges more on *any kind* of informing, without the civic minded examples provided of Glaser: "When the people formerly known as the audience employ the press tools they have in their possession to inform one another, *that's* citizen journalism" (Rosen 2008). Although, Rosen's conceptualisation still of course speaks to the *intent to inform*, and not merely the intent to say, entertain or amuse, for example.

In South Africa, there has been, in the first 10 years of citizen journalism,[2] appetite for both intentional civic-minded amateur journalism, with a participatory activist flavour, and for sharing of information that might just be useful to someone, or the sharing of opinions, either through blogs, or through the now ubiquitous ability to comment on online journalism stories, or leave comments on other blogs (and more recently, to annotate, 'like', rank or comment using social media).

CITIZEN JOURNALISM AS ALTERNATIVE MEDIA IN KENYA

However, in Kenya, rather than citizen journalism being a function of civic 'intent', it has instead been a reaction to long-standing editorial weaknesses within news organisations and fundamental structural failures within the broader media ecology. Kenya's media development is linked to its political history in very intimate ways. The 2007 political crisis particularly brought this aspect into sharp focus. According to Ogola (2009), the manner in which the media covered the 2007 post-election violence offered us a thorough reading of the state of journalism in Kenya. Ogola argues for a historical understanding of the relationship between the news media and the country's political history in order to understand that media's much criticised coverage of the post-election crisis. At the centre of this discussion is the notion of power and how the political elite mobilized it to suit their own agendas. One of the difficulties arising here is the fact that media ownership in Kenya has been closely tied to political patronage (Ogola 2009). This is true of media both before as well as after 1992, when the media sector was liberalised following the re-introduction of political pluralism in the country. The relationship between the media and the country's political elite became quite visible after the botched 2007 elections. As Ogola shows in his article, it was possible to trace dominant patterns of coverage that were extremely biased and that omitted what would otherwise have proved controversial. It is such omissions, gaps, partialities and weaknesses that draw attention to the question of quality journalism in Kenya. If one then attempts to define quality in the traditional paradigms of truth, objectivity and fairness, several news media institutions in Kenya fail to meet such standards. While the key media institutions have brought events and items considered newsworthy to Kenyans, the excessive bias and selectiveness of what stories to tell, as well as how to tell them, has undermined openness.

The fact that the Kenyan media has tended to favour the political elite does not in any way mean that Kenyans have not been able to gain access to news or information in other ways. As Dumisani Moyo has argued, in the absence of information from the media, "various alternative forms of communication ... take centre stage ... feeding on, as well as feeding from, an increasingly hungry rumour mill" (Moyo 2009, 552). Wallace Chuma has called this a "parallel market", describing the "explosion of rumour and hearsay in cyberspace" in the absence of other more formal avenues of information as similar to the thriving (informal) black market economy following the collapse of Zimbabwe's formal economy (2008, 26). The existence of such an alternative space particularly after the 2007 elections in Kenya has been both timely and significant. Already accused of blatant bias and political patronage, the Kenyan news media faced competition from alternative renditions of voices online (as well as through other new media platforms). The internet predominantly provided a space for a counterculture, destabilizing "the information infrastructure that had been built around the nation-state creating space for categories that before had been 'floating' in private and individualized sites, uncategorized, unacknowledged, and therefore easily dismissed" (Ligaga 2012, 4). We return to this discussion later in the chapter.

REACH, VOICE, VERACITY AND SUSTAINABILITY: FOUR SOUTH AFRICAN CITIZEN JOURNALISM INITIATIVES

Unlike Kenya, citizen journalism in South Africa has been more formally organized, *intentional*, better funded and mainly civic oriented, even if it is also broadly located within an activist tradition. This section looks at three landmark citizen journalism projects in South Africa.

Reporter.co.za

Inspired by Ohmynews in South Korea, Reporter.co.za was started in January 2005. Although a 'stand-alone' site, Reporter.co.za was funded by Johnnic (later Avusa, now Times Media Group), one of South Africa's 'big three' media houses, and aimed, it appears from interviews at the site's launch, to encourage and showcase 'incidental' journalism. No specific community was focused on or catered for; the site was explicitly for everyone in South Africa (or plausibly, further afield). The founding editor at the time, Juliette Saunders, told journalists, "people can do what they want, so it is a form of citizen journalism. We don't have any control over the product" (van Noort 2006).

In terms of reach, about 15 million South Africans had cell phones by 2005 (Abrahams and Goldstuck 2010), but only 1 in 12 had access to the internet, although, of course, among the socio-economic elite, numbers were much higher (Berger and Masala 2012).

Although Reporter.co.za was designed primarily to be a stand-alone destination, good stories were slated to appear on Johnnic's mainstream print titles (and probably on their web sites where these existed), including the national circulation-leading weekly *The Sunday Times* and the then still popular daily the *Sowetan*. Although no definite numbers were ever released, and given that the site closed in less than two years, it is probable that large audiences were not reached, except for the occasional story that was picked up by larger titles (Banda 2010).

In terms of voice, the editor said at the time, "I'm not afraid no one will read those stories because we won't write stories to bore other people" (van Noort 2006). The contributions and content was in English only, however. What stands out, given how closely associated citizen journalism was to become to hyper-local journalism, was the statement by the editor that Reporter.co.za's aim was to give "our readers the opportunity to determine what they regard as news. We welcome news reports, opinion pieces, columns, entertainment news, reviews, interview and *even community-oriented issues*" (Knight 2010, 44; emphasis added). The lexicon of the mainstream media's 'menu' of news reports and opinion pieces says a great deal about the timbre and style of stories sought.

Despite the editor's disavowal of control suggested in the notion 'people can do whatever they want', in terms of veracity, the site did have 20 newsroom journalists who did, at least, fact-checking. "We are looking for facts rather than opinions. And fact checking will all depend on the circumstance; of course we do a quality-control check. We are strict about accuracy" (van Noort 2006).

Nonetheless, despite some attempt at quality control, at least one commenter called the reports "half-baked, the sort you would expect from beginner reporters who would (usually) be sent back to plug the holes. The pictures have a charming amateurishness" (Harber 2006).

In terms of sustainability, it was not clear what the economic model was in terms of finances or retaining an audience. Backed by Johnnic/Avusa, it is likely that it was hoped the site would grow its audience and eventually be able to sell advertising (Banda 2010). It would also provide stories for existing publications, or at least story tips, and possibly serve as a talent spotting recruitment service. According to the editor of the time, "citizen reporters" would also be paid, if their stories or pictures appear, but rates were to be low if stories just appeared on Reporter.co.za (about US$5). They received much more if the stories were used in any of Johncom's newspapers (van Noort 2006). Apparently 6,000 people contributed pieces of citizen journalism in reporter.co.za's approximately two-year existence (van Noort 2006).

In retrospect, Reporter.co.za was a pioneering and reasonably large-scale experiment that, in between some actual journalistic successes, generated, in the editor's own farewell online message, "far too many pictures of Table Mountain and pets" (Knight 2010, 45). Its lack of geographical specificity, or clear 'demographic' market segments (although its content did seem to skew to younger people), the then still very low levels of internet access in South Africa and the 'newspaper English' style and tone may all have conspired against its prospects of success.

Thought Leader

Thought Leader, unlike Reporter.co.za, was not designed as a standalone site; it was and is part of the *Mail & Guardian* (*M&G*) web site. The then *Weekly Mail* was the first African paper to go online (and the 7th paper to do so in the world; M&G 2012). This 'internal' hosting of the site would give Thought Leader an immediate reach on what was then one of the most popular online news sites in South Arica. Unlike Reporter.co.za, Thought Leader was designed to be a "hybrid blog-media product" (Buckland 2007). This was a different kind of journalism entirely: not the eyewitness breaking news reporting focus of Reporter.co.za, but rather a platform that mostly carried the opinions and journalism of a selected and somewhat elite group of bloggers. According to one of its key architects, the site aimed to be a place where "M&G journalists, columnists and other writers, commentators, intellectuals and opinion makers across various industries and political spectrum meet" (Buckland 2007).

Although Thought Leader was also meant to be a 'home to some of the country's up-and-coming writers", to be accepted as a contributor required going through a vetting process. Additionally, the English-only register and the quality of the writing—often conceptual, argumentative and even academic at times—could not be described as easily accessible to all South Africa. This was a not a problem for the founders of the site, as the *M&G* readership niche is strongly elitist, as the *M&G* says on its rate card: "A large number of readers are professionals, captains of industry, public-sector officials, academics, diplomats and lobbyists". The 'contemporary' rate card also boasts 57% of readers currently having post school education (M&G Rate Card 2013).

Despite this elite target audience and style, it should be noted that, at least in 2013, 43% of the M&G's current readership does *not* have a school-leaving (Matric) qualification and that many of the Thought Leader contributors use a colloquial style and approach, despite the general air of sophisticated debate that Thought Leader tries to embody.

In terms of sustainability, Thought Leader incurred few costs, as contributors were not initially paid. Styled as an 'editorial blog' with content that "pass(es) through an editor . . . old fashioned traditional media style," the decision not to pay contributors was explained with these words: "Not everyone writes for bucks. But compensations do come in the form of a *quid pro quo*: the writers get an area for their profiles, where they may promote themselves" (Buckland 2008).

There were initial plans to attract advertising to the site and split some of the revenue with contributors; it is not clear if that has ever happened.

Thought Leader quickly became popular. After 18 months of operation, the site already sported almost 2,000 posts from 170 bloggers. From an audience point of view, 80,000 'uniques', i.e., different individuals, or at least people using different computers, were reading articles each month (Buckland 2008). Thought Leader continues to the present and appears, by the number of contributors—approximately 280 contributors—and very large number of comments that some posts inspire, to be a firm favourite of visitors to the M&G site.

As one of the site's initial architects notes, quality was key from the launch time and was the central consideration in the decision to open the site only to selected bloggers. "Making influential people part of your site attracts networks and builds audiences, quickly. User-generated content from a closed, selected network of users works best. It also ensures a high-quality product. Media is about quality content, and that is its key differentiator" (Buckland 2008).

Iindaba Ziyafika ('The News Is Coming')

Iindaba Ziyafika was an ambitious citizen journalism project (coordinated by the co-author of this chapter) that attempted to use rapidly developing cell phone capacity and ubiquity to experiment with citizen journalism in a small town (Grahamstown, South Africa) as an adjunct to the 'professional' journalism in South Africa's oldest independent newspaper, *Grocott's Mail*.[3] Funded by a generous Knight Foundation "News Challenge" Grant of US$500,000, *Iindaba Ziyafika* was designed to see if large scale, regular, citizen journalism could be integrated into a community newspaper, as well as have its own (sub)web site and, later, its own radio show based exclusively on citizen journalism.

Iindaba Ziyafika eschewed the model of enthusiastic volunteer, believing that in resource and income poor Grahamstown, with low levels of literacy and very high unemployment, some training and some remuneration would be both important to the success of the project. It would also be ethically appropriate. A citizen journalism training course was devised and delivered over six afternoon sessions over six weeks, and 'graduates' could be paid a small stipend for their stories after graduating from the course. Over two years, about 200 people were trained in the basics of doing citizen journalism, and about 350 stories got published, many in print and more online. A once-a-week citizen journalism radio show *Lunchtime Live*, which aired on the local community radio station, *Radio Grahamstown*, in the majority local language isiXhosa, seemed to be well received (although there is no research into the claimed listenership of the radio station; Tsarwe 2011).

In terms of reach, the paper and the radio station attracted reasonable audiences, estimated, in the newspaper's case, at about half of adults in Grahamstown. Other research indicates widespread though irregular readership of *Grocott's* print issue and listenership of *Lunchtime Live*, but limited access to the web site, outside of the university and in wealthier and mostly white private homes (Tsarwe 2011).

In terms of veracity, all copy that appeared online or in print was edited, and often heavily reworked, by professional journalists employed by either *Grocott's Mail* or the *Iindaba Ziyafika* project, both to improve language and for accuracy and legal reasons. This was very contentious, as it touched deeply on issues of voice. As critics pointed out, as many contributors were not comfortable writing in English (which was often a participant's 3rd or 4th language), *Iindaba Ziyafika's* initial reliance on conventional 'newspaper English' was problematic (Steenveld and Strelitz 2010). The early establishment of an SMS line for incoming text messages (and the promise of their publication) allowed for freer expression, including some use of popular mobile SMS 'shorthand' and township *patois*, but even these SMS messages were carefully moderated. This was done partly for practical and legal reasons: even publishing a seemingly 'fair comment' text message in print, where, for example, an (anonymous) author complained that a local fish shop was sometimes "dirty", brought a furious response from the fish shop owner, who was convinced that competing retailers were behind this demeaning SMS comment. Legal action was threatened, apologies made, and much energy expended for a citizen journalism 'story' of 30 or so words (Dugmore 2009).

Another reason for the caution on the part of the editors and professional journalists is that early research by the project managers showed that free or low paid journalists are more susceptible to 'undue influence'. Further interviews with citizen journalists (post the project's closure) indicated that some of the more prolific writers were approached, on occasion, to either keep certain details and names *out* of their stories, or, sometimes, to put certain things in (Dugmore 2012; Tsarwe 2011).

In terms of sustainability, the number of citizen journalists working regularly in the *Iindaba Ziyafika* rapidly reduced to a few regulars, less than 10 of the 200 trainees, over the two years. Most trainees wrote one or two stories, not even reaching the threshold for payment (only the third published story onwards attracted a small stipend). Many ex-participants said it was just too hard and even 'boring' or, in a small town, guaranteed to create enemies (Dugmore 2009). But a few contributors enjoyed the challenges of journalism, and some started to make some of their living from contributing two and more stories a week. This small crew, eventually about five or six regulars, spoke about how being part of a 'team'—where members could get mutual support, or allowed them to work out ethical dilemmas, gave them a sense of 'community of practice' and the courage to take on vested interests in Grahamstown. Having access to airtime, fax machines and computers (in the citizen journalism newsroom the project established) was facilitative of citizen journalism, and this would probably always be the case in resource poor environments (Dugmore 2012; Nyathi 2011).

As noted in later assessments of the project, citizen journalists who do a good job of getting their stories into print on a regular basis quickly start to see themselves as *journalists*, and the fuller moniker 'citizen journalist' comes to rankle (Dugmore 2012). When interviewed, these participants argued that when calling up the Mayor's office (or when speaking to any authority figure), for example, asking for comment, or trying to get a story done, few would volunteer that they were not 'real' but only 'citizen' journalists.

One of the key lessons from the project was that when speaking to those who hold power in society, even relatively 'minor' power (a school head-master or a health clinic director, for example), journalists require the kind of commitment, 'standing' and backing that both a formal institution, and being part of a community of practice, help engender (Dugmore 2012).

CITIZEN JOURNALISM AND KENYA'S POST-ELECTION CRISIS

As noted earlier in the chapter, citizen journalism in Kenya has not emerged from the kind of formal organization with institutional support such as has been the case in South Africa. Instead, it has been more spontaneous, perhaps even 'indisciplined'. As such, a clear historical trajectory of its development in Kenya is almost impossible. However, key moments in Kenya's political history provide opportunities for studying some of its most notable characteristics.

Much work has been done on Kenya's 2007–2008 post-election crisis and specifically on the role that was played by social media. Briefly, following a botched election in 2007, violence erupted in Kenya leading to the deaths of more than 1,000 people and the displacement of about 500,000. The clashes erupted after the Electoral Commission of Kenya (ECK) declared Mwai Kibaki winner of a closely contested election, following which Kibaki was quickly and secretly sworn in. Shortly after, a ban on live media was placed by John Michuki, then Internal Security minister, purportedly in the interest of public safety. The information vacuum that was created, coupled with a hunger for news, led to the creation of several alternative sources of news. As Zuckerman (2009), Makinen and Kuira (2008) and Goldstein and Rotich (2008), among others, have variously shown, the media black-out ignited the use of new media forms, whether in the form of SMSs or the internet. According to Zuckerman, Kenyan bloggers, especially Ory Okol-loh (of the Kenyan Pundit), Juliana Rotich (Afromusing) and Daudi Were (Mental Acrobatics), became active and visible citizen journalists. They took up the responsibilities of reporting what was taking place, inviting people to send in comments, photographs and SMSs. Their various blogs became depositories where Kenyans could drop in information about what was going on.

One lesson that can be drawn from the 2007 experience is the significance of alternative online voices that enabled Kenyans to receive news
where mainstream media had failed. Zuckerman (2009) also points out that
mobile phones were equally important, especially in circulating SMSs that
kept people abreast with what was going on. However, unlike the case of
online platforms, the government was able to shut down mass circulation of
SMSs for, ostensibly, public safety. In the absence of other formats, the internet became a key location for discussions, exchanges of information and
heated arguments. The more visible of these online blogs fall under what
David Domingo and Ari Heinonen (2008, 3) identify as "journalistic blogs"
(10), a "new category of news and current affairs communication" (3).

Bloggers such as Ory Okolloh were particularly active in the formation
of a web site that drew together a Kenyan community in search of a middle
ground in the aftermath of the crisis. Along with others, she started the
Ushahidi (from the Swahili word meaning 'testimony') web site, a site that
has been recognized internationally for its efforts to congregate citizen journalists in times of crisis. It has been described aptly as a "revolutionary
crowd sourcing utility that enables citizen journalists and eyewitnesses all
over the world to report incidences of violence through the web, mobile,
emails, SMS and Twitter" (Afropulse 2012). Okolloh participated in the
formation of the web site after her own blog, Kenyanpundit.com, became
saturated with information following the media ban. According to Okolloh,
Ushahidi was built by a team of volunteers who wanted to create a space for
people to tell their stories without fear of victimization. It was a landmark
technological event, creating possibilities for understanding how information could circulate in Kenya during that moment. Ushahidi is presently
global in its reach, allowing different contributors in places facing crisis to
report what they are witnessing, often countering information circulating
in mainstream media. The significance and contributions of Ushahidi were
noted when the web site received recognition at the 16th annual Webby
Awards in May 2012, for the outstanding use of innovative technology for
social good.

CITIZEN JOURNALISM AS THE 'FIFTH ESTATE'

Beyond the post-election moment, citizen journalism in Kenya also takes
place on other online platforms such as Twitter and Facebook. Twitter, especially, has become a key site, where well-known names of self-identified
citizen journalists are beginning to emerge to question information provided
in the media, or in some cases, to provide 'breaking news'. These citizen
journalists pride themselves in being transparent, and truthful, in the face of
mainstream media's practice of hiding information, and can be described,
following Nimmo and Combs (1992) who have called the internet the 'fifth
estate', as watchdogs of the other estates, including the media. Examples

of 'Twitter activists' include Robert Alai (@RobertAlai) and Dennis Itumbi (@OleItumbi). Robert Alai, for instance, was arrested in 2012 after he circulated a tweet accusing Kenyan government spokesperson Alfred Mutua of being involved in the murder of two human rights activists, Oscar Kingara and Paul Oulu. At the time of their deaths, Kingara and Oulu were doing some work related to the mass tortures and murders of suspected Mungiki criminals, reportedly by the Kenyan Police (*Mungiki* is the name of a vigilante group made up mostly of young Kikuyu men). The social media's 'report' of the assassinations by far surpassed the brief reports that appeared in the leading newspapers in Kenya. A discussion thread in one of Kenya's vibrant web sites, Jukwaa.com (discussed later in this chapter), was dedicated to the murders, providing details of the event, including shocking pictures of the bloody, lifeless body of Oscar Kingara, taken minutes after the assassination. The post included statements from politicians, journalists, activists, writers and colleagues. Much like the assassination of former Minister of Finance Robert Ouko (see Cohen and Odhiambo 2004) and British tourist Julie Ward (see Musila 2008), the deaths of Kingara and Oulu would have been silently but firmly pushed aside from public scrutiny were it not for citizen journalists who ensured the story sustained currency. They provided depth to the story and allowed for a far more substantive engagement with possible 'truths' about the assassinations.

Sometimes citizen journalists are borne out of misfortune and frustration, such as was the case with Kenyan photojournalist Clifford Derrick Otieno, who in May, 2005, was slapped by Kenya's first lady, Lucy Kibaki, after she caught him recording her illegal entry and subsequent outburst at a Kenyan newspaper newsroom. Otieno, seeking justice by reporting assault, quickly found that his life was in danger and had to flee the country. He has subsequently dedicated much of his time trying to speak about the lingering injustices that are not being exposed in the media, especially because information is still largely controlled centrally by the state.

While citizen journalism can be narrowed down to individuals, its lack of institutionalisation has meant that a wider variety of Kenyans have been able to engage with news in various ways. Still, on online content, it is interesting to note that most of what appears close to citizen journalism descriptively occurs in discussion forums. This is truly where the 'indisciplined' voices of Kenyans can be heard. While these sites appear to engage randomly with information, they remain crucial, especially in the absence of formalized spaces of citizen journalism. A good example is the discussion forum Jukwaa.com. Jukwaa is a discussion platform that deals exclusively with Kenyan politics. It is moderated by a Kenyan social media activist Onyango Oloo. Apart from Jukwaa, Oloo also runs a number of blogs, most visible among them the Kenya Democracy Project blog. Unlike several discussion sites, which are often a part of a larger bulletin board system, Jukwaa is dedicated to Kenyan politics. It has a limited number of members with the option for new members to join the forum presently disabled.

The moderator offers very clear rules of participation against any kind of discrimination and acts swiftly and harshly against any offenders. Also interesting about Jukwaa is the fact that its limited membership ensures a regular input by members of the forum who, though using pseudonyms, are well known by other members of the forum. This minimizes the number of troublemakers in the forum. Jukwaa has therefore become a dependable source of information to readers who want to find out more about an event or controversial news item in Kenya.

Lastly, while citizen journalism in Kenya seems untethered to any formal institution, it is interesting to note the kinds of projects that are beginning to emerge at the level of community that are provoking a sense of participatory journalism. The past two or so years have seen an emerging community of citizen journalists reporting on Nairobi's slum life, for instance, a project most of these slum dwellers feel is important if they are to retrieve their voices as inhabitants of what has now become a tourist attraction. Based on one of Nairobi's largest slums, Kibera, projects such as the *Ghetto Mirror*, *The Kibera Journal*, *Kibera News Network* and radio station *Pamoja FM* all variously constitute an emerging form of citizen journalism (Patinkin 2012). These are important projects that provide much more than a blanket idea of slum life and allow residents to engage in empowering ways with their communities. In engaging with citizen journalism's typology, therefore, one cannot ignore these kinds of marginalized but important voices.

CONCLUSION

As has been noted by several scholars, citizen journalism feeds off of mainstream media, often depending on professional journalists to break a story before picking it up and interrogating it. Lasica (2003) argues that institutionalised journalism and citizen media should be understood as existing in a symbiotic relationship and should not be read as either/or categories. Still, in the contexts of institutionalised censorial media-political regimes, such as Kenya, that deny citizens access to information, citizen journalism will continue to plug that gap by offering alternative readings of news. It is this role that will ensure it remains relevant in the future.

In South Africa, by contrast, with less formal censorship and much more media freedom, citizen journalism has morphed in either more formal and more widespread 'stringer' or 'freelance' arrangements (with and without payment), or is being superseded by the greater 'reach' and paradoxically greater intimacy of Facebook and Twitter. Many of the regular contributors to Thought Leader, for example, tweet to their 'followers' and alert their 'friends' when their new blog goes up on Thought Leader. Thought Leader itself can be followed on Facebook and Twitter. Like in Kenya, thousands of people in South Africa are experiencing the internet for the first time *every day*, and signing up to Facebook for the first time *every day*, and experimenting in forms of expression and participation, some of which is citizen journalism like. Veracity and quality can get lost in this mix, which is why projects and platforms like Thought Leader, with tightly selected bloggers, and the new Health-e based OurHealth Citizen Journalism project, which, like *Iindaba Ziyafika*, use selected, named, semi-trained journalists and then *curate* and edit their content. They are likely to continue to be an important part of the emerging hybrid forms of journalism that are coming to dominate contemporary media landscapes.

REFERENCES

Abrahams, Lucienne, and Arthur Goldstuck. 2010. "The State of e-Development in South Africa: A View from the End of the First Decade of the 21st Century." LINK Public Policy Paper 11. Accessed 24 February 2013. http://link.wits.ac.za/papers/abrahams-goldstuck-2010-edevelopment-sa.pdf.

Afropulse. 2012. "Ory Okolloh." 14 August. Accessed 31 January 2013. http://afropulse.blogspot.co.uk/2012/08/ory-okolloh.html.

Allan, Stuart and Einar Thorsen. 2009. *Citizen Journalism: Global Perspectives.* New York: Peter Lang.

Banda, Fackson. 2010. *Citizen Journalism and Democracy in Africa.* Grahamstown: Rhodes University, Highway Africa.

Bentley, Clyde. 2008. "Citizen Journalism: Back to the Future?" Paper presented at the Carnegie-Knight Conference on the Future of Journalism, Cambridge, MA, 20–21 June.

Berger, Guy. 1996. "The Alternative Press—Private and Community Newspapers and News Agencies." Paper presented at Reporting Southern Africa conference, Johannesburg, 14–16 October. http://guyberger.ru.ac.za/fulltext/Altiaj.rtf.

Berger, Guy. 1999. "Towards an Analysis of the South African Media and Transformation, 1994–99." *Transformation* 38: 82–116.

Berger, Guy, and Zikhona Masala. 2012. "Mapping Digital Media: South Africa." London: Open Society Foundations.

Buckland, Matthew. 2007. "Thought Leader." *Matthewbuckland.com*, 24 August. Accessed 22 January 2013. http://matthewbuckland.com/?p=323.

Buckland, Matthew. 2008. "Thoughts About the Leaders: The Columnists 2.0 Model." *Matthewbuckland.com*, 6 September. Accessed 22 January 2013. http://matthewbuckland.com/?p=449.

Chuma, Wallace. 2008. "Zim Media: Mugabe's Dodgy Tactics." *The Media.* 25–26.

Cohen, David, and Elisha Atieno Odhiambo. 2004. *Risks of Knowledge: Investigations into the Death of the Hon. Minister John Robert Ouko in Kenya, 1990.* Athens: Ohio University Press.

de Lanerolle, Indra. 2012. *The New Wave: Who Connects to the Internet, How They Connect and What They Do When They Connect.* South African Network Society Project, University of Witwatersrand.

Domingo, David, and Ari Heinonen. 2008. "Weblogs and Journalism: A Typology to Explore the Blurring Boundaries." *Nordicom Review* 29: 3–15.

Dugmore, Harry. 2009. "Moving Beyond Text for Cell Phone Citizen Media." 16 June. Accessed 23 January 2013. http://www.pbs.org/idealab/2009/06/moving-beyond-text-for-cell-phone-citizen-media152.html.

Dugmore, Harry. 2012. "Communities of Practice and the sustainability of Citizen Journalism." Paper presented at the International Association of Media and Communication Research conference, Durban, 15–20 July.

Gillmor, Dan. 2004. *We the Media. Grassroots Journalism by the People, for the People.* Sebastopol, CA: O'Reilly.

Goldstein, Joshua, and Juliana Rotich. 2008. "Digitally Networked Technology in Kenya's 2007–2008 Post-Election Crisis." Berkman Center Research publication 2008–09: 1–10.

Glaser, Mark. 2006. "Your Guide to Citizen Journalism." *MediaShift*, 26 September. Accessed 24 January 2013. http://www.pbs.org/mediashift/2006/09/your-guide-to-citizen-journalism270.html.

Harber, Anton. 2006. "Citizen Kane—Not." *The Harbinger*, 8 February. Accessed 22 January 2013. http://www.theharbinger.co.za/wordpress/2006/02/08/citizen-kane-not.

Hyde-Clarke, Nathalie, ed. 2010. *The Citizen in Communication: Re-Visiting Traditional, New and Community Media Practices in South Africa.* Cape Town: Juta.

Kessel, Ineke van. 2000. "*Grassroots:* From Washing Lines to Utopia." In *Media Under Apartheid,* edited by Les Switzer and Mohamed Adhikari, 283–326. Athens: Ohio University Press.

Knight, Megan. 2010. "Blogging and Citizen Journalism." In *The Citizen in Communication: Re-Visiting Traditional, New and Community Media Practices in South Africa,* edited by Nathalie Hyde-Clarke, 31–50. Cape Town: Juta.

Lasica, Joseph Daniel. 2003. "Blogs and Journalism Need Each Other." *Nieman Reports* 57: 70–74.

Ligaga, Dina. 2012. " 'Virtual Expressions': Alternative Online Spaces and the Staging of Kenyan Popular Culture." *Research in African Literatures* 43: 1–16.

"M&G Rate Card." 2013. Accessed 22 January 2013. http://cdn.mg.co.za/content/documents/2013/01/07/rate_card_2013.pdf.

M&G. 2012. "History." Accessed 22 January 2013. http://mg.co.za/page/history.

Makinen, Maarit, and Mary Wangui Kuira. 2008. "Social Media and Postelection Crisis in Kenya." *International Journal of Press/Politics* 13: 328–335.

Moyo, Dumisani. 2009. "Citizen Journalism and the Parallel Market of Information in Zimbabwe's 2008 Election." *Journalism Studies* 10: 551–567.

Musila, Grace. 2008. "Kenyan and British Social Imaginaries on Julie Ward's Death in Kenya." PhD diss., University of the Witwatersrand.

Nyathi, Sihle. 2011. "The *Iindaba Ziyafika* Project: A New Community of Practice?" MA diss., Rhodes University.

Nimmo, Dan, and James Combs. 1992. *The Political Pundits.* New York: Praeger.

Ogola, George. 2009. "Media at Cross-roads: Reflections on the Kenyan News and the Coverage of the 2007 Political Crisis." *Africa Insight* 39: 58–71.

Patinkin, Jason. 2012. *Think Africa,* 6 November. Accessed 31 January 2013. http://thinkafricapress.com/kenya/read-all-about-it-citizen-journalists-give-new-face-nairobi-slums-kibera.

Reisinger, Don. 2012. "CNET." 21 May. Accessed 25 January 2012. http://news.cnet.com/8301-1023_3-57438332-93/youtube-users-uploading-72-hours-of-video-each-minute.

Rosen, Jay. 2008. "A Most Useful Definition of Citizen Journalism." *PressThink,* 14 July. Accessed 25 January 2012. http://archive.pressthink.org/2008/07/14/a_most_useful_d.html.

Schoon, Alette Jeanne. 2011. "Raw Phones: The Domestication of Mobile Phones amongst Young Adults in Hooggenoeg, Grahamstown." MA diss., Rhodes University.

Silverstone, Roger, and Eric Hirsch, eds. 2002. *Consuming Technologies: Media and Information in Domestic Spaces.* London: Routledge.

Steenveld, Lynette, and Larry Strelitz. 2010. "Citizen Journalism in Grahamstown: *Iindaba Ziafika* and the Difficulties of Instituting Citizen Journalism in a Poor South African Country Town." Paper presented at World Journalism Educators Conference, Rhodes University, 4–7 July.

Tsarwe, Stanley. 2011. "'Too tired to speak?' Investigating the Reception of Radio Grahamstown's Lunchtime Live Show as a Means of Linking Local Communities to Power." MA diss., Rhodes University.

van Noort, Elvira. 2006. "Will Citizen Journalism Shake up SA Media?" *Mail & Guardian*, 6 January. Accessed 26 January 2013. http://mg.co.za/article/2006-01-06-will-citizen-journalism-shake-up-sa-media.

Wasserman, Hermann, and Arnold S. de Beer. 2006. "Conflicts of Interest? The South African Media and Its Role During the First Ten Years of Democracy." *Critical Arts* 19: 35–51.

Zuckerman, Ethan. 2009. "Citizen Media and the Kenyan Electoral Crisis." In *Citizen Journalism: Global Perspectives*, edited by Stuart Allen and Einar Thorsen, 187–208. New York: Peter Lang.

NOTES

1. There are many interpretations of the term Citizen Journalism, and its etymology. See especially Rosen (2008), Glaser (2006), Gillmor (2004), Banda (2010). Knight's overview (2010) provides a useful summary.

2. The periodization of Citizen Journalism, as a phenomenon of the Digital Age, closely linked to changes in the power and ability of digital technology, its cost and ubiquity. In South Africa, 2004 is arguably as useful a starting point for periodization of digital platform CJ as blogs start appearing (often penned by Journalists), early concepts of 'MoJo' (mobile enabled journalism) started to get off the ground as cell phones started to feature cameras, recorders, and email/web connectivity, including Wi-fi. The launch of Nokia 9500, Nokia's first camera-enabled 'smartphone' in 2004 enhanced this. Internet use in South Africa also increased, in 2004 to about 10% of the population (Abrahams and Goldstuck 2010) although not everyone had frequent access, and ADSL broadband, only introduced late in 2002, started to replace much slower dial-up connections. By 2010, it would be accurate to say that the South African socio-economic elite were online in ways that were similar to anywhere in the world, but that the vast majority of the population were not yet. A majority of South Africans are only predicted to be online by 2014 (de Lanerolle 2012).

3. Since the paper was bought by Rhodes University's School of Journalism and Media Studies in 2002, some journalism is done by students studying at the Journalism School.

Section V

Case Studies from India and the Arab World

14 Where More Is Not Better

Challenges Facing Quality News Journalism in 'Shining' India

Prasun Sonwalkar

In the very first month of *Indian Opinion*, I realized that the sole aim of journalism should be service. The newspaper press is a great power, but just as an unchained torrent of water submerges whole countryside and devastates crops, even so an uncontrolled pen serves but to destroy. If the control is from without, it proves more poisonous than want of control. It can be profitable only when exercised from within.

—Mahatma Gandhi (1982, 287)

Two inter-linked narratives stand out in recent western discourse about India and its media, which, when seen 'from below', as this chapter will show, present at best a superficial and otiose view of reality. The first narrative refers to India's status as one of the rapidly growing economies, often described as the next 'superpower' and an 'economic powerhouse' with an average GDP of nearly 7% in the last decade. India is one of the so-called BRIC countries (Brazil, Russia, India and China) that are supposed to be at an advanced stage of economic development. Influential columnists such as Tom Friedman of *The New York Times* often celebrate the recent rise in India's economic indicators: "If India were a stock, I would buy it" (*Economic Times* 2010). The context is massive and complex: a deeply diverse country of hundreds of languages and ethnic groups, following all major world religions, and of sub-continental size with a population of nearly 1.25 billion (65% below 35, according to the 2011 Census), India is estimated to have more than 350 million people belonging to a globalised middle class with increasing purchasing power. English, the language of colonial rulers, has a privileged, elitist and aspirational status in independent India and is used by nearly 10% of the population that controls domains that have social, cultural and professional prestige.

The celebratory economic view of a globalised India is shared not only by Western writers, politicians and captains of industry, but by large sections of the Indian elites and the middle class as well, including journalists and politicians (in the 2004 general elections, the then ruling Bharatiya Janata Party unleashed a high-profile media campaign titled 'India Shining', seeking to spread a feel-good message about its achievements in office; the party lost the election). In 1947, when India became independent amidst large-scale disturbances and killings and embarked on its uncertain path of democracy, the question often asked by Western observers was, 'Will India survive?' Sixty-five years later, the question has changed to: 'Will India become a superpower?' (Kitchen 2012).

The second narrative is about the efflorescence in India's media ecosystem since the early 1990s, when the liberalisation of the country's economy was accelerated, adding 'media superpower' to its recently acquired sobriquets. Drawing on the strength of its culture, the growing international reach and appeal of the Indian media (Bollywood films, television soaps, news channels) are often seen in cultural imperialist tones by its neighbours (Sonwalkar 2001), while influential writers and politicians such as Tharoor expound on the global influence of India's 'soft power' (2012). There are grounds for such optimism, with latest industry figures suggesting that India has one of the largest media and entertainment industries in the world. A media-rich poor country, India's media industry has recorded exponential growth—particularly since the early 1990s—in terms of the number of newspapers published, television channels, news channels, radio stations, internet access and mobile connectivity. And the growth is set to continue in the foreseeable future, attracting international media capital. As the World Association of Newspapers (WAN) noted in recent years, India is among only two countries—China being the other—where newspaper circulation has been increasing, while elsewhere it is in irreversible decline. There has been a proliferation in India of what I call the 'hardware' of journalism (enabling factors such as technology, capital, rising literacy, access, laws), which offers new opportunities for the 'software' of journalism—the quality of editorial content that empowers citizens, holds those in power to account, and strengthens democratic institutions—to flourish.

Some recent industry figures of India's largely privately owned media infrastructure are revealing. Overall, daily newspaper circulation in India is estimated to be 350 million, with vast scope for growth. *The Times of India* (established 1838) sits at the top of the table as the world's largest circulated English-language newspaper (4.3 million; 12 editions). According to the Registrar of Newspapers of India, there were 82,222 registered newspapers published in various languages in 2011, including 32,793 in Hindi (India's national language) and 11,478 in English. According to the Ministry of Information and Broadcasting, satellite television channels number 825, including 130 channels devoted to news in various languages. Mobile phone subscribers (mostly non-data subscribers) amount to nearly 900 million, and there are 21 million internet subscribers, according to the Telecom Regulatory Authority of India. There are 245 private FM radio stations (news is not allowed on private radio). Besides the largely privately owned media infrastructure, the state owns and operates one of the largest television and radio networks in any democratic country, broadcasting across the sub-continent and beyond in various languages, through Doordarshan (television) and All India Radio.

At the WAN convention in the southern Indian city of Hyderabad in 2009, India was hailed as the great global hope for media, especially print. According to the WAN invitation to the convention,

> Developing literacy and wealth are part of but far from all the story: Great credit needs also to be given to Indian newspaper professionals, who are re-inventing the newspaper to keep it vibrant and compelling in the digital age. Although broadband and mobile are booming in India, print newspapers are growing right along with them. The country has more daily newspapers than any other nation and leads in paid-for daily circulation, surpassing China for the first time in 2008. Twenty of the world's 100 largest newspapers are Indian. Newspaper circulation rose a further 8 percent last year. (quoted in Baru, 2011)

James Murdoch of News Corp went further by declaring at a conference in Mumbai in 2011, "The impressive achievements of the last two decades have not even begun to fulfil the potential of this great land. I believe India's creative force is a still sleeping tiger waiting to be awakened" (Murdoch 2011). While lauding India and its young population, he went on to describe the rest of the world as "grey and tired".

The celebratory trope about the Indian media is also evident in the titles of influential industry reports, which, significantly and seamlessly, club 'media' and 'entertainment' together and refer to them as 'M&E markets'. A joint report in 2011 by consultants KPMG and the Federation of Indian Chambers of Commerce and Industry (FICCI) was titled 'Hitting the high notes on the Indian media and entertainment industry in 2011'. It estimated that India's media and entertainment industries were growing rapidly: worth $13.2 billion in 2010 and projected to touch $25 billion by 2015. The report saw the biggest growth potential in television (up to $6 billion by 2015) and print (up to $6.3 billion). Despite television receiving increasing advertising, the print media's share had grown from $1.4 billion to $2.6 billion between 2005 and 2010. KPMG-FICCI's report for 2012, titled 'Digital dawn: The metamorphosis begins', says,

> The overall M&E market is expected to grow at a compounded annual growth rate of 15 per cent per annum over the next five years ... The potential for increase in media penetration, growing importance of regional markets, increasing consumption in tier 2 and 3 cities, impact of regulatory changes, more focused consumer research, innovation in content, marketing and delivery platforms to serve different niches,

increasing device penetration like mobiles, tablets, PCs etc., all point towards a very positive future for the industry. (from Foreword)

KPMG-FICCI's reports are among several accounts that project an optimistic view of the Indian media industry. These include reports from the Ministry of Information and Broadcasting, Registrar of Newspapers of India, Audit Bureau of Circulations, Indian Readership Survey, Media Research User's Council, Telecom Regulatory Authority of India and TAM India. If the 'entertainment' aspect of such reports is excluded, estimates and figures over successive years point to remarkable growth in the 'hardware' of journalism since the early 1990s. The growth across sub-continental India offers the potential of increasing interaction and integration among peoples, institutions, local economies, regions and cultures that do not have much in common, let alone share a singular conception of national identity. Some key reasons for the growth are rising literacy (from 12% in 1947 to more than 74% in 2011), new technology, intense competition to capture media markets, a growing middle class with purchasing power and what Jeffrey (1993, 2007) calls "political excitement". The preoccupation with politics in news discourse is rooted in India's colonial history, beginning with opposition to policies of the East India Company in the first Indian-language journals in the early nineteenth century, and then journalism playing a major role during the freedom movement, when a generation of leaders (such as Gandhi, Jawaharlal Nehru) and journalists cooperated to overthrow British rule. Television has added a visual dimension to the public sphere and has become the most pervasive medium in a country where literacy has not reached the entire population. Internet penetration is low but increasing and is creating new spaces and forums for India's ancient tradition of argument and debate through, for example, citizen journalism, which has the potential of extending forms of 'recognition' to regions and minorities that are usually marginalised or ignored in mainstream news discourse (Sonwalkar 2009).

However, scratch the surface and the reality is that this technologically deterministic, economy-driven 'feel-good' story in Western narratives has an equally valid part and counterpart: quantity is not the same as quality. The two are often conflated, but a distinction needs to be made between the state of the news media infrastructure (hardware) and the state of journalism (software); the two are not necessarily compatible. In many respects, concern over quality journalism in Britain finds a strong echo in India, which historically borrowed from the British model of journalism. If rampant commercialisation and rapacious pursuit of profit led to lowering of ethical standards in British journalism, resulting in several inquiries sparked by the phone-hacking row, there is similar concern and hand-wringing in India over the quality of journalism reaching new depths in recent years. International coverage too has dwindled in Indian news discourse, as owners seeking to cut costs rely more on news agencies and stringers to provide coverage to their young readers/audience who do not have the colonial baggage of previous generations.

The Press Council of India (PCI), a statutory watchdog body formed in 1956 to maintain and improve standards of newspapers and news agencies, among other objectives, has expressed serious concern over the increasing ethical and financial corruption in Indian journalism evident at the institutional and personal levels. The PCI is considered a toothless body due to its limited powers, but recent reports and controversial remarks about the news media by its chairman, Justice Markandey Katju, have helped raise awareness that all is not well with Indian journalism. Some hope for a Leveson-like inquiry into unethical practices in Indian journalism, such as the widespread phenomenon of 'paid news' (openly selling space in newspapers to candidates during elections), extortionist and blackmailing activities of sections of the news media, dumbing down of news content on television, and symbolically annihilating vast areas of public life in a country that continues to face serious challenges of poverty reduction, education, health, rural development, financial corruption in government and the private sector, and internal security. Gandhi's views about journalism, expressed in his journal *Indian Opinion* (launched in South Africa in 1903 to fight racial discrimination) find few takers in independent India, particularly since the early 1990s, when the nexus between politics, business and the news media became deep and all too pervasive.

India's Oxbridge-educated Prime Minister, Manmohan Singh, who has often favoured self-regulation to statutory controls to raise the quality of journalism, voiced the concerns of many in a speech to journalists (Singh 2005):

> With the rapid growth of media in recent times, qualitative development has not kept step with quantitative growth. In the race for capturing markets, journalists have been encouraged to cut corners, to take chances, to hit and run. I believe the time has come for journalists to take stock of how competition has impacted upon quality . . . How many mistakes must a journalist make, how many wrong stories, and how many motivated columns before professional clamps are placed?

Besides Singh, unease over the quality of Indian journalism has been expressed by several stakeholders, including journalists, who are increasingly helpless and frustrated at advertising and marketing professionals driving editorial decisions to maximise profit. Calls for self-regulation have not resulted in changes in journalism practice, as most owners of newspaper and television companies take assumptions and practices inherent in the idea of 'Murdochization' to levels that Rupert Murdoch may not have envisaged when he introduced his 'model' of journalism in Britain, the United States and elsewhere. Due to India's size and its many languages, the size of the media market is fragmented, which is also reflected in the complex ownership pattern of Indian media organisations. A large number of entities own media organisations, but a closer look reveals market domination by less than 100 entities that control what is heard, read or watched at the national and state levels. Absence of cross-media ownership restrictions means that the main players dominate content across platforms, and most owners have traditionally held business interests outside the media. Growing corporatization has resulted in large industrial houses acquiring direct and/or indirect interest in media groups, both leveraging and feeding off each other to maximise profits. There are already allegations that crony capitalism is leading to 'crony journalism' (Jagannathan 2012). Another key trend is political parties and individuals allied to political ideologies owning or controlling influential sections of the news media. Any attempts to restrict ownership and curb monopoly are strongly resisted in the name of freedom of the press. The result is that while the quality of journalism touches new lows, media companies are among the most profitable in any sector in India's economy; that is, the quality of journalism is inversely proportionate to the growth of the news media infrastructure. As T.N. Ninan (2011), chairman and editorial director of *Business Standard*, a leading financial daily, put it,

> We have never had such a vast audience or readership, but our credibility has never been so tested. We have never seen such a flowering of TV channels and such a spreading footprint for newspaper titles, but the market is more consolidated than ever around the top few players. The quality of what we offer to our public has never been better, but that same public can see that the ethical foundations of our actions have plumbed new depths. The impact of the media on India's public discourse has never been so instant and its reach so pervasive, but many ask whether that impact is for good or ill. It is unquestionably the best of times, and it is also, unfortunately, the worst of times.

The next section presents a brief analysis of journalism from the late 1980s, when the introduction of a corporate culture in the newsrooms of *The Times of India* changed the rules of the game not only in the mass circulation newspaper but in the entire news media. The chapter then sets out three key indicators that pose a serious challenge to the quality of journalism:

- the institutionalisation of a corporate culture in *The Times of India* Group and its adoption by most media owners across the country;
- the financial and ethical corruption involved in the practice of 'paid news' during elections; and
- the dumbing down of news content on television channels by focusing on celebrities, crime, cricket, the occult, superstitions and Bollywood to drive ratings, revenues and profits.

As a journalist in India since the early 1980s and a witness to the 'Murdo-chization' of journalism in *The Times of India* since the late 1980s (Son-walkar 2002), I suggest that the situation is fast reaching a stage where, unless checked soon, the deteriorating quality of journalism in India has the potential of endangering the viability and future of the much-celebrated 'world's largest democracy'. When politicians, who are usually delighted that news organisations are open and willing to be corrupted, criticise it, and when financial and ethical corruption in journalism become central themes in popular culture, such as Bollywood films ('Rann', directed by Ram Gopal Varma 2010) and thinly disguised novels by journalists ('News-room Live' by Prabhat Shunglu 2012), then there is a serious problem with the celebration of the recent growth in India's news media.

'MURDOCHIZATION' AND ITS EFFECTS

Print journalism began in India soon after the East India Company estab-lished itself in Calcutta in the late eighteenth century, and spread its influ-ence across the sub-continent. The first printed journal, the *Bengal Gazette*, was launched by James Augustus Hicky on 29 January 1780. By 1833, there were 33 English-language and 16 Indian-language publications in circulation, reflecting a nascent sense of nationalism that was later taken forward effectively by leaders such as Gandhi and Nehru, culminating in India's freedom in 1947. The press had matured in the acid bath of the freedom struggle, and when India became free, "she had already acquired a sophisticated press, experienced in agitation, but also knowledgeable in the arts of the government" (Smith 1980, 159). Due to the colonial con-text, the primary objective of journalists until 1947 was to assist in the goal of attaining freedom. After independence, the press—diverse, plural-istic, chaotic, but largely independent—developed a close relationship with India's new democratic institutions. Until the early 1990s, journalism pri-marily meant print journalism, practiced by privately owned newspapers, since news on television and radio was controlled by the state. According to Ram (2012, 270), there were two main positive functions of the relatively independent and pluralistic press: the credible-informational function and the critical-adversarial-investigative function. However, in the mid-1980s, a paradigm shift took place in Indian journalism, initiated first in *The Times of India* when Samir Jain, son of the chairman Ashok Jain, took over as its vice-chairman. The newspaper is owned by the Bennett, Coleman & Co Ltd (BCCL), which is controlled by the Jain family. The effect of several marketing-oriented changes introduced by Samir Jain has been so deep and far-reaching that analysts divide Indian journalism into pre-Samir Jain and post-Samir Jain eras. For good or for worse, Samir Jain—who interned at *The New York Times* and *The Times*, London, before joining BCCL—has been credited with single-handedly 'Americanising' *The Times of India* and changing the face of Indian journalism. As Coleridge observed in his book on global newspaper barons, "Of all the newspaper owners in the world, I met no one so single-mindedly wedded to marketing as Samir Jain" (1993). Coinciding with the liberalisation of the Indian economy in the early 1990s, Samir Jain initiated and effected the paradigm shift from the "by-line to the bottom-line" (Sonwalkar 2002) in Indian journalism, which is today seen as having led to widespread financial and ethical corruption at the institutional and individual levels.

Setting out his ethical compass in the early 1990s, Samir Jain famously told top editors and journalists of *The Times of India* that news is no different from soap or any other commodity. He had little patience with the traditional Chinese wall between the editorial and marketing departments of a newspaper. As several editors and journalists left the newspaper after their positions were downgraded and beats viewed as down-market abolished, Samir Jain shifted priorities by asking for 'light' editorial content, setting up trendy, up-market marketing departments and offering attractive packages to advertisers. Privileging the marketing side and marginalising the editorial attracted much criticism from journalists and other newspapers, but as circulation, revenue and profits of *The Times of India* soared, others were quick to profit by adopting similar practices. Samir Jain replicated the kind of newspaper price wars unleashed earlier in London by Murdoch, besides introducing innovative advertising and other marketing initiatives. *The Times of India* faced accusations of distancing itself from journalism's normative obligations and functions in a democracy. The keyword in its newsroom was 'aspirational', content that was to be targeted at a young, urban readership, which meant ignoring events and issues that were considered 'down-market'.

The result was what India's vice-president Hamid Ansari termed 'sunshine journalism': "When media portrayal is of a life that is always good, optimistic, going with the tide of those with discretionary spending power and their causes and pet themes, the role of the media as a defender and upholder of public interest is relegated to the background and its commercial persona takes over, replete with its allegiances to the market and the shareholders" (2011). Shah (1997) detailed the shift towards marketing within *The Times of India* over the years, of how a former cigarette company executive was designated the managing editor; how, when the editor went on leave, his place was filled by an executive; and how, finally, the editor's post was scrapped altogether. Sainath, a senior journalist who worked on *The Times of India*, observed,

> The 1990s have witnessed the decline of the press as a public forum. This can be attributed largely to the relentless corporate takeover of the Indian press and the concentration of ownership in a few hands. Around seven major companies account for the bulk of circulation in the powerful English language press. In the giant city of Bombay, with

over 14 million people, *The Times of India* has a stranglehold on the English readership. It also dominates the Hindi and Marathi language press. *The Times* is clear and unequivocal in its priorities. Beauty contests make the front page. Farmers' suicides don't. Sometimes reality forces changes, but this is the exception, not the rule. Most other large Indian newspapers are eagerly following *The Times'* philosophy, inspired by the press baron Rupert Murdoch: a newspaper is a business like any other, not a public forum. Monopoly ownership has imposed a set of values entirely at odds with the traditional role of the Indian press. (2001)

The Times of India group went on to introduce more financial lucrative marketing initiatives amidst continuing concerns over falling standards of journalism. In 2003, the group set up a company called Medianet, which offered space in the form of 'advertorials' in *The Times of India's* supplements for a price. The supplements, sold and distributed with the main paper, are called 'Delhi Times', 'Bombay Times' or after the name of the city where the edition is published. Anyone desiring visual and/or textual coverage in the brightly produced supplements could do so for a price. The initiative again attracted much criticism, but financially it was considered a major success as would-be celebrities, individuals seeking to register on the party circuit, PR and 'brand' professionals, and others rushed to buy newspaper space. The 'advertorial' content produced by Medianet is written by staff reporters, and the masthead of the supplement carries four words in tiny print: 'Advertorial, entertainment promotional feature', which, critics say, needs a magnifying glass to be seen. According to Santosh Desai, CEO of a brand consulting firm, "As far as advertising is concerned, it has always wanted to penetrate the sacred space of editorial, because that is where credibility lies. And now, here was editorial saying, penetrate me. So, of course advertising did just that, as PR" (Puri 2012). In 2010, a sub-committee of the Press Council of India reported that the practice and model of buying space introduced by Medianet had subsequently led to the "epidemic" of "paid news" during elections.

Another recent initiative of BCCL is what is called 'private treaties' or 'brand capital', under which a deal is offered to companies seeking to insert advertisements in *The Times of India*: BCCL accepts advertisements from such companies in exchange for equity in the companies. One-third of the amount decided is accepted in cash and the rest in equity or real-estate ownership. As a result, BCCL is now supposed to have a stake in more than 150 companies. Conflict of interest is obvious, with staff reporters unlikely to write against such companies. The initiative prompted renewed concern about journalism ethics, including from the regulator Securities and Exchange Board of India (SEBI), which wrote to the Press Council of India,

Private Treaties may lead to commercialisation of news reports since the same would be based on the subscription and advertising agreement entered into between the Media group and the company. Biased and imbalanced reporting may lead to inaccurate perceptions of the companies which are the beneficiaries of such private treaties ... It is our concern that such agreements may give rise to conflicts of interest and may, therefore, result in dilution of the independence of the press vis-a-vis the nature and content of the news/editorials in the media of companies promoting such agreements. (Sainath 2010)

Undeterred by criticism that *The Times of India* had ceased to be a journal of record, and unabashedly open about its ways of doing business, Vineet Jain, younger brother of Samir Jain and the managing director of the company, believes that "we are not in the newspaper business, we are in the advertising business ... if ninety per cent of your revenues come from advertising, you're in the advertising business" (Auletta 2012). According to an analysis of BCCL's performance, the company is not only one of the biggest media companies in India, it is one of the most profitable companies of its kind anywhere in the world: "While its flexible ethical standards have attracted criticism, BCCL's aggressive marketing strategies and marketing clout have often been successful in stifling competition" (Guha Thakurta 2012). The analysis quotes an interaction between Samir Jain and Inder Malhotra, who resigned as the resident editor of the New Delhi edition of *The Times of India* in 1986: "I told Samir that although he was fond of describing the newspaper as a product that was no different from a cake of soap, I had never seen a cake of soap that had to worry about its credibility and integrity. His reply to me was curt: 'Only profit matters, nothing else' ".

THE PHENOMENON OF 'PAID NEWS'

As the practice of offering news space for money through Medianet became an established feature, it assumed larger and more damaging proportions by 2009, this time in the charged atmosphere of electoral politics. After general elections were held in April-May of that year, it was revealed that large sums of money were paid by some candidates to representatives of media companies for favourable coverage or to ignore or produce negative content about rival candidates. The new practice was termed 'paid news', resulting in another round of concern about falling standards of journalism in India. A detailed report was produced by a sub-committee of the Press Council of India, which named newspapers and media companies, including *The Times of India* group and other prominent news organisations. According to the report, titled 'Paid News: How corruption in the Indian media undermines democracy', the deception or fraud takes place at three levels: The reader of the publication or the viewer of the television programme is deceived into believing that what is essentially an advertisement is, in fact, independently produced news content. By not officially declaring the expenditure incurred on planting paid news items, the candidate standing for election violates the

Conduct of Election Rules, 1961, which are meant to be enforced by the Election Commission of India under the Representation of the People Act, 1951. Finally, by not accounting for the money received from candidates, the concerned media company or its representatives are violating the provisions of the Companies Act, 1956, as well as the Income Tax Act, 1961, among other laws. The 71-page report submitted to the PCI described the practice thus:

> The entire operation is clandestine. This malpractice has become widespread and now cuts across newspapers and television channels, small and large, in different languages and located in various parts of the country. What is worse, these illegal operations have become "organized" and involve advertising agencies and public relations firms, besides journalists, managers and owners of media companies. Marketing executives use the services of journalists—willingly or otherwise—to gain access to political personalities. So-called "rate cards" or "packages" are distributed that often include "rates" for publication of "news" items that not merely praise particular candidates but also criticize their political opponents. Candidates who do not go along with such "extortionist" practices on the part of media organizations are denied coverage. (PCI 2010, 5)

The report is an important contribution to the ongoing debate about the quality of journalism, even if it did not lead to any action against the news organisations named. It cited several examples of 'paid news' in newspapers across the country, including in the Hindi-language *Dainik Jagran* (Daily Awakening), which is India's largest selling newspaper. Several candidates in elections were quoted in the report, describing their experience of 'paid news'. The Election Commission has several rules that, if implemented proactively, can curb the practice of 'paid news'. It issued new guidelines after the 2009 revelations and set up monitoring committees in constituencies during subsequent elections. In 2011, in the first case of its kind, Umlesh Yadav, a legislator elected in the north Indian state of Uttar Pradesh, was disqualified by the Election Commission for not disclosing expenditure spent on gaining favourable media coverage. She was found guilty of exceeding the limit on election expenses. To prevent the phenomenon of 'paid news' further impeding democratic processes, there are now suggestions that election laws be amended to declare exchange of money for 'paid news' as a corrupt electoral practice, but as of mid-2013 there was little movement on this. Ingenuous candidates and media houses are already reported to enter into arrangements for favourable coverage for a price before rules come into force when the dates of the 2014 general elections and other local elections are announced. As Ram observed, 'paid news' was "every bit of a rogue practice as the UK's phone hacking affair was… . It also led to some critical debate on a wider phenomenon—paid news not as a rogue practice but as a deeper and industry-wide phenomenon that was not confined to election coverage" (2012).

TELEVISION JOURNALISM IN THE DOCK

As in the case of print, there are pockets of quality journalism on Indian television, but the overwhelming picture remains bleak. There have been several recent examples of financial and ethical corruption. In October 2012, industrialist Naveen Jindal, who is also a member of parliament from the ruling Congress party, released a recording of a sting operation in New Delhi in which Sudhir Chaudhary and Samir Ahluwalia, editors of Zee News and Zee Business channels, were seen negotiating a deal with executives of his company to back off on a potentially damaging story in exchange for a five-year advertisement commitment to the channel running into millions of dollars. Releasing the footage, Jindal said, "The government gives channels a licence to show news. They are not given a licence for extortion or blackmail" (Jebaraj 2012). Jindal's company filed a complaint with the Press Council of India, while the Broadcast Editors Association expelled Chaudhary and removed him as its treasurer in the wake of the allegations. Zee News and Zee Business channels belong to the Zee group, which pioneered private television in India in the earlier 1990s. Zee denied Jindal's allegations, but the controversy raised fresh concerns over the quality of journalism in India—could it get any worse? There are also reports of individuals associated with some news channels being arrested for making extortionist demands.

Since economic liberalisation in the early 1990s allowed private satellite television, television has become the most important mass medium in the country, with entertainment dominating as the most viewed genre. News, too, is increasingly presented as a form of entertainment in an intensely competition-driven environment to attract and retain viewership. Idioms, images and songs from Bollywood are often used to cover important events, resulting in the trivialisation of issues involved. In order to attract eyeballs, news channels focus on emotion-driven issues such as religion, superstition, the occult, astrology, and crime, attracting strong criticism from the chairman of the Press Council of India, Justice Katju, among others. News channels are invariably part of the pre-release publicity of Bollywood films, to which much time and footage is devoted in exchange for money. Even news channels such as NDTV—often cited as an example of quality journalism—are not exempt from deriving ratings-driven benefits of using Bollywood themes in news programming.

As Thussu (2007, 111) points out, there is an obsession of almost all news channels with Bollywood-centred celebrity culture, besides events and issues related to crime and cricket:

> The lack of coverage of rural India, of regular suicides by peasants (more than 170,000, in the last 15 years, according to government figures), and the negligible reporting of health and hygiene, educational and employment equality (India has the world's largest population of

child labour at the same time as having vast pool of unemployed young people), demonstrates that such stories do not translate into ratings for urban, Westernized viewers and are displaced by the diversion of infotainment.

Television journalism, with a more recent history than India's print journalism, had a positive impact during times of crises, such as the large-scale Hindu-Muslim disturbances and killings in Gujarat in 2002 or the torrential rains in Mumbai in 2005. In a country with a long history of Hindu-Muslim clashes, for the first time, television journalism covered the Gujarat events—widely considered a pogrom against Muslims—live. It was termed 'India's first television riot', when the long-established rules in print journalism not to name the perpetrators or victims of riots to prevent escalation of violence proved superfluous. The rules were formulated by the Press Council of India in the 1950s, when there was no television, but in the charged atmosphere in Gujarat, they were also ignored by most of the local Gujarati language press, which was openly biased against the Muslim community. Coverage by NDTV and the English-language press stood out for highlighting the killings and atrocities against the Muslims and forcing federal authorities to take preventive measures (Sonwalkar 2007).

The quality of television journalism is directly related to the economics of the television industry. According to industry figures, the audience for television is in the region of 565 million and is growing by the day. The figure, though, is mainly for entertainment channels, with the more than 130 news channels accounting for only about 10% of the total television market. In the hyper-competition to attract audience and advertising revenue, journalism ethics often become a casualty, as the news channels struggle to survive at a time when the economics of both print and the broadcast sector has become tougher. Advertising budgets have shrunk, partly due to the global economic slowdown. In a field where audience or consumers are usually the metric to pull revenue, questions are being raised over the authenticity of ratings and circulation figures. Arriving at television ratings figures (or TAM—Television Audience Measurement)—on which most advertising expenditure is based—is an uncertain exercise, at best. In 2012, NDTV filed a suit in New York to recover about $1 billion from Nielsen and WPP, the world's largest communication services group, who jointly own TAM in India. The suit alleges, among other things, gross negligence, false representations, *prima facie* tort and corruption in the ratings system.

CONCLUSION

Quality journalism in India faces challenges partly due to the exponential growth in the last two decades: too many news organizations chasing fragmented audiences and shrinking advertising revenue, forcing them to cut corners and sacrifice ethics. The ability of citizens to make choices in a democracy based on a range of opinions available through the news media has been hampered by the narrow range of opinion allowed to be expressed, through 'paid news' and the trivialization of content on television. Challenges to quality journalism also come from little investment by news organizations in human resources. While a minority of top editors and journalists attract global-level salaries, the vast majority faces difficult employment and career options. There is also the important factor of journalism education. Thousands of journalism training institutes have sprung up in recent years, besides departments of journalism in universities, but editors and senior journalists despair at the quality of skills and knowledge of new recruits.

During India's freedom struggle and for several years after independence in 1947, journalism was seen as a mission. It may no longer be so, but it is also not just a matter of 'commission', motivated by institutional and personal profit. The declining quality of journalism has caused much concern, prompting criticism and demands in the social media for accountability from journalists, but the concern has not yet reached the stage where the vast majority of readers and viewers protest and demand change. There is much potential for quality journalism through the internet, with several examples of community journalism in villages and small towns in existence, but for the moment, the story of the quality of Indian journalism is similar to that of Indian democracy: imperfect, chaotic, diverse, compromised, noisy, corrupt and, in some aspects, magnificent.

REFERENCES

Ansari, M. Hamid. 2011. "Indian Media in a Challenging Environment." *The Hindu*, 16 July.
Auletta, Ken. 2012. "Citizens Jain: Why India's Newspaper Industry is Thriving." *The New Yorker*, 8 October.
Baru, S. 2011. 'The real greatness of Indians is that we are consensual', Second H Y Sharada Prasad Memorial Lecture, New Delhi. Accessed 13 May 2013. http://www.rediff.com/news/slide-show/slide-show-1-the-real-greatness-of-indians-is-that-we-are-consensual/20110420.htm
Coleridge, Nicholas. 1993. *Paper Tigers: The Latest, Greatest Newspaper Tycoons and How They Won the World*. London: Heinemann.
Economic Times. 2010. "If India Were a Stock, I Would Buy It: Thomas Friedman." 11 September. Accessed 14 February 2013. http://m.economictimes.com/opinion/interviews/if-india-were-a-stock-i-would-buy-it-thomas-friedman/articleshow/msid-6531292.cms.
Gandhi, Mohandas. K. 1982. *An Autobiography, or, the Story of my Experiments with Truth*. Harmondsworth: Penguin.
Guha Thakurta, Paranjoy. 2012. "The Times, the Jains and BCCL." *The Hoot*, 19 November. http://thehoot.org/web/TheTimestheJainsandBCCL/6425–1–1–4-true.html.
Jagannathan, R. 2012. "Rise of Crony Journalism and Tainted Money in Media." *First Post*, 10 September. http://www.firstpost.com/business/deccan-chronicle-rise-of-crony-journalism-and-tainted-money-449735.html.

Jebaraj, P. 2012. 'Jindal plays CD, claims Zee editors demanded Rs 100 crore', *The Hindu*, 25 October.

Jeffrey, Robin. 1993. "Indian Language Newspapers and Why They Grow." *Economic and Political Weekly* 28, 2004–2011.

Kitchen, Nicholas, ed. 2012. *India: The Next Superpower?* London School of Economics IDEAS Report SR010.

Murdoch, James. 2011. Keynote Speech at FICCI Frames Conference, Mumbai, 23 March. http://www.newscorp.com/news/news_479.html.

Ninan, T.N. 2011. "Indian Media's Dickensian age." CASI Working Paper 11–03. Centre for the Advanced Study of India, University of Pennsylvania.

Press Council of India. 2010. *Paid News: How Corruption in the Indian Media Undermines Democracy.* New Delhi: PCI.

Puri, Anjali. 2012. "Spotting the Astro Turf." *The Hoot*, 26 September. http://thehoot.org/web/SpottingtheAstroTurf/6330–1–1–5-true.html.

Ram, Narasimhan. 2012. "Sharing the Best and the Worst: The Indian News Media in a Global Context." James Cameron Memorial Lecture, City University, London, 3 October.

Sainath, P. 2001. "None so Blind as Those Who Will Not See." *UNESCO Courier*, 20 July. http://www.unesco.org/webworld/points_of_views/200701_sainath.shtml.

Sainath, P. 2010. "Private Treaties Harm Fair, Unbiased News: SEBI." *The Hindu*, 19 June.

Shah, Amrita. 1997. *Hype, Hypocrisy and Television in Urban India.* New Delhi: Vikas.

Singh, Manmohan. 2005. "PM's speech at the silver jubilee event of the Chandigarh Press Club." 24 September. http://pmindia.gov.in/speech-details.php?nodeid=193.

Smith, Anthony. 1980. *The Geopolitics of Information: How Western Culture Dominates the World.* New York: Oxford University Press.

Sonwalkar, Prasun. 2001. "India: Makings of Little Cultural/Media Imperialism?" *International Communication Gazette* 63: 505–519.

Sonwalkar, Prasun. 2002. "Murdochization of the Indian Press: From By-line to Bottom-line." *Media, Culture & Society* 24: 821–834.

Sonwalkar, Prasun. 2007. "Disturbing the Banality of Journalism: Political Violence, Gujarat 2002 and the Indian News Media." In *Media and Political Violence*, edited by Hillel Nossek, Annabelle Sreberny and Prasun Sonwalkar, pp. 247–267. Cresskill, NJ: Hampton Press.

Sonwalkar, Prasun. 2009. "Citizen Journalism in India: The Politics of Recognition." In *Citizen Journalism: Global Perspectives*, edited by Stuart Allan and Einar Thorsen, pp. 75–84. Oxford: Peter Lang.

Tharoor, Shashi. 2012. *Pax Indica: India and the World in the Twenty-First Century.* New Delhi: Penguin.

Thussu, Daya Kishan. 2007. *News as Entertainment: The Rise of Global Entertainment.* London: Sage.

15 (Re-)framing the 'Quality' Debate
The Arab Media and Its Future Journalism

George Ogola

INTRODUCTION

The Arab media's role in the Arab Spring has in recent times become the default discursive frame within which that media is discussed—transformative, progressive and highly politicised. The tectonic political shifts in the Arab world that have seen the fall of despotic regimes in Tunisia, Libya and Egypt—their intense and unrelenting mediatisation—have pointed not only to a new political order but also to a new Middle East and North Africa (MENA) media dispensation. It is a dispensation in which satellite television and new media are increasingly involved in the region's realpolitik. The Arab media are breaking old barriers inimical to open public communication and slowly adopting a new agenda—even ethos, in, for example, what constitutes news. Satellite television and new media are the key drivers of this transformation. While some of the claims especially made of new media have been rather extravagant and unqualified, they have unquestionably contributed to various progressive media developments the region has witnessed since the late 1990s. And yet, there are also factors, both old and emergent, that continue to threaten the future of the media and of quality journalism in the Arab world. This chapter seeks to explore some of these transformative changes, the emerging spaces for quality journalism in the Arab world, but also the threats the media sector continues to face. The aim is to provide a broad but critical overview that may inform more detailed and localised studies to extend the discussion. While it is true that the Arab world is so expansive and differentiated that its imagination as homogenous may even be rendered problematic, we can also conceivably agree that there are factors—historical, political and geographical—that make the construction of such a region as an analytical category valid, perhaps even necessary. In this chapter, by Arab world is meant the Middle East and North Africa, commonly referred to as the MENA region.

QUALITY JOURNALISM IN THE ARAB WORLD

The chapter takes as its point of departure the need to destabilise the assumed universalism of what constitutes quality journalism. My reading of quality journalism here is fundamentally inflected contextually by the political realities of the Arab world. Accordingly, quality journalism is stretched to take on multiple roles beyond the usual normative functions ascribed to journalism in the West. The Arab journalist wears many faces. For to them, politics and its corollaries, including religion, are at the centre of the mechanics of quality journalism. Indeed, as Pintak and Ginges (2009) argue, Arab journalists tend to "see their mission as driving political and social change in the Arab world" (171). It is therefore not uncommon that a number of Arab media figures "wear two hats—that of the journalist and that of a politician". Examples thus abound of journalists who are also either active politicians or political activists. We can cite the cases of Gibran Tueni who was the publisher of Lebanon's largest daily *An Nahar* until his assassination (Pintak and Ginges 2009), or more recently of Mona Eltahawy, a prominent U.S.-based Egyptian columnist. Indeed, in a widely cited survey of Arab journalists drawn from across the region by Pintak and Ginges (2009), 68% of the respondents completely agreed that it is permissible to engage in political activities. Meanwhile, nearly 70% said they had no objections to a journalist taking part in political demonstrations (171). The survey also found that Arab and American journalists tend to work with dramatically different agendas. While U.S. journalists ranked "investigating government claims" as their primary agenda, Arab journalists privileged "encouraging political reform" (172).

Arab journalism further goes beyond the newsroom in far more fundamental ways. They have also taken up the role of "border guards of an imagined Arab *Watan* [nation]" (Pintak 2009, 193). Pintak argues that these journalists "reflect a worldview that largely transcends borders, a sense of self-identity that sets region above nation and religion above passport" (193). Fuelled by feelings of Otherness in the face of perceived international, mainly Western anti-Arab sentiment, Arab journalists seek to forge a shared consciousness of pan-Arabism. In an interview with Joan Connell, Pintak describes this new identity as one in which "the region's three powerful political movements—pan-Arab nationalism, nation-state nationalism and Islamism—converge to take on the region's autocrats, to drive out foreign forces, to bolster human rights and to challenge Israel" (Connell 2011). Elsewhere, he notes that "Arab journalists are decidedly cross-border in their world-view" (Pintak 2009, 196). Their survey cited previously found an even split between those who identified themselves with the Muslim world and those who identified with the Arab world as their pre-eminent identity. Only 15% identified themselves with the nation-state (Pintak 2009, 196).

Quality journalism in the Arab world must therefore be understood within the context of the place that Arabness and indeed religion occupy in the Arab political imagination and social organization. In a study by Weaver, Beam, Brownlee, and Voakes (2007), 97% of Arab journalists polled categorized themselves as Muslim (88%) or Christian (7%). Religion thus remains a significant part of the Arab journalist's identity. One is therefore likely to encounter difficulty attempting to separate religion from Arabness, and both from Arab journalism. To be sure, journalism is in part a cultural product informed by but also constitutive of the culture within which it operates. Religion, and more precisely Islam, is constitutive of the Arabic culture. It follows then *mutatis mutandis* that Arab journalism is necessarily influenced by both Islam and Arabness.

As a matter of fact, news organizations such as Al Jazeera state rather unambiguously that they are a media "with an Arab affiliation and a global orientation" (www.AlJazeera.com). Similarly, the Saudi-owned Al Arabiya describes itself as an "Arabic station, from the Arabs to the Arabs, delivering content that is relevant to the Arabs" (www.AlArabiya.com). It is a role that was well illustrated in Al Jazeera's unique coverage of the banning of Muslim veils in French schools in 2005. In what was then unprecedented in the pan-Arab media, a famous anchorwoman Khadija Ben Gana decided to wear a veil when interviewing a French minister. Cherribi (2006) later argued that the 'veil story' was deliberately religiously inflected and covered 282 times in current affairs shows and news items by Al Jazeera. This was essentially a cultural, religious and political statement as well as a form of protest. It was an attempt to provoke new readings of modernity; one that was culturally shaped by Arabness and Islam. It demonstrated the way politics and religion overlapped in this part of the world and how culture is routinely mobilised as a form of political protest. Suffice to say that the pan-Arab satellite television is actively engaged in forging a new regional political consciousness, one that collapses not only national borders but, more importantly, Islamism and Arabism to create a new identity that can be appropriated to fight both the domestic as well as the international Other. The Arab world is inherently imbued with what Pintak (2009) calls the "classic touchstones of nationalism theory: language, media, and ethnie" (192). These are easy to mobilise in defence of a cause. Indeed in his book *Nations and Nationalism in a Global Era*, Anthony Smith notes how "regional associations based on 'Pan' nationalism can generate overarching cultures and identities that compete with, or even replace, national state and ethnic identities" (1995, 121; see also Lynch 2006). The pan-Arab satellite television has, therefore, since the 1990s attempted to construct a powerful transcendent identity that goes beyond the nation-state despite the existing intra-Arab rivalries in the MENA region.

ARAB MEDIA LIBERALIZATION: 'ISLAMIC GLASNOST' OR VICARIOUS POLITICS

Until the 1990s, the media in much of the Arab world was under state control (Amin and Napoli 2006; Sakr 2007). The media sector was constrained by highly repressive laws and other punitive regulatory mechanisms imposed by the largely autocratic political regimes in the region. The advent of satellite television in the late 1980s, however, forced Arab governments to marginally liberalise their airwaves, the result of which was the explosion of pan-Arab and Arab satellite television stations across North Africa and the Middle East (Gelvin 2012). From the late 1990s, a number of Arab governments even encouraged media organizations to invest in their countries. Countries such as Egypt, Bahrain, Dubai, Jordan and Yemen actively sought European-based Arab TV stations to shift their operations to the region by offering a number of incentives, including "tax exemptions and lower production costs" (Miles 2005, 331). The most successful of these was Egypt under the Mubarak government who went as far as creating a 'media free zone' in Cairo. Many Arab stations relocated to the zone and were given access to the Egyptian satellite Nilesat, which was much cheaper than the European satellites. Egypt also exempted these stations from its restrictive censorship laws (Miles 2005, 331). Today, Egypt remains arguably the most powerful political and regional media player in the Arab world with an influential and widely read press. Meanwhile, its TV and film industry supplies much of the Arab-speaking world with shows from its Media Production City (BBC 2013). Most of the leading Arab pay TV networks also continue to have a presence at the Media Production City (BBC 2013).

Yet a discussion about the state of the Arab media is incomplete without a study of Al Jazeera, arguably the region's most powerful media voice since the 1990s. Described by Miles (2005) as 'iconoclastic', Al Jazeera revolutionized television broadcasting and quality news in the Arab world. Its success has since led to the establishment of various 'Al-Jazeera generics' across the Arab world, including Abu Dhabi TV and Al-Arabiya. Much older channels such as ANN, Orbit, LBC, Future and ART have also all adopted its style and programming.

Al Jazeera's growth since its establishment in 1996 has been phenomenal. In 2005, an industry web site conducting a poll involving nearly 2,000 advertising executives in 75 countries identified it as the world's fifth most recognized brand (Clark 2005, cited in Sakr 2007, 116). The organization was founded by seed money provided by the Emir of Qatar with an initial five-year grant of nearly US$137 million (Miles 2005, 346). Over the years, the station has also had to rely on regular supplementary grants from Qatar. The station's International Division, now Al Jazeera English, has increased its world profile but with considerable financial implications. As a result, even after a decade of operations, the station's financial situation remains tied to the largesse of the Qatari government.

But Al Jazeera's success has also been the subject of much debate. Politically, the news organization continues to polarize opinion. Sakr (2007) observes that as world opinion shifted following 9/11 and the invasion of Iraq, the station's messages continued to elicit contradictory responses with both the West and the Arab world castigating it. She notes that being allied to the Qatar government, the station was put on the defensive in a way that seems to have altered the nature of the 'Al Jazeera project'. The station announced it was going "to build a communication bridge between the East and the West" and to "promote certain values" (Sakr 2007, 127). This decision raised significant concerns. Sakr, for example, asked whether "by self-consciously articulating a rationale for its own existence based on building bridges, the station moved from being a transparent media outlet to becoming a political actor in its own right" (2007, 127). Inferences on this decision may be varied. What is clear, however, is that over the years the station has had to navigate political landmines arising from long standing intra-regional rivalries, which have in part shaped the station's journalism. Thus, for example, it has had to fight accusations of being pro-American in the Arab world mainly because it is funded by a government that hosts one of the biggest American military bases in the region. At various times the station has also had its bureaus closed in Egypt, Syria, Algeria and the West Bank (Miles 2005). Some Arab countries often accuse Qatar of using the station to give it political weight and set it as major regional player (El-Nawawy and Iskandar 2003).

More recently, Al Jazeera has been accused of subtly, sometimes even overtly, supporting the Muslim Brotherhood. The Brotherhood's 'spiritual leader' Yusuf Qardawi is a prominent figure on the channel. He hosts a primetime programme 'Sharia Law and Life' watched by millions across the region. Qardawi is also head of the International Union of Muslim Scholars (IUMS) and therefore a hugely influential figure in the Arab world. Critics further argue that since the Arab Spring and the take-over of power by the Muslim Brotherhood in Egypt and groups associated with it in Libya and Tunisia, there has been a notable shift in the coverage of these countries with criticism of the new regimes far more timid, if at all (Khalil 2012).

There are also critics who caution that the celebration of the Arab satellite media proliferation should not mask the more fundamental debate about political freedom in the region. Miles (2005), for example, dismisses the common argument that the 1990s and satellite television brought about an 'Islamic glasnost'. He notes that the Arab world did not actually suffer from an information deficiency and that, except for the most authoritarian regimes, news has always been available. He cites the case of Algeria where the media went as far as threatening to sue the President when it was ruled by a military dictatorship. But while such examples are important, they are also rare. Indeed, one would argue that while having access to news is important, the content of the news is probably far more important, and therein lays my criticism of Miles. Still, he cites a useful intervention by Mamoun Fandi, an Arab writer and Professor. Fandi expresses his reservations at the mushrooming of satellite television in the Arab world, arguing that it is creating a situation where the media has now become the arena for politics with politics itself ignored. He calls it "living vicariously through the media" (cited in Miles 2005, 329). He further argues thus: "That is not actual living. This is vicarious politics, this is virtual politics. Governments in the Arab world are encouraging that trend whereby the media becomes a substitute for real politics . . . You allow people to participate in harmless politics, politics that does not lead to any serious political change. So everybody is happy". Fandi's argument reminds us of Achille Mbembe's arguments about the *mutual zombification* of polity and potentate. He argues that this relationship robs them of their vitality leaving them both impotent (*impouvoir*) (Mbembe 1992). But there's one thing he misses. These arguments ignore the changing relationship between the media and *actual* politics. Although this relationship is complex, it is the case that politics has become an increasingly mediatised process in which television has effectively replaced the podium. The attention governments in the region and beyond give the media is precisely because they acknowledge it as now a 'real' space with material consequences on the practice of politics and in the wider performance of power (Ogola 2009; see also Street 2001). Even then, we cannot ignore Miles's point that "power in the Arab world remains in the hands of the same individuals and small elite groups who have handled matters of state for decades" (2005, 329). Political power continues to rest within the broader institutional and political structures outside the media.

STATE OF THE ARAB MEDIA: NARRATING THE CHALLENGES

Sakr (2007) rightly notes that political liberalization in Arab states remains fragile and faltering (3). Although the Arab world has seen significant political changes over the last decade, more particularly in the last two years, the region's media still faces a number of challenges. Media legal regimes have generally been restrictive with ruling governments able to shut down media organizations or jail journalists arbitrarily (Hafez and Paletz 2001). Indeed, in some of the countries, there are worries that media freedom is actually shrinking as political power is dispersed away from the state. Cases of journalists being charged on flimsy grounds, intimidated or even killed abound. In December 2012, a court in Luxor convicted Tawfix Okacha, a journalist and owner of the TV station *El-Faraeen,* for defamation. Okacha was sentenced to four months in prison and fined 100 Egyptian dollars. He had been charged following a complaint by a former MP Nasreddine Moghazi after a programme highly critical of President Mohammed Morsi was aired on *El-Faraeen (Egypt Independent* 2012). The station is well-known for its opposition to Morsi and the Muslim Brotherhood. In the same month in Bahrain, Reporters Without Borders (2012a) reported that Sayed Yousef Al-Mihafda had been arrested for allegedly posting false information on Twitter. The said false information was a photo of an injured protester in Manama. Around the same time *New York Times* columnist Nicholas Kristof reported that he had been denied entry on arrival at Manama airport because he was on a persona non grata list (Shafaqna 2012). According to the BBC (2013), Bahraini journalists generally "risk prosecution for offences which include 'undermining' the government and religion, crimes which are ill-defined and interpreted in a manner that seeks primarily to intimidate journalists." Journalists are also routinely targeted, as was the case of three editors from opposition daily *Al-Wasat* who were sacked and later fined for publishing "false" news (BBC 2013). Similar abuses have been cited across the Middle East and North Africa, including in Egypt, Syria, Iran, Iraq, Yemen, Algeria and Morocco (Reporters Without Borders 2012a). Even in countries that have recently gone through regime change, these abuses are not atypical.

According to *Reporters Without Borders* (2012b) Press Freedom Index of 2011–2012, while the Arab spring gave birth to new political developments in the Arab world, media gains have been modest, with some countries actually getting worse. The report notes that Tunisia rose 30 places in the index to 134th but has yet to accept a free and independent press. Bahrain on the other hand fell 29 places to 173rd on the Index. The regime has continued to crack down on pro-democracy voices within and outside the media. The report further notes that Libya marginally improved (to 154th), while Yemen is further down the scale at 171st position. The much talked about Egyptian uprising did not translate into a freer media, with the country falling 39 places to 166th. The Index notes that there were three periods of exceptional violence for journalists—in February, November and December. The effect of the Egyptian 2012 constitutional referendum is yet to be seen. Meanwhile, Syria fell even further to position 176 on the Index.

The Index must, however, be put in perspective. While the cases mentioned previously confirm the fragile political environments within which these media operate, there are several progressive media developments in some of these countries that should equally be acknowledged. A massive 84% of journalists who participated in the *Inside the Arab Newsroom Survey* by Pintak and Ginges (2009) agreed that the Arab media is becoming freer, with just more than half saying that, as individual journalists, they were freer to practice their craft (167). Pintak and Ginges, however, caution that in interpreting this data, we need to be aware that the terms *freedom* and *control* in the Arab world mean something entirely different. They note that while American journalists in the same survey were referring to editorial interference and business pressures, Arab journalists usually have more fundamental threats in mind, including physical violence, threats from religious extremists or government intimidation (167).

The opening up of the media in the Arab world has, however, been undermined by the quality of Arab journalism. The Arab media continues to suffer from a professional deficit arising in part from journalists' lack of the relevant training. In a survey by Weaver et al. (2007) on journalists' qualifications, only 22% of Arab respondents held a journalism degree, while the same number had no professional training before being hired. This no doubt translated into the poor remuneration they received from their employers, which in turn made them particularly susceptible to corruption.

Indeed, most respondents to the *Inside the Arab Newsroom* survey earned less than US$500 a month, with print journalists especially poorly paid. Nearly 90% of the print journalists in the survey earned less than US$500 (cited in Pintak and Ginges 2009).

Many journalists and news organizations have therefore taken to unorthodox and corrupt ways to make ends meet. Pintak and Ginges (2009) cite the *Cash for Editorial Survey* done by the International Public Relations Association (IPRA) in which 40% of Arabic-language journalists said they would reprint a press release in return for a gift (165). The survey also found that 80% of those polled said journalists seldom or never refused free travel or products. Another 60% said it was common for favourable stories to be published for ad purchases (IPRA 2002).

News organizations were found to be compromised in a similar way. The Arabic Network for Human Rights Information (ANHRI) found that 25 stories published by Tunisian newspapers and magazines between 2006–2007 were paid for by Ben Ali's regime (ANHRI 2007, cited in Pintak and Ginges 2009, 164). Meanwhile, the leading Egyptian newspaper *Al-Ahram* reportedly gives top editors a percentage of the advertising the newspaper receives, which no doubt has an impact on editorial content (Pintak and Ginges 2009, 164). Similarly, in an Interview with Pintak, then editor-in-chief of the pan-Arab Palestinian daily *Al-Quds Al-Arabi* Abdel Bari Atwan claimed that he had been offered millions by Saudi and Kuwaiti governments both seeking favour with his newspaper (165).

The problems regarding the professionalization of the Arab media is also complicated by its active role in the complex geopolitics of the MENA region. A number of the region's news organizations are participants in intra-Arab as well as broader regional political rivalries. This has had particular implications on the professional conduct of the region's media. Nossek (2004) observes that there is a general agreement that "when a national or regional network broadcast news of a war or political violence in the region, this news becomes 'our news'. On the other hand when the news is from elsewhere then it becomes 'their news' and the coverage becomes more professional" (345). For example, Arab leaders and countries that did not support Hezbollah during the Lebanon-Israeli war in 2006 came under intense criticism from the Arab media. Meanwhile, during the Arab Spring, while revolutions in Libya, Egypt and Tunisia were given wide coverage by news organizations such Al Jazeera, similar Shia protests in Bahrain and Saudi Arabia against the ruling monarchies were barely given any coverage in the same channel or indeed by Al Arabiya (Khalil 2012). Regional and intra-regional affiliations and rivalries thus continue to undermine the openness of the Arab media.

Further, while it is the case that Islam is an integral part of the Arab culture and therefore of its journalism, it has also manifested itself as a threat to the emerging openness of the region's media. The role of Islam in the mediatisation of the Other and in the politicization of the region's media can be seen in the reaction of Arab journalists to the publishing of the infamous Danish cartoons in a number of newspapers around the world. Nearly 80% of the respondents to the Pintak and Ginges (2009) survey agreed with the statement that "journalists must balance the need to inform the public with the responsibility to show respect". Pintak notes that many Arab journalists "decried the action [of printing the Danish cartoons] as deliberate provocation" (171). In a similar survey assessing the role that religion played in Arab journalism, 40% of Arab journalists interviewed said it was necessary to believe in God to have good moral values against just 5% of U.S. journalists (Kohut and Doherty 2006).

Elsewhere in this chapter, I have also given the example of the Muslim Brotherhood's Yusuf Qaradawi whose presence in Al Jazeera has raised fears over the station's relationship with the Muslim Brotherhood and a particular brand of Islamism. In a related example, Al Jazeera once apologized to viewers when, in one of its programmes, one of the guests Richard Dawkins, who is an atheist, talked about his belief in the non-existence of God. The station later disassociated itself from the guest's comments. In another case, the station apologized after guest Wafa Sultan, a Syrian psychologist living in the United States, was accused by viewers of attacking Islam (MPAC 2008). While such an apology is not particularly unique to Al Jazeera, it still smacked of the kind of intolerance that may in the long run deny oppositional voices perceived too controversial, space to air their views within these media.

On the extreme end of the scale has also been the proliferation of fundamentalist religious TV stations such as *Al Majid,* which professes Salafism, and the Lebanese-based *Al-Manar,* which has consistently advocated for *intifada.* These stations make no apologies about their religio-political affiliations, but in the process, they close their media for public debate. These stations and many others associated with different strands of Islam continue to threaten the emerging tradition of public media as an important space and interlocutor of MENA politics.

Media ownership also poses a critical threat to the future of quality journalism in the Arab world. The region has seen phenomenal growth, especially in the broadcast sector, since the 1990s. There are now more than 300 free-to-air Arab satellite channels in various capitals across the region (Miles 2005). But Pintak and Ginges (2009) argue that "just as conglomerates dominate the American mediascape, a feudal corporatist model is threatening to replace state media control in the Arab world" (169). Most of the emerging media are owned either directly or by proxy by individuals "closely linked sometimes through blood—to the ruling elite" (169). Examples include the largest media conglomerate in the Arab world, which is reportedly owned by the brother-in-law of King Abdallah of Saudi Arabia (Miles 2005). Lebanon's Future TV is owned by the Hariri family (Sakr 1999), while several of Egypt's new channels were controlled by a wealthy businessman linked to the Mubarak regime before its fall (BBC 2013).

Meanwhile, Al-Jazeera's relationship with the Qatari government remains strong, with the King's blood relations sitting on the organization's board. It is also not known how much the Qatari government continues to spend on Al Jazeera, making the organization particularly vulnerable to state control. Indeed, Miles has argued that when foreign countries take umbrage with their coverage in Al Jazeera, those countries' diplomats approach the Qatari government first and the station's management second (Miles 2005). In 2001, for example, the U.S. Secretary of State Colin Powell famously told the Emir of Qatar to ask Al Jazeera to tone down its "inflammatory rhetoric" against the United States (El-Nawawy and Iskandar 2003, 176).

TOWARDS TOMORROW'S ARAB MEDIA

In the survey by Weaver et al. (2007), almost 80% of the Arab journalist respondents were 40 years old or younger (cited in Pintak and Ginges 2009, 160). This was in contrast with a similar cohort in the United States where journalists tended to be much older. The typical Arab journalist is a young to middle-aged male, an age group especially associated with the use of new media technologies. While it is true that the transformative potential of new media is often overstated, conjectural, even populist (Fenton 2010), few dispute its role or agency in shaping current journalistic trends and political discourse. There are various ways in which we may look at that agency. Joshua Meyrowitz's arguments on this agency are especially apposite for our purposes. He argues that new media "re-organizes hierarchies" (Sakr 2007, 10). He observes that new media "transforms the home and other social spheres into new environments and offer us quicker or more thorough access to events and behaviours if at the same time giving us new events and behaviours" (10). Meyrowitz argues that people "gain a different sense of their own potential when they can use electronic media to overcome restrictions on social interaction that are imposed by physical space" (11). New media tend to make power more diffuse, breaking down the rules and orthodoxies implicated in the exercise of and performance of power and politics. This is especially so in societies where such rules are traditionally stylised to follow particular forms, such as has been the case in much of the Arab world. In new media are opportunities to contest these hierarchies, rules and orthodoxies. The use of new media during the Arab Spring provides us a useful case study of how new forms of communication are helping confront traditional authority as well as contest and simultaneously develop alternative political narratives.

Although it might be the case, as Malcolm Gladwell once noted in an article published in *The New Yorker* in 4 October 2010, that "revolutions cannot be tweeted", arguably to dispense of suggestions about the possibility of a 'Twitter-inspired revolution', what is not in doubt is the fact that, in the case of the Arab Spring, new media gave the uprisings local and international visibility, helped sustain the visibility and transgressed traditional censorial barriers by introducing a new stylistic in what constituted news in the Arab world. It is significant to note that Twitter or Facebook feeds could themselves now constitute news or generate news ideas for organizations such as Al Jazeera. I am keenly aware of the fact that traditional media are often incredibly adept at appropriating new technologies while in fact remaining 'traditional' and that this has been the case in many countries. However, we cannot ignore the contribution these technologies have made in the generation of 'alternative' news streams and in the inclusion of voices or stories that were previously either ignored or inaccessible to mainstream media organizations. It is a trend bound to continue having an impact on Arab journalism. Indeed, it is important to note that, with the exception of Yemen, Syria, Jordan, Iraq and Saudi Arabia, internet penetration in the other Middle East countries was at more than 50% as of June 2012. Facebook subscribers were more than 23 million (Internet World Stats 2012).

Another emerging shift in the Arab media relates to the changes in the content, especially on television. Not long ago, most Arab TV stations mainly featured Western soaps, dramas and documentaries or their local versions (Miles 2005). These were not only popular but also cheap. While this is still the case in most stations, the growth of the television and film industry has also seen an exponential increase in local Arabic language programming tackling local problems. Although this does not necessarily mean quality journalism, it signifies the emergence of what may turn out to be an important new avenue through which to expand the Arab public sphere. Indeed, the popularity of local programming in both Al Jazeera and Al Arabiya, arguably some of the most watched TV stations in the region, demonstrates why local programming is becoming a new critical social and political space for the enunciation and discussion of things Arab.

The unambiguous political role that the Arab media has had to play in the region has naturally made it susceptible to political activism at the expense of professional journalism. This activism has led to the growth, for example, of fundamentalist politico-religious media organizations and activist journalists, some of whom are not particularly interested in expanding the Arab public sphere. The Pintak and Ginges (2009) study reveals that Arab journalists are acutely aware of their professional deficiencies. It is a reality that has prompted media organizations from within and outside the MENA region, policy makers, international and local NGOs and others, to establish journalism centres and training programmes for local journalists. Such initiatives include the Arab Reporters for Investigative Journalism (ARIJ), Al Jazeera Media Training and Development Centre, Media Centre for Arab Palestinian Journalists in Israel, Arab Women Media Centre and the ICT-focused twofour54 based in Abu Dhabi. Organizations such as the International Centre for Journalists (ICFJ) also partner with local news organizations to offer training opportunities to Arab journalists.

Many training initiatives have also been funded by organizations such as USAID and the EU. It can be hoped that these initiatives will see the growth of a more professional corps of journalists in the region who will ultimately help enhance the quality of the region's journalism. Meanwhile, there has also been an increase in the number of foreign journalists working particularly in the pan-Arab TV stations. For example, some of the most senior editorial managers working at organizations such as Al Jazeera are seasoned professional journalists from established Western news media organizations. Al Jazeera International was first headed by Nigel Parsons who had been a director at APTN. He joined the station with a number of seasoned professional journalists from major news organizations in North America and Europe, including the BBC, ABC, ITN, CNN, Sky and CBC. These journalists have been especially instrumental in professionalizing Al Jazeera.

Miles (2005) has also noted the attempt to standardize journalistic practice in the region. Such standardization is important and will not necessarily compromise diversity. Instead, it could provide useful benchmarks for quality journalism. For example, Al Jazeera has now managed to accustom Arabs to "a standard form of Arabic speech and led to a growing sense of regional integration. It set a new standard of excellence in translation and is used as a benchmark by professional translators all over the world" (Miles 2005, 335). When such standardization gains consensus, it will become easier to agree on the professional norms and practices with which to work in the region.

I have argued elsewhere in the chapter that state control of the media in the Arab world coupled with its historically fractious relationship with the West over the years easily made it a platform for fairly predictable and unitary narratives on pan-Arabism. In recent times, however, the region's media is simultaneously opening up to alternative narratives. Al Jazeera, for example, was the first to give Israelis an opportunity to speak directly to Arab audiences. This was unprecedented in the region not long ago. Yet such invitations have now become fairly commonplace. Within the Arab nations, satellite television stations are also slowly facilitating much more open public political debates. Programmes such as Al Jazeera's 'Opposite Direction', largely modelled on BBC's 'Crossfire', attempt to make politicians accountable, while also enabling broader debates between opposing political camps. Meanwhile, the adoption of the talk-show format by several of the region's TV stations is also increasingly allowing for public debates on issues that were previously censored (Lynch 2006). The format is slowly reconfiguring the relationship between power and the people. Sakr (2007) further observes that even in countries where ruling families still control the media, competing political forces are now able to employ "critical media content to create pressure for change" (7). Elite dissent thus also finds expression in these new spaces.

Lastly, one of the biggest problems that is, however, likely to endure and continue to affect the quality of journalism in the Arab word is the region's media ownership profiles. Even with the proliferation of satellite television, a number of the most well-funded and influential TV organizations in the region are still owned by an elite political class often with ties—both business and blood—to the ruling regimes. This class will continue to seek control over the editorial directions the media organizations take. Sakr (2007) notes, for example, that Saudi Arabia's ruling family has many branches, with members disagreeing on many issues and that "in the absence of channels for legitimising their policy preferences through the ballot box, they have invested in media operations at home and abroad in order to ensure favourable publicity for these preferences at the national and regional levels" (8). In just about all the MENA countries, the state retains significant control not only of the media infrastructure but also of the media. Unless the ownership structures are radically transformed, this is a problem that is likely to continue undermining quality journalism in the region.

CONCLUSION

The complexity of the Arab world and its conflicted realities makes it difficult to surmise its future, much less its future media. However, there are indications the region's media ecology will be radically different in the next decade. Already, there are signs of what we can expect of its expansion. The progressive developments taking place in the region will most likely incubate a better media and journalism. In the continued absence of free public spaces and structures for political expression, the media is likely to continue acting as the region's default 'parliament'. But to do so successfully, it will also have to confront a number of challenges, ranging from its lack of professionalization, an issue widely acknowledged by the region's journalists, to problems associated with media ownership. As long as the region's media remains in the hands of the dominant ruling and political forces, their transformative potential will always be under threat. This will work against the expansion of the Arab public sphere. However, a new media ecology with a new ethos, purpose and perhaps even a re-orientation of its understanding of quality that is less prone to crusading—for this role can be Janus faced—lays in broader and more fundamental political reform.

REFERENCES

Amin, Hussein, and James Napoli. 2006. *The Media and Power in Egypt.* London: Routledge.

BBC. 2013. "Bahrain Profile." BBC News Middle East, 29 January. Accessed 5 February 2013. http://www.bbc.co.uk/news/world-middle-east-14541053.

Cherribi, Sam. 2006. From Baghdad to Paris: Al Jazeera and the Veil. *Harvard International Journal of Press/Politics* 11: 121–138.

Connell, Joan. 2011. "The New Arab Journalist." Dart Center for Journalism Trauma, 29 January. Accessed January 2013. http://dartcenter.org/content/lawrence-e-pintak-on-new-arab-journalist#.UPu_fhweaiF.

Egypt Independent. 2012. "Okasha Found Guilty of Defaming Morsi, Gets Four Months in Prison." Accessed January 2013. http://www.egyptindependent.com/news/okasha-found-guilty-defaming-morsy-gets-four-months-prison.

El-Nawawy, Mohammed, and Adel Iskandar. 2003. *Al Jazeera: The Story of the Network that's Rattling Governments and Redefining Modern Governments.* Boulder, CO: Westview.

Fenton, Natalie. 2010. *New Media, Old News: Journalism in the Digital Age.* London: Sage.

Gelvin, James. 2012. *The Arab Uprisings: What Everyone Needs to Know.* Oxford: Oxford University Press.

Hafez, Kai, and David Paletz. 2001. *Mass Media, Politics and Society in the Middle East.* New York: Hampton Press.

International Public Relations Association (IPRA). 2002. *Unethical Media Practices Revealed by IPRA Report.* Paris: International Public Relations Association.

Internet World Stats. 2012. "Internet Usage in the Middle East." Accessed January 2013. http://www.internetworldstats.com/stats5.htm.

Khalil, Naela. 2012. "Al Jazeera: A New Type of Democracy." MA diss., University of Central Lancashire.

Kohut, Andrew, and Carol Doherty. 2006. *State of the News Media.* Washington, D.C.: Pew Research Centre for the People and the Press.

Lynch, Marc. 2006. *Voices of the New Arab Public: Iraq, Al Jazeera and Middle East Politics Today.* Lanham, MD: University Press of America.

Mbembe, Achille. 1992. "Notes on the Post-Colony." *Africa: Journal of the International Africa Institute* 621: 3–37.

Miles, Hugh. 2005. *Al-Jazeera: The Inside Story of the Arab News Channel that is Challenging the West.* New York: Grove Press.

MPAC. 2008. "MPAC Criticises Al Jazeera Apology for Featuring Critic of Islam." Accessed January 2013. http://globalmbreport.org/?p=611.

Nossek, Hillel. 2004. "Our News and Their News: The Role of National Identity in the Coverage of Foreign News." *Journalism* 53: 343–368.

Ogola, George. 2009. "A New Grammar of Dialogue: Media and the Cultural Restyling of Political Representation in Kenya." In *Oral and Written Expressions of African Cultures,* edited by Falola Toyin and Ngom Fallou, 3–18. Durham, NC: Carolina Academic Press.

Pintak, Lawrence. 2009. "Border Guards of the 'Imagined' Watan: Arab Journalists and the New Arab Consciousness." *Middle East Journal* 632: 191–212.

Pintak, Lawrence, and Jeremy Ginges. 2009. "Inside the Arab Newsroom." *Journalism Studies* 10: 157–177.

Reporters Without Borders. 2012a. "Authorities Use Arrests, Expulsions to Prevent Information Circulating." Accessed 31 January 2013. http://en.rsf.org/bahrein-authorities-use-arrests-expulsion-28–12–2012,43844.html.

Reporters Without Borders. 2012b. "Press Freedom Index 2011/2012." Accessed 31 January 2013. http://en.rsf.org/press-freedom-index-2011–2012,1043.html

Sakr, Naomi. 1999. "Satellite Television and Development in the Middle East." *Middle East Report* 210: 6–8.

Sakr, Naomi. 2007. "Approaches to Exploring Media-Politics Connections in the Arab World." In *Arab Media and Political Renewal: Community, Legitimacy and Public Life,* edited by Naomi Sakr, 1–12. London: I.B. Tauris.

Shafaqna (Shia International News Association). 2012. "NYT's Nicholas Kristof Detained at Bahrain Airport." 18 December. Accessed January 2013. http://www

.shafaqna.com/english/general/item/10345-nyt%E2%80%98s-nicholas-kristof-detained-at-bahrain-airport.html.
Smith, Antony. 1995. *Nations and Nationalism in a Global Era*. Cambridge, MA: Polity Press.
Street, John. 2001. *Mass Media, Politics and Democracy*. Basingstoke: Palgrave.
Weaver, David, Randal A. Beam, Bonnie J. Brownlee, and Paul S. Voakes. 2007. *The American Journalist in the 21st Century: US News People at the Dawn of a New Millennium*. Mahwah, NJ: Lawrence Erlbaum Associates.

Conclusion

Peter J. Anderson

This project has demonstrated several things. First, the importance of establishing precisely what is meant by quality news journalism when the term is used within debates about the future of the news media. Too often the concept is used in such a vague way that the level of discussion and analysis around it is debased. Chapter one set out in some detail the issues in this regard.

Equally, it is not helpful or enlightening to discuss the rise or decline of quality journalism without having some form of measurement. Chapter one set out a new and carefully reasoned approach to measuring news quality, to supplement other means of doing this that have been put forward within the literature. That discussion has informed the chapters that followed and has been used in a manner that is appropriate to the separate and individual contexts of each of those chapters.

An examination of those separate and individual contexts also has thrown up a number of interesting findings that have emphasised the extent to which it is dangerous to assume that the same technological and/or economic phenomena will have exactly the same or even similar results across the various continents and cultures of the globe. For example, Akinfemisoye and Deffor point out that the newspaper and broadcast media in parts of the intermediate and developing world are bucking the trend and performing well financially, but emphasise also that this good news is very much context specific and therefore not easily transferable elsewhere. Sonwalkar also notes a huge growth across the Indian news media industry as a whole, with print newspapers particularly bucking the trend apparent in developed states through continuing increases in their circulation. But he also identifies major problems in the form of quantity outstripping quality, with the fierce, profit-driven dash for growth leading to a serious cutting of corners and a lack of investment in the human resources necessary to ensure high quality hard news journalism across the range of the coverage.

It is interesting to note also that a number of authors are unconvinced by the view that old journalism and new journalism, mainstream journalism and citizen journalism, are simply competing entities, with the latter destined to replace the former. Bentley's chapter, for example, emphasises how, within an American cultural context, citizen journalism and mainstream journalism are interdependent, with a degree of crossover and absorption of the former within parts of the latter. Citizen journalism cannot replace all of the functions of mainstream journalism if the collapse of the latter becomes absolute, but neither can mainstream journalism do many of the things that 'the citizens' do.

What is more, citizen journalism and alternative journalism monitor and challenge the more complacent certainties and poorly performing parts of mainstream journalism, as Cook and Dickinson point out. For them, they play by different rules to some degree where conceptions of quality are concerned, with transparency, for example, being higher on the agenda than traditional notions of objectivity, but ultimately they are about trying to deliver as accurate a picture of the world as they can, even if that accuracy may often be checked by comments and crowd correction rather than the role of a traditional editor. Dugmore and Ligaga see a vital role for citizen journalism within the specific context of Kenya that fits with the Cook-Dickinson view, noting that it helps fill the information gap within Kenyan society that is left by institutionalised censorship of the mainstream news media. This is an excellent example of the ways in which citizen journalism can help facilitate the kind of participatory democracy outlined in chapter one.

For Bentley, citizen journalism also is a crucial ingredient in helping to expand or restore the appeal of mainstream media when incorporated within it.

However, to emphasise some of the key (and in the case of South Africa, for example, growing) roles of citizen journalism is not to imply that mainstream journalism is on the road to oblivion. As pointed out previously, in some countries, most particularly India, as Sonwalkar demonstrates, trends are being challenged, with the print and broadcast news industries continuing to prosper. Equally, while print news declines in terms of sales and advertising in developed economies such as the UK and the USA, Blackhurst shows how new models and experiments can still find success, with his examples of the birth and spectacular growth of the *i* and the re-birth of the London *Evening Standard* in the UK. As he admits, those successes do not yet extend to the traditional model of national print newspapers in the UK, just as they do not extend, for example, to the *New York Times* or *Washington Post*. But to assume that these 'old dogs' will die is to rule out without evidence the possibility of the creation of new print formats that depend not on the failures of the past, but the generation of new thinking in the future. Experiments are being conducted with, for example, interactive newsprint at the University of Central Lancashire, and the two success stories reported by Blackhurst emerged apparently 'out of nowhere'. This suggests that what is needed is a revolution in how print is thought of and marketed, the materials on which its hard copies are printed and the technologies that are incorporated within these—and the complementary technologies to which they can be hooked up. It could be argued that so far print as a whole hasn't been successfully re-thought because not enough of the most able brains have been engaged in the process.

Equally, with online mainstream journalism, while paywalls have had only very limited success, other than in the case of niche market products such as the *Financial Times*, and advertising has been generating nothing like the revenues enjoyed during the heyday of print journalism, this is not necessarily the whole story. As Blackhurst points out, thinking about new ways of, for example, telling the news in a virtual environment within which the viewer can be a participant is in many cases only in its infancy, but offers tantalising possibilities of being able to create something so novel and involving that significant parts of the audience might want to pay to become involved in it.

In addition, it is not all a worrying picture with regard to broadcast high-quality hard news across the developed states. Beers, for example, points to the ability of American citizens to access high-quality hard news on public radio and television *if they so choose*, to compensate for the declining quality of the traditional mainstream provision. He notes also the high value presence of CNN as a global quality hard news provider in competition with the BBC. Robinson and Hobbs, while noting the decline in UK commercial radio news, are much more optimistic about the continuing presence of quality television hard news from key providers such as the BBC and Sky, and their enhanced focus upon the needs of the audience and the accessibility of quality news. Ogola highlights how the plurality of perspectives internationally has been extended by the growth of al Jazeera.

However, some contributors identify real problems in the developed world's mainstream news industry. Among the most worrying are those relating to what many traditionally have seen as the pinnacle of quality hard news journalism in the form of investigative journalism. Ortolani's chapter, for example, points to worries about the extent to which it will be possible to fund investigative journalism from the disappointing advertising revenues that continue to come in from digital business models in the USA. Within a primarily UK context, Lashmar sees a mixed bag where high quality investigative journalism is concerned, with encouraging signs in terms of the emergence of albeit small, but in some cases highly effective, new providers of investigative journalism, but notes also the continuing problems of how to fund the largest mainstream part of the provision. Current suggestions for how to fund this by, for example, a relevant House of Lords committee, are far short of the needs of the kind of participatory democracy outlined in chapter one.

Other worries stretch right across the continents that have been examined here. Ownership issues are a good example, ranging from the limitations on both the freedom of expression within Middle Eastern news media and its transformative potential resulting from it being in the hands of the region's dominant political forces, as Ogola notes, to the censorship issues that Dugmore and Ligaga highlight in Kenya and the problems resulting from the media industry of much of the developed world having fallen into the hands of conglomerates that Egglestone identifies. For Egglestone, if the provision of mainstream television news is left to the free market, the corporate preoccupation with profit will always shape the debate and act as a limiting factor in terms of the extent to which quality hard news can be produced.

There were also concerns about the growing deterioration in the provision of local news. Beers, for example, noted an increasing tendency to share local television news production facilities in several American cities. The sharing of local/regional newsroom facilities in South Africa was also highlighted. Bentley pointed to losses of American local newspaper titles. Robinson and Hobbs commented on the reduction in regional news differentiation in the UK's ITV programming. On the other side of the coin, while hardly pretending that all is well with the UK local and regional newspaper press, Williams did note some positive signs, including new start-ups as well as closures.

These issues aside, there is ultimately a fundamental and interesting conclusion to be drawn that affects centrally the future of the news media in all of the societies examined here and that relates to the technology on which all of its forms and platforms depend. As pointed out explicitly or implicitly in several chapters, rapid technical/scientific development has now become a continuously destabilising factor within news economics, and, via the direct knock-on effects of the latter, on how much news can be delivered, at what quality levels, on what platforms and at what, if any, price and/or revenue level. This is a profit/investment driven phenomenon, facilitated by the ultra-sophisticated level of scientific knowledge that has been reached across the world's main research institutes and design and/or manufacturing companies. Now that materials science and design team skills and creativity have reached their current levels, the capacity for generating previously unimaginable communication devices at middle and mass market prices becomes limited only by the level of consumer interest in and ability to buy the new products. The free market driven competition by the producers of, for example, android and iPhone devices becomes so dependent on being 'the next with the best' that the pressure to continuously create game-changing innovations and products becomes almost unstoppable.

Where high quality hard news is held to be fundamental to the effective working of participatory democracies, all of this raises a fundamental question as to how its economic viability is to be protected if the economics of the news business are continuously being called into question by developments that damage or even destroy the business models of platforms that previously had been key means of getting quality hard news to the audience. Equally, the greater the range of alternatives to accessing the news that new technologies open to citizens, then the greater the range of 'Lucifer factors' (see chapter one) there are to tempt the news audience elsewhere.

The potential responses to this problem are several. The free market response, for example, is to say that, because the market is the most efficient means of delivering wealth across societies, there is little that can be done about this other than to ensure that the major quality hard news providers are managed ably enough for them to adapt and to innovate well engineered solutions to each technology driven news provision problem as it arises. One of the possible mixed market approaches argues that the market and its consequences are too dynamic and unpredictable for key news providers to be left without a safety net in case of sudden and potentially insurmountable challenges resulting from the rate of technological change and consequent shifts in audience loyalties and behaviour. Therefore, they should be protected so that they can at least stay afloat through the rough seas of over-rapid change, for example, through subsidies (preferably in a way that does not give governments influence over the news that depends on them) or a BBC style model of public funding.

It is worth considering in detail a line of thinking that might be called the 'interventionist' change management approach. The rate of technological and scientific development has far outstripped the corresponding rate of political development in any of the continents examined within this book. In consequence, governments have simply no adequate mechanisms in place to cope with the maelstrom that has been affecting large parts of the news industry (in the present in the developed world, in the future for the rest of the world as the new technologies become more widespread). In part at least, the functioning of their democratic political systems depends on that news industry, even those that operate one variant or another of the mixed market approach. If governments continue to sit back and watch ineffectually as the economic foundations of a quality news provision are repeatedly shaken by the sometimes startling rate of product innovation in the communication technologies field, they run the risk of the rocks upon which their own democracies are built beginning to crumble. As was suggested in chapter one, it could be argued, therefore, that what is needed now is the thinking through of a change management strategy relating to the core requirements of democratic societies.

Put simply, at the moment each new communication technology adopted by news and media organisations and the citizenry as a whole is governed largely by economic, fiscal, health and safety rules, in terms of how they are sold to end users. There is at the moment no mechanism for thinking through in advance any potential negative side effects they might have on the quality of hard news or its availability to the public—a public who, in theory, largely depend on it for the information that is required to enable them to be effective members of a participatory democracy, as defined in chapter one. It would be ridiculous to argue that the clock should stand still and that change in such politically important areas of technological development should be frozen. But it is not ridiculous to argue that democratic political systems should start to develop in ways that help them to catch up with the implications of such change. It could be argued that they need at least to start to consider frameworks for discussing with manufacturers during the testing and development stages of such new technologies their potential costs and benefits for the communication of hard news and political communication in general, within the states for which they are responsible. The argument that highly secretive manufacturers like Apple would be unlikely to share their new product details with their governments prior to launch is somewhat undermined by the now common knowledge that, for example, US security agencies and the UK's GCHQ have the capacity to penetrate their and other organisations' 'secrets' at will if they so choose. The news industry that will be affected needs also to be brought into the discussions (at a point where technology manufacturers are not afraid of possible leaks of their new developments leading to a loss of commercial advantage), which need to focus on possible ways of minimising the costs and maximising the benefits. This might from time to time, where possible, involve the slowing down of the introduction of new step-changing communication technologies within one or more democracies in order to allow news producers, manufacturers and, to use the jargon, other key stakeholders in the democratic process adequate time to work out ways of coping with their negative effects and harnessing the beneficial ones. That would bring greater stability to the news business and, in so doing, would bring another crucial benefit because stability is a key attracter of increased investment, and that also, in theory at least, should help provide the resources necessary to protect the budgets for quality news, should the owners of the relevant businesses choose to use the investment in this way and not channel it off into increased returns to shareholders.

It is important to emphasise here that such an approach does not mean that manufacturers and product innovators should be 'blamed' for the negative side effects of recent technological advances as far as the economics of quality news is concerned. That mechanisms for dealing with these are not in place could be argued to be the fault rather of governments that have been slow to catch up with the implications of what has been happening, or that have been blinded by ideological bias to the importance of any such involvement in the business sector. It should be remembered also that it was the newspaper industry largely on its own that made the mistake of flooding the internet with free copy without first having thought through adequately the economic consequences of doing this. The internet, the computers it has been built on and the companies that manufactured them did not force newspapers to provide their content without charge (although in the UK it has long been felt that free access to the BBC's news site has damaged the ability of quality newspapers to persuade the audience to pay or subscribe online). It is everyone involved who needs to start thinking at a higher level about how best to handle new technological advances.

Some might dismiss all of this as a mere theoretical possibility unlikely to be achievable in the real world. An obvious question is how could the likes of Apple be persuaded to tune their product features and launch timings to the requirements of such a process within those democracies that introduced it. There would be particular concerns that the process itself might be abused and used as back door protectionism. However, the inevitable watchfulness of corporate lawyers should help guard against the latter possibility, while the equal application of any scrutiny/slow down process to all manufacturers would help guard against fears of commercial disadvantage. Trade law may well require some modification domestically and internationally if such a process is to be fully legitimised, and some powerful states would not be enthusiastic about this on ideological grounds. However, if proposals for change are framed clearly in terms of their importance for the effective working of democracy, they would have a legitimacy that would give them an at least sporting chance of success in those states/transnational organisations most committed to democratic ideals.

The preceding chapters demonstrate why something significant needs to be done, and now. This particular prescription requires governments to think more deeply and more radically about the relationship between technology, the news and democracy than has so far been the case, and persuading them to do so would not be easy. The potentially best way of doing this would be to highlight clearly and in detail the possible consequences for democracy of the present situation being allowed to continue. The need for significant change is highlighted by newspapers online, simply because, as pointed out previously, most of the industry charged onto the internet without first having thought through the implications of the new technology and its likely impact on their business models—and their ability to continue to deliver quality hard news. As also was pointed out previously, citizen journalism has been able to fill part of the gap left by the significant downsizings of the staff needed to run 'online damaged' quality hard news operations at titles ranging from the *New York Times* to the *Guardian* and the *Independent*, but it is a long way short of being able to do an equivalent job.

Consideration of the plight of newspapers opens up another dimension to the process of change management, however, that also could be argued to be important. It does not include provision for any slowing down of technological developments. Instead, the argument is that in order to cope with the consequences of change, the news industry itself should enhance greatly its ability to generate new technological developments, new design formats and techniques and increase severalfold its creative resources. This could be done with help from government/university funded research and development and would enable news organisations to think through in much more detail the impact of each new technology on quality news provision. To return to an earlier example, such R&D and thinking space could focus on, among other things, the nature of the print newspaper and all the possible ways it can be designed, delivered, financed and reinvented in terms of its relationship with its audience. As pointed out previously, the *i* and the London *Evening Standard* are two illustrations of the fact that, four years ago, what many people were saying could not be done *could*. They represent two successful reinventions of the newspaper business model. There is in theory no reason why others should not follow, should sufficient brain power and investment be devoted to their genesis. If democratic states are seriously committed to the high quality news information flows that are necessary for their effective functioning, then they need to start thinking about frameworks within which such economic and intellectual investment could be facilitated—and as Egglestone pointed out in an earlier part of the book, ways of reducing the negative impacts of some of the ownership structures currently dominating large parts of the news business nationally and internationally.

There are possible other solutions to the news industry's technology-related plight but no space to mention them in this brief conclusion. Some have been discussed already, in Williams's chapter six, for example, and readers will have derived food for thought also from these. It is not claimed that the suggestions discussed here are the last word on the subject, but it is hoped that they might prompt at the very least a debate that will result in the finding of more effective solutions to the problems for the news industry than currently are being discussed.

So overall, this book, while acknowledging all of the worrying trends within the global quality hard news industry, also identifies others that are quite positive—together with something of the extent to which they are country and culture specific—and possibilities for the protection of hard news that, while existing in embryonic form, have not yet been either fully thought through or tried. What can and should be done to enhance, protect and promote quality hard news within each of the societies examined here varies according to the opportunities and limitations presented by their individual cultural, political, social and economic contexts. Even within the somewhat similar democracies of the UK and the USA, the different ideological variations of liberal free market economics means that there are significant differences in what can be done to preserve and promote quality hard news journalism. Put at its simplest, the USA is unlikely ever to fund an equivalent to the BBC because of the economic ideological barriers to this. Solutions to the quality and economic problems of the news providers within each of the societies examined have therefore to be found within the specific contexts of those societies. There is no universal prescription to remedy the problems that each has. Equally, those same societal differences make it at best unsafe to assume that what happens in the USA and the UK today with regard to quality hard news provision across the most advanced digital platforms will necessarily be what happens tomorrow with those same platforms in Kenya, South Africa or India. The problems that face the various continents are not uniform in their nature, and neither are the possible solutions to them, and nor should we expect this to be the case. One of the most variable factors examined here is the quality levels of the news available, with, for example, the huge range of problems that Sonwalkar identifies in India being different to those that Ogola, Rodny-Gumede, Dugmore and Ligaga found in South Africa and Kenya, that Bentley, Beers and Ortolani identified in the USA and that Robinson, Hobbs, Blackhurst and Williams noted with regard to the UK. The question of how to improve the position of the weakest news providers in this regard and enhance that of the strong is so complex that it is beyond the scope of this book, but what should be noted is that the notion of a 'quality news provider' currently varies enormously across these various societies, just as the notion of precisely what is involved in a democracy does. Again, solutions to the quality problems of each society need to be devised within the specific context of the country involved.

This book demonstrates that a number of possible solutions to these problems exist or are evolving and that the future of journalism is far from bleak across these continents, even in those where its challenges are greatest. What is in doubt, however, is the extent to which high-quality journalism in the senses set out in chapter one is widely achievable, given the huge range of obstacles that we have seen, or whether it remains predominantly the preserve of news providers like the BBC, CNN or the *New York Times*, supplemented, monitored and checked by the best kind of citizen journalism as identified by Dugmore and Ligaga, Bentley and Cook and Dickinson. In that regard, the book must end on a note of pessimism.

Bonus Chapter—More Core Material Available by Web Link

Why Mainstream News Still Matters, and Why New Business Models Must Be Found

Peter J. Anderson

Available at: http://clok.uclan.ac.uk/7824

Contributors

EDITORIAL TEAM

Peter J. Anderson is Reader in News Media and Research Coordinator for the School of Journalism and Digital Communication at the University of Central Lancashire, UK. He has published a variety of books, articles and book chapters on both communication and politics, including (with Geoff Ward, eds.) (2007) *The Future of Journalism in the Advanced Democracies*, Aldershot: Ashgate; (with Anthony Weymouth) (1999) *Insulting the Public? The British Press and the European Union*, Harlow: Longman; (with Christopher Williams and Georg Wiessala, eds.) (2000) *New Europe in Transition*, London: Continuum; and (1996) *The Global Politics of Power, Justice and Death*, London: Routledge. He also co-edited with Georg Wiessala the book-length *European Studies* volume 25, which was thematically focussed on 'The European Union and Asia'. He taught previously at the universities of Lancaster and Southampton and used to run a consultancy on the EU, the news media and the citizenry.

George Ogola is a Senior Lecturer in Journalism at Central Lancashire University and still writes as a columnist for *Business Daily*, a Nairobi-based financial newspaper. Previously he was a freelance correspondent for the UK-based *News Africa, a* Features Writer/ Sub-Editor for *East African Standard Newspapers,* and an Eastern Africa Correspondent for South Africa's *Sunday Times'* Africa Edition. Prior to his current post at Central Lancashire, he was Head of Department, Media and Communications, Midrand Graduate Institute, Johannesburg, South Africa. He has published a variety of academic articles and book chapters on East African literature and the Kenyan news media, including "The idiom of age in a popular Kenyan newspaper serial", in *Africa: The Journal of the International African Institute*, 76.4 (September 2006) pp. 569–589 and "The political economy of the media in Kenya: From Kenyatta's 'nation-building' press to Kibaki's fragmented nation", in *Africa Today* 57(3), 2011, pp. 77–95.

Michael Williams is a Senior Lecturer in Journalism at Central Lancashire University and is responsible for the prestigious series of *Harris Lectures*, which brings some of the leading figures in British journalism to speak at the university during the autumn and spring semesters each year. In addition to his teaching and research role, Michael continues to work as a leading journalist, writing for the *Independent*, the *Daily Telegraph*, the *Daily Mail* and the *New Statesman*. He also runs his own media company and blog in addition to being an author. He began his journalistic career as a graduate trainee at the *Daily Post* in Liverpool in 1971 and went on, among other things, to become one of the founding editors of the *Today* newspaper, Head of News and features at the *Sunday Times*, Deputy Editor of *New Society* and Deputy Editor of the *Independent on Sunday*.

Contributors

Motilola Akinfemisoye has worked as both a print and broadcast journalist in Nigeria. Currently she is one of the winners of an international scholarship at the University of Central Lancashire and is a PhD student in the School of Journalism and Digital Communication. Among other things, her PhD investigations focus on the extent to which alternative media are impacting the institutional practices of mainstream journalists in Nigeria. This research interest is finding expression also in her publications, with an article on the same theme included in the January 2013 issue of the journal *Ecquid Novi*.

Robert Beers was a Senior Lecturer in Journalism at the University of Central Lancashire. He was the winner of many U.S. national and regional journalism awards, including two Gold Medals at the New York International Film Festival and an Emmy. His distinguished career included a period as news manager of WTVJ/CBS Miami. After being hired by CBS News as a reporter to run their Miami Bureau, he covered Central and South America. He covered the conflicts in El Salvador and Nicaragua for CBS News in the 1980s. Subsequently, he went to BSP Americas and did work for Knight Ridder, CBS and the National Education Association, among many others. As a university teacher he was both highly respected and extremely popular with students on the university's international programmes. He passed away in February 2013, shortly after completing the final revisions to his chapter.

Clyde Bentley is Associate Professor in Convergence Journalism at the Missouri School of Journalism. He worked in the newspaper industry for 25 years and then completed a doctorate in journalism at the University of Oregon in 2000. Among other things, he was a reporter, photographer, copy editor and managing editor of the *Coeur d'Alene (Idaho) Press*. He spent some time as an advertising manager at the *San Antonio Recorder-Times and Irving News* before becoming the general manager of the daily *East Oregonian* in Pendleton in 1993. His research continues to focus on the habits, preferences and comfort levels of media consumers, especially users of digital media. He currently serves as a member of the Center for the Digital Global, Missouri's campus-wide project to study the future of the Internet. Among his recent research projects was a survey of MU computer users to determine their attitudes toward 'spam'. Bentley helped found MyMissourian.com, an 'open source' publication in which the readers are also the writers.

Chris Blackhurst is Group Content Director across the *Independent, i, Independent on Sunday* and *Evening Standard* titles and websites and London Local TV. Prior to that, between July 2011 and June 2013, he was Editor of the *Independent* newspaper and Group Editorial Director, *Independent* and *Evening Standard*. Formerly, he was City Editor of the *London Evening Standard* and is regarded internationally as one of the leading journalists and commentators on financial matters. His career began at *Euromoney* magazine. He then moved on to *Business magazine*, the *Sunday Times* business desk, its Insight investigative team, and then the *Sunday Express*. From there he moved to the *Independent on Sunday*, spending four years as a Westminster correspondent, and he was made deputy editor under Rosie Boycott. His journalism has appeared in numerous magazines and other publications, and he has written and presented two BBC Radio 4 Profiles. He has been nominated for a number of awards from, for example, the London Press Club and the British Press Awards.

Clare Cook is a Senior Lecturer in Journalism at Central Lancashire University. She was formerly an award-winning journalist working for the *Lancashire Evening Telegraph, the Nottingham Evening Post* and celebrity titles owned by the *Daily Express*. She is engaged currently in a number of projects focussing on social media and journalism that will be published during 2013.

Sally Deffor has an MA in Strategic Communication from the University of Malmo, and between January 2010 and January 2012, she was Communications Officer for the Coastal Resources Centre-USAID/ICFG programme in Ghana. Currently, she is one of the winners of an international scholarship at the University of Central Lancashire, and she is a PhD student in the School of Journalism and Digital Communication. Her doctoral project focuses on an evaluation of the impact, role and potential of digital platforms with regard to news storytelling.

Andrew Dickinson is a Senior Lecturer currently teaching digital and online journalism at the University of Central Lancashire, and he is course leader for the BA in Digital Journalism Production. In his spare time he edits television programmes, provides training for journalists making the move to digital and writes a thought-provoking journalism blog.

Harry Dugmore is Associate Professor and Director of the Discovery Centre for Health Journalism at Rhodes University's School of Journalism and Media Studies in Grahamstown, South Africa. Prior to starting the Health Journalism Centre, Harry was the MTN Chair of Media and Mobile Communication at Rhodes University. As part of the MTN Chair's work, Harry managed the US$500,000 *Iindaba Ziyafika* Citizen Journalism project between 2009 and 2012. This project explored ways of creating a more participatory local journalism as the transition from print to digital and mobile media gathers momentum in South Africa. Harry is currently on the steering committee of the Highway AFRICA conference, the largest annual conference for African Journalists. He is also Deputy Chair of the Board of the David Rabkin Project for Experiential Journalism.

Paul Egglestone is Director of the Journalism and Digital Communication School's Media Innovation Studio at the University of Central Lancashire. Currently he is involved in several leading-edge digital media research projects, and he has won significant amounts of external research funding for his work. He is Principal Investigator for the EPSRC-funded *Interactive Newsprint* project. A former independent television producer working for the BBC, ITV and Sky on regional and network programming, he has been focussing recently on international documentary and digital content generation for broadband and mobile dissemination. He sits on the steering group for Lancashire Economic Partnership's New Media and ICT group and also leads the Journalism Sector of Northern Edge, the centre of professional excellence for creative and cultural industries.

Andrew Hobbs is a Research Associate in the Journalism and Digital Communication School at Central Lancashire University. Prior to taking up an academic research career, he had twenty years experience writing and sub-editing for UK local, regional and national newspapers and magazines. He has published a number of academic articles on journalism prior to and since the award of his doctorate in 2010, including, for example, "When The Provincial Press Was The National Press (c.1836-c.1900)", *International Journal of Regional and Local Studies*, Series 2, 5:1 (2009) and "Just the local paper: Reading the local newspaper in the late Victorian era", *Quadrat* (Bulletin of research in progress on the history of the British book trade), 2008. He has also co-edited a special issue of the *International Journal of Regional and Local Studies* on the history of the provincial press. He is an associate editor of the online *Dictionary of Nineteenth-Century Journalism.*

Prior to taking up his current academic post at Brunel University, **Paul Lashmar** gained a reputation as one of the UK's leading investigative journalists. He is also a television producer and author and continues to write for UK newspapers on a freelance basis, including the *Guardian, Independent on Sunday* and *The Evening Standard*. He broke a long series of exclusive stories when working for *The Observer* and the highly respected *World in Action*, Granada Television's much lamented flagship investigative journalism programme. He has also produced a number of programmes for Channel 4's *Dispatches* series. During his last eight years at *The Observer*, Paul and David Leigh formed the paper's investigative team, and in 1986 they received the UK Press Awards "Reporter of the Year" accolade, primarily for revealing British security agency MI5's political vetting of BBC staff at that time. He has written also for *The Washington Post, The Daily Telegraph, The Sunday Telegraph, The Times, Miami Herald, Harpers, Africa Confidential, Africa Report (US)*, and *West Africa* and broadcast for BBC Radio's *"From Our Own Correspondent"*.

Dina Ligaga is a Lecturer in the School of Literature and Language Studies at the University of the Witwatersrand, Johannesburg. She gained her PhD from Witwatersrand in 2008. Her research interests stretch across popular culture, postcolonial discourse, representation and ideology, media audiences and processes of reception, and broadcasting. Her publications include "Ethnic Stereotypes and the Ideological Manifestations of Ethnicity in Kenyan Cyber Communities", *Africa Insight* (2009) 39.1; and *"Radio Theatre*: Interrogating the Developmental Narratives of Radio Drama in Kenya", in *Getting Heard: Reclaiming Performance Spaces in Kenya. Art, Culture and Society Vol. 3* (ed. Kimani Njogu), Twaweza Communications (2008).

Alex Ortolani is Senior Media and Content Officer at Asia Society in New York. He has reported for media outlets including Bloomberg News, the *South China Morning Post*, and the Associated Press. He holds MA degrees from Boston University and the University of the Witwatersrand.

Deborah Robinson joined the Journalism School at Central Lancashire University in October 2002. Previously she had spent ten years as a news reporter for the BBC. She worked out of the highly respected Oxford Road studios in Manchester on such news programmes as *North West Tonight* and *Northwestminster*. She worked also on the documentary series *Close-up North*. In addition, she has worked in regional newspapers, national magazines, radio and public relations. She is the School's course leader for the BA Single Honours Journalism programme.

Ylva Rodny-Gumede is a Lecturer in the Department of Journalism, Film and Television in the School of Communication at the University of Johannesburg, South Africa. Her research interests include political communication, media and development in transitional societies and the role of the media in conflict monitoring and resolution.

Prasun Sonwalkar teaches at The Media School, Bournemouth University, UK. A former journalist, he worked for *The Times of India, Business Standard, Press Trust of India,* and *Zee News,* among other news organisations. His research has been published in edited collections and journals such as *Media, Culture & Society, International Communication Gazette, Contemporary South Asia,* and *Modern Asian Studies.*

Index

1010 WINS 154
5G mobile phone technology 82
60 Minutes 149
7/7 bombings *see* London tube
  bombings

ABC (American Broadcasting
  Company) 74, 144, 145, 149,
  152–3
ABC News Now 145
Abrahams, Lucienne 253
Acton, Lord (John Dalberg-Acton), 40
Adamson, Andrew 118
Adegoke, Yinka 81
advertising: ad "skipping" technology
  79; aimed at older consumers
  75; and state broadcasters 96;
  classified 107, 113; growth in
  TV revenue 74; hidden 277;
  "narrowcast" 118; online 92–3,
  108; smartphones 82; targeted
  84, 118; television 81; *Times
  of India* 276; UK national
  newspapers 114; video 130;
  YouTube 68
"advertorial" 275
Afuah, Allan 88
Agence France-Presse 3, 10, 47, 69, 179
Agency and voice, Kenyan citizen
  journalism 260
aggregation 131, 139, 140, 177;
  Huffington Post 127
Ahlers, Douglas 93
Ahluwalia, Samir 278
Ahva, Laura 215
Aikat, Debashis 88, 90–2, 95
Ailes, Roger 147
Akinfemisoye, Motilola 88–100, 297
Akmal, Kamran 41

Al Arabiya 284, 289, 292
Al Jazeera: Al Jazeera English 73; Arab
  affiliation 284; brand 285;
  expansion 73, 285; links to Qatari
  government 291; political aims
  286; profitability 285; Richard
  Dawkins 290; selective coverage
  of Arab Spring 289; standardized
  Arabic translation 293; Western-
  trained journalists 293
Al Majid 290
Alai, Robert 259
Algeria 286
All India Radio 269
All Things Considered, NPR 155
Allan, Stuart 206, 210, 250
Allen, Jeffrey 88
all-news radio 154–5
Al-Manar 290
Al-Mihafda, Sayed Yousef 287
Al-Quds Al-Arabi 289
alternative media: Arab Spring 292;
  definition 205; Kenya 252;
  partnership with mainstream
  media 218–19; transparency 205
Althearn, Robert 185
Altmeppen, Klaus-Dieter 166
Al-Wasat 288
American Society of Newspaper
  Editors 19
America's Talking (cable channel) 148
Amin, Hussein 284
Amir, Mohammad 41
Amit, Raphael 88
An Nahar 283
Anderson, Chanders 127
Anderson, Chris 83, 109
Anderson, Peter J. 1–34, 9, 10, 20, 21,
  22, 167

Ansah, Paul 233
Ansari, Hamid 274
AOL 116
app: aid to reporting 172; BBC Radio 1
   Newsbeat 178; citizen journalism
   211, 242; *The Daily* 116; income
   118; popularity of news apps
   164; Zeebox social TV 76
Apple TV 80
"appointment viewing" 162
Arab identity 283
Arab journalism 282–96
Arab media liberalization 284–7
Arab satellite TV 285
Arab Spring: Al Jazeera coverage
   286; impact on media freedom
   288; new discursive frame 282;
   new media technology 291–2;
   selective coverage 289; U.S.
   audience interest 144, 147; user-
   generated content 172
Archers, The 30
Argus group, South Africa *see*
   Independent Group,
   South Africa
Arnett, Peter 146
Asif, Mohammad 41
"aspirational" newspaper content,
   India 274
Assange, Julian 37
Association of Media Women in Kenya
   (AMWIK) 239
Atieno-Odhiambo, Elisha 228
Atlantic magazine 127, 138
Atton, Chris 206
Atwan, Abdel Bari 289
audience material *see* user-generated
   content
Audience Research & Development
   (consultants) 150
audiences 16; data gathering 79, 118;
   decline in news consumption
   68; diaspora 93; education 19,
   29, 31; elite, Thought Leader
   254; fragmentation 68, 156,
   164; Hispanic 145; interactivity
   76; journalists' awareness of
   162–83; life experience 19;
   local radio, UK 164; metrics
   129–30, 165; NPR 155;
   participation platforms 206;
   perceptions of quality 109;
   ratings, India 279; regional

versus national newspapers,
   U.K. 107; segmentation 138;
   trust newspapers 91; TV decline,
   U.S. 144; TV growth 74; TV
   news, UK 163; young people
   consuming less news 75
Audioboo 209
Auletta, Ken 276
Avusa, South Africa 231–3
Axford, Barrie 13

Baden-Fuller, Charles 89
BAFTA (British Academy of Film and
   Television Arts) 168
Bahrain 287, 288
Baker, Edwin C. 231
Baker, Jonathan 171
Bakersfield Californian 192
balance 9, 147, 149, 157
Ball, James 46, 210
Banda, Fackson 253, 263
Baraza Limited, Kenya 236
Barclay brothers 105, 120
Barnett, Steven 122, 164, 166–7, 169,
   174, 176, 177, 179
Barringer, Felicity 195
Barton, Frank 229
Battelle, John 80
BBC: Academy 171; Appreciation
   Index 165; competitive pressures
   13; College of Journalism 171;
   "Delivering Quality First" 175;
   economic reporting and story
   boxes 16; editorial guidelines
   170; hyperlinking policy 216;
   iPlayer 84; licence fee 73, 171;
   Parliament channel 164; Radio
   1 165, 170, 177–8; skews UK
   news market 115
BBC Trust 171
BCCL *see* Bennett, Coleman & Co Ltd
Beam, Randal A. 283
Beckett, Charlie 122
Beers, Robert "In Memoriam" 143–61,
   299
Bell, Emily 121, 127, 207
Ben Gana, Khadija 284
Bengal Gazette 273
Bennett, Coleman & Co Ltd (BCCL)
   273
Bennett, W. Lance 72
Bentley, Clyde 184–201, 250, 297–8
Bercovici, Jeff 155

Berger, Guy 230, 234, 240,
    249, 253
Bezanson, Randall P. 89
bias 9, 251, 279
Bibel, Sara 146
Big and Emerging Market (BEM)
    economies *see* South Africa;
    Brazil; India
Bin Laden, Osama 144, 147, 165
Bird, William 229
Birt, John 167, 170
Blackberry Messenger 210
Blackhurst, Chris 55–66, 298
Blatter, Sepp 37
Blogger, platform 188
blogging 119, 188–92, 204, 251;
    BBC 215; "journalistic" 258;
    "mommy blogging" 191;
    NYMag.com 134–37; Okolloh,
    Ory 258; South Africa 254;
    unpaid on Thought Leader 255
Bloomberg News 128
Blottr 215
Boaden, Helen 18, 22, 163–5, 170–3,
    177–8
Boardman, Hamilton 133–4, 140
Bock, Mary Angela 209
Boczkowski, Pablo J. 215
Bogart, Leo 19
Boler, Megan 69
Bollywood themes in news presentation
    278
Borra, Erik 211
Bosch, Tanja 230
Bougalt, Louise 229
Boyd-Barrett, Oliver 231
Boyle, Brendan 93
Bradshaw, Paul 44, 46, 47, 118
Brady, Jim 190
Brand, Russell 213
brands 117–8, 122, 198
"brand stretch" 63
Brazil: local newspapers 95; media
    growth 90; newspaper paywall
    92; pay TV revenue 74; private
    media ownership 96; tabloid
    newspapers 94
bribery 289
BRIC nations (Brazil, Russia, India and
    China) 74
Brinkman, Inga 93
Bristol 119
Bronner, Fred 209

Brooks, Rebekah 38
Brown, Maggie 171, 175
Brown, Perry 185
Brownlee, Bonnie J. 283
Bruns, Axel 204, 209
Buckland, Matthew 254, 255
Bukh, Per N. 89
Buncefield oil fire, 2005 208
bundling of news and other content *see*
    business models: bundling
Bureau of Investigative Journalism 37,
    38, 42, 45, 50, 117
Burleson, Brant R. 14
Burlington, Vermont 152
Burrell, Ian 42
Bush, George W. (military service
    record) 189
Business, 57
business models: bundling 78, 113–14,
    118; citizen journalism 198;
    collaboration 117; concept
    of 88–89; crowdfunding 83,
    117; differentiated products
    94; diversification 117, 120;
    donations 83, 117; licence
    fee 96; micro-payments 115;
    national newspapers, UK 55–66;
    newspaper sales 92; paywalls
    92, 114–15; public funding 72;
    public-private partnerships 83;
    subscriptions 115, 131; subsidies
    116–17
Business Standard, India 272
Butt, Salman 41
Byrne, Dorothy 43, 170, 171, 179

cable TV: pay TV 77; bundling of news
    78; data harvesting 79; *see also*
    CNN; Fox; MSNBC; Sky
Calcutt inquiry 113
Callaham, John 81
Cameron, David 113, 177
Campbell, Anne 113
Campo-Flores, Arian 145
Canada 72, 77
Capital FM, Kenya 235
Caplan, Scott E. 14
Capus, Steve 71
Care Quality Commission 168
Carey, James 8
Carter, Ian 118
Casey, Joe 168, 170
casualisation 110

Caxton Publishers, South Africa 231
CBS: all-news radio format 155; foreign
　　news cuts 143; glory days 144;
　　lack of cable channel 145; local
　　TV stations 153; news values
　　156; radio stations 154; shared
　　newsrooms 152; *60 Minutes*
　　149; viewing figures 74
Celebrity Big Brother 112
celebrity news 36, 112
cell phone *see* mobile phone
Centre for Investigative Journalism 39
Chadwick, Alexander 207
Chaharbaghi, Kazem 89, 97
Chalaby, Jean 103
Chandler Jr., Alfred D. 88
change management 303
Channel 4: audience involvement;
　　current affairs output 167;
　　Dispatches 43; journalistic
　　innovation 166; malicious
　　complaints against 170; news
　　audience figures 163; reality-
　　format current affairs 169; well-
　　resourced 171, 178–9; *see also*
　　Byrne, Dorothy
Channel 5 112, 163
Charities Commission 49
"Charlie Bit My Finger" video 68
Chaudhary, Sudhir 278
Cheeseman, Nic 232
Cheredar, Tom 79, 81
Cherribi, Sam 284
Chesbrough, Henry 88
Chester, Jeffrey 80
China: rising pay TV revenues 74;
　　media expansion 90; Morecambe
　　Bay cockle-pickers 173;
　　newspaper growth 90–1; online
　　paid content 92; tabloid local
　　newspapers 95
Chisholm, Jim 108, 114, 117, 119
Chittum, Ryan 92
Chomsky, Noam 229
Choudhury, Barnie 48
Christakis, Nicholas 215
Christian Science Monitor 127
Chuma, Wallace 252
Chung, Deborah Soun 215
"churnalism" 111, 112
citizen journalism 202–19, 248–63;
　　activist tradition, South Africa,
　　249–50; agency and voice
　　260; as Fourth Estate 259;
　　"community of practice" 256;

data journalism 47; definition
　　195, 202, 204, 249–50,
　　251, 263; distribution by
　　mainstream 208; editing of
　　196, 253, 256; gatekeeping by
　　mainstream media 211; history
　　of 184–8; Kenya 251–2; lack of
　　institutionalization, Kenya 259;
　　making enemies 256; paid on
　　Iindaba Ziyafika 255; quality
　　criteria 248, 249; relationship
　　with mainstream media 207,
　　213; reporting emergencies 207;
　　self-correcting 189–90, 196;
　　SMS text messages 257; South
　　Africa 249–51; status 257;
　　Twitter, Kenya 258; *see also* user-
　　generated content
citizen news wires 216
City AM 61
City University, London 45
Clarke, R. 80
Clear Channel Communications 154
Clemens, Samuel 186
Clinton, Bill 143, 148
Cloud, Barbara L. 186, 187
CNN (Cable News Network): audience
　　knowledge 148; awards 149;
　　breaking news 135–6; CNN2
　　146; CNN International
　　71, 146–7; history 145–6;
　　impartiality 78; *iReport*
　　196; number of bureaux 73;
　　relationship with network TV
　　145; profits 146; quality 157;
　　ratings 146–7
Cobbett, William 39
code of conduct, Kenya 234, 239
cognitive complexity and news 14
Cohen, David 259
Cohen, Jeff 147, 148
Cohn, Dave 83
Cole, Peter 106, 123
Coleridge, Nicholas 274
Collins, Richard 88
Columbia Missourian 194, 196
Columbia space shuttle 195
Combs, James 258
Comcast 71
comments on blogs 190
commercial good, news as 72; *see also*
　　public good, news as
community radio, South Africa 242
comparativeness as quality
　　indicator 203

Competition Commission 118
competitive democracy 10
Condé Nast 133
Conduct of Election Rules, India 277
Connell, Joan 283
Conservative Home 116
Conservative Party 105, 117
consolidation of ownership *see*
    ownership: consolidation
content-sharing 231
converged newsrooms 120, 127–42, 241
convergence, South Africa 242
Cook Report, The 41
Cook, Clare 202–23, 298
Cook, Roger 41, 43
corruption, paid news (India) 276–7
corruption, Arab journalists 289
Coulter, Richard 119
Cover, Rob 76
Cranberg, Gilbert 89
Crawford, Alex 172
Crisell, Andrew 171
Cronkite, Walter 144
"crony journalism" (India) 272
Crowcroft, Jon 47
Crowdfunding *see* businessmodels:
    crowdfunding
Crozier, Adam 167
cultural imperialism, Indian 268
culture of contentment 18
Culture, Media and Sport Committee,
    House of Commons 111, 118,
    121, 122
curation 136, 172–3
Currah, Andrew 36, 51, 90
Curran, James 68, 103
Cushion, Stephen 177, 179
CW Network 153

Dacre, Paul 110
Daily Beast 116
Daily Express 110
Daily Mail 105, 121, 170, 213
Daily Nation 96, 228, 229, 242;
    website 93
Daily Star 112
Daily Sun (South Africa) 94, 230
Daily Telegraph 105; and Demotix
    citizen newswire 216; adaptation
    120; MPs' expenses scandal 37;
    profitable 108; paywall 114, 115
Daily, The 37, 41, 105, 116
Dainik Jagran 277
D'Angelo, Paul 11
Danish cartoons controversy 290

data harvesting *see* privacy and TV
    data-collecting
Dateline 71
Davies, Nick 35, 109, 111, 177
Davies-Carr, Charlie 68
Davies-Carr, Howard 68
Dawkins, Richard 290
Day, Robin 179
de Beer, Arnold S. 229–30, 238
de Bruijn, Mirjam 93
de Burgh, Hugo 39, 40, 51
de Lanerolle, Indra 263
deception *see* working practices:
    deception
decline, narrative of 35
Deffor, Sally 88–100, 297
deliberative democracy 10
Deloitte 74, 80
democracy, types of 9
democratic deficit 111
Demotix 216
Denmark 179
Der Spiegel 47
deregulation: Kenya 96; United States
    153, 157
Desai, Santosh 275
DeShano, Cathy 206
Desmond, Richard 112
Deterritorial Support Group 214
Detroit Free Press 127
Deuze, Mark 204
development journalism 228–30
Diário Gaúcho 94
Dickens, Charles 39
Dickinson, Andrew 202–23, 298
Digital Video Recorders (DVR) 79
disability, coverage of 169
Dish Network 79
Dispatches 43, 167
Doherty, Carol 290
Domingo, David 210, 258
Doordarshan 269
Douglas, Torin 206, 208
Dowler, Milly 113
Downie Jr., Leonard 69
Draper, Derek 213
Drury, Kenneth 42
DSTV 237
Duffy, Margaret 191
Duggan, Mark 209
Dugmore, Harry 248–63, 256, 257, 298
dumbing down 110–1, 166, 179;
    Kenyan radio 243; not inevitable
    7; or "relevance" 170, U.S. TV
    consultants 150

Duncan, Jane 229, 230, 236, 237
Dvorak, John C. 208, 209
Dwyer, Tim 68

e.tv, Ghana 97
East African Standard 228, 229, 242
EasyFM (Kenya) 96
economic crisis (2008), coverage of 15
economic pressures 84, 89
Economic Times 267
Economist, The 115
editions, reduction 108
editor, abolition of post, *Times of India*
    274
editorial independence, *Standard* UK 60
editorial integration, *Standard* UK 63
editorial redundancies 105, 107, 109,
    144, 152, 175, 231
Edmonds, Rick 127
Eggerton, John 155
Egglestone, Paul 20–1, 67–87, 164,
    177, 300, 304
Egypt 287, 288
Eisenhower, Dwight D. 14
Eko, Lyombe 96
El País 47
electronic news-gathering 150
El-Faraeen TV, Egypt 287
Ellison, Sarah 219
El-Nawawy, Mohammed 286, 291
Eltahawy, Mona 283
Enders Analysis 108, 114, 121
Enders, Claire 121
Entwistle, Clive 41
Entwistle, George 42, 117
Environment Investigation Agency 44
Ess, Henk van 48
ethics: India 271, 275; Kenya 234;
    national versus local newspapers
    113
etv, South Africa 237
Evans, Harold 39, 110
Evans, Rob 44
Evening News, CBS 143
evening newspapers 58–9, 61, 91,
    107
Evening Standard, London 51, 56, 59,
    61, 64–6, 116
Everatt, David 229
Exaro 38
exclusives 58
extortion, Indian TV 278

Facebook 18, 80, 165–6, 195, 258,
    260, 292
fact-checking 137
Fairclough, Norman 9, 15
Fairness Doctrine 147
Fandi, Mamoun 286
Farrelly, Paul 213
Federal Communications Commission
    147, 152
Federalist Papers 185
Feist, Sam 146
Fendt, Christian 89, 97
Fenton, Natalie 109, 111, 291
Fenton, Tom 143, 144, 145
Fielding, Nick 36
FIFA 37
"fifth estate" 258
Filton Voice 119
Financial Times 1, 55, 64, 106, 108–9,
    114
Finland 108
First Amendment 187, 197
First Tuesday 167
Flanders, Stephanie 170
Fleming, Ken 191
Flickr photo-sharing site 209
Foerstel, Herbert N. 143
Folha de Sao Paulo 92, 94
foreign news 73, 110, 143, 166, 167,
    172; decline in India 270
Foster, Patrick 85, 162, 171–2, 174–5
Foster, Robin 70
Fourie, Pieter J. 230
Fourth Estate 8, 9, 39; citizen
    journalism 259; requires
    institutional backing 257
Foust, James C. 205
Fowler, James 215
Fowler, Neil 119
Fox network 79
Fox News: and breaking news 128; bias
    147; history 147; ill-informed
    audiences 148; largest cable
    audience 144, 146; misreporting
    Buncefield oil fire 209;
    presentation style 78
"Foxification" 147, 177
framing: "story boxes" 11–12, 14;
    "mind boxes" 16–17
Franklin, Bob 35, 70, 89, 92, 107, 109
Frediani, Richard 165–6, 171, 174,
    176, 178

free newspapers *see* newspapers: free
    newspapers
Freedman, Des 109
Freedom of Information Bill 2007,
    Kenya 240
Freedom of Information requests UK 47
free-market response to change 301
Friedman, Tom 267
Fuchs, Christian 205
Full Fact 25
Fulton, Mary Lou 192
fundamentalist religious TV stations
    290
Future TV, Lebanon 290

G20 protests, London 2009 209
Gabbert, Mike 41
Gaber, Ivor 164, 202
Galbraith, John K. 18
Gandhi, Mahatma 267
Gans, Herbert J. 89, 98, 202, 203,
    204, 219
Gardam, Tim 92
Gardner, Frank 170
gatewatching 209, 214
Gawker 137
Gelvin, James 285
Geneits, Anne 70
General Electric 71
Germany 179
Ghana 88, 91, 93, 95, 97
Giles, Tom 169, 170
Gillmor, Dan 184, 263
Ginges, Jeremy 283, 288–92
Gladwell, Malcolm 291
Glaser, Mark 251, 263
Global-L 48
Global Witness 44
Godwin, Tim 210
golden age *see* nostalgia
Goldstein, Joshua 257
Goldstuck, Arthur 253
Goode, Luke 206
Goodier, Holly 211
Google 74, 85, 131, 177
Google Fusion 210
Graham, Frank 150
Grahamstown, South Africa 255
Granada Reports 173–4
Greenpeace 43, 117
Greenslade, Roy 40, 41, 42, 109, 113,
    116, 117, 213

Greenwald, Glenn 149
Greig, Geordie 60
Grey, Stephen 36, 46
Grocott's Mail 255
Groseclose, Tim 149
Guardian 105–6; collaboration with
    NGOs 43, 117; crowdsourcing
    Blair finances story 215;
    diversification 118; expansion
    from 1980s 104; ensuring
    citizen journalism quality
    211; falling revenue 114;
    investigative journalism 41;
    losses 108; Masterclasses 118;
    mobile news 17; phone-hacking
    investigation 50; popular
    website 114; predicted survival
    121; respected quality brand 1;
    "Reading the Riots" research
    project 210; relationship with
    citizen journalists 210; social
    media sourcing 46; staff cuts 36;
    Trafigura injunction 213; use
    of Audioboo app 209; use of
    Demotix citizen newswire 216;
    WikiLeaks 47
Guardian Media Group 119
Guardian Unlimited 210
Guido Fawkes 116, 213
Gujarat Hindu-Muslim violence (2002)
    279
Gulf War (1990–1991) 146
Gulyas, Agnes 107, 114, 115
Guskin, Emily 127, 157

Hadland, Adrian 230
Hafez, Kai 287
Halavais, Alex 195
Hall, Ben 106, 109
Hall, Stuart 14
Hamilton, Alexander 185, 186
Hamilton, James F. 206
Hannity, Sean 147
Harber, Anton 230, 253
Harbert, Ted 79, 80
Harcup, Tony 106, 123
hard news, Indian neglect of 278
"hardware" of journalism 268
Hari, Johann 214
Harrison, John 80
Haugerud, Angelique 232
Hawken, Andrew 164, 165, 176, 178

HBO (Home Box Office) 71
Heaton-Harris, Chris 44
Heikkilä, Heikki 215
Heinonen, Ari 210, 258
Helal, Carla 91, 94, 95
Henry, Patrick 186
Herman, Edward S. 99, 229, 231
Hermida, Alfred 209, 215
Hewlett, Steve 176
Hezbollah 289
Hicky, James Augustus 273
Hindustan Times 128
Hirsch, Eric 250
Hirst, Martin 80
Hitler, Adolf 17
HLN *see* CNN2
Hobbs, Andrew 119, 162–83, 299
Holliman, John 146
Honolulu 152
Howell, Deborah 190
HT Media Ltd 128
Hu, Yu-Wei 187
Huffington Post 116, 127, 212, 215
Hume, Brit 189
Hunt, Jeremy 47, 111, 176
Hutton Inquiry 168
hybrid forms of journalism 261
Hyde-Clarke, Nathalie 250
hyperlocal content in India and China 95
hyperlocal publications 118
hyperlocal web sites 118
Hyun, Kideuk 215

i, the (newspaper) 63, 65, 66, 116
Ibelema, Minabere 230
ideology 15, 16
Ifill, Gwen 149
Iindaba Ziyafika 255–57
Ilanga 94, 95, 232
Iliffe News and Media 117
Independent Group, South Africa
    230–1
Independent News & Media, Ireland 62
Independent on Sunday 62, 63, 104
Independent Radio News 163
Independent, The 61–2, 106; celebrity
    editors 112; editorial choices 58;
    editorial integration 63; future of
    print edition 64; history 104; no
    staff photographers 110; website
    64
India 267–81, 298; as case study 2;
    independence and the press
    273; "India Shining" campaign
    268; local newspaper growth

95; media and entertainment
    industries, value 269; media
    growth 90; newspaper history
    273; paid content news sites
    92; politically partisan TV 147;
    reasons for growth of media 270;
    rising newspaper circulation 90;
    rising pay TV revenue 74
Indymedia UK 212
Inglewood, Lord 49
Ingram, Matthew 115, 118
Inkatha Freedom Party 232
Inside Out 175, 176
instrumentalities of order 228, 232
Intel 81
interactive mapping 210
interactive newsprint 122
International Criminal Court 235
International Financial Law Review 56
International News Safety Institute 48
internet: "fifth estate" 258; and news
    diversity 17; economic impact
    on news 36; free content
    116; monetisation 64; news
    organisations' response 68;
    newspapers' slow response 62;
    penetration 107; penetration,
    Arab world 292; penetration,
    Kenya 241; penetration,
    South Africa 91, 253, 263;
    psychological effects 19
Investigative Dashboard 48
investigative journalism 35–52, 299;
    and democracy 49; BBC's role 49;
    Daily Telegraph 120; evolution
    of 43; fewer practitioners 36;
    funding 49; golden age 39;
    growth in practitioners 49;
    history 38; House of Lords
    inquiry (2011) 38; NGOs 38,
    43–45; not-for-profit bureaux
    45–46; subterfuge 41
iol.com 231
iPhone *see* smartphones
Iraq War (2003 to present) 36
iReport 196
Iskandar, Adel 286
"Islamic glasnost", 1990s 286
Isolezwe 94, 95, 231, 232
Israeli voices on Al-Jazeera 293
ITN (Independent Television News) 165
Itumbi, Dennis 259

Jagannathan, R. 272
Jain, Ashok 273

Jain, Samir 273, 274, 276
Jain, Vineet 276
Jarvis, Jeff 217
Jay, John 185
Jeffrey, Robin 270
Jenkins, Henry 68, 71
Jeong, Jaekwan 215
Jindal, Naveen 278
Johnnic, South Africa *see* Avusa, South
    Africa
Johnson, K. 209
Johnston Press 107, 115
Jonsson, Anna Maria 169
journalism: as information provider
    8; as truth 13; as "vicarious
    politics" 286–7
journalism training: Kenya 239; South
    Africa 238
journalists as activists in Arab world 283
Jukwaa.com 259

Kahney, Leander 188
Kalita, S. Mitra 137–40
Kameme FM Kenya 234, 235
Kaminski, John P., 185
Kanter, Jake 74, 169
Kanter Media UK 74
Karmazin, Mel 155
Katju, Markandey 271
Kawamoto, Kevin 128
Kaye, Jeff 55, 69
Keeble, Richard 35, 44, 47, 48, 50
Kempson, Trevor 41
Kenya 232–6, 299; 2007 election
    257–8; as case study 2; citizen
    journalism 251–52, 257–60;
    convergence 241–2; diaspora
    audiences 93; historical
    background 228–29; indirect
    political pressure 233; internet
    advertising 93; internet
    penetration 241; Kenya
    Broadcasting Corporation (KBC)
    96, 229; Kenya Democracy
    Project blog 259; Kenya News
    Agency (KNA) 228; Kenya
    Television Network (KTN) 235;
    Kenya Union of Journalists (KUJ)
    239; Kenyan Pundit blog 257–8;
    local language newspapers 95;
    local language radio 234–5;
    Media Council of Kenya 240;
    media growth 235–6; media
    independence 239; misuse of
    media power 251; mobile news
93, 242; Nation Media Group
    (NMG) 96, 232; newspapers
    trusted 91; oppositional
    journalism 232–3; paid news
    234; professionalisation 239;
    repression of media 239–40
Kenyatta, Jomo 228
Kershaw, Ian 17
Kessel, Ineke van 249, 250
KFAX San Francisco 154
KFWB Los Angeles 154
Khalil, Naela 286, 289
Kibaki, Lucy 259
Kibaki, Mwai 233, 235, 240, 257
Kimotho, Jane 234
King, Lila 196
Kingara, Oscar 259
Kitchen, Nicholas 268
Klatell, David 76
Klein, Jonathan 189
KM Group 118
Knautz, Rob 185
Knight, Megan 253, 263
Knight Foundation 83, 255
Koang-Hyub, Kim 19
Kohut, Andrew 290
Korea, South 72, 184, 191, 198
Koss, Stephen 103
Kristof, Nicholas 287
Kuira, Mary 241, 257
Kunelius, Risto 215
Kurtz, Howard 145, 150, 152
Kuypers, Jim A. 11
KYW Philadelphia 154

Lacy, Stephen 191
Laird, Sam 191
Lakeland Radio 163
Lashmar, Paul 35–52, 299
Lasica, Joseph Daniel 202, 260
Lay, Samantha 175, 176
Le Monde 47
Lebedev, Alexander 59, 66, 106
Lee, Jonathan, 216
"legacy" newsrooms 127
Lehman Brothers 114, 119
Leigh, David 116
Leth, Goran 185
Leveson Report 37, 51, 107, 108, 110,
    112, 113
Levies *see* business models: subsidies
Levy, David 48
Levy, Gideon 214
Lewinsky, Monica 143
Lewis, Justin 35, 177, 179

Lewis, Paul 44, 46, 177, 210, 211
Libya 288
Ligaga, Dina 248–63, 298
Linder, Jane C. 88
Link Media 83
LinkTV 83
livemint.com 128
Lloyd, John 45
lobby journalists 214
local news under threat 300
local newspapers: closures, 108; falling
    revenues, 108; local language, 95;
    new launches, 95, 118; profits,
    107; quality monitoring, 111
local programming, Arab TV 292
local radio 107, 118, 164, 171, 175,
    179; hate speech, Kenya, 235;
    US, 154–6
local TV news: US, 149–54; UK, 176
Local World 107, 117
localism 119, 150
London riots (2011) 209
London School of Economics 210
London tube bombings 205; BBC 206
long-form journalism, 116, 127, 135,
    137, 140, 149
Luscombe, Anya 162, 166
Lynch, Marc 284, 293

MacArthur, Brian 104
MacFadyen, Gavin 39
Macharia, Samuel Kamau 235
MacIntyre, Donal 35, 43, 50, 51
Macnamara, Jim 68, 69
Maddow, Rachel 148
Madison, James 185, 186
Magro, Maira 94
Mahmood, Mazher 41
Mail & Guardian 231, 254
Mail Online 114
Mail On Sunday 112
mainstream media: definition 204; lack
    of transparency 218
Mair, John 35, 36, 37, 44, 47, 48, 50
Majeed, Mazhar 41
Makinen, Maarit 241, 257
management 174; South Africa 238
Manchester Evening News 105, 116, 120
Manifold, Laurie 41
marginalized voices in citizen
    journalism 248
market segmentation *see* business
    models: differentiated products

Marr, Andrew 202
Marsh, Kevin 173
Masala, Zikhona 253
Massa, Lorenzo 88
match-fixing, Pakistan cricket 41
Matter, San Francisco 117
Mazotte, Natalia 92
Mbembe, Achille 287
McAlpine, Lord Alistair 13, 37, 42,
    117, 171
McAvoy, Kim 153
McBride, Damian 116
McCann, Madeleine 112
McChesney, Robert 69, 70, 72, 83, 231
McHugh & Hoffman, TV news
    consultants 150
McIntosh, Neil 210
McKenzie, Rod 165, 170, 178, 179
McLellen, Michele 196
McNair, Brian 7, 68
McQueen, David 168
Media Appeals Tribunal, South Africa
    240
Media Council of Kenya (MCK)
    239–40
Media Development and Diversity
    Agency, South Africa 242
Media Lens 212
media ownership *see* ownership
Media Production City (Cairo) 285
Media24 (South Africa) 230
Medianet 275, 276
mediatisation of Arab politics 287
Meehan, John 122
Meet the Press 71
Mellor, David 113
MENA region (Middle East and North
    Africa) 282
Mental Acrobatics blog 257
Meraz, Sharon 212
merged newsrooms *see* editorial
    integration
Messham, Steve 42
Metro (UK free newspaper) 59, 61, 115
Metro Citizen (South Africa) 231
Meyer, Philip 19, 123
Meyrowitz, Joshua 291
Michuki, John 257
Microsoft 71, 81, 148
Middle East 90, 128, 282–94
Miles, Hugh 285, 286, 291
Millington, Bob 30
Mills, Elinor 80

mind boxes 11–13, 16, 18–19
Mint, India 128, 138
Mirror Group 62, 117
Mitchell, Amy 127, 158
Mitchelstein, Eugenia 215
mixed-market response to change 301
mobile phones 82–3; Blackberry
    Messenger 210; for news 82,
    242; high penetration, Africa
    93; Kenya 242; live video 82;
    London tube bombings (2005)
    206; mobile television 83;
    SMS news alerts 93; SMS news
    blocked (Kenya) 258; South
    Africa 242, 253; user-generated
    content 195, 205–6, 242,
    250; young audiences 178; *see
    also* phone-hacking scandal;
    smartphones
Moghazi, Nasreddine 287
Moi, Daniel 232
Montgomery, David 117
Moonves, Les 145
Morecambe Bay cockle-picker deaths
    174
Moreira, Sonia 91, 94, 95
Morgan, Mary F. 89
Morning Edition (NPR) 155
Moro, Nikhil 88, 90, 91, 92, 95
Morris, Michael 88
Morsi, Mohammed 287
Moyo, Dumisani 252
MPs' expenses scandal 37
MSNBC 145; history 148–9;
    knowledgeable audiences 148;
    liberal bias 146; opinion channel
    147; new digital service 71;
    ratings 146
Mtwana, Nonceba 229
Mtykova, Monika 109
Mubenga, Jimmy 46
Mullins, Andrew 59, 60
multichannel television 68
multiperspectival news environment
    203
multiplatform news distribution 107,
    129, 153
Munthe, Turi 216
Murdoch, James 269
Murdoch, Rupert 113, 123; and
    BBC 177; defeats print unions
    104; launches Sky News 105;
    subsidises UK newspapers 121;

supports investigative journalism
    41; *The Daily* 116
"Murdochization" (India) 271, 273–6
Murrow, Ed 144
Murthy, Dhiraj 211
Musila, Grace 259
Muslim Brotherhood and Al-Jazeera
    286
Muslim identity of Arab journalists 283
Muslim veils (French ban) 284
Mutua, Alfred 259
"mutual zombification" of polity and
    potentate 287
MyMissourian.com 194

Napoli, James 284
Narisetti, Raju 128–32, 140, 141
narrative of decline 7, 39, 166
Naspers *see* Media24 (South Africa)
Nation Media Group 96, 233, 235
National Public Radio *see* NPR
nationalism 283
National Union of Journalists 204
NBC (National Broadcasting
    Company): awards 149; local
    TV stations 153; multiplatform
    journalism 71; participatory
    advertising 81; profitable 145;
    News Innovation Center 71;
    news-sharing 151–2; viewing
    figures 74, 144; *see also* MSNBC
NDTV 278
Negrine, Ralph 233
Neijens, Peter C. 209
Neil Report 168, 171
Nel, Francois 55, 88, 117
Netherlands 80
Netshitenzhe, J. 230
Network (film) 67, 70
Neuberger, Christoph 204
New Statesman 116
New World Information and
    Communication Order
    (NWICO) 229
New York Mag 134–7
New York Times: paywall 115, 131;
    user-generated content 195;
    website 114, 133–4; WikiLeaks
    47
Newman, Nic 70, 164, 179, 209
news: as public good 12, 69, 72, 158;
    as commercial good 12, 275
News Corporation 71

news cycle 109, 120
News Hour, PBS 157
News International 38, 41, 114, 121
"news junkies" 164
News of the World 38, 41, 113
News on Sunday 104
news: platforms 69; sharing 151, 154; sources 46, 95, 103
news24.com South Africa 230
Newsbeat 165, 170, 178, 179, 180
newsgroups 188
Newsnight: cuts 50; Jimmy Savile scandal 42, 45, 112, 117, 171, 177
newspapers: circulation decline in South Africa 232; circulation figures 61, 63, 65, 105–6, 108; circulation growth in India 268; circulation growth in developing and intermediate nations 90; *City AM* 61; distribution 59, 60, 91; free newspapers 59, 60, 108, 115–16, 231; management 108, 114; *Metro* 59, 61, 115; numbers of Indian titles 268; of record 106, 139; ownership 66; print version 64; tabloids 41, 62, 94, 95, 216, 230, 231; UK national 55–66, 103–26; UK regional 103–26
Newsquest 107
Newsroom Live (Indian novel) 273
news-sharing 151, 152
newswires 128
NGOs 117
Ng'weno, Hillary 236
Nicholas, David 19
Nichols, John 72
Nielsen ratings agency 149; veracity of 80–1, 279
Nielsen, Christian 89
Nigeria: local language newspapers 95; mobile phone use 93; newspaper-sharing 92; paywalls 92; trust in newspapers 91
Nightingale, Virginia 68
Nightly News, NBC 71, 143, 144
Nilesat 285
Nimmo, Dan 258
Ninan, T.N. 272
Nisbet, Matthew C. 11
Nord, David Paul 8
North Africa 90, 282, 285, 288

Northcliffe Media 117, 119
North West Evening Mail 216
Northern Rock 119
Northwest Voice, The 192
Norway 108
Nossek, Hillel 289
nostalgia *see* narrative of decline
NPR 155, 158
NUads 81
NUJ *see* National Union of Journalists
Nyamnjoh, Francis 93, 229, 234
Nyathi, Sihle 257
NYMag.com 134–7

O'Huiginn, Daniel 48
O'Neill, Deirdre 175, 176
O'Reilly, Bill 147, 148
O'Reilly Factor, The 144
O'Reilly, Tony 62, 230
Oakley, Chris 107–9, 117–19
objectivity 204
Observer 52, 57, 108, 114
"Occupy Nigeria" protests (2012) 91
Odhiambo, Elisha Atieno 259
Ofcom 49, 109, 111, 121, 163, 175
Ogola, George 227–47, 249, 251, 287, 282–96, 299
Oh, Yeon-ho 184, 191, 193
OhmyNews 184, 191, 192, 193, 194, 198, 199, 252
Okacha, Tawfix 287
Okolloh, Ory 258
Olbermann, Keith 148
Oliver & Ohlbaum Advisory 111, 117
Oloo, Onyango 259
Olympics 2012 82
omnivision deficit 13
online-first publishing 138
Open Society Foundation 70
Operation Desert Storm 146
Opposite Direction 293
Orchard, Mark 73
Organized Crime and Corruption Reporting Project 48
Örnebring, Henrik 169, 216
Ortolani, Alex 127–42, 299
Otieno, Clifford Derrick 259
Ouko, Robert 259
Oullette, Laurie 169
Oulu, Paul 259
Outing, Steve 195
outsourcing 120
Overton, Iain 42, 45

ownership: advantages of private
ownership 96; consolidation
96, 117, 118, 153, 154, 290–1,
231; consolidation, India 272;
cross-media ownership 118;
cross-media ownership in India
272; diversity, Kenya 236;
diversity, South Africa 236; lack
of regulation, Kenya 235; local
119, 150; local newspapers 107;
political, India 272

paid journalism (Kenya) 234
"paid news" (India) 271, 276–7
Paine, Thomas 186
Paletz, David 287
pan-Arabism 283
"pan" nationalism 284
Panorama 37, 42, 168–71
Papper, Bob 152
"parallel market" of news 252
Parliament Channel, BBC 179
Parsons, Nigel 293
Parsons, Richard 145
participatory democracy 10, 49, 69,
154, 166, 197, 219, 298, 299,
300, 301
"participatory journalism", South
Africa 249
Pasick, Adam 134–37
"passive discovery" 151
Paterson, Chris 150
Patinkin, Jason 260
Patterson, Thomas E. 72, 75
Paulson, Ken 187
Pavlik, John 69
paywalls *see* business models: internet
paywalls
PBS 149, 157
Pembroke and *Pembroke Dock
Observer* 118
People, The 41
Perez-Pena, Richard 127
Perspectives 167
Peston, Robert 119, 170
Peter, Jeremy 127
Pew Research Center 74, 144, 146–8,
151–4
Phillips, Angela 89, 90
Phillips, Dom 91, 94
phone-hacking scandal 37, 38, 113,
177
photographers 110

Picard, Robert 69, 89, 95
Pierce, Roger 197
Pilger, John 39
Pintak, Lawrence 283–4,
288–92
plagiarism 214
Plunkett, John 202
Poell, Thomas 211
police corruption 42, 43
Politico 146, 148
politics: non-participation 29, 30, 110
Postgate, Matthew 82, 164, 178
Potter Foundation 45
Powerline blog 189
Poynter Institute 195
PR *see* public relations
Prato, Lou 156
Prescott, John 30
Presidential Press Unit (PPU), Kenya
228
Presley, Elvis 156
Press Council of India (PCI) 271, 275,
276, 278
press freedom, Kenya 233, 239
Press Freedom Index 288
Preston, Peter 45
Primark 171
primary definers 14
print unions 104
privacy and TV data-collecting 80, 81
private detectives 110
"private treaties" in India 275
procedural democracy 9
professional identity of
journalists 208
professionalization: of Kenyan
journalism 239; of Arab
journalism 289
profitability *see* business models
programmes of record 173
ProPublica 38, 45, 127
Protection of State Information Bill,
South Africa 240
public connection theory 215
public relations: celebrity journalism
112; citizen journalism as PR
193; as news source 36, 111,
177; "paid news" (India) 277;
primary definers 14; smear
campaigns 170
"Publius" 185
Puri, Anjali 275
Purvis, Stewart 164

Qardawi, Yusuf 286
Qatar 73, 285, 286, 291
Qik 209
quality: audience measurement 26; awards scheme 26; criteria for citizen journalism, Kenya 249; crowdsourced monitoring 25; cultural context 304; defined as oppositional, Kenya 232; defined by the crowd 215; definition 1–34, 9; definition, Arab world 283; definitions in developing countries 227; elite bloggers 255; matrix 24; measurement 1–34, 9, 19; monitoring 20
quality indicators: accuracy 22–3; causality 23; comparativeness 23; comprehensibility 23; comprehensiveness 23; context 23
Quartz 128, 137, 138, 140, 141
Quinn, Stephen 55, 69

Rabaino, Lauren 195
Radio Grahamstown 255
radio licensing, Kenya 235
radio news UK, amount of 162
Radu, Paul Cristian 48
Ram, Narasimhan 273
Ramsay, Gordon Neil 164
Randewich, Noel 81
Rann (film) 273
Rantanen, Terhi 231
Rather, Dan 147, 189
Rawporter (citizen journalism app) 211
readership *see* audiences
Reagan, Ronald 14
Real News Network, The (TRNN) 83
reality TV 169
Rebillard, Franck 215
Redmond, Phil 30
Reese, Stephen D. 215
Reeves, Ian 113
regional differentiation 175
regional TV news 173–76
regulation: of broadcasting 177; Kenya 240
Reilly, Hugh J. 186
Reisinger, Don 250
religious identity of Arab journalists 283
"relevance" 170
relocation of Arab TV stations 285
Reporter.co.za 252–4
Reporters Without Borders 288

repression: of Arab media 287; of journalists in Bahrain 288
Reprieve 44
Republican Party 147
research and development in newspapers 303
Reuters 128
Reuters Institute for the Study of Journalism 36, 70
Rhodes University 263
Ricchiardi, Sherry 73
Ridder, Jan A. de 209
Riffe, Daniel 191
Roberts, Jim 133
Robinson, Deborah 162–83, 299
Robinson, Sue 206
Rock Center 71
Rodny-Gumede, Ylva 227–47
Roku 80
Rosen, Jay 195, 204, 208, 251, 263
Rosenbloom, Richard 88
Rosenstiel, Tom 127, 157, 158
Ross, Jonathan 213
Rotich, Juliana 257
Royal Media Services, Kenya 235
Royal Television Society (RTS) 168
Rusbridger, Alan 105, 111, 213
Rutigliano, Lou 215
Ryley, John 171, 172, 179

Sabbagh, Dan 108, 109
SABC (South African Broadcasting Corporation) 236–7, 242–3
Sachs, Andrew 213
Saddleworth News 119
Sainath, P. 274, 276
Sakr, Naomi 284–7, 290–1, 293–4
Sambrook, Clare 46
Sambrook, Richard 207
Samsung Mobile 81
Sands, Sarah 60
Sang, Joshua Arap 235
Santana, Arthur D. 190
Santhanam, Laura Houston 158
satellite radio 155
satellite TV: Africa 237; Arab liberalization 285; Arab public debate 293; bundling of news 78; data harvesting 79; growth of Arab channels 290; impact on Arab region 286; India 268, 278; news-free channels 29; pan-Arab TV 284; pay TV 77; ownership of Arab channels 294; *see also* Al Jazeera; CNN; Fox; MSNBC; Sky

Saturday newspapers 58, 63
Saunders, Juliette 252
Savile (Jimmy) scandal 13, 42, 69, 112;
    see also *Newsnight*
Schindehutte, Minet 88
Schlesinger, Philip 165, 179
Schlosberg, Justin 108, 109
Schmidt, Eric 74
Schmitt, Ernesto 76
Schnews 212
Schoon, Alette Jean 250
Schudson, Michael 69
Scollon, Ron 165
scope of book 1, 8
Scott Trust 105, 121
search engine optimization 109,
    137
second screen 76, 77, 164
secret filming 43, 166, 168, 170
Secret Millionaire 169
Select Committee on Communications,
    House of Lords 170, 171,
    179
self-regulation, Kenya 239
"service journalism" 215
seven-day newspaper operation 104
Shafer, Scott M. 88
Shah, Amrita 274
Shah, Eddy 104
Shapiro, Ivor 9, 20, 21
Sharia Law and Life 286
Sharpton, Reverend Al 148
Shaw, Bernard 146
Shirky, Clay 30, 122, 127, 202
Shott, Nicholas 176
Shunglu, Prabhat 273
Silverstone, Roger 250
Simpson, Alan K. 186, 187
Singapore 72
Singer, Jane 208, 215
Singh, Manmohan 271
Sirius XM 155
Skipworth, Mark 120
Sky News: audience 26, 164; audience
    measurement 165; audience
    share 164; business model 84;
    cross-platform use 164; fall of
    Tripoli coverage 172–3; less
    popular than CNN 146; mobile
    news 178; quality 179; resources
    171; rolling news 105; Sky News
    Radio 163; Sky Tyne and Wear
    176
Slashdot.org 215
Slattery, Brennon 127

smartphones: as journalistic tools 172,
    209; citizen journalism 209, 263;
    impact on news consumption
    164; impact on newspapers 107;
    impact on TV 82–3, 163; live
    video 82–3; making radio visual
    178; mobile news consumption
    132, 155, 165; popularity in
    Kenya 241; presentation of
    news 17, 29; second screens
    76
Smith, Anthony 273, 284
Smith, Chris 76
Smith, Jeffrey H. 88
SMS text journalism 256
social media 76, 165, 202–19, 251;
    2007 Kenyan elections 257; as
    news distributors 209; definition
    204; in investigative journalism
    46
"software" of journalism 268
Soloski, John 89
Sonwalkar, Prasun 267–81, 268,
    273–4, 279, 297
Sophos, Marc 153
Sorensen, Eric 143
South Africa: as case study 1;
    broadcasting liberalization
    236; new broadcasters 237;
    citizen journalism 248–9,
    249–57, 263; community radio
    242; convergence 242; cost-
    cutting 231–2; local language
    newspapers 95, 232; media
    history 227, 229–30; media
    ownership 231; MSNBC 236–7;
    newspaper advertising growth
    92–3; newspaper business
    models 91; professionalism
    238; regulation 240; resilience
    of private media 96; rising
    newspaper circulation 90;
    tabloid newspapers 94, 238–9
South African National Editor's Forum
    (SANEF) 238
Sowetan 253
specialisation 110
speed in news-gathering 23
Spinwatch 212
Spot.US 83
Sreenivasan, Hari 149
Sri Lanka 170
Stafford-Smith, Clive 44
Staines, Paul 116, 213
Stanistreet, Michelle 42

Star, Kenya 242
Starkey, Guy 171
Starsuckers 111
State control of Arab journalism 284
Steel, Emily 146
Steenveld, Lynette 256
Stellavision, Kenya 236
Stelter, Brian 144, 145, 147, 152, 186
Stewart, Christopher S. 145
Steyn, Elanie 229, 238
Steyn, T.F.J. 238
Stone, Martha 88
Storm, Hannah 48
story boxes 11, 12
Storyful 216
storytelling 30, 130, 169; Bollywood
     themes, 278
Stourton, Ed 36
Stout, David 155
Street, John 287
Strelitz, Larry 256
Stromback, Jesper 8, 9, 10, 21
Suarez, Ray 149
subsidy of news providers 69
Suffolk Constabulary 113
Sultan, Wafa 290
Sun, UK 41, 57, 104, 112, 114
Sunday Correspondent 104
Sunday newspapers 58, 104, 113, 231
Sunday Times UK 36, 51, 57, 104,
     108, 214; Insight team 36;
     investigative journalism 39
Sunday Times South Africa 231, 253
"sunshine journalism" in India 274
Supernanny 169
Super Notícia 94
Surowiecki, James 213
Surrey University 82
Sweden 216
Sweney, Mark 116
syndication 231

tablets: as future of news 178; causing
     newspaper decline 107; *The
     Daily* tablet newspaper 116; data
     harvesting 79; evening use 165;
     Folha de Sao Paulo paywall, 92;
     growth 127, 132; impact on TV
     163; news consumption 164;
     ownership predictions, UK 108;
     radio 155; second screens 76
"tabloidization" 94, 166
talk-show format on Arabic TV 293

tax breaks 117
technological determinism 17
technology: Arab Spring 291–92;
     declining news consumption
     31; government intervention to
     promote journalism 303; impact
     on democracy 302; improved
     reporting 172; user practices
     17, 28
Telemondo 153
television: broadband 77, 79, 145;
     consolidation of ownership 71;
     convergence 70, 82; hyperlocal
     84; Internet Protocol TV (IPTV)
     77; linear experience 76; national
     news, United States 143–49;
     "Over-The-Top" (OTT) delivery
     70, 77, 80; pay TV 77, 84;
     quantity of UK news 162; Smart
     TV 84; smartphones 83; Video-
     On-Demand (VoD) 77; *see also*
     cable TV; satellite TV
Temple, Mick 110
Tettey, Wisdom 232, 234, 238, 239
Thakurta, Guha 276
Thalidomide scandal 39
Tharoor, Shashi 268
This Week 39, 167
ThisDay 231
Thompson, Mark 68
Thorson, Esther 191
Thought Leader, South Africa 254–55,
     260–1
Thurman, Neil J. 208
Thussu, Daya Kishan 278
Time Warner 71
Times of India 268, 270–5; "paid
     news" 276
Times, The 106; 1992 price war 62;
     circulation 61, 62; growth in
     pagination 104; investigative
     journalism 41; losses 108;
     move to Wapping 104; paywall
     114–15
Time-Warner 145
Tindle Newspapers 118, 119
Tivo 79
Today (NBC TV programme) 59, 71,
     156
Today (UK newspaper) 104
Today programme (BBC radio) 164
Tomlinson, Ian 46
Tonight 168

Touboul, Annelise 215
Toynbee, Polly 30
Toyota 81
Trafigura injunction 213
training of journalists 171; Arab world 288, 292; India 280
Tran, Mark 199
triangulation 197
Tribune Broadcasting 153
Trinity Mirror 107, 117
Tripoli 172
trust 155, 194
Tsarwe, Stanley 255, 256
Tueni, Gibran 283
Tulisa: My Mum and Me 169
Tunisia 288
Turner Broadcasting System 71
Turner, Ted 145
Tweetminster 216
Twitter: aids understanding of audience 165–6; Arab Spring 291–2; Bahrain 287; breaking news 136, 209; citizen journalism 195, 258–9, 260; dispelling rumours 30, 210; promotional tool 46; "Sachsgate" 213; second screen 76; Trafigura injunction 213; use by mainstream media 211; Ushahidi 258

U.S. Constitution 187
UmAfrika 232
'Undercover Care: The Abuse Exposed' 168
University of Central Lancashire 122
University of Missouri School of Journalism 186, 193
Univision News 145
Urban75 blog 209
USA Today 104
user-generated content (UGC) 207, 250; 2005 London tube bombings 206; apps 211; definition 205; *Guardian* 211; tabloid newspapers 216; *Truthloader* channel 172; verification 172, 216; *see also* citizen journalism
Ushahidi 258
Usher, Nikki 215

Van Dijk, Jan A.G.M. 215
van Noort, Elvira 252, 253

Van Zoonen, Liesbet 169
Vandenbroucke, Guillaume 185
Varma, Ram Gopal 273
Verizon FiOS 153
vernacular language journalism, South Africa 236
vernacular language radio 234
Viasat1 97
Vice-Presidential Press Unit (VPPU), Kenya 228
Vickery, Graham 205
video journalism 130
visual stories 150
VJ (video journalist) 151
Voakes, Paul S. 283

Wall Street Journal: newspaper of record 139; pay wall 115; website 127, 128–32
Wall, Melissa 215
Wanta, Wayne 187
Wapping 104, 106, 109
Ward, Geoff 9, 10, 22
Ward, Julie 259
Wardle, Claire 172, 178, 205
Ware, John 171
Warner, Jack 37
Warner, Margaret 149
Washington Post: converged newsroom 129; online comments 190
Washingtonpost.com 190
Wasserman, Herman 94, 230, 249
Watergate 39
Weaver, David 283, 288
web 1.0 definition 205
web 2.0 definition 205
web 3.0 definition 205
web-only news organisations 127
websites: cannibalisation 115; newspapers 114; user figures 105, 106, 115
Weezel, Aldo van 95
Weinberger, David 215
Weldon, Michele 188
Weprin, Alex 149
Were, Daudi 257
Westinghouse 154, 155
Weymouth, Anthony 9
Whelan, Brian 214
Whitman, Walt 186
Whittemore, Hank 146
Wiedenbeck, S. 209
Wiener, Joel H. 103

Wife Swap 169
Wigston, David 230
WikiLeaks 37, 46–7, 218
Wikinews 212
Wilberg, Erik 88
Willcox, Elaine 173, 174
Willemsen, Lotte M. 209
Williams, Andrew 35, 172, 205
Williams, Jon 173
Williams, Michael J. 121, 103–26, 300
Williams, Walter 186
Willis, Robert 89, 97
Wingfield-Hayes, Rupert 173
Winterbourne View 37 *see also* "Undercover Care: The Abuse Exposed"
wisdom of crowds 213
Witschge, Tamara 89, 90
Women in Journalism (campaign group) 112
Wood, Ian 116, 120
Woodruff, Judy 149
Woodward, Robert 149
working practices 109, 133, 134, 139; converged newsrooms 127–42; crowdsourcing Tony Blair's financial portfolio 215; deception 168; helicopters 151;

individual versus institutional use of social media 214; journalists versus bloggers 189; newsroom "hub" structure 120; outsourcing of social media curation 216; "passive discovery" 151
World in Action 35, 39, 51, 167
Woza news site, South Africa 242
Wunsch-Vincent, Sacha 205

Xbox 81

Yadav, Umlesh 277
young people 121, 156, 164; consuming less news 75
Your.TV 80
YouTube 68; advertising 130; quantity of uploads 250; *Truthloader* channel 172
YouView 80

Zee Business 278
Zeebox 76
Zee News 278
Zero Hora 94
Zimbabwe 252
Zott, Christoph 88
Zuckerman, Ethan 241, 2

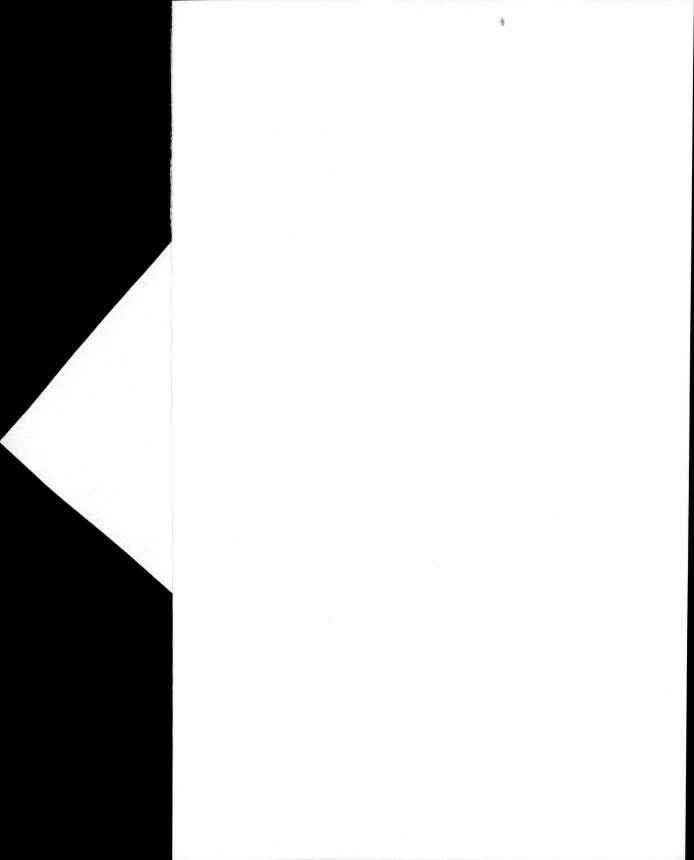

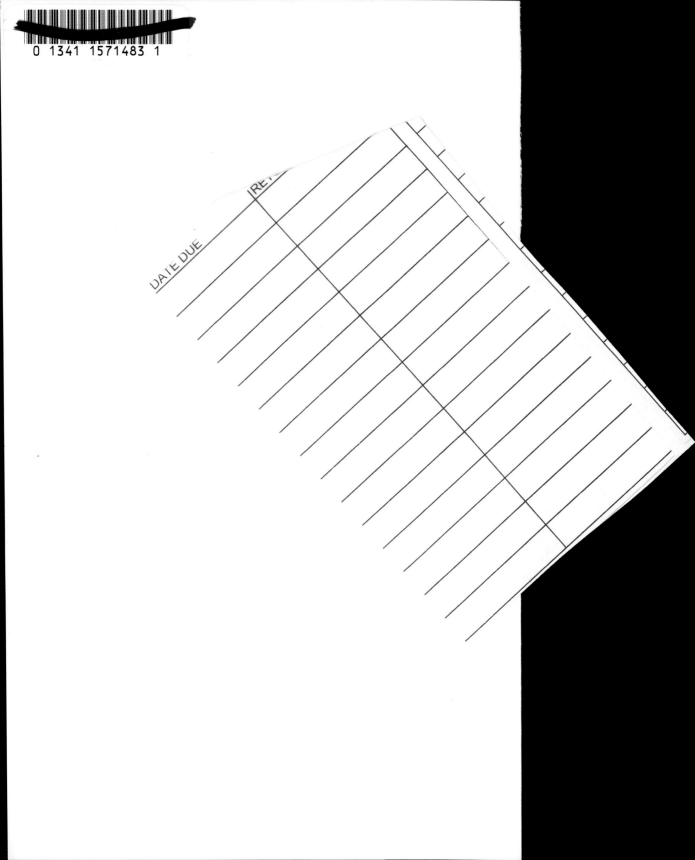